The Presidency of
HARRY S.
TRUMAN

AMERICAN PRESIDENCY SERIES

Donald R. McCoy, Clifford S. Griffin, Homer E. Socolofsky
General Editors

George Washington, Forrest McDonald
John Adams, Ralph Adams Brown
Thomas Jefferson, Forrest McDonald
James Madison, Robert Allen Rutland
John Quincy Adams, Mary W. M. Hargreaves
Martin Van Buren, Major L. Wilson
William Henry Harrison & John Tyler, Norma Lois Peterson
James K. Polk, Paul H. Bergeron
Zachary Taylor & Millard Fillmore, Elbert B. Smith
Franklin Pierce, Larry Gara
James Buchanan, Elbert B. Smith
Andrew Johnson, Albert Castel
Rutherford B. Hayes, Ari Hoogenboom
James A. Garfield & Chester A. Arthur, Justus D. Doenecke
Grover Cleveland, Richard E. Welch, Jr.
Benjamin Harrison, Homer E. Socolofsky & Allan B. Spetter
William McKinley, Lewis L. Gould
Theodore Roosevelt, Lewis L. Gould
William Howard Taft, Paolo E. Coletta
Woodrow Wilson, Kendrick A. Clements
Warren G. Harding, Eugene P. Trani & David L. Wilson
Herbert C. Hoover, Martin L. Fausold
Harry S. Truman, Donald R. McCoy
Dwight D. Eisenhower, Chester J. Pach, Jr., & Elmo Richardson
John F. Kennedy, James N. Giglio
Lyndon B. Johnson, Vaughn Davis Bornet

The Presidency of
HARRY S. TRUMAN

Donald R. McCoy

UNIVERSITY PRESS OF KANSAS

Published by the University Press of Kansas (Lawrence, Kansas 66049),
which was organized by the Kansas Board of Regents
and is operated and funded by Emporia State University, Fort Hays State
University, Kansas State University, Pittsburg State
University, the University of Kansas, and Wichita State University

Library of Congress Cataloging in Publication Data

McCoy, Donald R.
The presidency of Harry S. Truman.

(American presidency series)
Bibliography: p.
Includes index.
1. Truman, Harry S., 1884-1972. 2. United States—
Politics and government—1945-1953. I. Title.
II. Series.
E814.M38   1984   973.918'092'4   84-3624
ISBN 0-7006-0252-6
ISBN 0-7006-0255-0 (pbk.)

Printed in the United States of America
10 9 8 7 6

For
Sandy

CONTENTS

FOREWORD

The aim of the American Presidency Series is to present historians and the general reading public with interesting, scholarly assessments of the various presidential administrations. These interpretive surveys are intended to cover the broad ground between biographies, specialized monographs, and journalistic accounts. As such, each will be a comprehensive, synthetic work which will draw upon the best in pertinent secondary literature, yet leave room for the author's own analysis and interpretation.

Volumes in the series will present the data essential to understanding the administration under consideration. Particularly, each book will treat the then current problems facing the United States and its people and how the president and his associates felt about, thought about, and worked to cope with these problems. Attention will be given to how the office developed and operated during the president's tenure. Equally important will be consideration of the vital relationships between the president, his staff, the executive officers, Congress, foreign representatives, the judiciary, state officials, the public, political parties, the press, and influential private citizens. The series will also be concerned with how this unique American institution—the presidency—was viewed by the presidents, and with what results.

All this will be set, insofar as possible, in the context not only of contemporary politics but also of economics, international relations, law, morals, public administration, religion, and thought. Such a broad approach is necessary to understanding, for a presidential administration is more than the elected and appointed officers composing it, since its work so often reflects the major problems, anxieties, and glories of the nation. In short, the authors in the series will strive to recount and evaluate the record of each administration and to identify its distinctiveness and relationships to the past, its own time, and the future.

The General Editors

ACKNOWLEDGMENTS

I owe thanks to many people and institutions for assistance and support. The limitations of space and the quirks of memory prevent me from naming all of them. It is appropriate to mention my gratitude to the late Philip C. Brooks of the Harry S. Truman Library and Francis H. Heller of the University of Kansas for firing my scholarly interest in the Truman administration.

Philip Lagerquist, Elizabeth Safly, and Benedict K. Zobrist are only three of the many staff members at the Truman Library who have cheerfully provided me with assistance. I am also indebted to archivists beyond count at the National Archives and to archivists and librarians at the University of Kansas, especially John Nugent, for many favors. A platoon—or was it a company?—of researchers at the Truman Library over many years have supplied encouragement, intellectual stimulation, and good fellowship.

Special thanks for reading and commenting on my manuscript belong to a superb quartet of scholars: Clifford S. Griffin and Theodore

A. Wilson of the University of Kansas, Richard T. Ruetten of San Diego State University, and Homer E. Socolofsky of Kansas State University. Moreover, I appreciate the financial support of my research efforts, which was generously granted by the National Endowment for the Humanities, the Harry S. Truman Library Institute, and the General Research Fund of the University of Kansas.

Donald R. McCoy

Lawrence, Kansas
October 1983

1

★ ★ ★ ★ ★

ARRIVING AT ARMAGEDDON

''Boys, if you ever pray, pray for me now. I don't know whether you fellows ever had a load of hay fall on you, but when they told me yesterday what had happened, I felt like the moon, the stars, and all the planets had fallen on me.''[1] Thus the new president of the United States spoke to the press on April 13, 1945, the day after Franklin D. Roosevelt had died of a massive cerebral hemorrhage. Indeed the night after President Roosevelt's death Harry S. Truman had impressed his old friend Harry Vaughan as being panicky and his own daughter, Margaret, as being stunned. Truman had known that Roosevelt was tired and ailing, but the vice-president had believed that his chief's health would improve during his vacation in Georgia. Like most Americans, Truman had been astonished by Roosevelt's death.

This was not the only way in which Truman was unprepared to assume the leadership of the nation. Although he had been attentive to duty during his scant eighty-three days as vice-president, his work had chiefly involved him in the operations of the Senate and in making routine speeches. The president and Truman had seen each other infrequently, and their meetings had been of negligible value in preparing Roosevelt's understudy to take center stage.

Harry Truman was not, however, without pertinent experience and inner resources in assuming the presidency. Born on May 8, 1884, in Lamar, Missouri, he had lived a full and varied life during his almost sixty-one years. He had been raised in a close and affectionate family. His father, John A. Truman, was a peripatetic farm operator. Following

1

their father's fortunes, Harry, his brother, Vivian, and his sister, Mary Jane, moved often. Harry's school years were spent in Independence, Missouri. As a child, he seemed to have plenty of everything—family, friends, and fun. Although poor eyesight limited his athletic activities, he compensated for that by learning to play the piano and, especially, by reading everything he could lay his hands on. He was particularly motivated to study the history of government and leadership, an interest that, along with reading the Bible, he retained throughout his life. Although Truman's reading of history was often uncritical, he relied heavily on what he considered to be the lessons of the past in guiding himself and, later, the country.

Young Truman's book learning was only a part of his early preparation for leadership. There were also his ability to get along with other people, his industry, his honesty, and his adaptability—all of which had their roots in his childhood. As the oldest child, he had plenty of chores; and he had parents, especially his mother, Martha Ellen, who expected much from him. Yet his parents gave him considerable leeway in his personal activities, in part because they believed that such freedom would help him to develop into a responsible and self-confident person. Although the family was also prosperous enough that it could provide the necessities, his parents expected him to work for the luxuries that he enjoyed.

John Truman's finances became tight about the time of Harry's graduation from high school in 1901. There was not enough money for young Truman to attend college, although he did become a part-time student at the Kansas City Law School from 1923 to 1925. He held various jobs after he left high school: in succession, he worked as a timekeeper for a railway contractor, in the mail room of the *Kansas City Star*, and as a clerk in one bank and a bookkeeper in another. In 1906 he went to work on his Grandmother Young's large farm, which his father operated. Harry stayed there until 1917. When his grandmother died in 1909, she left her farm to her children, Martha Ellen Truman and Harrison Young. In 1916, when Uncle Harrison died, he bequeathed his share of the farm to Martha Ellen and her three children, Harry, Vivian, and Mary Jane. The farm was a haven, both financially and socially, for Harry Truman, where his responsibilities steadily increased, especially after his father's death in 1914.

By then, however, there was more to Harry Truman's life than farming. He joined a National Guard artillery battery in 1905 and the Masons in 1908. Both of these affiliations would be important to his development as a leader, for he rose gradually to become a colonel in the National Guard by 1927 and grand master of Missouri's Masons by 1940.

Harry became involved in politics in 1906, when he began serving as a Democratic election clerk in Jackson County. Moreover, he succeeded his father, after the latter's death, as road overseer in Washington Township. He also felt confident enough to enter a business in 1916, when he joined with a Kansas City lawyer and an Oklahoma oilman to form an oil company. The entry of the United States into World War I and the resultant manpower shortage put an end to this enterprise, however.

With the expansion of the Missouri National Guard during World War I, Truman became a first lieutenant. His outfit was sworn into federal service in August 1917 as part of the Thirty-fifth Division's 129th Field Artillery. In September he left for active service at Camp Doniphan, Oklahoma, where in addition to his other duties he served as regimental canteen officer. He embarked for France on March 30, 1918. Soon Truman was wearing captain's bars, and in July he assumed command of Battery D of the 129th Field Artillery. He and Battery D began their combat service early in September, seeing action in the Vosges, St.-Mihiel, Meuse-Argonne, and Metz operations. His men considered Captain Truman to be a splendid line officer, effective and firm, but fair. This assisted him not only in his rise to a National Guard colonelcy later but also in his political career. His military service fortified attitudes that would explain much of his decisiveness and patriotism as well as his aggressiveness and saltiness. Truman had found his model for manliness in his army experience, and he would never abandon this model. Moreover, his long National Guard service documented for him the lesson that he had gained from his reading of history that "a leader is a man who has the ability to get other people to do what they don't want to do, and like it. . . . It takes a leader to put economic, military, and government forces to work so they will operate."[2]

Truman arrived back in the United States in April 1919. He was almost thirty-five years old and eager to move on with his life. It is not surprising, therefore, that he quickly made two very important decisions. The first, and the more important, was to wed Bess Wallace, whom he had been courting for years. They were married on June 28, and after a honeymoon they settled down in Independence. Truman's other significant decision was to launch a haberdashery business in Kansas City with Eddie Jacobson, a comrade from the 129th Field Artillery. Their first year went well, but their hopes for success dwindled in 1921 as the postwar depression struck. In 1922 Truman and Jacobson had to close their store, and for years they struggled to pay off their debts. Jacobson filed for bankruptcy in 1925, but Truman ulti-

3

mately satisfied his creditors. Already an ardent Democrat, Truman blamed the Republican administration of President Warren G. Harding for his failure in business.

Yet as Truman's business career was collapsing, his military service opened the door to a career for him in politics. One of his customers was Jim Pendergast, who had been a fellow officer in the 129th Field Artillery. In 1921 Pendergast asked Truman if he would consider running for judge of the county court (Missouri's equivalent of county commissioner) for eastern Jackson County. The question had some force, because Jim Pendergast's father, Mike, was an important county Democratic leader. Truman was initially noncommittal, but by March 1922 the upright citizen and model war veteran announced his candidacy. It was a heated primary-election campaign. Although Truman had the support of the Pendergasts and many veterans, there were four other candidates of standing. The Ku Klux Klan, moreover, attacked Truman as being the errand boy of Catholic machine politicians. His intensive campaigning made the difference in the August primary election, and he won the Democratic nomination for county judge by a slender plurality. The voters overwhelmingly elected Truman in the general election in November.

In his new position, Truman won a reputation for being honest and conscientious. Neither this nor his affiliation with the Pendergasts could guarantee his reelection in 1924, however, for there was a wide-open split among Democrats at this time of unusual Republican strength. Truman joined many other Democrats in defeat that year in Jackson County. Once again he was in a straitened situation economically, especially as his only child, Margaret, had been born in 1924. Fortunately, he found remunerative work with the Automobile Club of Kansas City. He also served as president of the National Old Trails Association and continued his political, military, and Masonic activities. As he put it, such things ''widened my acquaintance and kept me in contact with many people, [who] no doubt played some part in my political fortunes.''[3]

Still, politics fascinated him, and at the suggestion of Mike Pendergast's brother, Tom, Truman ran for presiding judge of the county court in 1926. Tom Pendergast, who had become the Democratic boss of Kansas City, succeeded that year in uniting his party, which won most of the available county offices in the November elections. Truman was among the victors in 1926, and for the next twenty-six years he would continuously hold elective public office. He had found his métier.

Holding the key job in Jackson County government, Truman made the most of it. He initiated a much-needed program of improvements in public roads and buildings, and he put the county's finances in excellent shape. Not only was he a competent county administrator and legislator, but he performed honorably and honestly. Jim and Mike Pendergast accepted his ways (although Boss Tom occasionally grumbled). They did so partly because of a fondness and loyalty that had developed between them and Presiding Judge Truman; partly because he did things their way, to sustain their power, when this was ethical; and partly because his honesty and works reflected well on the often-venal Pendergast machine. As for Truman, he remained tied to the Pendergasts partly because without their support at that time, no Democrat would have had much chance of political success in Jackson County.

Truman's governmental accomplishments boded well for his political advancement. In 1930 he was reelected by a wide margin. He was acquiring much knowledge about state as well as local politics, because, in Missouri, county government also served state functions. He took care to broaden his governmental and political contacts as, for example, when he organized and headed the Greater Kansas City Regional Planning Association. By 1931 Truman was ready to ascend the political ladder, intending to run for governor in 1932. Boss Tom Pendergast, in his political wheeling and dealing, made other arrangements, though, so Truman abandoned his campaign. He expected to run for United States representative in 1934. Although he was maneuvered out of doing this, it would soon redound to his political benefit.

The term of Republican United States Senator Roscoe C. Patterson was to expire in 1935, and the Democrats anticipated that they would easily pick up his seat. The rub was that Missouri's Democrats were bitterly split as to who should run against Patterson. The St. Louis machine, in alliance with U.S. Senator Bennett Champ Clark, set out to become dominant in Missouri by backing the candidacy of St. Louis Congressman John J. Cochran. Another congressman, Jacob L. Milligan of Richmond, also was seeking the Democratic nomination, hoping to carry the rural and small-town vote. The Pendergast organization had to enter a candidate in order to attempt to maintain parity with its St. Louis counterpart in federal patronage and influence. Several leading Missouri Democrats had already rebuffed the Kansas City machine, however. In effect, it was left with Harry Truman. He was ambitious; at age fifty, he had nowhere else to turn for political advancement; he was a fighter; and he had a good reputation. The Pendergasts could do worse, and they knew it; Harry Truman could do much worse, and he knew it. When Jim Pendergast asked him if he would run for the Senate, Truman's answer was yes.

Missouri's 1934 primary election for the United States Senate was hard fought. The contest turned out to be more of a struggle between the Kansas City and St. Louis Democratic machines than one between the two veteran congressmen, Cochran and Milligan. Truman did his part as he mustered considerable support from his fellow county officials in Missouri and emerged as the strongest champion of President Franklin D. Roosevelt and his New Deal program among the three senatorial candidates. He was also an indefatigable campaigner, delivering from six to sixteen speeches a day. On primary-election day, Jackson County outdid itself in producing votes for its candidate, and Truman edged out his opponents in most other places in the state except for St. Louis. His plurality was some forty thousand votes. In Missouri during the Great Depression, winning the Democratic nomination for the United States Senate turned out to be tantamount to election.

Harry Truman was one of thirteen newly elected Democratic senators when he took his seat in Washington in January 1935. Before long he had earned a reputation for industriousness and honesty. These two attributes, as well as his ability to get along with people, guaranteed that the Senate's leadership and the Roosevelt administration would consider him acceptable. And he was reliable, faithfully supporting Franklin Roosevelt, his party, and its leaders in the Senate. Truman also emerged as a spokesman for antimonopolism. This impressed many congressional Democrats at a time when most of them viewed large corporations as part of Satan's domain. Although President Roosevelt and his New Deal lieutenants only just accepted the Pendergast-tainted Truman by the late 1930s, he was able to forge solid friendships with the Senate's Democratic worthies.

Truman was a happy senator, for the work and the leadership of the upper chamber suited him well. If he could remain in the Senate, he believed that some day he would advance to the highest circle of legislative leadership. Staying in the Senate, though, was the problem. Although competent and diligent, Truman was neither brilliant nor powerful. He needed help from others, and 1940, when he was up for reelection, was not the most-favorable year for finding it. Neither President Roosevelt nor the country then valued faithful supporters of the New Deal as they had earlier. Moreover, the Pendergast machine was crumbling; Tom Pendergast, indeed, had been convicted of income-tax fraud. Roosevelt had no wish to back a loser in Missouri, indicating that he would rather appoint Truman to the Interstate Commerce Commission and have Governor Lloyd C. Stark run for the Senate.

Although Truman had little campaign money and organized backing, he decided to run for reelection. Governor Stark and United States

Attorney Maurice Milligan, who had successfully prosecuted several Pendergast men, opposed Truman in the 1940 primary election. Truman's prospects were not encouraging, but this did not stop him and his handful of supporters from working vigorously for his reelection. They rallied to his cause organized labor, for which he had done much, and most black voters, to whom he had been polite in a considerably racist milieu; his many personal contacts over the state were used to good advantage; and his small organization worked efficiently and effectively. Milligan did not have the appeal that he anticipated, and Stark made several political blunders, which Truman exploited. The 1940 Missouri senatorial primary campaign was bitterly fought, and Truman won, but just barely. Although almost as much on his own as during the primary campaign, he won the general election by a respectable margin.

Not only had Harry Truman been certified for another six years in the Senate, but he was obligated neither to a machine nor to the Roosevelt administration. Now he had his opportunity to rise in leadership. This he did in a time-tested way, by becoming the chairman of an important Senate committee, the Committee to Investigate the National Defense Program. The task of Truman and his committee was to make sure that the government got the most for its money in America's huge defense production program as World War II intensified. Known as the Truman Committee, it did an admirable job in promoting economy, efficiency, and effectiveness in defense production. And under Truman's able leadership, it did so with a minimum of controversy, which the administration, business, labor, and most of his fellow senators appreciated. Thus, his influence in Washington grew steadily, as did his reputation among Democratic leaders for excellent service.

The prize that Truman's committee chairmanship and his mounting political reputation brought him was something that he probably had not contemplated, the vice-presidency. Important he had become, but he was not nationally prominent by 1944. Once again Truman would benefit by being available and acceptable at the right time. The best-known possibilities for the 1944 Democratic vice-presidential nomination were the ultraliberal incumbent, Henry A. Wallace, War Mobilization Director James F. Byrnes, and Supreme Court Justice William O. Douglas. None of them was able, however, to gain President Roosevelt's full endorsement or to muster enough strength among the Democratic convention delegates. Each was considered to have serious flaws by too many important Democrats, including ultimately the president. Many party leaders, therefore, looked elsewhere for a vice-presidential nominee. After much Byzantine maneuvering, they—and

7

apparently Roosevelt—agreed that Truman was a good compromise choice. He was an experienced, reliable, and reasonably influential senator. Moreover, he seemed unlikely to make trouble for anyone—at least not as vice-president. Interestingly, few Democrats thought to ask what he might be like as president. Perhaps this was for no reason other than that he excited no fear in the various quarters that opposed the possibility of having a strong-willed Wallace, Byrnes, or Douglas succeed to the White House. No, Harry S. Truman would do for vice-president, for most Democratic leaders felt comfortable with this only slightly above the ordinary senator. Thus it was that the 1944 Democratic National Convention nominated Truman for vice-president of the United States.

Truman knew that others were better qualified for the vice-presidency. Yet if he added little to the strength of the Democratic national ticket, he did what was expected of him. He followed orders, gave his quota of speeches and statements, and shook his share of hands. Roosevelt won by a smaller majority in 1944 than in his three previous presidential election contests. Yet he, and Truman, won by a comfortable margin of almost 3.4 million votes out of a total of some 47.8 million cast in the November election. In the months since his nomination, Truman had been catapulted from the lower circles of senatorial leadership to take office as the nation's second-ranking official on January 20, 1945. Less than three months later, he would become the country's chief of state and head of government.

What was this nation that Harry Truman as president was charged to preserve? It was a large land mass of approximately 3 million square miles, which had dependencies scattered about the Caribbean Sea and the Pacific Ocean. Thanks considerably to the World War II and postwar baby boom, the population of the continental United States had increased from 131.6 million in 1940 to 139.9 million in 1945 and 159.6 million in 1953. Slightly more than one-tenth of those living in the States were classified as nonwhite, and the vast majority of these were black, with smaller numbers of Hispanic-Americans, American Indians, and Americans of Asian backgrounds. The number of foreign-born Americans was roughly 11.6 million in 1940 and 10.3 million in 1950, continuing a downward trend since 1930. Although the majority of Americans were Protestant during the Truman era, the largest single religious group was the Catholic Church, which embraced almost one-third of the nation's church membership. Jews numbered about 5 million.

Most of the population lived in the Northeastern States and those bordering the Great Lakes, but Americans were spreading out to the

West and the Southwest. Another trend, enhanced by World War II, was reflected in the rapid growth of urban areas, which swelled from some 74.5 million to 89.0 million people between 1940 and 1950, contrasted to the slower increase in rural residents from roughly 57.3 million to 61.8 million. Migration remained an important part of American life, as the percentage of people living in the states of their birth declined from 77.1 in 1940 to 73.5 in 1950. The impact of better health care was mirrored in the increased rate of life expectancy from 62.9 years in 1940 to 65.9 in 1945. It would reach 68.8 by 1953.

Between 1940 and 1953, there was no significant change in the percentage of those from age five to seventeen who were enrolled in school. This indicated that the American school system had reached what was then sometimes considered to be the saturation point. As for college graduates, the demands of war had caused the number of degrees awarded to decrease from 216,521 in 1940 to 157,349 in 1946. This would soon change startlingly, thanks largely to the educational benefits that the federal government was providing to veterans. By 1950, colleges in the United States would award 496,874 degrees.

There had been important changes in occupational patterns, which were part of an ongoing trend accelerated by the war. Between 1940 and 1950, white-collar workers increased the most in number, from approximately 16.1 to 21.6 million; manual and service workers rose from about 26.7 to more than 30.4 million; while those who toiled on farms declined from some 9 to 7 million, reflecting in part the growing impact of technology on cultivation. World War II had reopened the doors of the job market to women, so that there were almost 18.5 million of them in the labor force in 1944, compared with 13.8 million in 1940. The number declined after the war to about 16.3 million in 1947, but rose slowly to reach 19.3 million in 1953, which was attributable to the increasing search of married women for work.

The nation's economy had boomed during the war, and it stood at a record peak when Truman became president. The demand for labor was so great that large numbers of people who were not usually considered part of the labor force had taken jobs. Purchasing power for working people rose significantly (in 1914 dollars) from an average of $943 to $1,318 between 1940 and 1945. The gross national product index (1958 = 100) had mounted from 43.9 in 1940 to 59.7 in 1945. During these years, agricultural and manufacturing income increased immensely, respectively, from $6.1 to $15.2 billion and from $22.5 to $52.2 billion. The national income rose from $81.1 billion in 1940 to $181.5 billion in 1945, although during the same five years the consumer price index (1914 = 100) increased from 139.5 to 179.3. Trade-union membership mounted from some 8.7 million in 1940 to 14.3 million in 1945. The index of nonfarm productivity per man-hour increased from 66.1 to 76.8 between 1940 and 1945, and of farm output per man-hour, from 42.7 to 47.9.

World War II had brought substantial economic and social changes to the United States, most of them for the better for most Americans. It was plain, however, that the emergency economic system that had developed during the war would not fit the requirements of peacetime. And it was arguable whether an extension of the regulatory system built by Franklin D. Roosevelt's New Deal would promote economic stability after the war. What was not debatable was that various powerful economic and social groups were girding for political battle to determine whether there would be, after the war, more or less federal regulation, and of whom and what. Labor unions, business groups, farm organizations, and many other citizen and even governmental interests would early demand that the Truman administration take action on these questions. Few of them would agree on what the result would be in a healthy economy and society.

One of the uglier facts of American life had been the antagonisms among the nation's diverse ethnic, racial, and religious groups. This was just as much a problem in 1945 as it had been earlier. If the prejudice directed toward European immigrants by native-born Americans and even fellow immigrants had lessened, it had been intensified during the war toward certain other groups, especially those of Japanese and Mexican origins. If anti-Catholicism had declined, anti-Semitism had mounted. If blacks had advanced in some ways during the war, there were those who stood ready "to put them in their place" afterwards. And if the overall position of American Indians had changed significantly, it was not readily apparent. The number of peacemakers in America had increased during the war, thanks in part to an idealistic, war-inspired growth of believers in the brotherhood of man. Moreover, the resolve of black and Jewish leaders to improve the position of their peoples in American life was clear. There were, however, many in society who harbored prejudice against whoever was different from themselves. The Truman administration would have to face the consequences of this potentially explosive situation.

The requirements of the war itself had had and would continue to have substantial impact on the United States. More than 16 million Americans had seen military service during World War II, 10 million of them as conscripts. Some 405,000 of them had died in service, and some 670,000 had been wounded. Although these casualties were relatively small compared with those of many other countries, they did not seem small to most Americans. Moreover, many of the servicemen and women who had survived now held different attitudes toward life from what they had held before. They expected, among other things, to find a decent, secure place in postwar society, as well as lasting peace. There was also the fact that new economic opportunities during the war had improved the situations of tens of millions of civilians. Many of these Americans had heightened expectations, which the new administration had to take into account. Furthermore, wartime needs had dictated that the industrial and agricultural capacity of the nation be greatly increased. The United States had shown its power during the war as the world's largest producer of goods and services; and not the least of its products were prosperity, technological dominance, and awesome military might. The country that could do this during war, many Americans believed, ought to be able to maintain peace in the world as well as to provide its own citizens with a decent standard of living. There were also those, probably more than ever before, who thought that the United States ought to be able to improve the lot of its minorities. The key question—a vexing one for the Truman administration—on all these matters was how to do this.

The responses to this question would be forged in an atmosphere not only of conflicting views but also of much impatience. This is not surprising, given that in many ways the United States was unique. No major nation, after all, had been more isolated from major world currents. During their short history, Americans, by force of circumstance, had often been pioneers in a broad range of human endeavors. Most Americans had, moreover, been remarkably free from the constraints found in older societies. Americans therefore had been substantially touched by a concern for the practical instead of the philosophical, the immediately relevant instead of the traditional, and the democratic and egalitarian instead of the authoritarian. Many of them also took great pride in their accomplishments, even when these were pedestrian. The result was that Americans usually had little patience with whatever was complicated or frustrating.

Despite the bafflements caused by the Great Depression, many Americans interpreted their performance during World War II as proof that they had not lost their ability to do the difficult immediately and the impossible soon. They expected that their society could bring this ability to bear on postwar challenges. What Americans had in reserve was their country's vaunted material abundance. With this abundance, the United States should be able to afford to accomplish its goals once it had reached agreement on how to do so. It seemed that there was substantial unity on the nation's paramount postwar objectives, and with this,

11

Harry Truman had no quarrel. There should be no return to the economic and political problems that had followed World War I; there should be no return to the Great Depression; and the approaching Allied victory in World War II should lay the basis for enduring peace. Opportunity, security, and peace seemed to sum up the goals of the American people. And these objectives, even if the important question of how they should be attained remained unresolved, did not seem unrealistic to most Americans. After all, a rich country led by "can-do, take-charge" people should be able to implement the necessary programs.

This uncomplicated, pragmatic, and, one might say, impatient approach was buttressed by the understanding that most Americans had of history and of the world. It was enough that people be frank, able, and well intentioned. This was how the United States had been built, so there was no reason that the world could not be similarly reconstructed. Certainly, most of the world's peoples must by now have the motivation to work for opportunity, security, and peace. The world was at a crossroads, and most Americans and their leaders were concerned that mankind take the right fork. Theodore Roosevelt's famous declaration of 1912 that "we stand at Armageddon, and we battle for the Lord" seemed to fit the mood of much of the United States at the beginning of the Truman era.

Americans in 1945 were eager to harvest the fruits that their past had promised them. They were especially unwilling to let peace and prosperity elude them again, not after the sacrifices and advances that they believed they had made. This is not surprising, considering that Americans often had interpreted their nation's history as a series of stands at Armageddon. After all, there were the Pilgrim Fathers, the Revolution, and the Civil War, as well as the struggles of pioneers, immigrants, and slaves, which almost everyone could cite. Most adult Americans in 1945, moreover, had had their own Armageddons in World War I, the Great Depression, and World War II. If one considers Harry S. Truman's personal experience, there was also the post–World War I depression. This understanding of history, along with the frequent assumption that most of mankind wanted what Americans wanted, colored the response of the people and even of the leaders of the United States to the challenges awaiting them as World War II drew to a close. Most Americans, Truman among them, were not prepared to react patiently to anything that threatened the accomplishment of peace, opportunity, and security, even if they were not united on how to achieve these ends. Sweeping though these ideas are, they are generalizations in which most Americans and their leaders concurred by the end of World War II. They are, therefore, the attitudes that set the stage for the development of the Truman administration's policies and actions at home and abroad. In short, no one can comprehend the United States and the presidency of Harry Truman without understanding the vague and often idealistic assumptions that most Americans shared by the last half of the 1940s.

2

★ ★ ★ ★ ★

TO END A WAR

Harry S. Truman, as the new president, was in an ambivalent position. Without reservation, he accepted his duty to serve. He found himself, however, inheriting policies and executive personnel about which he knew little. He was also keenly aware that he had succeeded to the job on Franklin D. Roosevelt's coattails, that he had no significant network of personal political support, that he was not well known, and that his personal make-up was very different from that of his urbane predecessor. To complicate matters, Truman would have no time to compensate for his actual or perceived deficiencies. He had, after all, become president as of the moment of Roosevelt's death; he would be held accountable if he did not immediately act the part, especially with World War II yet to be concluded.

Truman's character enabled him to make much of his on-the-job training as president. He was brisk, decisive, direct, industrious, practical, and tough—qualities that most Americans admired. He drew upon these attributes immediately. His first official action was to confirm that the United Nations conference would meet on April 25, 1945, as scheduled. He met with the cabinet and asked its members to stay on for the time being in order to provide continuity. He told them that he would continue Roosevelt's foreign and domestic policies, although he would be responsible for all decisions. Then, just hours after Roosevelt's death, Truman gave his first public statement as president. It was to the point: "The world may be sure that we will prosecute the war on both fronts, east and west, with all the vigor we possess to a successful conclusion.''

The beginning was easy; it was continuing as president that was difficult. Truman's paramount objective was to staff his administration appropriately. The new president needed reliable people to help him determine and carry out policies, all the more so since he was not familiar with so many ongoing policies. He had no love for doctrinaire, professional liberals—in other words, New Dealers who happened to be Democrats—whom he considered to be "the lowest form of politician." What he wanted primarily were people like himself—practical, liberal, and forthright Democrats who happened to be committed to most of the New Deal program. Yet, Truman could also respect conservative Democrats, if they played by his rules. His rules were fairly simple, and he outlined them for the cabinet on May 18. Cabinet members were to help the president "carry out policies of the Government; in many instances the Cabinet could be of tremendous help to the President by offering advice whether he liked it or not but when [the] President (gave) an order they should carry it out. I told them I expected to have a Cabinet I could depend on and take in my confidence and if this confidence was not well placed I would get a Cabinet in which I could place confidence."[1] More than Roosevelt, Truman applied these rules to those who served under him in the cabinet and in other positions. This was certainly one of his strengths, although it led to some notably explosive situations and to the appointment of some officials who offered the president little more than dependability.

Truman also relied more heavily on his top subordinates than had Roosevelt. Truman believed that this would make for a better-organized and more-methodical administration than Roosevelt's. And Truman did his part, for he was temperamentally incapable of being a remote guiding star. Thus he was accessible throughout his administration to the White House staff, heads of executive agencies, and lesser federal appointees. He had daily meetings with his chief White House aides and at least weekly meetings with cabinet members. He met regularly with the Joint Chiefs of Staff and, later, with the National Security Council and the Council of Economic Advisers. And Truman found time to meet with a variety of other advisory committees. This was, of course, in addition to his exhausting schedule of conferences with senators, representatives, diplomats, and private citizens. All this was used as an aid in keeping himself informed and in supervising or influencing the people with whom he had to work. In this respect, Truman was outstanding, for a wide range of federal officials knew more what he expected from them than they had under Roosevelt. Truman's great reliance on his staff was dictated by his initial relative ignorance of governmental policies, but it would be reinforced by their increasing complexity. The result was that a giant step was taken toward the institutionalization of the presidency, the emphasis being on organization and hierarchy at the expense of other factors. Under Truman, the president was to be less the formulator of policy and more the arbiter among policy formulators. It was no wonder that he would be greatly concerned about his appointees.

Getting a staff was no easy task for the new president, especially considering that initially he had so little idea about whom to choose. One thing he did know, however, was that there could be no Truman administration unless he had his own people in office. He acted quickly to assemble his own White House staff. He brought with him from the vice-president's office Matthew J. Connelly as appointments secretary, Rose Conway as personal secretary, and Harry Vaughan as military aide. Soon he named a high-school classmate, Pulitzer Prize winner Charles G. Ross, as press secretary, and a National Guard comrade, James K. Vardaman, Jr., as naval aide. He chose several current members of the White House staff to remain on, including Correspondence Secretary William J. Hassett, Chief Executive Clerk Maurice Latta, and David K. Niles, the administrative assistant for minority affairs. Fleet Adm. William D. Leahy continued on as the president's military chief of staff until 1949; Samuel I. Rosenman, as counsel to the president until 1946; and Harold D. Smith, as director of the Bureau of the Budget until 1946. Advisers in various specialized areas were brought in, most significantly John R. Steelman, a labor expert.

Given the time available, Truman had generally chosen his early White House aides well. Most of them were loyal, able, and easy to be around. Although there were some cronies among them, there were no more than among the aides of other presidents. Moreover, members of the White House staff were not peas in a pod, for their personalities and their points of view were divergent. There were also problems among them. Vardaman and Vaughan were reservists, which caused trouble with elements of the regular navy and army; serious questions would also be raised about their expertise and tact. Vardaman would not remain long at the White House, but Vaughan retained Truman's confidence throughout his presidency. On the whole, it was a highly satisfactory group in carrying out assigned duties, serving as sounding boards, and performing tasks beyond what others could be expected to do. Though Truman had experience and reliability among his early aides, what he needed were freshness, a broader range of ability, and better integration of staff efforts. This would not emerge until 1947 on the White House staff.

Truman also moved rapidly to reconstruct the leadership of the federal government. He moved in this direction on his first night as president, when he asked banker John W. Snyder, another Missourian and National Guard friend, to become federal loan administrator. With this appointment, Truman indicated that he was concerned with fiscal responsibility. Soon he would reappoint David E. Lilienthal to the Tennessee Valley Authority, which was a significant gesture to Democratic liberals. Moreover, Truman named a Supreme Court justice, Robert H. Jackson, to lead America's effort to prosecute German war criminals, showing that he meant business in this respect. In June he nominated the popular Gen. Omar N. Bradley to take the helm of the ailing Veterans Administration. In September the president surprised almost everyone when he appointed a Republican friend, Senator Harold H. Burton, to the Supreme Court. Clearly, Truman was looking for men of ability, but his appointments also demonstrated that he intended to reduce the liberal flavor of the government in order to make it seem more practical and, presumably, more appealing to Congress. This would be true of his cabinet appointments, too.

The president early decided to alter the make-up of his cabinet. He told Democratic National Chairman Robert E. Hannegan on May 19, "I could not possibly outline a policy for my own administration unless I had a Cabinet who was in entire sympathy with what I wanted to do and unless I had a Cabinet with administrative ability."[2] Truman had already named the Missourian Hannegan as postmaster general. On May 23 Truman announced that he would nominate Congressman Clinton P. Anderson of New Mexico as secretary of agriculture, former Senator Lewis B. Schwellenbach of Washington as secretary of labor, and Assistant Attorney General Tom Clark of Texas as attorney general. By July he had appointed former Senator James F. Byrnes of South Carolina, whom many considered the mainstay of the wartime Roosevelt administration, as secretary of state and former Congressman Fred M. Vinson of Kentucky as secretary of the treasury. Undersecretary Robert P. Patterson of New York was named secretary of war in September. In many ways, this was an astonishing shake-up. Four of the seven new cabinet members had been in Congress, most of them were from the West, and all were considered, like the president, to be good party men more than New Dealers. Practicality had been Truman's chief guideline in making these appointments. Supposedly, his new cabinet members would have more influence with Congress, be good administrators, and be people whom the new president could depend upon.

There were, of course, other reasons for the cabinet changes. Truman viewed the departing cabinet officers, except for Secretary of War Henry L. Stimson and Postmaster General Frank C. Walker, as being too much Roosevelt's people. He liked Labor Secretary Frances Perkins personally, but she did not seem to him to be strong enough to handle the anticipated postwar confrontations with organized labor. Perhaps his real reason was suggested in his comment that he "did not want any woman in the cabinet."[3] Truman relegated her to the Civil Service Commission. He believed that Secretary of State Edward R. Stettinius, Jr., was "a fine man, good looking, amiable, cooperative, but never an idea new or old." Then too, it seemed clear that, being next in line under current law to succeed to the presidency, Stettinius had no qualifications for that office. Truman named him to what Stettinius seemed to be best suited, permanent representative of the United States to the Preparatory Commission of the United Nations. Claude R. Wickard had seemed to be a caretaker secretary of agriculture, so it was no problem to give him the job he wanted as head of the Rural Electrification Administration. Truman leapt to the conclusion that he had nothing in common with the patrician Attorney General Francis Biddle, who was sent to serve on the War Crimes Court. In an uncharacteristic reversal, the president in 1952 assessed Biddle as able, efficient, and honest. Treasury Secretary Henry Morgenthau, Jr., had been far too close to Roosevelt and was the leading proponent of making Germany into a pastoral state, a controversial plan that few people took seriously. Truman viewed Morgenthau as a "block head, nut," who "fired himself from my cabinet by threatening what he'd do to me under certain circumstances." Morgenthau was to play no further role in the administration. The president thought that Walker was "my kind of man, . . . but no new ideas." However, before Roosevelt died, Walker had indicated that he wanted to resign. The outgoing postmaster general became alternate representative to the United Nations General Assembly. The aging, ailing Stimson was the only one of the group whose departure Truman regretted. He put the secretary of war in a class by himself as "a real man—honest, straightforward and a statesman sure enough."[4]

Truman thus was left, by six months after he became president, with only three of the ten cabinet members whom he had inherited. They were Secretary of the Navy James V. Forrestal, Secretary of the Interior Harold L. Ickes, and Secretary of Commerce Henry A. Wallace. Truman kept Forrestal on because he found him to be able. He retained

Ickes because of his outstanding administrative record; Wallace because of his popularity with many elements in the New Deal coalition. Although Truman did not, for the most part, regret his decision about Forrestal, he would come to regret having kept Ickes and Wallace in the cabinet.

The new president would have no shortage of advisers. Indeed there was a rush, by those who considered themselves important, to tell him how to run the government. Some of Truman's comments on his appointments schedule illustrate this. Maj. Gen. William J. Donovan of the Office of Strategic Services "came in to tell . . . how much he could do to run the Government on an even basis." Rear Adm. Richard E. Byrd "came in to tell how to settle world peace." Senator W. Lee O'Daniel of Texas "came in for purpose of reading me a four-page letter, paragraph by paragraph, on how to run the Government of the United States."[5] Truman saw many of these people only to strengthen his political contacts or to size them up. Some of his visitors did have, however, things of importance to say to him about federal policies and programs. Fortunately for him, Truman had a great capacity for talking with people as well as for reading, which were essential parts of his job.

The big question was, as it has increasingly been for modern presidents, could his ability to absorb information and to be reflective about it match his need to be decisive? Truman believed that it could not, although he never stopped trying. This is an important reason that he—and his successors—came to rely so heavily on aides, experts, and special committees for facts and opinions, that the presidency became so captive to organization during the Truman era. And this is why Truman never stopped trying to master great quantities of facts and ideas. He knew that he had to try to know what the policy formulators were talking about if he were successfully to be the arbiter among them. As with his emphasis on practicality in administration, Truman's criticism of Roosevelt was implicit. His predecessor had not known enough in an increasingly complicated world. Truman did not intend to make this mistake, at least not as often as he thought Franklin Roosevelt had.

Whether or not he was capable of remedying Roosevelt's mistakes or of building on his accomplishments, Truman had to press on as president. He addressed a joint session of Congress on April 16, 1945, where he praised Roosevelt and pledged himself to "support and defend [his] ideals with all my strength and all my heart." Truman enlisted himself in the campaign to achieve "a speedy victory" over Germany and Japan, and he reaffirmed that the United States would demand of them "Unconditional Surrender!" Moreover, he declared, "There will be no relaxation in our efforts to improve the lot of the common people." He ended his address by emphasizing the need to create "a sound international organization" for lasting peace and to have the "continued cooperation" of the Allies in building that peace.

Truman began to indicate specifics about programs at his first news conference, on April 17. By then, these included the Bretton Woods agreements, which established the International Monetary Fund and the International Bank for Reconstruction and Development; trade reciprocity; and the extension of public power. In the coming weeks he would add to this list the Good Neighbor Policy, price and wage controls, the Fair Employment Practices Committee, Social Security, full employment, and independence for the Philippine Islands. There were also war measures to be considered. Congress extended the lend-lease program in April and the Selective Service System in May. The president had to veto legislation in May, however, that would have reduced the pool of men who were eligible for conscription by making a wholesale exemption of those who were engaged in farming. He was able to beat back organized labor's attempts to increase the government's anti-inflationary wage formula, although the anthracite miners were able to force a favorable settlement despite his seizure of the coal mines.

The war in Europe was running smoothly toward a victorious conclusion. When Truman succeeded to the presidency, Allied armies had already driven deeply into various parts of Germany. By April 27 he could announce jubilantly that Anglo-American forces had met Soviet units, thus cutting Germany in two. Five days later, he was able to tell the nation that German forces in Italy had surrendered. In his news conference on that same day the president also confirmed the death of Adolf Hitler. Truman was delighted to announce on his sixty-first birthday, May 8, 1945, the complete surrender of Germany. Victory in Europe had finally arrived after years of horror for so many people. He warned Americans, however, that "we are only half through"; victory "must now be won in the East."

Truman's early weeks as president had gone well. This he understood, for as he wrote in his diary on May 27: "Luck always seems to be with me in games of chance and in politics. No one was ever luckier than I've been since becoming the Chief Executive and Commander in Chief. Things have gone so well that I can't understand it—except to attribute it to God. He guides me, I think."[6] It was more than luck and God, of course. Truman had taken command of the ship of state when its momentum was high and when the crew and equipment were in excellent working condition. He had also been granted a honeymoon by most elements in the American body politic, so that they could assess him and reassess their own positions. Furthermore, his own contribution was not small, for he had exercised command vigorously. Yet his luck, as he would have it, was due to run down.

Many important international agreements had already been decided. These included plans to stabilize world monetary and financial systems, to improve food and agriculture, to revive cooperation for better health practices, and to launch a new world organization for peace, the United Nations. By the end of July, Congress had approved these, as well as renewal of the reciprocal tariff and expansion of the Export-Import Bank. Many Americans held high hopes for the effectiveness of these approaches to securing world peace. These were, however, largely to be vain hopes. There were to be no shortcuts to achieving peace on earth. Agreements on various crucial matters either had not yet been reached, were only in the preliminary stages, or were subject to controversial interpretations. As it turned out, there was not enough time to resolve vital differences among and even within nations before the war ended.

Even the plans for winning the war against Japan were far from settled. America's goals were clear, of course. They were to achieve victory in Asia as quickly as possible, with as few casualties and as little expense as possible. The American government also stood for unconditional surrender of the Japanese Empire. There were those leaders, however, who believed that this would only spur the Japanese to greater resistance, so that peace might better be negotiated. These people included British Prime Minister Winston Churchill, Secretary of War Stimson, Secretary of the Navy Forrestal, Acting Secretary of State Joseph C. Grew, and Army Chief of Staff George C. Marshall. The struggle to change the unconditional-surrender policy had begun soon after President Roosevelt had announced it for Germany, Italy, and Japan in January 1943, partly to calm Soviet fears that the United States might negotiate a separate peace with the Axis powers. Presumably, Roosevelt's policy referred to the unconditional surrender of enemy governments and armed forces. There were American officials, however, who interpreted it as only an unconditional surrender of enemy military forces, and others who thought that peace could be negotiated. Indeed, there had been, in effect, a negotiated peace with Italy. Truman's succession to the presidency offered new opportunities to alter the policy with respect to Japan. The new president conceded, however, only to the extent of publicly explaining on May 8 that the policy required that "Japanese military and naval forces lay down their arms in *unconditional surrender*." He added that "unconditional surrender does not mean the extermination or enslavement of the Japanese people."

22

The situation was complicated by the stiff resistance that United States forces encountered in securing Okinawa, immediately south of Japan. During the almost three months before victory was achieved on the island in June, the Americans sustained almost fifty thousand casualties. How could the United States propose a negotiated peace when the Japanese appeared to be so determined to resist? Nevertheless, by July 2 the government was thinking about demanding Japan's surrender, with the proviso that the emperor could be retained. It was argued that this might encourage Japan's surrender without the need for a long and bloody conflict; it should also make the Allied occupation of Japan easier, if it were done with the emperor's cooperation.

There were, however, more basic issues, assuming that Japan was not ready to surrender, unconditionally or otherwise. These stemmed from the fundamental question of how a military victory could be won. United States forces, with some help from their British and Commonwealth allies, had rolled back the Japanese from their vast island empire by spring of 1945. These forces had largely destroyed the Japanese navy and had inflicted serious damage upon enemy air forces and industry. British forces had also progressed in forcing the Japanese out of Burma; and the Chinese, with American assistance, had advanced against the enemy in China. Good strategy seemed to dictate that while the enemy was being kept on the defensive on the Asian mainland, the main blow should be struck against the Japanese homeland.

The question of how to strike against the Japanese homeland had also not been settled. Naval and air blockades and offensives would probably work. Such a war of attrition might, however, take a long time and be very costly. And what if it did not work? What if the patience of the United States and its allies wore thin? What if other exigencies arose meanwhile that required their attention? What if Japan exploited these possibilities to negotiate a peace that was less than humbling? No, a war of attrition could not be seriously contemplated, for it would be unacceptable to the war-weary and victory-expectant American leaders and people.

Another possibility, one seriously considered, was an invasion of Japan, which might lead to undisputed victory. Although there was not complete military agreement on this, the advice given Truman was that, to be successful, an invasion would probably take a year from its initiation, perhaps in November, and that it would cost at least half a million American casualties. The Americans could not count upon their British and Chinese allies for much assistance in this undertaking, but they did hope to enlist the help of the Union of Soviet Socialist Republics. President Roosevelt had broached this question to the

Soviets and had received something of a commitment at the Yalta Conference of February 1945. Russian participation had its problems, of course, especially that the USSR would expect to share in the fruits of victory in the Far East. Yet Truman decided in May to confirm Russian entry into the struggle against Japan. In this way, more power would be brought to bear against Japan, and the expense and the casualties would be shared to a greater extent. It would also be better from the American standpoint for the Russians to be engaged against Japan than for them to have freedom of action elsewhere in the world. Nor was there anything to prevent the Soviet Union, for completely its own reasons, from fighting Japan. Therefore, such a war might as well be a cooperative effort, which might offer opportunities for the United States and Russia to straighten out their other problems.

There was another possibility, one that seemed to be right out of the pages of science fiction. This was the employment of a weapon so devastating that it would immediately bring Japan to its knees. Of course, this was the atomic bomb. Albert Einstein had spurred American development of it when he wrote President Roosevelt in 1939 about the possibility of such a weapon. By 1942 the atomic bomb had become an important consideration in American strategy, and Great Britain had become a partner in research on the weapon. The United States and Britain did not inform Russia about their work on a nuclear bomb. Indeed, at Prime Minister Churchill's insistence, Roosevelt agreed in September 1944 that "the matter should continue to be regarded as of the utmost secrecy" and that there should be an Anglo-American monopoly on the development of atomic energy "until terminated by joint agreement." They also agreed that the bomb "might perhaps, after mature consideration, be used against the Japanese, who should be warned that this bombardment will be repeated until they surrender."[7] Since the atomic bomb was not yet available, the British and the Americans considered using, if necessary, a deadly anthrax bomb against Germany.

What Truman inherited in the atomic-bomb program was a projected weapon of devastating potential that was 90 percent sure of working. By April 1945 most of those who were connected with the program were eager or willing to use the atomic bomb. The chief questions were how to use it and whether to share atomic information with other countries. Alexander Sachs, a liaison officer between the atomic scientists and the government, was among those who wanted to have an international demonstration of the weapon in the hope that this would end the war. The Danish physicist Niels Bohr was among those who wanted to share information as a way to gain cooperative use and control of atomic energy. And some scientists, such as Leo Szilard, had doubts about using the weapon at all. Scientists and others connected with the atomic project might raise these questions, but the administration would decide them.

Henry L. Stimson had, after Truman's first cabinet meeting on April 12, told the new president darkly and vaguely of a probable "new explosive of almost unbelievable destructive power."[8] The secretary of war waited until April 25 to elaborate. Then he also told Truman that the United States would probably not remain in a controlling position indefinitely, because knowledge of the bomb's bases and access to the materials for it were too widespread. Stimson emphasized that the key questions to be resolved about the bomb were its use, the sharing of knowledge about it, and a system to control it. He recommended establishing a committee to treat with these questions, which Truman approved.

The resulting Interim Committee consisted of fourteen scientists and government officials, in addition to General Marshall and, as chairman, Secretary Stimson. Given the pressure of time under which members of the committee operated, not to mention their lack of knowledge, it is not surprising that they gave largely platitudinous answers to the questions before them. The Interim Committee gloried in the significance that atomic energy had for military purposes and industrial development. They recommended that there be continued research, further exploration of sharing atomic information and of controlling the use of nuclear weapons, and, vaguely, that a way be found to use America's knowledge of atomic energy so as to improve relations with Russia. The committee's essential, alarmingly contradictory recommendation, on which there was general agreement was that

> we could not give the Japanese any warning; that we could not concentrate on a civilian area; but that we should seek to make a profound psychological impression on as many of the inhabitants as possible. At the suggestion of Dr. [James B.] Conant the Secretary agreed that the most desirable target would be a vital war plant employing a large number of workers and closely surrounded by workers' houses.[9]

Even if President Truman had had doubts about using the atomic bomb or if he had known of the Roosevelt-Churchill agreement of September 1944—and there is no evidence that either is true—he was prepared to consider the deliberations of his expert advisers as constituting "mature deliberation." Moreover, there is no reason to doubt that he shared the Interim Committee's assumption that the bomb could be the deciding factor in the war against Japan. In effect, the die was cast on this issue. What Truman did not share was their recommendation that there be no warning; what he was not prepared to resolve was how to share atomic information and how to control the use of atomic energy; and what he probably wanted was a way in which to use America's atomic secrets to advantage in dealing with the Soviet Union. As for Stimson, he had failed to get others to work out solutions to his profound concerns about sharing and controlling the atomic bomb and not aggravating relations with the Russians. The issue of sharing atomic information would be resolved before too long, thanks largely to Soviet espionage and research efforts. The question of controlling the use of atomic energy would remain unanswered far beyond the Truman era. Much the same was true in the case of relations between Russia and the United States.

One should not jump to the conclusion that the decision to use the atomic bomb was largely motivated by the Truman administration's concern about dealing with the USSR. True, some American leaders viewed using the bomb against Japan as an implied threat against the Russians if they were refractory. More often discussed was the possibility of trading information about the bomb with the Soviet Union for something of value. The concern about the Russians was not, however, primary then with the Americans. If it had been, much more attention would have been given to the issue. It is also unlikely that the Americans would have been willing for the USSR to enter the war against Japan, which could only have strengthened Russia's bargaining position against the United States. No, America's prime concern was to gain victory over Japan speedily. A quick end to the war would permit the United States to get out of a business that it was sick of, that was costly in blood and treasure, and that was delaying the pressing matter of postwar reconstruction at home and abroad. Even so, by June 1945, everything had not fallen into place with respect to ending the war against Japan. The atomic bomb was still only a probability, for it had not yet been tested. Secretary Stimson later wrote, "The bomb as a merely probable weapon had seemed a weak reed on which to rely, but the bomb as a colossal reality was very different."[10]

This reality was aggravated by problems in which Russo-American relations were central. Although the Grand Alliance had been highly successful in prosecuting the war against Germany, relations among the Americans, the British, and the Russians had suffered from serious misunderstandings. Only a fool would have expected Russia's leaders to relinquish their instruments of power and not to seek the buffer zones that they regarded as being necessary to their nation's security. The

Soviets saw no reason to trust the candied words of Western statesmen, for the Soviets had suffered too much from the German invasion and the past hostility of other powers. Moreover, there had been hard bargaining during the war as to what assistance the USSR would receive from its Western allies. Candor often seemed to be lacking, and the Russians had reason to fear that the Anglo-American powers might make a separate peace with the enemy. The Soviets also believed that the Americans and the British were not contributing as much as they could in fighting the Germans.

The Western Allies, for their part, were often disturbed by the USSR's war objectives. The Russians clearly did not intend to give up what they had gained early in the war—Estonia, Latvia, Lithuania, eastern Poland, and Bessarabia. Moreover, they were on record as wanting Bukovina and more of Finland; special interests in Bulgaria, Czechoslovakia, Germany, Greece, Hungary, Iran, Poland, and Yugoslavia; military bases in the Dardanelles; and a Russo-Danish condominium over the Baltic Straits. The keen observer could only conclude that the Russians wanted to dominate eastern Europe, to make the rest of the Continent militarily impotent, and to better their position in the Middle East. Nazi Germany, by invading the USSR in 1941, had opened the door for the Soviets to accomplish this and to have an excellent rationale for it. Despite the Atlantic Charter and similar idealistic proclamations, the inconsistency and reluctance with which London and, especially, Washington challenged Moscow's ambitions encouraged the Russians to believe that they could achieve their goals. When Americans raised pointed questions toward the end of the war, their timing seemed inauspicious. Maxim Litvinov said to Edgar Snow in Moscow in 1945: "Why did the Americans wait until now to begin opposing us in the Balkans and Eastern Europe? . . . You should have done this three years ago. Now it's too late and your complaints only arouse suspicion here."[11] Why, indeed, had the Americans waited? The answer is, in part, they did not believe that Soviet expansionism would be virtually unnegotiable by the end of the war and that they did not want to risk breaking up the Grand Alliance by challenging the Russians during the war. Moreover, they were not that sure of themselves and their own objectives beyond committing the USSR to the establishment of a world organization that would allow for the fair and amicable solution of international problems.

Franklin D. Roosevelt and Soviet Generalissimo Joseph Stalin in many ways accommodated each other successfully during the war. Yet Russo-American differences grew, and the Americans could not always count on agreement from their British allies. There were squabbles about a postwar United Nations, that centerpiece of American idealism, which Churchill and Stalin had less faith in than did Roosevelt, who was unhappy in 1944 when the British and the Russians agreed upon establishing spheres of influence in the Balkans. In September, to the former Archduke Otto of Austria, Roosevelt blurted out his concern about keeping "the Communists out of Hungary and Austria."[12] Poland was, however, the biggest issue. Roosevelt and Churchill advised Stalin that they could not recognize the Soviet-created Polish government—the so-called Lublin regime—which was waiting in the wings in Russia. The Western leaders were irritated by Stalin's refusal to assist the Polish uprising in Warsaw against the Germans in 1944. At Yalta in 1945, Roosevelt pressed Stalin to agree to free elections in Poland, which the Russian leader did. The president had his doubts about Stalin's pledge, however, and he wrote Churchill that there must be free elections in Poland. Roosevelt also hoped to extend this principle to other areas where the Western Allies had a chance of wielding influence. He wrote to Churchill on April 6: "We must not permit anybody to entertain a false impresson that we are afraid. Our armies will in a very few days be in a position that will permit us to become 'tougher' than has heretofore appeared advantageous to the war effort."[13]

What would have happened had Roosevelt lived is impossible to say, given his style of personal diplomacy. He may have been telling Churchill less of what he thought and more of what the British leader wanted to hear. No fox was Harry Truman, however. He was more literal-minded, relied heavily on his advisers, and was pressed for time in making his early decisions. His study of the situation indicated that relations between his country and Russia were deteriorating and that Roosevelt had intended to take a stiffer line. The United States ambassador to Moscow, W. Averell Harriman, rushed back to tell Truman that although the Soviets were willing to cooperate in several respects in order to rebuild their shattered economy, they were also moving to take over bordering states in a "barbarian invasion of Europe."[14] Admiral Leahy, chief of staff to Truman in the latter's role as commander in chief, often voiced suspicions about the Russians, as did Acting Secretary of State Joseph Grew. British Foreign Secretary Anthony Eden also soon got to the president to brief him on Britain's profound concerns with respect to the USSR. There were those, like Secretary Stimson and former ambassador to Russia Joseph E. Davies, who counseled Truman to go slowly with the Russians, but the preponderance of advice he received was to stiffen the American line.

The evidence seemed to support this. After the Yalta Conference of February 1945, the Soviet Union had intensified its actions in eastern Europe and had announced its intention to scrap its nonaggression treaty with Turkey. Moreover, Stalin's resolve to push as far west as possible with his armies was becoming plain, and Russia's unanticipated delay in activating the occupation machinery in Austria was irksome. Poland was, however, the prime concern of the Western Allies. They expected the Russians to fulfill their pledges, made at Yalta, for free elections in Poland and an enlargement of the provisional government to include non-Communist figures. The Anglo-American concern was genuine. After all, the British had gone to war to aid Poland, and the Americans had a large Polish-American constituency to satisfy. The Western Allies also viewed Poland as a test case for two of their war aims—national self-determination and the rebuffing of aggression. It just would not do to allow the exchange of one foreign imperialism for another in Poland. The problems were that the Western Powers had not been firm enough, if that would have made any difference, and that the Russians, not the Americans and the British, were occupying Poland.

Matters seemed to be scheduled to come to a head when Russian Foreign Minister Vyacheslav Molotov met with Truman. On April 22 the president, spurred by the British, told Molotov that the implementation of the Yalta agreements could no longer continue to be a one-way street. Truman was irritated by the news that Russia had just recognized the Lublin government. The next day he met with his key advisers on the Polish issue. Secretary Stimson, General Marshall, and Admiral Leahy advised against going too far on Poland, lest the Soviets delay entering the war against Japan. James F. Byrnes, who would soon become secretary of state, counseled a stronger stand, and Navy Secretary Forrestal declared that the United States should let Russia know how we felt about eastern Europe. Truman decided to make it icily clear to Molotov that he expected a representative Polish provisional government to be formed. This he did on April 23, adding that postwar American assistance to Russia might hinge on the satisfactory solution of the Polish question. When Molotov suggested that the United States was trying to impose its will on the USSR, Truman shot back that all that Stalin needed to do was to carry out his commitments on Poland. It may have been, as Truman later wrote, that Molotov told him, "I have never been talked to like that in my life," and that Truman retorted, "Carry out your agreements and you won't get talked to like that."[15] If these exact words were not exchanged, those who were concerned believed that they summed up what took place.

The Soviet reaction can only be a matter of conjecture. If the Russian leaders thought that Truman was inclined to bargain harder than had Roosevelt, this did not lead them to shelve their plans to join the United Nations or to enter the war against Japan. Nor is there any evidence that the Molotov-Truman meeting by itself influenced the Russians to intensify their actions in Europe. Too many other things would have affected the course of events. One was that Truman could not adhere to a stiff line on everything, partly because he believed that it was essential to have Russia participate in the UN and in the war against Japan. Moreover, neither the president nor most of his advisers were sure what to be firm on, especially since all of them wanted to keep the door open for negotiations. In short, the United States had not learned how to bargain effectively for its own interests. It had not even determined what its postwar interests were. One can say that if Russia had caused the postwar world crisis by its overreaching, America had contributed by its inconsistency.

Events were fast paced between the Molotov-Truman meetings in April and the Potsdam Conference of July. Lurking in the background was the horrifying story that the Soviets had massacred several thousand interned Polish officers at Katyn in 1940. There were, however, more immediate concerns. Late in April 1945, Russian paratroopers were landed in Denmark, and the Soviets unilaterally installed a provisional government in Austria. The USSR obviously intended to develop its influence in these two countries while their armies were seeking to occupy Berlin and Prague before American or British forces could get there. By June the Russians had unilaterally established political parties in their occupation zone of Germany and had prevented the effective operation of the Allied Control Council in Berlin until all Allied forces had withdrawn to their occupation zones. There was also a squabble over whether the Western Allies would have access to Berlin through the Soviet zone. The Russians in June had demanded a voice in Norway, too, and had indicated their interest in Lebanon, Syria, Tangier, Iran, and Turkey. London and Washington interpreted these actions as being contrary to their understandings with the Soviet Union.

Most spectacular was the Venezia Giulia crisis, although the Russians did not initiate it. The partisan forces of Josip Broz (Tito) had, with American, British, and Soviet support, gained control of Yugoslavia. Tito soon moved to acquire the Italian territory of Venezia Giulia, which included the important seaport of Trieste. The supreme Allied commander in the Mediterranean, British Field Marshal Sir Harold Alexander, advised the Yugoslavians that he intended to occupy and administer the area; and by May 2, British units had entered Trieste.

Although the Americans and the British now saw Tito's forces as being aligned with Moscow, London wanted to stand up to the Yugoslavs in order to combat the threat of communism to Italy, while Washington worried lest fighting should break out. Despite their bickering, the Western Allies built up their military strength in the disputed area and advised Tito and Stalin that the Allies would not permit Yugoslavian encroachment on Italy. The crisis was temporarily resolved in June, leaving Anglo-American forces in control of Trieste, and Yugoslavian troops dominant in most of its hinterland. The Venezia Giulia question continued to be a problem until it was settled in 1954, which gave Trieste and ninety square miles of the area to Italy and two hundred square miles to Yugoslavia. Before then, however, Yugoslavia had broken with Russia and had become friendly to the Western Powers.

Then there was the lend-lease imbroglio. This operation, initiated by the United States in 1941, had provided massive amounts of supplies to the nation's allies during the war, including some $10 billion worth to Russia. There was strong sentiment on Capitol Hill not to use such assistance for postwar reconstruction (despite Roosevelt's wishes to the contrary). Truman was sensitive to congressional sentiment. Shortly after Germany's surrender in May, he ordered the cessation of lend-lease shipments that were not needed for operations in the Far East or for the completion of industrial plants that were under construction. The Foreign Economic Administration interpreted his order too literally, however, going so far as to direct outbound ships to return to port. Within a day this order was rescinded, but damage had been done. Stalin was infuriated; he viewed the order as being aimed solely at Russia, even though it applied to all of America's allies. The incident pointed up a great problem for the world. Given the devastation caused by the war, how was economic reconstruction to be achieved? The few international arrangements agreed to, such as the United Nations Relief and Rehabilitation Administration, were woefully inadequate. Engrossed in concluding the war, America, Britain, and Russia had not given the question enough attention.

Truman was becoming aware of the need for emergency food and medical relief. He was also sensitive to the political implications, for as he declared in a public letter of May 22, ''A chaotic and hungry Europe is not fertile ground in which stable, democratic and friendly governments can be reared.'' Yet the resources that he could command were limited. It is to his credit that he soon adopted former President Herbert Hoover's suggestion that the United States Army provide relief to liberated countries in western Europe. This would, however, only begin to turn the tide against serious threats of famine, pestilence, and political chaos. The formulation of an effective policy of reconstruction lay in the future, and it would be spurred for political and economic reasons as well as for humanitarian ones.

The president also had problems with allies other than Russia and Yugoslavia. Of these, France was the most irritating. The French, largely as a matter of good will, had been granted occupation zones in Austria, Berlin, and Germany, but they often managed to vex the Americans about occupation matters. More irksome were France's efforts to reinstate itself by force in Lebanon, which Britain, at America's insistence, halted with a show of military strength. The Americans forced the French to relinquish their unauthorized occupation of Stuttgart in Germany and of the Val d'Aosta area in Italy. All this and more Truman chalked up to France's provisional president, Charles de Gaulle, whom the American characterized as a "son-of-a-b----" who was disobeying orders.[16] It is not surprising that by 1946 the United States Army ranked the interception and breaking of secret French messages as its third-highest priority, just behind those of Russia and Yugoslavia.

Truman plainly had his hands full just contending with the war against Japan, relations with the Western Allies, international relief, and domestic problems. It was the increasing worries about the Soviet Union that vexed him most. The big question was how could the United States be firm with the Russians when America's wartime actions, agreements, and announcements were open to differing interpretations? A related question was how could the administration enlist the cooperation of the Soviets in joint ventures when the concessions that might be required could ruin any policy of firmness on other issues? The carrot and the stick might work with a mule, but it could be dangerous when applied to a bear. Time was short, information was limited, and confusion was substantial. Clearly, the Truman administration could reassess its strategy toward Russia only with great difficulty.

America's illusions would keep getting in the way of the administration's reassessment of strategy. The positive reaction of so many Americans to the wartime portrayal of their Soviet allies as being gallant and progressive had not erased the suspicions of other Americans about an anticapitalistic, atheistic, and expansionistic Russian dictatorship. This was complicated by what most Americans, according to public-opinion polls, believed the world should be like. Nations should enjoy self-determination, but they should also be more like the United States. There should be a world government—one that would foster American ideas of peace, prosperity, and democracy, though not one that would frustrate America's freedom of action. These illusions, however well intentioned, were clearer to people abroad than they were to Americans.

Moreover, American illusions collided with the need to recognize the aspirations of other states and to deal with them pragmatically and patiently.

There were two other aggravating factors. One was that the American system did not often allow for quick, consistent responses to rapidly developing situations. Too many elements in a complicated body politic had to be considered. It was little wonder that the Russians had trouble interpreting United States policy when Americans themselves had such problems with it. The other factor was of recent development. Not only did the United States possess enough strength to become a dominant power internationally, but many Americans had also come to agree that events elsewhere in the world could affect them, largely because of rapid advances in military and economic technology. Now the United States had the power and increasingly the resolve to bring American ideas to bear all over the world. Consequently, the country might not retreat into its shell after its sally onto the global scene during World War II.

Truman and most other leaders did not yet understand that the American tide would not recede after the war. Thus the administration worked hard, before the end of the war, on behalf of its ideas with regard to peace, prosperity, and democracy. This in part explains the government's concern with unconditional surrender, the United Nations, and firm agreements with the other victors. Although the United States might not retreat as far from world involvement as it had after World War I, the nation would have to rely upon some mechanisms to ensure an international order that would be comfortable for Americans. This also partly explains the rising agitation in Washington. Russia, not to mention other countries, was not acting as the Americans had hoped it would. Therefore, the Truman administration felt pressed not just to defeat Japan as soon and as cheaply as possible; the administration also felt the need to create the United Nations so as to achieve the effortless perpetual peace that the United States craved and to arrive at solid understandings with other powers as to how things would be in the brave new postwar world.

The concern of the United States to achieve its grand objectives was just as sensible as Russia's race to acquire as much territory and influence as it could before the end of the war. The problem was not so much one of understandable objectives as it was of different tactics and levels of tolerance for what the other one did. In this situation, both the United States and Russia had their triumphs and troubles, with the troubles often growing out of the triumphs. The conquest of the Axis Powers would open a vacuum into which the victors would flow on a collision course with each other. Moreover, it would lead the wartime allies to reconstruct their erstwhile foes in ways that would be expensive and disturbing. The United States got the United Nations, but the latter often turned out to be little more than a shadow force and occasionally an embarrassment. The understandings between the United States and the Soviet Union were too often not solid. And of considerable importance, the competition between the two powers to gain their objectives often fueled their hostility toward each other.

What was the new American president to do? One cannot in fairness ascribe to Harry Truman weaknesses that were inherent in the situations and system that he inherited. No vice-president had succeeded to the presidency with such high stakes at issue. Of elected presidents, only Abraham Lincoln and possibly Franklin D. Roosevelt had assumed office under such pressure and with such complications. They had been elected to their high estate, however; had had some time to prepare to assume it; and were not obligated to carry on the policies of their predecessors. Truman did not have the time, the prestige, the mental preparation, or the luxury of concentrating on only one crisis. He had, in fact, two major crises to resolve simultaneously—winning the war and securing the peace—and the one complicated the other. And waiting in the wings for him were the challenges of domestic and world reconstruction.

The tactic that Truman initially followed with respect to Russia was to use the lure of the carrot and the encouragement of the stick. This, he believed, was in line with Roosevelt's intentions. Truman had applied the stick at his April meeting with Molotov. To consider the carrot, the president counseled in May with the former United States ambassador to Moscow, Joseph E. Davies, and Roosevelt's top confidant, Harry L. Hopkins. Subsequently, Truman sent Davies to London to tell Prime Minister Churchill that the United States would not be the agent of British interests and that the three powers must trust one another. As the president put it, he wanted to counter Generalissimo Stalin's "opinion we're ganging up on him."[17] Truman also dispatched Hopkins to Moscow to tell "Uncle Joe Stalin" that Tito should be restrained but that eastern European nations interested America "only so far as World Peace is concerned. That Poland ought to have a 'free election,' at least as free as [American bosses] would allow in their respective bailywicks. . . . Uncle Joe should make some sort of gesture—whether he means it or not to keep it before our public that he intends to keep his word."[18] This certainly gave the Soviet leader considerable latitude. Truman could not, however, adhere to such a policy as other conflicts arose.

Hopkins had other business with Stalin during their meeting in late May. This included requesting a summit conference, seeking agreement on voting procedures for the UN Security Council, and setting a date for Soviet entry into the war against Japan. Stalin had his own agenda, most important on which were the disposition of German naval and merchant vessels and the continuation of lend-lease. Hopkins reassured him about lend-lease and Russian claims to German ships. Stalin agreed to non-Communist participation in the Polish government, holding free elections there, and not extending the veto to determining the Security Council's agenda. He further agreed to a meeting with Truman and Churchill, fixing the place at Berlin, and told Hopkins that Soviet forces would be ready to fight Japan by August 8. Truman was pleased with the results of the Hopkins mission. It appeared that Truman had achieved what he wanted at this point and that other issues could be dealt with at the forthcoming summit meeting with Stalin and Churchill.

Despite constantly arising problems among the Allies in June and July, the omens seemed favorable. The Venezia Giulia crisis had been handled; there was improvement on questions of the occupation of Germany and Austria; and a broader-based provisional government of Poland had been established, with a commitment to hold free elections. Moreover, the delegates of fifty nations had approved the Charter of the United Nations in San Francisco. Yet Truman was not euphoric. He knew that many things remained to be settled. After a meeting on July 4 with some of his closest advisers, he jotted down: ''Discussed Russia & Jap War, Government for Germany, *Food,* fuel and transportation for Europe, Sterling Block etc. Don't feel happy over situation.''[19]

The atomic bomb was still to be tested. Until this happened in July, American strategy against Japan could not be decided. Other questions were involved. One concerned the reliability and strength of the peace feelers that had been extended by some elements in Japan. Another concerned how useful the bomb would be if it did work. Still another concerned whether the Russians could be counted on to enter the war in August. To be on the safe side, on June 18 Truman approved General Marshall's plan for an invasion of Japan in the fall.

The president meanwhile was preparing for the meeting with Russian and British leaders at the Berlin suburb of Potsdam. En route by ship to Europe, he wrote in his diary: ''How I hate this trip! But I have to make it—win, lose or draw—and we must win.''[20] The summit conference began on July 17. Truman became chairman of the meetings, and he moved briskly through the agenda. He was also in good spirits throughout, because he was steadily getting information on the success of the experimental explosion of the atomic bomb in New Mexico. By

July 21 the president knew of the full impact of the new weapon. During the Potsdam meeting, he and his secretary of state, James F. Byrnes, gained in self-confidence from this knowledge. They now believed that they held the trump card to use against Japan. Moreover, they believed that when the Russian leaders learned about the bomb, they would be more cooperative. Truman and Byrnes were right in their first surmise, but they were off the mark on the second.

The American leaders quickly made decisions with respect to Japan. After consultations among Truman, Byrnes, Stimson, Marshall, Leahy, and a few others at Potsdam, it was decided to use the atomic bomb, against military objectives, before August 10. It was also agreed that an ultimatum would be issued to Japan by Truman, Churchill, and China's Generalissimo Chiang Kai-shek. The American leadership ruled out the suggestion of an international demonstration of the bomb, because only two of the atomic devices would be available. The president's concern that ''soldiers and sailors are the target and not women and children''[21] was taken less seriously by those in the military hierarchy who chose the objectives than were the ideas of the Interim Committee as to what constituted military targets. The warning to Japan was so diluted that it had to seem inscrutable to anyone who was not privy to the existence of the atomic bomb. The closest the ultimatum of July 26 came to suggesting that something most unusual was afoot was in the last point, ironically number 13: ''We call upon the government of Japan to proclaim now the unconditional surrender of all Japanese armed forces, and to provide proper and adequate assurances of their good faith in such action. The alternative for Japan is prompt and utter destruction.''[22] There was no mention of retaining the emperor.

Speed dictated most of the thinking of Truman and his advisers: speed in ending the war quickly in order to save lives and resources, especially American, and to turn to other pressing matters; speed probably in order to lessen Russian intervention in the war. It is equally clear that during the discussions with his advisers, Truman became less concerned with giving the Japanese clear warning and less careful about making sure that the targets were purely or largely military. The need for speed also made those American officials who believed that the ends justified the means less thoughtful in considering the consequences of United States actions against Japan. Moreover, Truman and most of his advisers were so eager to end the war that they deluded themselves into believing they had given the Japanese a reasonable amount of time to reply to the ultimatum. A puzzled president was soon to note that it was strange that there had been no clear response to the ultimatum of July 26. Had he had more understanding of the divided and confused counsels in Japan, he would have known why a quick, clear-cut reply was not possible. The sharing of the responsibility with the British and Chinese governments did not save Truman and his administration from the stigma of having acted hastily in using the atomic bomb. Nor did the later explanations that its use saved more lives, Japanese as well as Allied, than it took. At least, clearer warning about the bomb, additional time for Japanese decision making, an offer to allow Japan to retain the emperor, and the choice of targets that were plainly military in nature would have left the United States in a better moral position. Although the odds are against it, more thoughtful consideration by Truman and the men around him might have led to a Japanese surrender without the horrors visited upon Hiroshima and Nagasaki.

As for the belief that United States possession of an atomic weapon would encourage Russia to be more conciliatory, again, too little thought was given to the matter. At Potsdam, Truman told Stalin that America had a new, powerfully destructive weapon. The Soviet leader only indicated that he hoped the United States would make "good use of it against the Japanese."[23] What the president did not know was that the Russians had received covert information about America's nuclear program. The Soviet reaction was to continue their espionage and to accelerate their development of atomic weaponry. Far from being intimidated, the USSR's leaders apparently felt confirmed in their suspicions with regard to American hostility and, therefore, in their secretive and aggressive ways. One can surmise that Soviet leaders doubted that the United States would share the secret of the bomb with them. It also seems that they doubted that the United States would launch a preventive war against them, so long as they stopped short of war in their own actions. Truman's error at Potsdam was in not entering into a full-scale discussion of the bomb with Stalin in the hope of preparing the way for negotiations that might lead to international control of atomic energy. Given Soviet suspicions of the United States, this probably would have made no difference. Then again, there is just the off chance that it might have. American haste and suspicions of the USSR militated against taking that chance.

The decisions of Truman and his advisers about the atomic bomb probably were the most important things that took place at Potsdam. Yet, other matters of significance occurred before the conference adjourned on August 2. The United States and Russian heads of state had impressed each other. Truman came away with respect for Stalin's directness and charm, but with distrust of other Russian leaders, which he never completely shook. Stalin seemed to be impressed by Truman's briskness and decisiveness despite the president's relative lack of experience and knowledge. An unresolved question is whether the Soviet leadership considered Truman dangerous or weak as a result of the impressions that they had gained of him. It was also during the Potsdam Conference that British voters decided to replace Winston Churchill's wartime coalition with a Labour government. Even at Potsdam the new prime minister, Clement Attlee, and his associates began to give the Truman administration closer support in dealing with Russia.

At Potsdam, the Americans, British, and Soviets reached agreement on a broad range of important issues. They agreed to eliminate all vestiges of Nazism in Germany; to restore local self-government on a democratic basis; to respect basic freedoms of speech, press, and religion; and to treat the vanquished country as a single economic unit, with the goal of making the German people self-sufficient. In principle, each of the occupying powers could take reparations from its own zone, except that 10 percent of surplus industrial equipment in the western zones would be transferred to Russia and another 25 percent would be set aside to be exchanged for specified commodities. The United States, Britain, and Russia would parcel out German naval and merchant vessels equally among themselves. The Soviet Union's interest in gaining more influence in Turkey was met with a statement affirming that the three powers would negotiate with Turkey for widening Russia's access to the Black Sea Straits. Left over for later negotiation were the determination of the Polish border and Russia's interest in being involved in the control of Tangier and in the disposition of Italy's colonies. The USSR agreed to the United States and British governments' having a real voice in the operations of the Allied Control Commissions in Bulgaria, Hungary, and Rumania. Western concern for the prompt withdrawal of Allied forces from Iran was put off for later determination, as was Truman's suggestion to open the inland waterways of Europe to free navigation by all. The three powers agreed to proceed expeditiously with war-crimes trials and in drafting peace treaties with Bulgaria, Finland, Hungary, Italy, and Rumania.

Truman left Berlin in an optimistic mood. The Big Three had addressed the chief issues and had decided them on a basis that he believed was fair to all concerned. The Americans had bargained particularly hard to prevent the Russians from stripping Germany so that the United States would not have to finance a large share of Soviet reparations. Moreover, the president was pleased with the establishment of the Council of Foreign Ministers. Representing China and France as well as the United States, Britain, and Russia, this council was left with working out many of the details of the Potsdam Agreement and deciding many of the unresolved questions. The Potsdam Agreement gave the impression that the Grand Alliance was still intact. Truman indeed told the American people by radio on August 9 that the "Three Great Powers . . . shall continue to march together to a lasting peace and a happy world!"

The president's mood soon changed. He decided that he did not like his negotiating experience and that he did not want to participate in another such conference. In fact, he never did. Although he would by-and-large hold to the Potsdam Agreement and hoped that Russia would too, he became less optimistic that the accords would be implemented and that the Council of Foreign Ministers would be very successful. Truman's growing pessimism was based on his conclusion that the USSR could not be counted on to negotiate fairly in the interest of lasting peace. He thought that the Russians believed that the United States was due for a depression and that it was "planning to take advantage of our setback."[24] Whatever their reasons, the Soviets would strive to extend their power. Truman was unwilling to have agreements flouted or to see any authoritarian power try to dominate the world. His response increasingly would be to apply the stick instead of offering the carrot to the Russians.

There was, of course, the war against the last of the Axis Powers to be concluded. When Japan had not replied affirmatively to the Sino-Anglo-American ultimatum for surrender, the atomic bomb was dropped on the city of Hiroshima on August 6. The most-responsible party, Truman, was concerned with the killing of "all those kids" and the future effects of atomic weaponry. Yet he blurted out, "This is the greatest thing in history."[25] He was not alone in his jubilation, which was general in the United States. Indeed, in a poll taken on August 8, 85 percent of Americans approved the use of the atomic bomb on Japanese cities. As most Americans saw it, nuclear attack would soon end the long and bloody war against a nation of treacherous and brutal yellow-skinned fanatics. As had been true increasingly during World War II, for the United States as well as other powers, the ends seemed to justify the means.

The United States released the second atomic bomb, on Nagasaki, on August 9. Hastiness obviously played a role in this action, for the administration had left the decision about the follow-up explosion to commanders in the field. The situation had also been expanded on August 8, as Truman excitedly announced in the shortest presidential news conference on record, "*Russia has declared war on Japan!* That is *all!*" After receiving news of the Soviet invasion, Prime Minister Kantaro Suzuki recommended, to an assembly of Japan's eminences, that Japan surrender. They were still debating when word arrived of the bombing of Nagasaki; even then, military leaders refused to contemplate surrender. Finally, Emperor Hirohito intervened, and the issue seemed to be settled.

On August 10 a Japanese broadcast reached the United States, reporting that Japan would surrender on Allied terms, provided that the emperor's prerogatives were not prejudiced. President Truman called together Secretaries Byrnes, Forrestal, and Stimson and Admiral Leahy to consider the Japanese offer. After some discussion, they decided to accept the surrender with the stipulation that the emperor would be retained subject to the authority of the supreme Allied commander for Japan. The cabinet approved this formula, as soon did Great Britain, China, and Russia. The Allies dispatched their reply on August 11, although Japan did not agree to it without further opposition from military leaders. Finally, at 7 P.M. on August 14, Truman was able to announce that Japan had accepted the surrender terms. He also announced a two-day holiday, and celebration swept the land. The long, bitter war was over.

3

★ ★ ★ ★ ★

RECONVERSION

Serious problems would quickly follow in the wake of Allied victory in 1945. For the United States, economic reconstruction at home was one of the most important of these challenges. President Truman was sensitive to the fact that the war had interrupted the struggle in the United States to decide how the New Deal initiatives would be worked out. Moreover, he was keenly aware of the economic difficulties that the United States had encountered after most of its wars as well as being apprehensive about the return of the depression of the 1930s. His prime domestic objective—one shared by almost all Americans—was to avoid a repetition of either the Great Depression or the economic troubles that had followed World War I. The pressing question was how to do so.

One of the Truman administration's greatest problems in tackling postwar economic questions was the inadequate preparations that had been made for peace during the war itself. It was not a matter of lack of concern in America about reconversion. The problem stemmed more from uncoordinated, sharply competitive thought and planning. Congress in 1943 had eliminated the National Resources Planning Board, the agency that President Roosevelt had most looked to for help on reconversion. The legislators had also shown themselves incapable of providing leadership on most questions of reconversion as on many other matters. There was, however, a plethora of interests that gave some attention to postwar planning—the Bureau of the Budget, various congressional committees, many private groups, several old-line executive agencies, and elements in most of the fifty-three wartime federal organizations. Out of this welter of concern emerged the International Monetary Fund, the World Bank, and the Serviceman's Readjustment Act (or the GI Bill of Rights), among other things. Yet most of the ideas that were bandied about in administration, congressional, and private circles were not acted upon because of lack of agreement.

The main problem that would confront the United States after the war seemed clear. During the war the nation had come to enjoy full employment and record income levels. Yet most of America's industrial production was devoted to winning the war, the cessation of which would pose great problems of converting to enough peacetime production to sustain a high level of economic opportunity. Concern for this had led to some action. In 1942 Congress authorized the extension of basic agricultural price supports for two years after the war, and in 1944 the Office of Contract Settlement was created to cushion the termination of government contracts at the end of the war. There was the establishment of the Surplus War Property Administration, which was to sell surplus federally owned goods and production facilities at discounted prices in order to help business and yet realize some income for the government. Moreover, it was anticipated that the new Retraining and Reemployment Administration would assist people who had lost their wartime jobs in finding employment.

These preparations were potentially useful, but they did not deal significantly with the central concern of stimulating production for civilian purposes after the war. In late 1943, Chairman Donald M. Nelson of the War Production Board (WPB) had sought to increase the output of civilian commodities. His efforts had been rebuffed by those, including President Roosevelt, who had feared that such a program would endanger war production. During 1944 Roosevelt had eased Nelson out of effective leadership of the key federal economic-control agency by sending him on a mission to China. There was also interest, within the WPB, to perpetuate governmental control over production during the transition period from war to peace in order to try to maintain high levels of employment. But opposition from industry, the military, and certain other federal agencies had led WPB officials to talk publicly only in terms of retaining a few controls over production.

This meant that the government would not seriously address the problem of production reconversion until after the war with Germany had been won. Federal officials generally believed that there would be enough time to act later, an attitude that was based on the assumption that the war against Japan would last for at least a year after victory in Europe. Moreover, the Roosevelt administration was counting heavily on the tremendous accumulation of savings during the war. Amounting to more than $200 billion, this sum should somehow result in investment, spending, and production that would tide America over the anticipated postwar employment problem. In its obsession with economic salvation through the spending of accumulated savings, the administration discounted many other possible instruments of reconstruction. The government's concern to win the war quickly and to avoid political controversy reinforced this attitude. The Roosevelt administration seemed oblivious, therefore, to the danger of postwar inflation as pent-up civilian demand, backed by an abundance of dollars, might collide with an insufficient amount of consumer goods. Furthermore, there had been no planning to resolve the inevitable disputes between labor and management after wartime controls expired. The director of War Mobilization and Reconversion, James F. Byrnes, demonstrated the administration's smugness when he declared at the beginning of 1945, "all administrative actions which pave the way to orderly transition from war to peace and which are feasible at this time have been taken."[1] Even though far more planning had been done to cope with postwar economic problems than ever before in America's history, Byrnes's statement was wildly optimistic.

The inadequacy of the government's preparation for postwar reconstruction had not been Truman's only legacy. He had also inherited the reasons for that inadequacy. It had been a long time since Franklin D. Roosevelt had been in command of Congress except on clear-cut emergency issues. This had been partly because of his diminishing personal powers, his political mistakes, and his concentration on winning the war. Moreover, the proportion of conservative Republicans and even Democrats had been relatively high since 1938. The Seventy-ninth Congress with which Truman would have to work was certainly not one that would be very responsive to initiatives for increased federal programs and controls. In this, Congress reflected a shift in the attitudes of much of the electorate, which was feeling prosperous and was wearying of Big Brother in Washington. Roosevelt's lesser attention to party matters during the war contributed to this situation. To aggravate affairs, the more-conservative breed of war managers had replaced many of the New Dealers in government.

This was, however, only part of Harry Truman's inheritance. The prescriptions for postwar reconstruction also were wide-ranging. This mirrored the variety of men in power and the rise of conservatism as well as the new prestige and resources acquired by business, which had done so much and profited so much in helping to win the war. There may have been substantial unity in America on winning the war, but clearly there was widespread division on the shape of reconversion.

Moreover, not enough of the New Deal economy or the wartime economy was relevant to postwar problems. This further spurred the scramble to decide who would choose and manage the changes. The variety of thought—and even of ignorance—among interested private and public elements guaranteed that the reconversion period would be a time of confusion.

This situation left Truman with many disadvantages. Yet it also had some advantages for him. He had considerable choice in defining his problems, priorities, and policies. What emerged was a Truman administration program that was more than a warmed-over New Deal. Yet the problems were enormous, and confusion and controversy would mark reconversion under Truman. Many have assessed him unfavorably, ascribing his problems to economic ignorance. The new president had had no formal education in economics. He did, at least, have a rich occupational background as a bank clerk, farmer, merchant, and salesman; Truman also had often dealt with economic and budgetary matters as a county official and a United States senator. Much of his work, indeed, as chairman of the Truman Committee, had been concerned with the wartime economy and postwar reconversion. One could make a case that he was better prepared to deal with economic issues than most presidents have been, probably better than his predecessor Roosevelt and certainly better than his successor Eisenhower, whose presidential economic experiences had been relatively narrow.

Thus, when he became president, Truman knew that economic reconstruction would be one of the major challenges facing him. Like Roosevelt, he found, however, that he had to devote almost all of his efforts to winning the war and to handling foreign relations. He was sensitive to economic problems when he found the time for them. For example, Secretary of Commerce Henry A. Wallace told him on May 18, 1945, of his department's estimate that by 1947 there would be 7 million unemployed Americans. This potential situation appalled Truman and strengthened his resolve to use governmental powers to prevent it. Nor was the president unaware of the threats of inflation and labor-management strife after the war. He and his advisers believed that the government would have more time to act than was the case. Nevertheless, Truman did encourage appropriate executive agencies to consider policies to deal with economic reconstruction. He also acted occasionally, as when in May 1945 he initiated the cutting of war-related expenditures.

After Germany's defeat, the administration focused more attention on economic questions. Truman's advisers did not speak with one voice, however, whether on controls, employment, inflation, labor, or whatever. One important example is pertinent. Chairman Julius A. Krug of the War Production Board had authorized an increase in the production of selected civilian goods. Krug believed that the removal of federal direction of production directly after the war would produce prosperous economic readjustment more quickly. In this, Krug encountered opposition from directors Chester Bowles of the Office of Price Administration, William H. Davis of the Office of Economic Stabilization, and Fred Vinson of the Office of War Mobilization and Reconversion, who was Truman's chief adviser on reconversion. As they informed the president, they feared the possibility of a disastrous postwar inflation if reasonable controls on wages, prices, and taxes were not continued. They were not zealots one way or another. There had to be, however, as Bowles wrote in June, "a thorough re-examination of the scope of price controls as well as other wartime controls generally. Price controls must be lifted as rapidly as the need for them disappears."[2] Thus the main issue was joined: namely, to have enough controls to restrain inflation and yet not so many as to discourage the speedy development of civilian production and peacetime jobs.

While Truman was primarily engaged in the conduct of the war and foreign relations, Krug largely got his own way on domestic economic matters. Krug not only encouraged production for peacetime uses; he also removed more than one-third of the War Production Board's regulations governing industry. The situation was assisted by Vinson's being appointed as secretary of the Treasury in July and the decision of his successor at the Office of War Mobilization and Reconversion (OWMR), John Snyder, to delay action until President Truman's return from Potsdam in August. Truman would by then have to make many decisions on questions that no longer permitted delay, because the end of the war was imminent. Within less than a month he would have to map out a plan for America's economic reconstruction.

Some ideas had been broached earlier. On May 1, Truman had publicly commended the Office of Price Administration (OPA) for having controlled inflation, and he suggested that Congress extend price-control authority for a year or more. The legislators did not act on this recommendation. Nor did they act on the president's request later in May to extend unemployment benefits to all nonfarm workers and to increase the individual payments to at least twenty-five dollars per week for as long as twenty-six weeks. Meanwhile, George W. Taylor of the National War Labor Board had drawn up a plan to keep key wage rates at least the same during the reconversion period. The Office of Economic Stabilization (OES) agreed and also suggested that wage increases be encouraged in order to stimulate greater business and employment opportunities. No formal policy was adopted, however, to implement either the Taylor Plan or the OES's response to it. Some action came from an unexpected quarter when Congress, before it adjourned on August 1, passed the Reconversion Tax Act. This legislation, which was aimed at providing more capital for reconversion activities, increased the exemption on the corporate excess profits tax from $10,000 to $25,000. It proved to be a boon for small businesses.

Agricultural, business, and labor elements were becoming nervous because of the mounting evidence that the government was basically not prepared to deal with reconversion. The old Truman Committee, now headed by Senator James Mead of New York, also sharply criticized the administration in late July for inadequate planning. The committee's report singled out the OWMR for confining "itself to umpiring disputes" when it should "plan and issue orders." The report further declared that if the war were to end soon, "we will find ourselves in a sorry state economically."[3] Such criticism was to the point, for the end of the war was near, and the administration did not have a reconstruction policy. Krug of the War Production Board hewed to the idea of rapidly terminating controls in order to stimulate the economy. The Office of Price Administration, organized labor, and much of small business dissented, for it was apparent that the OPA could not operate effectively without the continuance of WPB controls.

John Snyder of OWMR knew that it was time to set a course. Indicating his own sense of urgency, he met Truman's ship when the president arrived from Potsdam the day after the bombing of Hiroshima. Snyder outlined the problems for Truman, who consulted others but acted quickly. On August 9 he requested Krug to use the WPB's powers in order to spur civilian production by facilitating distribution of the necessary materials. Krug was also to remove production controls except as these were necessary to prevent speculative hoarding. In short, the president had elected to combat both recession and inflation by emphasizing economic growth while using controls where necessary. He had chosen to travel down the middle of the road, and it would prove to be slippery.

Truman's request of Krug was only the beginning of the president's offensive against the problems facing the nation's economy. On August 11 the president called Congress into session for September, asking federal agencies to submit proposals for a major presidential message to Congress. Reconversion was now Harry Truman's top priority. Indeed it was an emergency situation, and planning to meet it was paroxysmal. Truman spent a great deal of time consulting with agency heads, many of whom were new at their jobs. Most of them were overflowing with ideas, alarmed at the situation, and far from united on what to do about it. It was the president, therefore, who had to take the lead.

He tried to set the course in Executive Order 9599 of August 18. This directed executive agencies to "assist in the maximum production of goods and services required to meet domestic and foreign needs," to "continue the stabilization of the economy" through controls, and to facilitate the removal of these controls when they were no longer needed. There should not be either "inflation or deflation." Collective bargaining would be allowed to secure wage and salary increases as long as prices did not rise except to remedy gross inequities. Work disputes that would interfere with military production or the "effective transition to a peacetime economy" would be deemed contrary to the national interest. The director of War Mobilization and Reconversion, John Snyder, was to coordinate the government's efforts to achieve these goals.

Truman's next important step was to prepare to announce his administration's overall domestic program for postwar America. He charged his counsel, Samuel I. Rosenman, with coordinating the input to this message, which would be delivered to Congress on September 6. Rosenman rallied all interested federal agencies to make sure that their points of view were considered. He also used his pivotal role, with support from Press Secretary Charles Ross, to instruct Truman about Roosevelt's ideas. Rosenman later crowed, exaggeratedly, that he put Truman "on the path of New Deal thinking from which he never strayed."[4] Snyder considered the resulting presidential message to be too liberal, and Rosenman thought it was too long. Truman later saw it as the beginning of the Fair Deal. It is doubtful, however, that the exceedingly busy president had any profound grasp of what he was saying at the time he made the speech.

The president's September 6 message to Congress was liberal and long—it was a catalog of his good intentions. He set forth a program of twenty-one points that he urged the legislators to consider in recon-structing postwar America. Truman had already requested some of the points, such as better unemployment compensation, reorganization of the executive branch, a permanent Fair Employment Practices Commit-tee, improved disposal of surplus property, and continued authority for economic controls. Others dealt with immediate problems. These in-cluded increasing the mimimum wage, legislation to encourage full employment, improved collective bargaining, extension of the U.S. Employment Service until 1947, increased security for farmers, support of scientific research, tax reduction, additional public works, assisting world reconstruction, regulation of atomic energy, unification of the armed services, and universal military training. Among his long-range programs were those aimed at providing the American citizen with a decent home, adequate medical care, and a good education. He was also concerned with heightened assistance to small business as well as the development of river valleys and facilities for air transportation.

This was a party platform, inaugural address, and state of the union message all in one package, and only its high points have been covered here. Republican Congressman Charles A. Halleck of Indiana declared: "This is the kick-off; this begins the campaign of '46." House Minority Leader Joseph W. Martin, Jr., remarked: "Not even President Roosevelt ever asked for as much at one sitting."[5] They had a point, for Truman had presented too many recommendations, politically charged ones at that, for Congress to do much more than gag upon. He had also provided his critics with many targets. Yet he would hew to most of his proposals until they were enacted or until he left office. Central to it all was his vision, one shared by most of his aides and especially John Snyder, that full production was the key to the reconstruction of United States society. As Truman saw it, it was a magic circle. Full production thus meant full employment, which spelled the perpetuation of full production. It also meant an increase in governmental revenues so as to provide more public services. Additionally, the president believed that full production and employment in America would expand international trade and would lead to "greater economic security and more opportunity for lasting peace throughout the world." If Truman's message had New Deal overtones, it also had his own particular emphasis on looking to private enterprise as a full partner in achieving a new and better America. If he would be less than successful in securing the New Deal aspects of his program, he would be highly successful in promoting peacetime American production.

Officials of the Truman administration did not sit back to await congressional action. They used the tools at their disposal to facilitate reconversion. On the night of Japan's formal surrender, September 2, the government canceled some one hundred thousand contracts worth about $23 billion. Very few contracts—only those for essential military production—would be left by the end of 1945. The administration planned to demobilize 5 million of the 12 million military personnel within a year after the end of the war. This goal was soon increased to 9 million, however, partly in response to public pressure to "bring the boys home" and partly in order to slash federal expenditures. The administration lifted manpower controls immediately, and it continued rationing only of tires, meats, fats, oils, sugar, and shoes. The War Production Board moved faster on removing production controls than both the Office of Price Administration and, apparently, Truman wanted. By September, the WPB had dropped 229 of the remaining 389 production controls. The OPA was more cautious, lifting price controls only on nonessential goods such as furs and sports equipment.

The administration's primary concern was to maintain employment. Industrial production had dropped steadily since February 1945, and by August, administration officials were seriously alarmed. It was widely held that 6 million Americans would be unemployed by the end of the year. Indeed, 1.8 million people lost their jobs during the first ten days of peace. This gave new impetus to the administration's peacetime production policy as well as for the rapid removal of controls. Interest rates were kept low; Treasury Secretary Vinson on October 1 asked Congress to lower taxes by $5 billion; only fifty-five production controls remained by November; and by 1946, only sugar was being rationed, and most restrictions on exports and imports had been abandoned. Moreover, the administration encouraged the use of the nation's savings, which totaled $239 billion by the end of 1945, to stimulate production. Thus did the government move to win the battle of conversion from wartime to peacetime production in order to deal with the threat of large-scale unemployment.

One of the most worrisome impediments to expanded peacetime production was conflict between management and organized labor. Industry was eager to take advantage of the removal of controls, the availability of capital, and pent-up consumer demand. Labor had no objection to this, provided that it got its full share of whatever prosperity there might be. Not only did the unions and management disagree as to what that share should be, but labor was smarting from having had to sacrifice during the war. The Little Steel formula of 1942 had largely frozen labor's basic hourly wage rates and had prohibited strikes. The unions had been galled to see business profit hugely from federal production incentives, while working people prospered only when they labored beyond a forty-hour week and collected overtime pay rates. The end of the war meant that there would be little overtime work available and that large numbers of employees might be laid off. Moreover, the unions believed that they had lost influence in Washington and knew that they had no friend in management. With the Japanese surrender, labor's no-strike pledge would be void. The end of hostilities overseas promised, therefore, to lead to the beginning of hostilities at home.

Caught off base by the speedy termination of the war, the government had not prepared any labor policy for the reconversion period. Truman's guidelines in his executive order of August 18 were vague and offered little hope to labor to deal with smaller pay packets, lessened job opportunities, and possible inflation. In August, Republican Senator Arthur H. Vandenberg of Michigan proposed the convening of a conference of representatives from government, labor, and management to work out the guidelines for industrial peace that might ensure maximum production and employment. Secretary of Labor Lewis Schwellenbach endorsed the idea, and soon the administration was making arrangements for such a conference. No less was hoped for from the conference than to get labor and management to agree on ways in which to settle their disputes without strikes and to cooperate in wage and price stabilization. Somehow a way also had to be found to increase wage rates without raising market prices. Some very optimistic federal officials believed that the growing supply of surplus labor would make unions more cooperative and that the promise of large postwar profits would result in cooperation on the part of business. How wrong they would prove to be.

On September 11 the United Steelworkers demanded a wage hike of two dollars a day. Other unions were quick to present their demands, which averaged a 30 percent increase in wage rates, and the United Mine Workers announced a strike in order to organize foremen. President Truman was stung by these demands, for he had taken the paucity of response from business and labor as agreement to his August 18 executive order, at least until the labor-management conference could deliberate. He wrote in his diary on September 20: " 'Labor' has gone off the beam. The job now is to bring them back. And it is going to take guts to do it."[6] The next day he blew off steam to his staff, saying that some time he might tell labor and management to "go to hell."[7] Truman did act to the extent of transferring all labor matters to Labor Secretary Schwellenbach's jurisdiction. The president could not, however, get the labor-management conference going in September, as he had planned, because of disagreements over the agenda. Meanwhile, Price Administrator Chester Bowles explored with union and industrial leaders the possibility of agreeing upon a formula to keep the peace. There seemed to be a good chance that agreement could be reached on raising wage rates by 10 percent, while the OPA minimized the impact on prices. Secretary Schwellenbach would have nothing to do with using controls in the formula, however, for he did not believe inflation was a threat.

The administration urged the use of collective bargaining in the hope that labor and management might thereby compose their differences at least until the labor-management conference met. Meanwhile, Truman indicated that the government would not tolerate strikes in crucial industries. He seized the plants of twenty-six petroleum producers and refiners on October 4, on national security grounds.

"Nothing," he asserted in a public statement then, "will be permitted to stand in the way of the adequate supplies of *any* kind for our armed forces." As all knew, however, the president could use such a weapon only selectively, because it was legally questionable and politically dangerous. The administration was still counting on the labor-management conference to develop a formula that would enable the nation to avoid industrial strife and thus to maintain maximum production and employment.

The president opened the Labor-Management Conference on November 5 by calling upon the representatives of the unions and industries "to handle their own affairs in the traditional, American, democratic way." He raised the bogy of congressional action in case labor and management failed to maintain production and employment. He suggested that collective bargaining could avert strikes and lockouts. If that failed, however, "some impartial machinery for reaching decisions on the basis of proven facts" might be used. Truman admonished the conferees that contracts, once agreed to, should be abided by. Perhaps he should have been more forceful in his presentation; perhaps he should have insisted upon having voting representatives of the government at the conference. In any event, it soon became clear that labor and management had rather different ideas than Truman did of what was the "traditional, American, democratic way" to resolve disputes. The proceedings of the conference resembled less a Quaker meeting or a legislative session than the shoot out at the OK Corral. Perhaps the conference just came too late. While it was meeting, strikes began to plague the land, thus demonstrating collective bargaining's ineffectiveness in the face of labor's long-pent-up demands and industry's conviction that it was strong enough to resist union action. It was unlikely that the representatives of labor and management at the conference could reach agreement while industrial combat was erupting across the country. On November 30 the conference adjourned without making any significant recommendations on how to avoid work stoppages.

Meanwhile, the United Automobile Workers had called out 175,000 workers in its dispute with General Motors, and other large-scale strikes were impending. By early December, half a million American workers were off the job. Truman told Congress on December 3 that the Labor-Management Conference had not agreed on a way to avert work stoppages when collective bargaining and conciliation had failed. He recommended that in disputes "vitally affecting the national public interest," which had not been resolved by existing machinery, Congress should authorize the president to appoint fact-finding boards, which would investigate the disputes and issue reports before work stoppages could begin. The recommendations would not be binding. The public would know, however, what impartial investigation had revealed; and Truman hoped that this would facilitate the settlement of labor disputes. Anticipating congressional action, he appointed fact-finding boards for the General Motors strike and a dispute at United States Steel. He was to be disappointed, for Congress delayed considering approval of this tactic. The nation would soon pay the price in terms of intensified industrial disputes.

Indeed, Congress gave Truman little of what he requested in the fall of 1945. The legislators did give him a better-organized surplus-property agency, and they joyously supported his efforts to cut federal expenditures. They also gave him much of the authority that he wanted so that he could reorganize the executive branch, chiefly to eliminate wartime agencies. They renewed his war powers, including price-control authority, though only for six months instead of the year that he had asked for. They happily reduced taxes, but by almost $1 billion more than the administration's recommendation of $5 billion. On Truman's other recommendations, Congress took no action except waywardly to return the Employment Service to the states, a move that he vetoed. Congress was, however, to have its way on this issue in 1946.

Elsewhere, there were some pleasant surprises for the Truman administration. There was the speedy reconversion of industrial facilities, 93 percent of which were ready to begin civilian production by December 1945. The settlement of wartime contracts proceeded smoothly, as most of them were satisfactorily negotiated by the end of the year. This was a stabilizing factor for federal finances, as well as a way to supply many industries with funds for reconverting quickly. Moreover, unemployment did not reach the predicted 6 million by the end of 1945. It was indeed only 2 million as a consequence of employers' retaining more workers than had been anticipated and of the heavier retirement from the labor force of the elderly, housewives, and teenagers. The GI Bill of Rights also affected the situation significantly. Many veterans started businesses of their own with federally guaranteed loans. Even more returned to school with federal funding in order to extend their education, while others decided to take advantage of the special unemployment benefits that were available to veterans. Whatever provision of this enormously popular legislation was used, it kept large numbers of veterans off the job market at the right time, pumped billions of dollars into the economy, and vastly expanded the pool of educated Americans.

The pleasant surprises were offset partly by the Truman administration's increasing worry about inflation. Business, labor, and agriculture were pressing for gains that would contribute to inflation. Strikes were threatening to stymie production, while consumers were eager to buy. The president began to fear that the government's economic controls were being lifted too quickly. Indeed, there were speculative hoarding and delayed shipping of products in order to see whether time would not bring an end to controls and therefore generate higher prices. The administration, with its fears of deflation calmed, began to cope with inflation during fall 1945. The administration's course was erratic, partly because federal officials were not united in the fight against inflationary pressures. Nor were they sure that deflation could not become a problem. Therefore, the administration sometimes seemed to be alternately giving the patient depressants and stimulants. While Congress cut taxes by almost $6 billion, for example, largely at the administration's behest, the Treasury floated a bond drive, partly to siphon off excess spending power. The government stabilized interest rates, which stood at slightly over 2 percent on short-term business loans. While this prevented inflationary interest payments, it encouraged borrowing, which put more money into circulation.

Truman tried to spur clearer-cut anti-inflationary action. On December 14, he told the cabinet that he was giving full support to Chester Bowles and the Office of Price Administration in dealing with inflation through controls. Moreover, some production controls, especially on construction materials, were reimposed that month. In January 1946 the OPA placed price ceilings on cotton. It was a situation, however, that the proponents of controls ultimately could not handle, because controls created animosity, often from those whose political support was needed. Moreover, in order to solve other problems, control programs were breached, particularly in coping with agricultural and labor-management problems. The administration sought other approaches in restraining inflation. One was to get surplus federal property on the market, so as to stimulate reconversion at low prices. This did not work out well, for it proceeded too slowly, although ultimately it provided businessmen and even consumers with $20 billion of material at cut-rate prices. More effective were the administration's efforts to slash federal expenditures. The goal was no less than a balanced federal budget eventually. The administration cut federal outlays from some $98 billion in fiscal year 1945 to about $60 billion in fiscal year 1946, while federal receipts declined only from some $50 billion to about $43.5 billion. It was an outstanding accomplishment, one that the Truman administration is seldom given credit for, one that kept the government from contributing significantly to inflation.

Events in the agricultural sector constituted one of the central economic problems confronting the nation. Instead of selling on the open market, farmers fed more of their grain to livestock or sold it to brewers and distillers in order to command better prices. This would lead to shortages and higher prices for consumers. The Department of Agriculture, under Clinton P. Anderson, contributed to the situation by warning that farmers had to guard against marketing surpluses, which would depress prices. Thus, underestimating future demand, governmental and private spokesmen for agriculture bridled at continued rationing of and price controls on food. They and Anderson also discouraged increased production. Ironically, the president had appointed Anderson to be secretary of agriculture partly because Anderson had fought in Congress against wartime agricultural scarcity. Anderson instead, as secretary, continued the very policies that he had earlier opposed, because he relied heavily on his department's experts, just as Truman initially had relied too heavily on Anderson.

During the infighting between the government's price controllers and farm interests, rationing was removed from foods except sugar before the end of 1945. The result was that domestic consumption of food rose, and prices threatened to do the same. Moreover, before 1945 had ended, news came that foreign needs for American grain during the first half of 1946 would far exceed the estimates. Even Secretary Anderson was moved to act after learning in January 1946 that Europe alone required more than one-third of the American wheat on hand. He immediately advised the cabinet that a food crisis had arrived. The administration had to reimpose some controls and to exhort Americans to ration themselves voluntarily. Truman, on February 6, told the country that "more people face starvation and even actual death for want of food today than in any war year . . . it is apparent that only through superhuman efforts can mass starvation be prevented." The president called upon Americans to conserve food; he ordered that grain used in the making of alcoholic beverages be restricted and that the amount of flour coming from wheat be increased from 70 to 80 percent; he commanded the Agriculture Department to control inventories of wheat and flour; and he directed that less grain be fed to livestock and fowl.

The administration's food-emergency program did not work satisfactorily, for farmers were reluctant to market their grain. Truman grumbled about one of their defenders toward the end of February 1946: "It is too bad [he] couldn't be taken to Poland and be allowed to spend the rest of the winter and spring in a Polish village on the rations they have to eat."[8] To encourage farmers to sell their grain, Anderson proposed that prices be raised where permissible. This was blocked, however, by the fear on the part of Truman and his price-control advisers that it would result in an unacceptable amount of inflation. One compromise was to allow farmers to exchange their wheat for certificates which they could cash in at the market price available at any time that they chose until April 1, 1947. Farmers were unmoved by this offer, and the international food crisis remained unresolved. By April 1946 the diets of tens of millions of people over the world had fallen to starvation levels. The administration, on April 19, offered a bonus of thirty cents a bushel for wheat delivered by May 25 and for the first 1.3 million tons of corn marketed before May 11. This was basically the plan of Chester Bowles, the government's leading price controller, to get grain flowing to market without incurring price increases. Even this failed. On May 10 Truman and his administration surrendered and raised the price ceilings on wheat and corn, respectively, by fifteen and twenty-five cents a bushel. Producers had achieved what they wanted, and soon the government would get what it had begged for—food for the hungry of the world. Six million tons of American grain had been shipped or were available for delivery abroad by July 1. Although the Truman administration had fallen short of its promises to supply meat, fats, and oils, it still had done a remarkable job under trying circumstances. The United States had sent one-sixth of its food stocks overseas during the first half of 1946. As one scholar has observed, "It is no exaggeration to say that American relief shipments in 1945–46 were the salvation of Europe."[9]

This was accomplished at a price, however. American consumers not only had to tighten their belts; they also had to pay higher prices for their food. Meat and butter, as well as grain and flour, became scarce in America in 1946. Moreover, much of the available beef and pork moved through expensive black-market channels of trade. Indeed, by May, thefts of meat from civilian and even military sources were being reported. A federal program, launched in April to supply a fair number of animals to approved slaughterhouses, did not significantly improve the situation. Public pressure mounted for the abandonment of price controls, which Secretary Anderson seemed to support in testimony before a Senate committee on May 1. Two days later, House Speaker Sam Rayburn declared that cattle should no longer be under price controls. President Truman countered that as long as the situation warranted and the government had the power, price controls would be maintained on livestock and meat. Livestock raisers had learned from grain producers, however; so they slowed down the marketing of their animals. They could only have been encouraged by the leisureliness of Congress in considering Truman's request to extend federal authority over price controls beyond July 1.

Congress finally enacted a new price-control measure. After a sharp discussion among his chief economic advisers, Truman decided to reject it. The bill, as he said in his veto message of June 29, gave the nation only "a choice between inflation with a statute and inflation without one." He urged Congress to send him a bill that would give him genuine authority to combat inflation, not one that would allow prices to increase between 11 and 100 percent. The president had a great deal of public support. For example, a Fortune poll of June reported that 67.2 percent of those answering believed that price control was the best way to keep the cost of living within reason. Truman received additional public backing, judging from the mail arriving in the White House and on Capitol Hill, when prices rose rapidly after controls lapsed on July 1. Prices had earlier increased only by 3 percent since Japan had surrendered. During July 1946 they rose an unprecedented 5.5 percent, with food increasing by 13.8 percent. Congress consequently acted with unusual speed, and the president was able to sign a new price-control law on July 25.

Truman pointed out that the statute was not as good as the one that had lapsed on July 1. In fact, the new law turned out to be a failure from his point of view. Many items were exempt from price controls either temporarily, such as meat, or even permanently. The new Price Decontrol Board decided to leave grain, poultry, and dairy products uncontrolled. Prices continued to rise on these commodities, and black markets flourished on a number of controlled items. On October 14 the president announced the lifting of price controls on meat and the acceleration of the decontrol of many other prices. These concessions did not improve the situation, and the election of a Republican Congress in November gave no promise that he could obtain better legislation. On November 9 Truman surrendered, announcing the termination of price controls—except on rents—and of residual controls on wages and salaries. He was reduced to telling the public that "good wages, full employment and sound business profits must depend upon management and workers cooperating to produce the maximum volume of goods at the lowest possible price." By then, inflation had about run its course, and volunteerism in the market place had gained its victory. The discussion never seemed to end, however, as to whether more-effective federal controls or speedier dismantling of wartime controls would have alleviated the painfulness of postwar inflation and commodity shortages.

Strife between labor and management contributed at least as much to America's postwar economic woes as did the revolt of the farmers. Almost 2 million workers had walked off their jobs by February 1946 as strikes erupted all over the country. It was the worst wave of strikes in the nation's history: 22.9 million man-days of work were lost through work stoppages in February alone. As a consequence, there were also layoffs in many other industries because of material shortages. The Truman administration's production and employment goals were imperiled, as was the whole idea of controlling inflation by matching supply and demand. Ironically, the government's quick settlements of contracts, as well as tax reductions and refunds, which were intended to finance high production, often encouraged management to be obdurate in dealing with organized labor.

The president's fact-finding board on the General Motors dispute reported on January 10. Although the United Automobile Workers accepted the board's recommendations, the company did not. Truman constantly put pressure on management and labor to reconcile their differences, but the General Motors strike dragged on into March before it was settled. He gave even more attention to the impending steel strike, because it would immobilize so many other businesses. On January 12 the president told the industry and union representatives to reach a settlement and to "cut out the monkey business."[10] Benjamin Fairless of United States Steel requested more time to check with other steel producers, which Philip Murray of the United Steel Workers agreed to. Meanwhile, Price Administrator Chester Bowles blazed into warfare with John W. Snyder, director of War Mobilization and Reconversion, over whether to allow steel prices to increase by $2.50 or $4.00 a ton. As it turned out, the steel companies demanded more—$7.00 a ton—than either Bowles or Snyder was prepared to give. On January 18 Murray accepted Truman's offer of a wage increase of 18.5 cents per hour. Fairless rejected this, however; and the steel workers went out on strike.

Truman was furious, holding capital and labor equally to blame for creating a situation for which only the public would pay. On January 24 Fairless suggested calling all of the steel industry chieftains into conference. Truman replied that all he wanted was acceptance of his offer. After all, he asked his staff, "Who is going to run the country?" When Snyder defended Fairless, the president bristled, saying, "He lied to me in the first place."[11] In February the government offered the steel companies a price increase of $5.00 a ton. It was accepted, and the steel strike was soon over. The significance of the strike was clear, however, to labor and to management. Within reason, they could extort what they wanted from the government. The result was that industrial price controls had been seriously breached in order to spur production. Defeated in the test case with steel, Bowles fumed and offered his resignation. Truman in turn growled that he should have accepted Bowles's resignation when it had been offered earlier, in 1945. The administration still needed Bowles, however, for he was its chief symbol of holding the line against inflation. The president placated him by promoting him to head the Office of Economic Stabilization, which added wage and production matters to his jurisdiction. The administration used the steel settlement as a basis for modifying its wage-increase policy by roughly 18.5 cents per hour. The resultant inflation, Truman thought, would be acceptable if price controls otherwise held.

During March the number of workers on strike fell to less than two hundred thousand, and industrial production rose for the first time since November 1945. Matters would deteriorate again in April and May 1946, when first the United Mine Workers (UMW) and then the railway workers struck. The UMW's John L. Lewis was courting federal seizure of the bituminous coal mines, for he believed that the government would grant his union's demands for a health-and-welfare fund as well as pay and other increases. He had to be wary of public opinion, for many Americans and certainly Truman considered him public enemy number one of the union set. Lewis was probably the inspiration for a classic memorandum that the president wrote to himself at about this time. Truman proposed summoning union leaders in order to "tell them that patience is exhausted. Declare an emergency—call out troops. Start industry and put anyone to work who wants to go to work. If any leader interferes court martial him. Lewis ought to have been shot in 1942, but Franklin didn't have the guts to do it. . . . Adjourn Congress and run the country. Get plenty of Atomic Bombs on hand—drop one on Stalin, put the United Nations to work and eventually set up a free world."[12] Writing this must have helped Truman get through another frustrating day. It did not solve the labor problems, however. As the railway strike loomed on the horizon in May, Lewis sagely announced a twelve-day respite in the UMW strike while negotiations continued. It became plain, even under these relaxed conditions, that the miners and the mine operators would not agree. Moreover, because of the scarcity of coal, other industries were being forced to curtail their operations. The president therefore ordered governmental seizure of the bituminous mines, effective May 21. Lewis had gotten what he wanted. Indeed, at the end of May, his union tried the same tactic in the anthracite coal mines, winning success by June 8 in negotiations with the mine owners.

Truman had also been exerting pressure on Alvanley Johnston of the Locomotive Engineers and A. F. Whitney of the Railway Trainmen to reach agreement with the railroads within the guideline of an 18.5 cents per hour increase in wages. His efforts failed, and on May 23 the engineers and trainmen struck against the railways for the first time in the nation's history. Unless resolved immediately, this strike could clog most of the arteries of American transportation and shut down most of the country's industry. The president had threatened to seize the railways in the event of a strike. On May 24 he made good on his promise, pointing out that this was now a strike against the government. He demanded that the railroaders return to work by 4 P.M. on May 25, and he announced that he would address Congress on the subject of industrial peace. Angered, Truman considered conscripting the railway workers. In his private fulminations against their leaders, he declared that the "government's being flouted, vilified," and he suggested, "Lets . . . hang a few traitors."[13]

Cooler heads than Truman's prevailed in the administration, however. The president toned down his statements and accepted Secretary of War Robert Patterson's suggestion that the army run the trains. Johnston and Whitney were alarmed now, protesting that Truman had incorrectly conveyed the impression that the railroaders would not work for the government. They wrote to him of their willingness to negotiate an interim agreement based on a wage increase of 18.5 cents per hour. Truman did not read their letter. Indeed, he had announced the termination of mediation, for he was intent upon taking the matter up with Congress. Nevertheless, Presidential Assistant John Steelman decided to talk with Johnston and Whitney on May 25. By 3 P.M. Steelman had telephoned the White House that an agreement might be reached before the president began to address Congress an hour later. Steelman and the union leaders came to agreement at 3:55 P.M. Time was needed, however, to type and sign the settlement.

Truman, steely faced, entered the chamber of the House of Representatives to an ovation, and began his address on time. His was tough talk, although—or because—he must have been aware of Steelman's efforts. The president spoke of a strike that "threatens to paralyze all our industrial, agricultural, commercial, and social life." He confirmed that he intended to have the army run the railroads. Then Truman requested legislation to stop strikes against the government, to deal with the "obstinate arrogance" of men like Johnston and Whitney. This would (1) include the authority to start injunctive proceedings to forbid a union leader from encouraging workers not to work; (2) strip workers of their seniority rights if they persisted in striking against the government; and (3) fix criminal penalties for employers and labor leaders who violated the law relating to a federally seized industry. Truman also asked for authority to set wages that would be fair to labor and capital in such an industry; and to encourage management to settle rapidly, he asked that net profits flow into the national treasury. Then he threw in his bombshell, asking for the power ''to draft into the Armed Forces of the United States all workers who are on strike against their Government.'' At this dramatic point in Truman's message, Secretary of the Senate Leslie L. Biffle hurried to the rostrum to hand Truman a note containing news of Steelman's agreement with Johnston and Whitney. Pandemonium swept the House chamber as Truman announced ''that the railroad strike has been settled, on terms proposed by the President.'' Anticlimactically, he ended his address, asking for a new labor law that would protect the rights of workers, capital, and the public alike.

At last, Truman had won a major battle. Both labor and management were impressed, if irritated, and they would subsequently handle their disputes more cautiously. Those disputes would occasionally get out of hand, but the threat of economic collapse would not, at least for a generation, be as great as it was in May 1946. Nor would there be another year like that following the end of the war, when 5 million workers had been involved in 4,630 work stoppages and 120 million man-days of labor had been lost. Industrial productivity rose in June, and the United States was on its way to attaining the growth economy that Truman wanted. Yet in the process of reconversion, labor had suffered. In the year after Japan's surrender, hourly wages had risen by 9.6 percent, but weekly earnings had dropped by 8.1 percent because of the loss of war work and overtime pay. Worse was the loss of real income because of inflation amounting to 12.4 percent. In short, labor was back to its 1942 purchasing power, while that of Americans in the agricultural and white-collar sectors had risen. Organized labor, through its tactics, had encouraged the breaching of price controls, which adversely affected it. Furthermore, the unions had lost political standing, which would in 1947 result in stiff regulatory legislation that they adamantly opposed. The government bore some of the responsibility for the results, of course. In 1945 the Truman administration had, for whatever reasons, failed to devise a comprehensive reconversion program: for example, there could have been wage increases of between 10 and 15 percent, some compensating price increases, and temporary continuance of the no-strike, no-lockout pledge. Yet, in fairness, it must be said that there was no guarantee that Congress, labor, management, and agriculture would have accepted such a program.

What had happened during America's postwar reconversion was nevertheless impressive. Unemployment had reached only 2.27 million, or 3.9 percent, in 1946, which was less than it was even in 1942. The government had greatly cut its expenditures, with the result that the growth of the federal debt had almost been stopped. Purchasing power remained high and, with it, productivity. In fact, wages and salaries only declined from $117.5 billion in 1945 to $112.0 billion in 1946, while consumer credit rose from $5.7 billion to $8.4 billion. Despite the strikes, manufacturing productivity dropped by only about 11 percent. What disturbed Truman was that in the process he had been defied and vilified and that the country could have done even better, as he saw it, if he had received greater cooperation. It was little wonder that in May 1946, given the revolts of farmers, workers, and management, he sometimes responded more like Captain Harry of Battery D than like the chief of state.

Truman's problems with Congress contributed to presidential perturbation. Indeed, in 1945 and 1946, Congress had been largely unresponsive to his requests for reconstructing the postwar United States. As early as September 1945 he had shown his temper over a clash with his former colleagues in Congress. After a meeting with the Democrats on the House Ways and Means Committee, he recorded, "I told 'em either I am the leader of the Dem party or I'm not; that the Senate had let me down."[14] This outburst settled nothing. Truman, like most senators and representatives who have become president, would seldom be in command either of Congress or even of his fellow partisans in it. After all, he had not been a prime leader in Congress, so why should the lords of Capitol Hill look to him for direction now? It might have been different if he had had a powerful constituency of his own, if he had been more than just the fellow who had slipped into the presidency much as a matter of chance. It might even have been different if Truman had been more the lion or the fox or had possessed a strong, united administration. Yet even if Congress had deemed him stronger, this would not have led to presidential triumph after triumph. There were still the tremendous number of foreign and domestic problems that confronted him as president. Moreover, there were the growing independence of Congress and the weariness of so many Americans of being dictated to from Washington.

Truman's greatest legislative success so far came in February 1946 with the passage of the Employment Act. This measure declared that it was the "responsibility of the Federal Government . . . to promote maximum employment, production, and purchasing power." The president was required to report to Congress annually on the state of the economy and to recommend programs that were designed to achieve the purposes of the act. To assist him, Congress created the Council of Economic Advisers, composed of three persons who were trained and experienced in economic matters. Congress also established the Joint Committee on the Economic Report, which was composed of members of the House and Senate, to make recommendations to further the purposes of the act. Although Congress had wrangled over the legislation, the Senate passed it unanimously, and the House overwhelmingly. This was easy to do, however, for it was much like voting for God, Mother, and Country—it cost very little. And who knew, it just might be useful. Late in July, admittedly a bit late, Truman appointed the members of the Council of Economic Advisers. It would be some time before the council's influence would be felt, but now its work could begin and it would make a considerable contribution to developing the government's economic policies.

Congress also responded favorably to the administration's requests to improve the school-lunch program, aid the newly independent Philippines, give veterans priority in purchasing surplus property, strengthen the Foreign Service, create the Indian Claims Commission, expand agricultural research, lend money to Great Britain, and, with enthusiasm, increase congressional salaries. Few of these measures were, however, among the most important in the president's program. Indeed Congress defeated most of Truman's key requests. These included legislation dealing with labor, health care, housing, unemployment insurance, poll taxes, universal military training, scientific research, unification of the armed forces, the mimimum wage, the Fair Employment Practices Committee, and the Employment Service. Congress passed many other bills in forms that Truman did not like, some of which he felt compelled to veto. Indeed he employed the veto twenty-one times in 1945 and thirty-three times in 1946. Congress did not override any of these vetoes, probably because he rarely disapproved legislation that was of great interest at the time. Nevertheless, the veto was a significant weapon in Truman's arsenal, and he was among the presidents who used this weapon most often.

Truman had other serious problems. Among the most important was staffing the government. He often complained about the difficulties of retaining good people and of finding replacements for them if they left. When asked in his January 24, 1946, news conference if the chairman of the Canadian-American Defense Board had submitted his resignation, Truman replied: "I haven't received it as yet. I don't think I have. I have a drawer full of them. It may be among them." At his May 2 news conference, he explained why he was slow in making appointments: "Difficult to find the men to fill the jobs. Should we find somebody that we think is capable of taking the job, he has got a better job, or doesn't want to consider Government service. That has been true ever since the war ceased. The good men are flocking to private industry for bigger pay. It's the most difficult thing we have to face, is finding men for the places."

There were also a remarkably large number of troubles in Truman's official family. James F. Byrnes was too independent at the State Department. Fred Vinson was so good at the Treasury that the president promoted him to the chief justiceship in 1946. Truman's conservative and able friend John W. Snyder took Vinson's place. Robert Patterson at War, James V. Forrestal at Navy, Tom Clark at Justice, and Robert E. Hannegan at the Post Office Department were satisfactory to Truman, to Congress, and to most of the public. Clinton Anderson had caused problems at Agriculture by underestimating the demand for food. He partly redeemed himself, however, by his later strenuous efforts to increase the availability of agricultural commodities. At the Labor Department, Lewis B. Schwellenbach was hampered by serious illness. Most of what went wrong on the labor front was not his fault, but that did not keep him from often being blamed.

During 1946, the departments of the Interior and of Commerce were the most troublesome spots in the cabinet. Interior Secretary Harold L. Ickes bucked the president on the latter's nomination of oilman Edwin W. Pauley to be undersecretary of the navy. It was a bitter clash, spurred by disagreements on oil questions, which resulted in Truman's accepting Ickes's resignation in February and failing to secure Pauley's confirmation. As for Commerce Secretary Wallace, he had publicly, if not in private, always supported Truman. In a monumental display of ineptitude by both of them, however, Wallace spoke out critically on foreign policy. As shall be considered later, Truman concluded in September that he had to request Wallace's resignation. The replacement for Ickes was Julius Krug, chairman of the War Production Board. If Krug was no Ickes in ability and attitudes, he was a seasoned player of bureaucratic warfare on the state and federal levels. The president called W. Averell Harriman, the talented businessman and diplomat, from the United States embassy in London to take Wallace's place. During the eighteen months that Truman had been in office, his cabinet had taken on a more conservative hue. It was a cabinet with which he believed he could be comfortable, even if he could not depend upon it as much as he wished.

There were also serious problems of discontinuity in the administration. One example was John Snyder, who within a year's time was federal loan chief, director of War Mobilization and Reconversion, and secretary of the Treasury. One can also look at it in terms of a position—say, the directorship of War Mobilization and Reconversion—which was held by Byrnes, Vinson, Snyder, and finally John Steelman, who also served simultaneously as assistant to the president. It was often confusing and sometimes demoralizing. Certainly, it adversely affected the continuity in the making and execution of policies. The situation was aggravated by sharp differences of opinion among administration officials: for example, Bowles versus Snyder, Wallace versus Byrnes, and Forrestal or Ickes versus almost everyone. And leaks of information about disputes in high places were common. They sorely vexed Truman, who kept telling his subordinates that this was no way to run a government. By 1947 the clashes and leaks would lessen, as the administration became more Truman's than a transitional one; but they never ceased to plague him.

Troubles among the White House staff also surfaced in 1945 and 1946. There were complaints that too many aides sat in on the morning conference, and then, when this was changed, that too few were invited. Steelman complained of Secretary Schwellenbach's lack of knowledge about labor affairs and of Snyder's big-business orientation. Some of the staff were critical of George E. Allen's informal involvement in White House matters as a friend of the president. Many worried about the easy access to the White House that was enjoyed, through Harry Vaughan, by Jack Maragon, a controversial lobbyist. General Vaughan was indiscreet in other ways. After a meeting on the coal crisis in May 1946, the press asked him if the meeting had concluded. He replied: "I assume it has. The President is in the swimming pool—by himself. The world may be going to hell but the President has got to keep clean."[15]

The White House staff saw changes in 1946. Most notably, Samuel Rosenman left with Truman's genuine regrets in January, and the president appointed naval aide James K. Vardaman, Jr., to the Federal Reserve Board, partly because of his ability to irritate the navy. This left the way open for a dynamic Naval Reserve officer from St. Louis, Clark Clifford, to replace Vardaman and soon to perform Rosenman's duties. Clifford would quickly take his place alongside John R. Steelman in encouraging the professionalization and stabilization of the president's staff. The crucial episode here was the railway strike in May, when Steelman's initiative led to settlement of the dispute and when Clifford's speech-writing and coordinative skills impressed everyone. By June, Clifford's many talents had led Truman to make Clifford his chief speech writer and, in effect, his national-security assistant, with the title of special counsel. This coincided with the president's emergence as a supremely tough, decisive leader.

Truman had other problems, though. Too often, his toughness came across as insensitivity; his self-confidence, as provincialism; and his anger, as pettiness. He did not handle the Ickes and Wallace resignations well, which contributed to the disenchantment of New Dealers with him. Through the economic storms of the time, he had outraged much of labor, business, and agriculture. His continued personal contact with the Pendergast family, often carried on surreptitiously, was widely deemed to be inappropriate for a president. He was often criticized for his public statements—for example, his use of the presidential news conference to oppose the renomination of Kansas City Congressman Roger C. Slaughter. Ironically, Slaughter was a Pendergast favorite. It was never concealed that Truman liked to play poker and to have a drink of bourbon now and then, which offended many strait-laced voters. And there were some who were irritated by his love of bestowing decorations. This probably went too far when he handed out Selective Service Medals to a squad of draft-board representatives and then surprised their chief, Gen. Lewis B. Hershey, by pinning a Distinguished Service Medal on him. Not to be outdone, Hershey whipped out a Selective Service Medal to pin on the commander in chief. There were also tales about Truman and cronies like Vaughan and Allen and their jests and pranks, which too often made the White House sound like an American Legion hall. Moreover, the president's public vindictiveness against some members of Congress was handled so artlessly that it reinforced the negative picture of him. His public criticism of Republican Senators Robert A. Taft and Kenneth S. Wherry for being in league with profiteers and his barring of two representatives—Republican Clare Boothe Luce and Democrat Adam Clayton Powell, Jr.—from the White House because of slurs that they had allegedly cast upon Mrs. Truman stand as illustrative examples.

Whatever the cause—issues, personality, partisanship, factionalism, or some combination—Truman's popularity dropped precipitously in 1946. For example, in a Fortune poll in January, 82 percent of the respondents thought that he was doing a good or excellent job; by June that number had fallen to 52 percent. With the summer came inflation and increasing frustration over foreign policy. The president may have believed that labor and most farmers and consumers had no reasonable choice but to support the Democratic party in the fall elections, but he was wrong. The Republicans exploited the issues well, and Democrats were often lackluster in defending their party and president. It was common to hear the pun "To err is Truman." By the time of the

November elections, the opposition had saturated the nation with the challenge "Had Enough? Vote Republican." Many Americans responded affirmatively to this; many others, who could not shift to the Republicans, stayed away from the polls. The voters elected 245 Republicans and 188 Democrats to the House of Representatives and 51 Republicans and 45 Democrats to the Senate, thus creating the first Republican-controlled Congress since the presidency of Herbert Hoover. Clearly, the Truman administration had reached a crisis of confidence.

4

★ ★ ★ ★ ★

THE IRON CURTAIN DESCENDS

Americans were jubilant with the coming of peace in September 1945. Still there was unease in many quarters. Despite Harry S. Truman's public professions that America and Russia were marching in step in peace, there were signs that the wartime allies were following different paths. There were also indications that America's leaders did not know what to do about it. Many of them looked to the developing United Nations organization for a miracle of peacekeeping, including people of otherwise divergent views, such as Assistant Secretary of State Dean G. Acheson and Secretary of Commerce Henry A. Wallace. As Acheson said after receiving news of the atomic bombing of Hiroshima, "If we can't work out some sort of organization of great powers, we shall be gone geese for fair."[1] Truman shared this sentiment to the extent of often publicizing the prospects for a better world that the UN offered. Its golden promise of peace would not be fully realized, however. The major reasons were implicit in a comment written by Michigan's Senator Arthur H. Vandenberg after the Senate ratified the UN Charter in July. This Republican apostle of a bipartisan foreign policy asserted that the UN Charter would "work," though "everything, in the final analysis, depends on Russia (and whether we have *guts* enough to make her behave)."[2]

The Wilsonian panacea of a world organization was only one concern of the United States during the immediate postwar period. Intertwined with it was the widespread attitude that it was time for peoples everywhere to join hands in order to eliminate war and to cooperate in solving the globe's problems. In contrast was a spirit of xenophobia, a good deal of which had survived the war. In the United States, the wartime alliances with Britain and Russia had not done away with suspicion and even dislike of those countries, especially of the Soviet Union. When in late 1943 Stalin asked Roosevelt to turn over a share of captured Italian naval vessels, the president's chief of staff, Adm. William D. Leahy, exploded: "Russians are the damnedest double crossers. . . . God, I hate to give destroyers to those dirty crooks."[3] Henry Wallace's diary reeks of hostility toward Great Britain and his fear of having the United States become its catspaw, an attitude that was shared by many Americans. Truman, too, was suspicious of British as well as of Soviet leaders. And one can add his dislike of Chinese and French leadership.

Xenophobia in the United States had deep roots. Generally, it was based on the country's relative geographical isolation and the rather different development of its institutions. There were also specific reasons for disliking given nations. For example, distrust of the British could be traced back to colonial and revolutionary times, and there were plenty of instances since when they had offended Americans. Many thought the Russians crude and brutal and Russia very likely "a world bully,"[4] as Ambassador Averell Harriman said; and they saw the Communist regime as an expansionist power that stood contrary to everything that was dear to the United States. The pride that most Americans had in themselves supported their often-lofty attitudes about other peoples. This sense of superiority had been reinforced by the nation's experience with immigrants, its considerable degree of racism, and its involvements abroad. Foreigners were not all deemed to be equally bad, nor did Americans see all of them as being suspect. At least among better-educated Americans, there were favorites, and often for reasons that were as specious as those for disliking other foreigners. Again as examples, some Americans could like the British for their culture and the Russians for their heartiness.

Whether it was a case of disliking or even liking other people, the reasons for it usually either reinforced or dictated one's perceived self-interest in doing so. So, if an American liked the Russians or believed that good relations with them were vital to peace, it would take a great deal of aggravation from the Soviet Union for such a person to become hostile to that nation or its ideology. Henry Wallace, for example, could overlook much from the Russians but little from the British, while Dean Acheson could be very understanding of Britain but easily alarmed by the Soviet Union. This analysis must, of course, be tempered by the insight contained in what Counselor Benjamin V. Cohen of the State

Department said about those who had to deal with Russia and foreign policy in 1945: "There was considerable conflict not only between people involved, but also within each individual."[5] This applied to President Truman and Secretary of State James F. Byrnes, who wanted to stand up to the Russians and yet negotiate with them on a friendly basis.

Xenophobia and national pride would play another role in the development of postwar United States foreign policy. Now that American leaders had the means—and, some believed, the responsibility—to become world leaders, their national pride would lead them to make alliances with other countries, usually on the basis of their fears of the Russians. Therefore, it became less difficult to supply aid and arms to regimes and peoples for whom many Americans had little liking. Moreover, for those whom many Americans liked more than they disliked, especially in western Europe, assistance was often tinged with an attitude of superiority—that the United States knew best. Americans might like Costa Ricans, love the Dutch, consider Australians as being almost like themselves, and tolerate the Italians. America's leaders increasingly left no doubt, however, that, in alliance, only the United States could be a full partner. This was partly because of the abundance of American money and resources. But it was also national pride and some xenophobia that led United States leaders to believe that their world vision was superior to that of others.

There were other strands in postwar American thinking about the world. One was that the United States had fought World Wars I and II and had been the deciding factor in both. Its leaders did not intend to fight a third one unless it was on American terms. The nation would not appease those who might jeopardize American conceptions of peace, prosperity, and democracy. Secretary of the Navy James V. Forrestal said to the cabinet in September 1945, with regard to the Soviets: "It seems doubtful that we should endeavor to buy their understanding and sympathy. We tried that once with Hitler."[6] The superior means as well as motives of the United States entered into this determination. There was also a personal factor, for the contemporary crop of American leaders had backgrounds that encouraged them to think in terms of governmental power. Military experience, either in the First or Second World War, or occasionally in both, led many leaders to consider military solutions, especially now that the United States had military power. Past governmental experience, especially in a government that was stronger than ever, conditioned officials to use governmental solutions to problems. In short, those Americans who held high office after the war were more accustomed to using the power of government, both economically and militarily, than had been their fathers and grandfathers. They had no intention of rolling back government, United States military strength, or the nation's competitive edge in world trade to their dimensions of the 1920s or earlier. It was not so much a matter of hunger for power as it was a belief that it all constituted a positive good for their country and for the world. Many people elsewhere in the world would have been surprised if postwar United States leaders had thought otherwise. Indeed, leaders in many others countries feared that the United States would turn back the clock. It was now time for the United States to play a major role in world affairs permanently.

This knowledge did not solve the problem of how the United States would act on the world stage. Its idealism and residual xenophobia, its schemes for good and new, and its fears of Russia did not add up to a foreign policy. This was complicated by the fact that few American leaders had the information or vision to cope comprehensively with postwar challenges. Henry Wallace said in May 1945: "Truman's decisiveness is admirable. The only question is as to whether he has enough information behind his decisiveness to enable his decisions to stand up."[7] Wallace might just as well have applied this comment to himself and to other American leaders. They all were seeking knowledge and coming up short, partly because, as Senator Vandenberg began calling it in 1945, Russia's iron curtain obscured everything. Vision was also a problem that led Truman, for example, within a single day, to talk about cutting military budgets and not cutting them too much, about being patient with the Soviets and being tough with them.

The vacillation was remarkable, yet understandable. The Americans had never experienced anything like the Russian leaders before—with their sweet talk at one moment and their invective at the next. March and countermarch was not a tactic that was unknown to American politicians, but not in the proportions used by the Soviets. Moreover, American leaders were engaging in world politics at a time when everything was in unusual flux, when things at home were nettlesome enough for any administration. This reinforced the impatience for which they were known. United States officials, including Truman, wanted everything to be resolved at Potsdam or, if not there, then at the next meeting of the Council of Foreign Ministers. Patience, for American leaders, seemed too often to be a matter of weeks, when it should have been a matter of years. Little wonder that Truman chose for secretary of state James F. Byrnes, whose reputation as a negotiator and compromiser seemed to promise a quick settlement of all problems. As Byrnes would soon discover, speedy negotiation was not the order of the day for the Soviet Union, nor was it possible in all situations. The Wilsonian world vision of self-determination, free trade, world cooperation, and an end to war, which was shared in principle by Americans from Herbert Hoover to Henry Wallace, was not necessarily a vision that appealed to leaders elsewhere. Nor was it something that, even with the best of intentions, could be accomplished in a year or even in a decade. Their patience blunted, their information inadequate, their experience wanting, and their vision impaired, United States officials would have to find substitutes for good will and speedy agreements in a quickly changing world composed of peoples of diverse interests. One result was that the United States would try to checkmate Soviet activities on the world scene. In doing so, the United States heightened many of Russia's fears that it was under attack by an ambitious capitalist power.

This was the great irony of the postwar period. If Soviet leaders had been less suspicious and less defensive, their prophecies of an American threat would have been less self-fulfilling. After Japan had capitulated, the United States could hardly wait to discharge most of its troops and to reduce its foreign commitments. In August 1945 the administration was already preparing to end the draft after obligations in regard to occupation had ceased. Truman was serious about replacing conscription with short-term national service, not necessarily military, for young men. And even this stood little chance of obtaining congressional approval. On August 21 American lend-lease aid was terminated, which dashed hopes abroad that it would be used as a reconstruction program. During that fall and into 1946, official discussions of foreign assistance were limited. True, the United States assumed a considerable burden in providing food to tide Europe over the menace of starvation in 1945 and 1946. It would help out elsewhere through the instrumentalities of UNRRA (the United Nations Relief and Rehabilitation Administration) and special gifts. Moreover, the United States would employ the limited resources of its Export-Import Bank to assist in world reconstruction as it would encourage the development of the World Bank and the International Monetary Fund. All of this, however, meant little in view of the world's needs. It is questionable whether the United States would later have gone much further in developing foreign-aid programs if it had not been for blustering Communist aggrandizement. In short, Russia obligingly made itself seem to be a menace to the United States, just as it interpreted whatever the United States did as a threat to Russia itself. This is the greatest tragedy of world politics in the period immediately after World War II.

The Potsdam Conference had probably been more successful than many Americans, in their impatience, had interpreted it as being. If few questions were resolved there, the United States and Russia had laid a basis for what should be discussed in the future. The next consideration of these matters came up in London in September 1945, at the first meeting of the Council of Foreign Ministers. Secretary Byrnes approached this meeting optimistically, but the Soviet tactics of intransigence, invective, and diversions took their toll of the impatient and inexperienced Americans. The United States demanded democratic governments in Rumania and Bulgaria, even though it lacked a power base there. Molotov responded by suggesting that affairs should take their course in those areas, as they had in Italy. Byrnes then pointed out that the United States had recognized Finland, as well as Poland, despite disturbing events there, and had made no reservations with respect to Hungary. Molotov rejected British Foreign Minister Ernest Bevin's proposal to send an investigatory commission to Rumania. Indeed, the Russian foreign minister indicated that the United States and Britain would have to recognize the new Balkan governments before they would consider a peace treaty with Italy. The Russians had plainly come to London prepared to trade on the basis of strength, while the Americans believed that they were standing on agreements that had been arrived at previously. Molotov also returned to Russia's earlier demands for possession of Italy's former African colony of Tripolitania and bases in the Dardanelles, and he argued that the USSR should participate actively in the occupation of Japan. The Russian also reversed his field and declared that France and China should be limited in regard to which peace treaties they could consider. Byrnes returned to Truman's proposal to internationalize the Danube, which Molotov said was unfriendly to Russia. The American also offered, as a concession, to demilitarize Germany for twenty-five years, which the Russians took under advisement.

The London Conference ended on October 2. It was largely a failure from the American viewpoint. Byrnes told a radio audience, "We are willing to make concessions but the United States does not believe in agreement at any price."[8] There was much to the later comment of his Republican aide, John Foster Dulles, that at London "our postwar policy of 'no appeasement' was born. . . . We refused to pay international blackmail."[9] Yet Byrnes was far from through in trying to negotiate with the Russians. Even the president, though disappointed, was not prepared to admit defeat. He told his news conference of October 8 about the London Conference: "I don't think it's a failure. I think it was one step in arriving at a final conclusion. I am not in the slightest alarmed at the world situation. It will work out." Truman was, of course, putting a happy face on a bleak situation. If he and his advisers had really seen matters in this patient way, the history of the world might have been different. There was little wrong with standing as firm with Russia as it was standing with the United States, thus allowing agreements to emerge slowly but solidly. Among the problems of America's leaders were trying too often to combat the adversary's strength—for example, the occupation of disputed areas—with principles; considering stalemate to be failure; and being in a hurry. The Russians would make mistakes, but these were seldom among them.

Despite Truman's calming words, Americans were increasingly upset by what they saw happening in the world. In addition to being perturbed over Soviet attempts to exclude the United States from eastern European affairs and to seek power elsewhere, Americans saw evidence of Russia's bullying of people in occupied areas and of brutality toward the some 2 million Soviet citizens who were repatriated. Word coming out of Japan was pessimistic. Gen. Bonner Fellers, one of Gen. Douglas MacArthur's aides, wrote in October that "the Soviets want blood and revolution in Japan; hence to them all stabilizing influences are taboo."[10] Also in October the Joint Strategic Survey Committee reported to the Joint Chiefs of Staff that it was distressed over "the recent aggressive and uncompromising attitude of the Soviet Union."[11] The committee cited ominous developments throughout eastern Europe; Russian demands in Europe, the Mediterranean, and the Far East; and subversion in Latin America. On November 5 Assistant Secretary of War John J. McCloy returned from a trip around the world. His report was brimming with accounts of widespread economic dislocations, malnutrition, unemployment, and unrest, as well as fear of Russia among leaders in non-Communist countries. The United States, he indicated, was often looked to as the savior among nations.

China was one of the greatest areas of American concern. There were a million Japanese soldiers in China, who had to be disarmed and repatriated; and the United states had committed itself to assist in the process. Moreover, the long antagonism between Nationalist government forces and the Communist Chinese persisted. In the Truman administration there were those, such as Labor Secretary Lewis Schwellenbach, who wanted to withdraw United States marines from China as soon as possible and those, such as Navy Secretary Forrestal, who wanted a United States presence there in order to discourage the flow of the Russians into the power vacuum created by Japan's surrender. The United States compromise position was to help the Nationalists disarm the Japanese and to promote peace between the conflicting Chinese forces. The situation was brought to a head when the flamboyant United States ambassador to China, Patrick J. Hurley, unexpectedly resigned in

November and damned the administration for having no China policy. Affairs were complicated by Britain's desire for a weak China and Russia's looting of machinery from Manchuria and its turning over of Japanese arms to the Chinese Communists.

The administration acted quickly. It decided to keep United States marines in China, to move additional Nationalist forces to northern China, and to arrange a political settlement between the Nationalists and the Communists. The problem with this policy was that it put the United States in the inconsistent position of supporting the Nationalists while trying to be the honest broker of peace between them and the Chinese Communists. Given the bitter antagonism between the two groups and given the ineptitude of the Nationalist government under Chiang Kai-shek, it would have taken a miracle for this policy to succeed. In late 1945 Truman chose General of the Army George C. Marshall to go to China as his special ambassador to attempt to perform the miracle.

Truman may have believed, as he wrote in his private papers, that ''we are merely winding up the war. . . We are not mixing in China's internal affairs.''[12] But few people saw it this way, for the idea of having a strong, united, and democratic government in Peking was not in line with powerful interests in China, London, or Moscow. Marshall strained as much as Sisyphus in trying to roll his boulder up the Chinese mountain. Chiang Kai-shek belabored Marshall for trusting the Communist Chinese; the Communists saw him as a dupe of the Nationalists; and the Russians hindered him by their slowness in observing their agreement to depart from Manchuria. Nevertheless, Marshall arranged truces in 1946 that reduced the fighting between Nationalist and Communist troops as well as agreements for the unification of China. Success was not to be Marshall's, however. By the end of July, civil war had flared up again, and it was clear by October that negotiations could not be successfully resumed. Despite Forrestal's delaying actions, most United States forces had been removed from China by the end of 1946.

By 1946 Truman had already concluded that the world resembled a gigantic minefield. Even issues that should have been easily resolved took on unforeseen difficulties. One was that of displaced persons (DPs), who had no safe place to which to return after the war. The displaced persons of Asia were largely left to shift for themselves. The United States placed its emphasis on the hundreds of thousands of European DPs, particularly Jews. President Truman pressed the British to allow Jewish DPs into the British protectorate of Palestine, and he inquired as to where else they and other DPs could be admitted. No country, including the United States, wanted to accept many Jewish

DPs, most of whom, small wonder, did not want to remain in Germany. This led to wrangles among nations in accommodating the new Diaspora, as well as to conflict within the United States over modifying its immigration policy. In 1946 the Truman administration persuaded the United Nations to create the International Refugee Organization (IRO) to deal with the resettlement of DPs. Congress passed the Displaced Persons Act in 1948, which authorized the United States to shoulder much of the load. By 1952 the IRO had arranged for the resettlement of more than 1 million people, with the United States receiving almost four hundred thousand.

The most prickly aspect of the problem was arranging for Jewish DPs to enter Palestine. The United Kingdom resisted fulfilling its promise to make that Middle Eastern land a national home for the Jews. It was more than a matter of resources and prejudice, for the British believed that their hands were already full in dealing with tensions between the Arabs and Jews in Palestine. Furthermore, for commercial and military reasons, Britain did not want to offend Arabs elsewhere. There were numerous Americans, too, who feared jeopardizing their nation's future in the Arab world, especially in view of its rich oil resources and the Soviet interest in the area. Thus the battle lines were being drawn in 1945 and 1946, not only in the Middle East, but also in Washington and between the United States and Britain.

The British believed that they might stabilize the situation in Palestine, since they had strictly limited Jewish emigration and had forbidden Jews to obtain Arab land. Truman upset his ally's plans, however, by expressing his sympathy for resettling one hundred thousand Jewish DPs in Palestine immediately and for establishing a Jewish national home there. Navy Secretary Forrestal and some people in the State Department opposed him, because they thought that this would not only damage United States relations with the British and the Arabs but would also invite violence and Russian intrigue in the Middle East. In response, the president agreed only to try to find a solution to the Palestinian problem through the instrumentality of the Anglo-American Committee of Inquiry, which was created in late 1945. In April 1946 the committee recommended the establishment in Palestine of a federated Arab-Jewish state under a UN trusteeship, along with the easing of restrictions on immigration and the transfer of land and with bringing Arab living standards up to those of the Jews. The committee's report only exacerbated the situation. Arab spokesmen complained bitterly, while Jewish representatives demanded the immediate implementation of the recommendations. Violence among Arabs and Jews and even the British became a serious problem in Palestine. Tensions were accelerated after Foreign Minister Bevin refused to facilitate the acceptance there of Jews, who were, he said gratuitously, central to the policy of the Americans "because they did not want too many of them in New York."[13]

By July, Truman felt that he was being besieged. The Arabs had defamed him; the British, he believed, were double-crossing him; the Jews were pressing him hard, even discourteously, for action; his official family was divided; and Congress was in an uproar. Moreover, he was sickened by growing Jewish terrorism in Palestine. New negotiations with the British and with representatives of the Jews and Arabs during that summer and fall were unsuccessful. On October 4, 1946, during Yom Kippur, Truman implied his endorsement of the Jewish Agency's plan to create within Palestine a Jewish state that would control its own economic and immigration affairs. As part of this plan, one hundred thousand immigration certificates would be issued immediately. The British and the Arabs were infuriated, and Truman's Yom Kippur statement was attacked at home as a blatant bid for the Jewish vote in the November elections. He had several motives, not the least of which were his compassion for the Jewish survivors of the Holocaust during World War II and his frustration with the bloody stalemate in Palestine. Whatever his motives were, his tactics did not work with the British. The response from London was to refer the issue to the UN in 1947, which meant that there would be a great deal of the Palestine question in everybody's future.

No foreign issue was deemed to be more important in Washington than the deteriorating relations between the United States and the USSR. This came into focus again at the December 1945 meeting of the Council of Foreign Ministers in Moscow. Molotov was his usual intractable self, but Secretary Byrnes's discussions with Stalin led to some agreements. Stalin said that Soviet troops would remain in Iran until March 1946. Stalin indicated, however, that if Iran were to challenge, before the UN, Russia's total control of its occupation area, "We will do nothing to make you [the U.S.] blush."[14] The Russian leader reaffirmed his support of the Nationalist Chinese government, saying that Soviet troops would be withdrawn from Manchuria by February. His influence probably facilitated the agreement to establish a four-power commission to work out the bases for an independent Korea within five years. Nothing came of this, however, for the Russians did not permit the commission to operate. Molotov and his comrades seemed to be more amenable to UN involvement in the control of atomic energy and to Byrnes's proposal to demilitarize Germany for a generation. Although there continued to be a stalemate on the issues of forming representative governments in and Western recognition of Bulgaria and Rumania, the meeting made progress on planning for a World War II peace conference.

Byrnes returned from Moscow feeling more optimistic than he had upon his arrival there. He did, however, face an unhappy president. Truman believed that Byrnes had not kept him adequately informed as to events in Moscow and had released information to the public before consulting with his chief. Truman had learned that he could not be his own secretary of state; but Byrnes soon discovered that he could not be his own president. Truman summoned Byrnes to meet with him directly upon the latter's return from abroad. In later accounts, the two men disagreed as to what had transpired. The upshot was, however, that Byrnes kept his president better informed and that Truman became more direct in instructing his secretary of state. Truman also wrote a harsh letter to Byrnes, which, Truman said, he read to him on January 5, 1946. Byrnes denied this, and there is no evidence to contradict him. What is important about the letter is that it shows that Truman reached different conclusions about the Moscow meeting and other recent developments than had Byrnes. The president was outraged by the situations in Bulgaria, Rumania, and especially Iran, which had been Russia's "friend and ally" during the war. Moreover, he believed that Russia intended to invade Turkey. Truman asserted, "Unless Russia is faced with an iron fist and strong language another war is in the making." His program was: do not recognize Rumania and Bulgaria until there are free elections and representative governments there; vigorously support Iran; internationalize key European waterways; retain "complete control of Japan and the Pacific"; and work for stable governments in China and Korea. "I'm tired of babying the Soviets."[15] Truman was clearly ready to take a tougher stance toward the Soviet Union, even though some of his toughness in the letter of January 5 was a result of his frustration with the secretary of state. However Byrnes received the presidential message, he, too, would be tougher in dealing with the Russians, as well as less independent of Truman in carrying out his duties.

Postwar United States foreign policy had begun to emerge in 1945, and it would take further shape in 1946, largely in the crucible of Soviet–United States relations. It was not ideally what most Americans wanted, but it seemed as close to it as conditions would permit. Trade liberalization was part of the policy, as the United States launched initiatives to reduce trade barriers and to facilitate commerce among nations. This took on a Cold War complexion in the development of a network to strengthen "free nations." Moreover, it was meant to include working people, as the United States threw out lines of communication with European non-Communist labor organizations. Related to this were American attempts to promote cooperation among nations. This was seen not only in support of the United Nations and its panoply of affiliated organizations but also in negotiations on a wide range of projects with other countries. Obviously, peace was intended to be served by having the United States stand up to perceived threats of aggression and by trying to defuse conflicts through negotiations. Democracy and individual freedom would be encouraged through the development of propaganda and educational programs.

One problem with the emerging United States foreign policy was that the principle of national self-determination sometimes became compromised. As United States leaders became increasingly concerned with the creation of a strong anti-Communist front, they became more assertive in telling their country's allies how they should act (as well as less concerned with the degree of democracy and freedom that they practiced). Instead of the Golden Rule of "Do unto others as you would have them do unto you," which Truman invoked as a basis of American foreign policy in 1945, increasingly the dictum would be "What contributes to the struggle against communism is good for the world." The problem with this was that American leadership, in its obsession with thwarting communism, was sometimes blinded to the needs of other peoples. Moreover, America's power was often intimidating to actual or potential allies, which were left with insufficient leeway to pursue their own interests. What Washington could not achieve through reason it could often buy (though sometimes at outrageous prices) or could gain through intimidation. Even an official United States reproof was enough, in some countries, to jeopardize economic stability or the perpetuation of a government. However acceptable this seemed to be in order to promote an international anti-Communist front, it did not always serve the causes of national self-determination, democracy, individual freedom, and voluntary cooperation among nations.

There was no doubt that the Truman administration, which was impatient in its quest for world peace and harmony, considered Soviet expansionism to be a grave threat. By early 1946 it was clear that the Russians would soon have their way in Poland, Rumania, Bulgaria, and probably Hungary. Albania and Yugoslavia were already beyond the pale of Western influence. Czechoslovakia and Finland were still in doubt, and Iran festered. Japan was safe, but the situations in China, Greece, and Germany were unsettling. Korea would soon be formally divided into Russian and United States protectorates. The USSR was expanding its international agitational and propaganda forces, and it continued to place pressure on Turkey and to seek outposts in North Africa, the Mediterranean, and Scandinavia.

In a speech on February 9, 1946, Stalin sent shock waves through the Western world. He indicated that peace among nations was impossible so long as capitalist forces—which he declared to be the cause of World War II—remained in control of the non-Communist world. Therefore, he announced that it was necessary for the USSR greatly and rapidly to expand its production of defense materials. This led, at the request of the State Department, to the writing of the so-called Long Telegram of February 22 by George F. Kennan, the United States chargé d'affaires in Moscow. Kennan interpreted the Soviet world view as being based on the "traditional and instinctive Russian sense of insecurity." For this reason, Russia's rulers had to sound the tocsins of defense against the outside world, which they were afraid to be compared with. They also used this fear to justify dictatorship at home and infiltration and subversion abroad. Kennan concluded, in effect, that one could not do business with Moscow.[16] The Long Telegram was widely read in Washington. It probably had greater influence after Forrestal circulated in January a study by a Smith College professor, Edward F. Willett, which questioned whether there could be accommodation between Russian communism and Western democracy. Both the Willett and the Kennan documents helped lay the groundwork for the increasingly pessimistic view that United States leaders would take toward the Soviet Union. Events in 1946 would appear to prove what Willett and Kennan had written.

During the last week of February, everything seemed to go wrong. Iran had taken to the UN its complaint that the USSR was preventing Iran from dealing with uprisings in Iran's northern territories. Russia blocked Iran's appeal, however, before the Security Council. Meanwhile, the Soviets intensified the pressure on the Turks to share control of Turkey's strategic areas; and the beginnings of a Communist government were laid in northern Korea. Truman was so discouraged that on February 25 he told some of his aides that the United States was going to be at war with Russia, and on two fronts. The president could do little about Iran and Korea but to await developments. He had an opportunity, however, to show the flag in Turkish waters without being provocative. So, on February 28, he dispatched the battleship *Missouri*, with an escorting task force, to Istanbul to take home the body of the recently deceased Turkish ambassador to the United States.

Others responded quickly to the new pressures. On February 27 Senator Vandenberg, the Republican leader on foreign policy, recited for the Senate the USSR's transgressions around the world. He asked pointedly, "What is Russia up to now?" Aiming at the administration, he declared that "the situation calls for patience and good will; it does not call for vacillation."[17] Secretary of State Byrnes also called for firmness on February 28, in a speech that pundits labeled the "Second Vandenberg Concerto." In addition to stressing the need for "frank discussion," he asserted that in order "to do our part to maintain peace in the world we must maintain our power to do so."[18] Byrnes was no doubt responding to congressional, press, and even presidential criticism of his tactics. And the criticism seemed to be matched by a shift in public opinion, for in February the Gallup poll found that only 35 percent of those polled thought that Russia would cooperate with the United States; this figure was down from 54 percent the preceding August.

All this was spiritedly reinforced by Winston Churchill's visit to the United States in February and March 1946. Britain's former prime minister talked with the American leaders, urging that Britain and the United States unite in opposition to an aggressive Russia. He became the focus of world attention when he journeyed to Fulton, Missouri, to speak at Westminster College on March 5. There, in President Truman's presence, he declared that from the Baltic to the Adriatic "an iron curtain has descended" across Europe, basically with police states to the east and free nations to the west. The result of this and Russia's "expansive and proselytizing tendencies" elsewhere was "a growing challenge and peril to Christian civilization." Churchill suggested that an Anglo-American military alliance was in order.[19] His address had considerable force, coming as it did at the time of the Iranian crisis, mounting Soviet pressures on Turkey, Communist acceleration of civil war in Greece, and revelations of Russian atomic espionage in Canada. It is no surprise that a Gallup poll in March showed that 60 percent of the respondents thought that the United States was being too soft with Russia.

As for Iran, Soviet troops were supposed to leave there by March 2. They lingered on, however, although American and British forces had departed. Secretary Byrnes sent stiff notes to Moscow on March 5 and 8, asking for the withdrawal of Russian troops; and Iran took the issue to the Security Council again. Finally, on March 26, the USSR announced that it would withdraw its forces within six weeks, although it extracted an agreement for the establishment of a Soviet-Iranian oil company and left behind a potent Communist movement in northern Iran. Truman played down the situation, declaring at his March 14 news conference that "I am not alarmed by it." His concern was great, however. On March 23 the president told the new United States ambassador to

Moscow, Gen. Walter Bedell Smith, that because of the Iranian episode, he no longer believed that Stalin was "a man to keep his word." Truman directed Smith to "urge Stalin to come to the U.S.A."[20]

Ambassador Smith had a long talk with Stalin early in April 1946. The Soviet leader could not have liked being summoned to Washington, however sugar-coated the invitation was. He told Smith that his physicians had instructed him not to travel. Stalin reaffirmed his desire for peace and was cordial, although he made clear his belief that the United States and Britain were allied in trying to thwart the USSR. Meanwhile, Soviet policy had become more conciliatory. The Russians had not only begun to withdraw from Iran, Manchuria, and Denmark's Bjornholm, but they were also being less obstreperous on the Allied Control Council in Germany. If February and March had marked a serious and stiffer turn in United States foreign policy, the less-combative Russian attitude appeared to confirm the wisdom of hard talk from Washington. It also seemed to indicate that the United States did not have to build up its military strength or make great outlays for foreign aid beyond what the administration had already committed itself to.

The world's attention seemed to be focused on what would happen at the next meeting of the Council of Foreign Ministers, scheduled to begin in Paris on April 25. As usual, Truman was publicly optimistic. He told a news conference of April 18: "Our relations with Russia are as cordial as they have always been. When two horse traders get to bargaining, they sometimes get pretty rough with each other, but they hardly ever wind up in a fist fight. They usually make a trade. That is what we propose to do with Russia." Molotov began the conference on a promising note by reversing his opposition to France's full participation in the formulation of European peace treaties. But he made few concessions after this. Indeed, the conference stretched out, often acrimoniously, until July 12. The Russians rejected Byrnes's proposal to demilitarize Germany for twenty-five years, thus missing an opportunity to neutralize a traditional enemy. Agreement was reached on draft treaties with the minor Axis nations, although in a form that was more satisfactory to Russia than to the Western powers. What the United States, Britain, and France got in return concerned matters that they thought should not have been on the agenda—the dropping of the Soviet demand for a trusteeship in Libya and agreements on the cession of the Dodecanese Islands to Greece and on Italian reparations. At least the way was better paved for the meeting of the World War II peace conference.

The renewal of the question of Venezia Giulia was the most upsetting one at the Paris meeting of the Council of Foreign Ministers. The 1945 settlement had only been temporary; so Russia felt free to press Yugoslavia's demands for the entire area, including Trieste. Yugoslavia aggravated the situation during the conference by executing Marshal Tito's wartime rival for leadership, Mikhail Mikhailovitch, who was a favorite in some Western quarters. It was agreed at Paris, to no one's satisfaction, to continue the status quo in Venezia Giulia, except for forming the Free Territory of Trieste under the control of the UN. The Americans were explosive on this issue, which reflected their impatience. As Byrnes saw it, the Russians were getting increasingly difficult to deal with. And there was some truth to this, if only because the Soviet representatives interpreted United States impatience as something that they could exploit. The problem with this was that it confirmed the growing American view that one could not negotiate with the Russians.

Of course, the Russians could not be pleased with evidences of American hostility, even if they often provoked it. And those evidences were many, for a large variety of Americans openly criticized the Soviet Union. On April 29, during the conference of foreign ministers, Navy Secretary Forrestal went so far as to charge that "the capitalistic and communistic concepts could not live together in the same world."[21] Except for Henry Wallace, no one was encouraging the president to be more patient with the Russians. Truman usually asked those with whom he talked for their opinions, but the views that he received about the Soviets were almost always dismal. For example, when he conferred with Herbert Hoover in May about world food problems, Truman alluded to his problems with the USSR. The former president's advice, which was hardly uncommon, was that "there was only one method of treating this present group of Russians and that was with a truculent spirit. They treated us that way and we should be truculent."[22]

Truculence seemed to be the order of the day. On May 15 the State Department published a secret report on Russia. Combining Willett's and Kennan's analyses with other pessimistic views, this remarkable document detailed United States grievances against the USSR. It declared: "A strong U.S. military establishment . . . will serve as a powerful deterrent to a bold and adventurous Soviet policy of aggrandizement. . . . The language of power backed by reason and right is the only language the Kremlin understands. . . . The U.S. must also be alert to the possibilities for lending prompt and adequate support to its friends." The conclusion was that the Russians would back down, for they were not then interested in war.[23] This was not yet the policy of the

United States, but it was on its way to becoming so. Little was needed except the will to spend the necessary money.

As it was, more money was being devoted in 1946 to coping with Communist combativeness than had been anticipated in 1945, when little was being done beyond expanding the radio propaganda operations of the Voice of America. The nation decided to retain many of its World War II military bases, from Alaska to Iceland and from Japan to Eritrea. The United States sought trusteeships over the former Japanese mandates in the Pacific. Congress, though reluctantly, approved a $3.75 billion loan to the economically ailing United Kingdom. The United States accelerated arms shipments to Latin America. The Philippines Military Assistance Act and a trade agreement with that new nation became forerunners of similar programs to shore up the defenses of non-Communist countries. Even the Fulbright Act of 1946, which established educational exchanges, took on Cold War overtones.

Further testing of the atomic bomb meanwhile took on new urgency. Also, the American impulse of 1945 to share information about atomic energy became more guarded in 1946. Russian statements that they would soon acquire the bomb, as well as news of the USSR's refusal to agree to an international inspection system, did this openness in. Two results were that there would be no significant intergovernmental sharing of atomic information and that no international controls would be imposed on atomic weaponry and energy. Another consequence was that there was greater secrecy and more military control of atomic energy in the United States than might otherwise have been the case. None of this was without popular approval. In four Gallup polls taken between August 1945 and September 1946, the percentage of Americans who wanted their country to retain full control of the atomic bomb ranged between 68 and 75.

The administration also labored long and hard, though unsuccessfully, to reorganize its armed forces into a unified defense establishment and to impose a universal service requirement. Truman tried to spur scientific contributions to the nation, but he and Congress did not reach agreement on a National Science Foundation until 1950. The Central Intelligence Group, which began operating early in 1946, proved to be ill equipped to coordinate United States intelligence activities abroad. Therefore, the administration drew up plans to create a new agency that could carry on various intelligence operations in foreign countries.

Expectably, in a time of growing international tensions, concerns also arose about the security of the nation. The administration not only continued the wartime loyalty-security apparatus, including legally questionable wiretapping provisions, but Attorney General Tom Clark also called for better organization of it. In November, after Republican insinuations during the 1946 election campaign that the administration was soft on communism, President Truman established the Temporary Commission on Employee Loyalty. In March 1947 he instituted a permanent loyalty program for civil servants. The goal of this was to exclude from federal employment any persons of questionable loyalty; the way of doing this was to add Communist organizations to the list of suspect groups that one should not either belong or have belonged to. Although in low gear, the post–World War II Red scare was on. Most scholars believe that the federal program led to injustices being perpetrated by overzealous supervisors, investigators, and loyalty boards. It seemed fair only in comparison to the unbridled investigative activities of some congressional committees and the harsh restrictions imposed by several state governments.

Meanwhile, the World War II peace conference began in Paris on July 29, 1946. The conference would be long and often acrimonious. Even after it ended in October, work on the peace treaties with the lesser Axis Powers was not concluded until the meeting of the Council of Foreign Ministers in November and December. The Western powers fairly well got what they wanted in Italy, but they were forced to recognize that Bulgaria, Hungary, and Rumania were within the Soviet sphere of influence. Again the United States was frustrated in seeking the internationalization of the Danubian waterway and the demilitarization of Germany for a generation. Although a peace treaty with Germany was not on the agenda, the Russians pressed for $10 billion in reparations from that country. It was agreed that this would be subject to negotiation, so that the United States would not wind up financing German reparations.

Other things occurred that affected the peace negotiations. Disagreements intensified between Russia and the Anglo-American combine over the administration of occupied Germany, with France playing its former allies off against one another. While Russia was rapidly establishing communism as the dominant political force in its zone of occupation, the United States was rethinking its policy of deemphasizing the industrial development of Germany. In July the economic integration of the United States and British zones of occupation began, signifying the political and economic division of Germany between East and West. Although the Soviets obstructed the negotiation of an Allied peace treaty with Germany, they stole a propaganda march on the Western Powers. Molotov, in July, declared that Russia's objective was to transform Germany into a peaceful, democratic state that could develop its own industry, trade, and agriculture.

Both Byrnes and Gen. Lucius D. Clay, who was in effect the United States viceroy in Germany, were alarmed by this. It was agreed that the secretary of state had to make clear what United States policy toward Germany was and that he should do so there. On September 6, Byrnes entered the old State Opera House in Stuttgart, ironically accompanied by a band playing "Stormy Weather." He lashed out at the situation, obviously the result of Russian intransigence, that was complicating the governing of Germany. He then endorsed the development of industry and self-government in Germany in order to earn it "an honorable place among the free and peace-loving nations." As much to reassure Britain, France, and even Germany as to stand up to the Soviets, Byrnes declared that "as long as an occupation force is required in Germany the army of the United States will be a part of that occupation force."[24]

The peace conference in Paris was also affected by Yugoslavian and Turkish affairs. There were still tensions in Venezia Giulia, where Anglo-American and Yugoslavian forces faced each other. On August 19 Yugoslavian warplanes shot down an unarmed United States supply plane, killing five people. Washington filed stiff protests over this and other incidents, and it replaced the transports with armed bombers on United States supply runs. Although Yugoslavia agreed to pay indemnities, tensions continued as a result of its trying Catholic Archbishop Aloysius Stepinac for treason. As for Turkey, in August, Russia pressed its demand to participate in the defense of the Black Sea Straits. The United States saw this as evidence of Soviet interest in dominating Turkey, outflanking Greece, and threatening the Middle East. Therefore, the United States supported Turkey's rejection of Russian demands. Washington's firmness in these cases was matched by its nervousness as to how to back up its position if necessary. Navy Secretary Forrestal used these situations in order to complain about cuts in defense funds and to force a review of America's capabilities to meet emergency military challenges. He also used these as opportunities to develop the United States naval presence in the Mediterranean.

In September would come a crisis in the Truman administration itself. The postwar development of United States foreign policy had disturbed Secretary of Commerce Henry Wallace, who had become the chief source of cautionary remarks to the president and within the cabinet. Truman did listen to Wallace and, as often as not, told him that he shared his qualms about the direction of events. It is impossible to say whether Truman was primarily humoring Wallace as his one ultraliberal cabinet member, encouraging discussion of the issues, or agreeing with a number of Wallace's apprehensions. Probably it was a combination of all three, as well as of some less-obvious motives. By summer 1946, Wallace became more direct in expressing his concerns. On July 23 he wrote to Truman at length, explaining his view that Russia had as much reason to fear the United States as the United States had to fear Russia. The United States, he declared, had to "be prepared, even at the expense of risking epithets of appeasement, to agree to reasonable Russian guarantees of security."[25]

This conviction led Wallace to give an address in New York City on September 12, in which he criticized United States foreign policy and called for allaying Soviet suspicions about the West. This showed questionable judgment on the part of a cabinet member, but Truman had seen the speech and had praised it to Wallace, which demonstrated even-more-questionable conduct. To top this, in his speech, Wallace said that Truman had approved it as representing the administration's policy. The president said, astonishingly, in his news conference of September 12, that this was correct. When Secretary Byrnes in Paris heard about the speech, he felt that he had been torpedoed by one of his own while he was in combat with the enemy. He expressed his deep displeasure with Wallace's remarks. On September 14 Truman back-tracked, lamely explaining that he had only approved Wallace's right to make the speech, not the contents of it. Meanwhile, Wallace's letter of July 23 found its way into print. Truman wrote a memo to himself on September 16, noting that the "Wallace affair is very embarrassing." He demonstrated that he had been hazy on foreign policy when he added, "There were one or two things in the [speech] which I thought were a little wild but I did not interpret them as contrary to the general policy."[26]

The uproar over Wallace's speech led to negotiations between Truman and him, with Byrnes threatening to resign if the president could not control his secretary of commerce. Wallace agreed to stop speaking out until after the Paris peace conference, but this was not good enough for the secretary of state. On September 19, Byrnes radioed Truman: "You and I spent fifteen months building a bipartisan policy. We did a fine job convincing the world that it was a permanent policy upon which the world could rely. Wallace destroyed it in a day." Then Byrnes asked to be relieved of his duties.[27] Wallace was now not just "a little wild" to the president, especially as other high officials were pointing out how his and Wallace's remarks had undermined Byrnes in the conduct of foreign relations. "Henry is a pacifist 100%," Truman confided privately. "He wants us to disband our armed forces, give Russia our atomic secrets and trust a bunch of adventurers in the

Kremlin Politburo who have no morals, personal or public."[28] The president had shifted in a few days from seeing less to seeing more than there was in Wallace's address. On September 20 he asked for Wallace's resignation, convinced that the time and the issues were too crucial to allow his secretary of state to leave.

With Wallace's departure from the administration, Truman lost his last intimate link to serious, if often exaggerated, criticism of the developing United States foreign policy. During the rest of his time in office, the president would be highly vulnerable to the thinking of those who more often than not advocated a hard-boiled approach to the Soviet Union. Very soon after Wallace had resigned, Truman was exposed to this. The president himself indeed initiated it. On July 12 he had told his special counsel, Clark Clifford, that if the Paris peace conference failed, the truth about the Russians would have to be revealed. He asked Clifford to provide him with a list of international agreements that the Soviets had violated. Clifford turned the job over to his aide, George M. Elsey, a young naval reservist who had seen wartime service in the White House Map Room. Elsey recommended, instead, that they prepare a report on the entire scope of Russian-American relations. The president agreed that this would be more useful. Clifford made inquiries of numerous top governmental sources, and other materials were gathered on Soviet transgressions, duplicity, and aggrandizement.

Elsey was largely reponsible for preparing the resulting eighty-two-page top-secret document. It had strong overtones of Kennan's and Willett's views and of the State Department's secret report of May 15 on the USSR. The Elsey-Clifford report was pessimistic about Soviet-American relations, based on what seemed to be strong evidence of Russia's interest in dominating the world. Powerful medicine was recommended so as to contain Soviet aggrandizement. The report stated that "as long as the Soviet Government adheres to its present policy, the United States should maintain military forces powerful enough to restrain the Soviet Union and to confine Soviet influence to its present area. All nations not now within the Soviet sphere should be given generous economic assistance and political support in their opposition to Soviet penetration." War might eventuate, of course, so the United States "must be prepared to wage atomic and biological warfare" in response to Russian military action. Yet the report left room for accommodation, even economic aid to and increased trade with Russia. The authors reflected the hope, however dim, that Soviet leaders would change their minds about the irreconcilability of communism and capitalism and would "work out with us a fair and equitable settlement when they realize that we are too strong to be beaten and too determined to be frightened."[29]

The report was presented to Truman on September 24, and he read it that night. He believed that it was "so hot" in terms of trying "to develop some relationship with the Soviet Union" that instead of circulating it, he had all of the copies of the document locked up in his safe.[30] Nevertheless, the president had read it, and it had had its impact on him. Moreover, what was in the report represented the thought of most of his chief military and foreign-policy advisers. It would just be a matter of time until a policy consonant with this thinking would be developed and financed. Secretary Byrnes might not then have agreed with the contents of the Clifford-Elsey report, but he intended to resign by 1947, if for no other reason than that Truman and he were too often in disagreement. Those who remained in the most influential positions would be sympathetic to the thrust of the report. All that was needed was for the Russians to continue their intransigence and agitation, and in that they would cooperate fully.

There were, of course, other developments. The British and the Americans had begun to make informal joint military plans by August 30. A month later, units of the United States fleet were being permanently stationed in the Mediterranean, as Navy Secretary Forrestal wanted. What vitally concerned America's military chieftains that fall was what Forrestal called the "many signs of a gathering drive to cut down our Armed Forces and to persuade the people that we should haul out of Europe."[31] Truman's perserverance in cutting military expenditures to balance the budget was part of this concern. Clearly, the president was relying on America's possession of the atomic bomb, not expansion of the armed services, to back up his administration's increasingly tough foreign policy.

James Byrnes's last act was to be played out in November and December 1946. At the meeting of the Council of Foreign Ministers in New York, Molotov tried to change the draft peace treaties, despite the agreements arrived at during the Paris peace conference. Byrnes and Bevin forced the Soviet foreign minister to settle for some slight alterations in the language of the treaties. In December the secretary of state spoke to the United Nations on disarmament, especially the control of atomic weapons. This paved the way for the Security Council to approve a United States plan, with Russia abstaining. The UN was now on record in favor of an international system of inspection and control of atomic weapons, to be defined by treaty. Over the years the Soviets blocked any treaty because it would not control all arms, and Americans became increasingly less interested in such an agreement.

Byrnes did not take any part in this, for he left the secretaryship on January 20, 1947. With his departure, the foreign policy of the United States would place less emphasis on negotiation. Whatever hopes President Truman had previously held for developing "some relationship with the Soviet Union" grew slim when he received the Clifford-Elsey report. After Byrnes left Washington, they were nonexistent. The search for a modus vivendi had ended.

5

★ ★ ★ ★ ★

THE EIGHTIETH CONGRESS
AND THE HOME FRONT

If the fall and early winter of 1946 was a time for regrouping in foreign policy, the same was true for domestic policy. Truman's popularity rating in the Gallup poll had fallen to 32 percent, and the Democrats had lost control of Congress in the November elections, which was widely seen as a vote of no confidence in the administration. Indeed, many people, including some Democrats, called upon the president to resign. This was a suggestion that Truman did not take seriously, knowing that nineteen other presidents had served at one time or another when their parties were not in control of Congress. He would serve out his term; he would do his job the best he could; and he would strive to get the public's approval of what he had done.

Truman had plenty to do on the home front before the new Congress opened in January 1947. One thing was to deal with a serious labor crisis. In October 1946 John L. Lewis took advantage of the fact that Congress was out of session and that the election campaign was in progress in order to demand a new contract from the government for the United Mine Workers. Better benefits for the mine workers were at stake, but so were the nation's economic stability and, as winter approached, the heating of America's homes. The administration negotiated with the UMW, skillfully trying to spin out time until after the elections without a strike being called or the labor vote being affronted. The government then took a tough line, following Interior Secretary Julius Krug's recommendation that Lewis negotiate with the mine owners, not with the government, which was only temporarily in control of the coal mines. The idea was that it was better to risk a strike than to be a party to boosting inflation and treating the UMW as though it were a sovereign state. On November 15 Lewis rejected Krug's position and announced that the UMW's agreement with the government would end on November 20. The administration mobilized to dramatize the situation, playing up Lewis's seeming unreasonableness and the possibility of economic hardship. Attorney General Tom Clark successfully applied for a temporary injunction to keep the UMW from striking. In response, miners began to walk off their jobs; by November 20 the bituminous coal fields had been shut down.

Lewis tried various and often Byzantine ways to reach accommodation, including a direct conference with Truman, which the president turned down because, as he said privately, Lewis had called him a "sonofabitch."[1] The president had decided to finish the fight that Lewis had started, and he intended to beat the UMW leader at his own game. The government hauled Lewis into court to face contempt charges, of which he was found guilty on December 3. On the next day, the court fined him $10,000 and the UMW $3.5 million, with an additional fine for the union of $250,000 for each day that the strike continued. Lewis called off the strike on December 7, ostensibly to avert a national coal shortage and to permit the Supreme Court to hear his appeal without any hint of economic pressure. (The next March the Supreme Court upheld the fines but reduced the union's liability to $700,000.) Truman had won, and his stock with the public rose considerably.

Meanwhile, the administration was preparing for the coming of the Republican Eightieth Congress. Some softening of legislative requests took place: for example, shifting the emphasis from encouraging inexpensive housing for veterans to supporting the initiatives in public housing that were being championed by Republican Senator Robert A. Taft. The administration also further trimmed budget requests in line with the president's and the Republican leadership's policy of trying to balance the budget. More of a concession was Truman's proclamation that on December 31 World War II hostilities had ended. This meant the termination of numerous emergency powers and authorizations; it also removed an area of battle in which the administration could not win; and it might demonstrate the president's reasonableness to some Republicans. Truman planned to continue having frequent meetings with the House and Senate leadership, even though it was now Republican. At the suggestion of the Senate's new president pro tempore, Arthur H. Vandenberg, Truman even included Senator Taft, the chairman of the Republican Senate Policy Committee, a man with whom Truman had seldom agreed.

The president believed that he could command the necessary support in Congress for most of his foreign-policy initiatives, which would prove to be the case. Truman even believed that he could do well on several domestic issues. He had support among leading Republicans for certain measures—for example, from Taft on public housing; from Senator Arthur Capper on civil rights; from Senator Hugh Butler on insular affairs; and from Congressman James W. Wadsworth, Jr., on universal training. Moreover, Truman had pleasant relationships with a number of Republican worthies on Capitol Hill. What he overlooked was that senior members of Congress did not always get what they wanted and that personal relationships did not necessarily translate into legislative support. Then, too, the complexion of Congress had changed. If the Democrats, split between their liberal and conservative contingents, had seldom mustered a majority for the president on domestic issues, the Republicans were less likely to do so. Too many Republicans had too many axes to sharpen, and for the distinct purpose of felling Democratic trees. When, during the Eightieth Congress, Republicans were in a mood to cooperate with Democrats, it was usually with those who, for their own reasons, were intent upon stymieing the administration's programs.

Truman approached the new year with some confidence for other reasons. His stock had risen in the Gallup poll, reaching a 48 percent approval rating in January. Moreover, America's economic problems had eased. Meat and most other groceries were plentiful by December 1946, and more appliances and other gadgets were available to eager consumers. Equally good news was that the government's index of all consumer prices increased by less than 1 percent that month, while food prices dipped by 1 percent. The nation had reabsorbed most of the discharged servicemen without seriously swelling the number of unemployed, which stood at about 2 million. The administration had achieved large cutbacks in federal spending, and a balanced budget was actually a possibility in the near future. In short, the United States appeared to have vanquished the chief postwar threats to the economy, and the government was ready to capitalize on that accomplishment.

It was in this spirit that Truman prepared his legislative proposals. There were no surprises, for the administration had outlined its domestic program during 1945 and 1946. The task now was to present its components in ways that would be most acceptable to Congress. Therefore, Truman approached the Republican Congress on January 6, 1947, to deliver his State of the Union message. He was conciliatory, almost genial, in talking of the need to "work together" despite "honest differences of opinion." The president emphasized five points in his address. They were, first, the promotion of harmonious relations between management and labor; second, the restriction of monopoly and the encouragement of free enterprise; third, the continued fostering of home construction; fourth, the balancing of the budget; and fifth, the achieving of a fair income for farmers. Truman added several subsidiary points to these, including "adequate medical care to all who need it," the protection of civil rights, and the development of natural resources. In support of his domestic program, he made clear his conviction that domestic advancement and the conduct of foreign affairs were closely linked. The United States had to be strong at home "to fulfill our responsibilities to ourselves and to other peoples."

Two days later, on January 8, the president sent his first Economic Report to Congress. This document showed the importance of the new Council of Economic Advisers in buttressing the factual and intellectual bases for the administration's program recommendations. The report's goals were clear. Paramount among them was the promotion of economic growth, now that the worst threats of inflation, unemployment, shortages, and industrial disruption seemed to have passed. The government's primary role would be to foster growth in employment, productivity, capital formation, and consumer purchasing power. There should be a new labor law to facilitate collective bargaining in dealing with disruptive disputes between labor and management. There should also be a serious study of taxation, aimed at making the burdens more equitable and deciding when—though not in 1947 or 1948—taxes could be reduced. These matters, along with long-range efforts to promote foreign trade, social-welfare programs, and the better use of labor and other resources, would permit the best development of the economy, with benefits for all.

Essential to the achievement of these goals was the balancing of the federal budget, which Truman took up with Congress on January 10. He proposed expenditures of $37.5 billion for fiscal year 1948, set against estimated revenues of $37.7 billion. If Congress continued wartime excise levies and raised postal rates, expenditures could be lowered to $37.1 billion, and revenues could be increased to $38.9 billion. Either way, the budget would be balanced, with a surplus left to be applied against the national debt. The success of this budgetary program would require cuts in expenditures for defense and international affairs, but it would allow for increases in expenditures for social-welfare, natural-resource, and agricultural programs. The Truman budget was a continuation of his 1945/46 fiscal policy. In following this policy, the president had fought against inflation and excessive tax burdens while striving to meet emergency challenges and to extend domestic programs that he deemed to be important to the economic advancement and security of the United States.

The administration's legislative and budgetary program seemed to be reasonable. It had been packaged only after arduous White House efforts to reduce federal spending. It had been carefully formulated to appeal to a conservative Congress and yet to allow the administration to retain its liberal credentials. It seemed to have popular support (Truman's popularity in the Gallup poll shot up to 60 percent by March). It was achievable within the revenues projected to be available. Moreover, the program gave Congress considerable leeway in deciding on how the administration's goals could be reached. In January 1947 Truman and many of his associates believed that they could have as much success as they had had with the Seventy-ninth Congress; but they were soon to be disillusioned.

Congress was not in a cooperative mood. Now that the Republicans, for the first time since 1931, had majorities in both houses of Congress, they were fully prepared to exercise their power. They were strongly representative of the small-town, farming, and business elements that had often felt left out during the long years of Democratic rule. Things were going to be different. Even if the Republican legislators did not always agree on their own goals—for agricultural, business, and small-town America did not always think with one mind—they were fairly united on what they did not want. This was an extension of New Deal policies, however expertly they might be trimmed and softened by Truman. In this, the Republicans could often count upon significant support from Democrats. The proportion of liberal Democrats in Congress had declined over the years, while the Democrats who remained were more likely to represent farming, business, and small-town interests. Therefore, many Democratic congressmen often found it appropriate to cooperate with their Republican colleagues. The president soon discovered that instead of working with Congress on many domestic issues, he would be the target of legislative offensives. Truman wrote to his sister, Mary Jane, in late March: "I am having the usual amount of trouble and bickering. When the Congress gets all snarled up it is necessary for them to find someone to blame—so they always pick on me."[2]

One of the first items approved by the Eightieth Congress was what would become the Twenty-second Amendment, which in effect limited presidents to two terms in office. This constitutional amendment, which the states ratified by 1951, did not apply to Truman, but it was an overt Republican rebuff to Franklin D. Roosevelt's scrapping of the two-term tradition. More substantial was the eagerness of congressional Republicans to reduce income taxes, contrary to Truman's wishes. Indeed, this was the objective of the first bill introduced in the House of Representatives in 1947. The president vetoed it on June 16 as being inflationary, favoring the rich, and unbalancing the budget. It was, in short, "the wrong kind of tax reduction, at the wrong time." Unable to override his veto, Congress quickly passed a similar tax bill. Truman rejected this on July 18, for much the same reasons. The income-tax-reduction battle was over for 1947. It was renewed in 1948, however, when Congress emerged the victor.

The administration more than achieved its overall budget goals for fiscal year 1948, but not in the way that Truman wanted. Thanks to slightly lower appropriations than he requested and to additional administration economies, expenditures for fiscal year 1948 totaled only some $34 billion, while receipts ran higher than expected—more than $42 billion. Deducting money that was set aside for the Foreign Economic Cooperation Trust Fund, this meant a surplus of almost $5.5 billion. What Truman had requested and what Congress had appropriated funds for were, however, rather different. Less was appropriated for defense, housing, veterans, education, agriculture, transportation and communication, business, labor programs, and general governmental expenses. Congress approved more for international, natural-resource, and social-welfare programs, largely because of the exigencies of the time.

This did not mean that the administration and Congress in 1947 never agreed on domestic issues. In February, Truman reiterated his call that provision be made for the Speaker of the House to succeed to the presidency, assuming there was no vice-president, in case of the death, resignation, removal, or inability to act of the president. His reason was that the office should be filled by an elected officer. Not surprisingly, the Republican Congress acted favorably on this proposal. Presidential and congressional interests also coincided in reorganizing the executive branch in order to promote economy and efficiency. Truman had earlier used limited powers, conferred upon him by Congress, to effect some useful reorganizations in the executive branch. Now it appeared that this should be done on a wider scale. Truman was agreeable to having it spurred by a bipartisan commission, which was to study the situation intensively and then make recommendations after the 1948 elections. Congress established and the president approved this commission in July 1947. In a brilliant stroke, Truman named former President Herbert Hoover, who had long been a champion of reorganization, as chairman of this Commission on the Organization of the Executive Branch. The Hoover Commission, as it became popularly called, quickly settled down to its work, which led to significant results during Truman's second term.

Yet, on most domestic issues, Congress and the president did not see eye to eye. Inflation was one important example. At issue basically were economic controls, of which Truman wanted more and the legislators wanted fewer. The president usually lost, so he largely was left with the ineffective tool of persuasion in coping with the threat of inflation. He told business and farmers to hold the lines on prices so that there would not be pressures for wage increases, which in turn would lead to more price rises. His drive to restrain price and wage increases met with resistance—from business, for fear that it would trigger a recession; from farmers, for fear that their income would drop; and from labor, for fear that it would not catch up with earlier price increases. This resistance reinforced Congress's willingness to cut back on existing controls. Truman complained bitterly, criticizing Congress for weakening rent controls, for allowing sugar controls to lapse, and for not strengthening controls on consumer credit. Whatever the causes, and they considerably transcended the issue of controls, consumer prices rose an alarming 14 percent between 1946 and 1947.

This was just one case of the inability of Congress and the administration to cooperate on domestic legislation in 1947. It was repeated again and again, on questions dealing with monopoly, health, housing, agriculture, education, Social Security, and natural resources. And it was not just a matter of Congress's blocking administration initiatives, for the president's jousts with the legislators were highly productive of vetoes, a total of thirty-two in 1947. Most of Truman's vetoes and pocket vetoes were applied to minor legislation. There were, however, in addition to the two vetoes of income-tax-reduction bills, his disapprovals of legislation to weaken the Interstate Commerce Act, to exclude newspaper and magazine vendors from the Social Security program, and to subsidize the production of copper, lead, manganese, and zinc. The most important and highly publicized case, and the only one in which Congress overrode the president's veto, concerned the rewriting of the National Labor Relations Act of 1935.

Strife between labor and management had been a highly significant problem in the United States in 1945 and 1946. The resulting strikes had led to many inconveniences and had contributed to driving prices skyward. Increasingly, tempers had flared, and many Americans were blaming the unions for initiating industrial turbulence. Many members of Congress considered the results of the 1946 elections as a mandate to crack down on organized labor. The controversial strike by the United Mine Workers in late 1946 aggravated the situation, so much so that

Navy Secretary James Forrestal feared that "dangerous . . . restrictive and overpunitive labor legislation" was on the way.[3] Truman tried to deal with this by calling for objective study of industrial problems and by encouraging labor and management to negotiate with each other in better faith. He gave little guidance to Congress on the matter of labor regulation, however, apparently in the belief that it would not be heeded. Despite requests from some Democratic leaders on Capitol Hill, the president remained aloof while Congress considered new labor legislation.

What emerged from legislative consideration were separate measures sponsored by Fred A. Hartley, Jr., chairman of the House Labor and Education Committee, and Robert A. Taft, chairman of the Senate Labor and Public Welfare Committee. In April 1947 the House exultantly passed the Hartley bill, which in its more-extreme provisions would have placed unions under antitrust laws, outlawed mass picketing and most industry-wide collective bargaining, and eliminated bargaining on fringe benefits. The Senate could not accept anything so extreme. In response, however, it wound up passing a measure, the Taft bill, that was stronger than it might otherwise have been. A conference committee in June recommended compromise legislation, which resembled Taft's relatively reasonable bill more than Hartley's. Under this Taft-Hartley bill, employees no longer had to be union members before being hired, but only afterwards and only if the employees voted so. Now, unfair labor practices as well as unfair management practices were dealt with in the law. Unions became liable for violations of contracts, and they had to make annual financial reports to their members and to the Labor Department. Neither unions nor corporations could make financial contributions to election campaigns. In order to retain their organizations' rights under the law, union leaders had to swear annually that they were not Communists. The president was authorized to appoint a fact-finding board when he believed that a strike could jeopardize the national interest. After receiving the panel's report, he could direct the attorney general to secure a court injunction to delay a strike for eighty days to allow for its settlement. Secondary boycotts and jurisdictional strikes were also forbidden.

Congress passed the Taft-Hartley Act in June. Truman now had to decide whether he would veto or sign the bill, and he had to do this in the greatest glare of national publicity that he had yet experienced. The legislation was top news. Moreover, labor and liberals raged publicly against the bill, while business and conservatives responded in kind. Truman's prime political advisers urged a veto, and cabinet members mostly recommended signing the bill. The president was on the spot. If he approved the measure, he would antagonize liberals and the unions; if he vetoed it, he would further irritate Congress and conservatives. Whatever his decision, it had to be political in nature, for it was clear that Congress would override a veto. Truman decided on the veto so that he might improve his ability to rally labor and liberal support on later issues and for the 1948 elections. Furthermore, he knew where he stood with Congress, and his veto could do little to change that. The president told Congress on June 20 that he had disapproved the measure because it was unworkable, divisive, discriminatory, and "a clear threat to the successful working of our democratic society." Truman went on the radio that evening to inform America's voters of his reasons. He knew that the voters would be the judges, in the 1948 elections, of who had been right on the issue. As expected, Congress voted to override his veto, and the Taft-Hartley Act became the law of the land.

It can be argued that Truman was both right and wrong in his action. By his veto, he had taken a giant step toward winning the support of many liberals and of organized labor for his 1948 election campaign. Moreover, he was correct in pointing out the divisiveness of the new law. In some ways it discriminated against labor, and some of its provisions turned out to be unworkable. Yet the heart of the Taft-Hartley Act—those provisions that gave the government more power to intervene in industrial disputes—did regulate labor activity without seriously impairing the legitimate power of unions, just as the Wagner Act of 1935 had restrained outrageous actions by management without crippling it. Truman and his successors used the law effectively to enhance the results of collective bargaining and to maintain a reasonable level of industrial peace. There is no doubt that the Taft-Hartley Act was the most important domestic legislation of the Truman presidency.

As a sidelight, it was poetically just that the first major labor dispute in which the Taft-Hartley Act was invoked concerned the United Mine Workers. The miners walked out on March 15, 1948, over the issue of old-age pensions. On April 3 Truman directed the attorney general to seek an injunction to stop the strike. The miners ignored the injunction, and on April 19 John L. Lewis and the UMW were found guilty of contempt. Soon afterward the miners returned to work, and the dispute was settled in an orderly fashion. Truman later had other industrial troubles, but they were usually subdued, thanks to the powers placed in his hands by the law. He would be in the enviable position of reaping the political benefits of his celebrated veto and the administrative benefits of the Taft-Hartley Act.

Meanwhile, another problem of vital importance was arising in 1947. The administration had anticipated that Europe would again be short on foodstuffs. Severe winter weather and drought during the spring and summer aggravated the situation. American production had also fallen off, while domestic demand had climbed (this also contributed to the resumption of inflation at home). It appeared, by September, that the problem would be worse than in 1946. Soon Truman appointed the Citizens' Food Committee to promote voluntary food conservation. To him, the issues were clear. First, the United States had an obligation to prevent starvation in Europe, partly for humanitarian reasons and partly to offset the appeal of the Communist parties in western-European elections. Second, the nation had to combat inflation at home. Both of these things were possible, even though the growing season was over, if consumer demand could be decreased.

The Citizens' Food Committee met on October 1, 1947, and immediately challenged Americans to cooperate in conserving food, especially grain. The committee received much publicity, which had little effect, however, because its members could not agree on any dynamic program. The committee's chairman, Charles Luckman of Lever Brothers, did produce a radio program and a television show, emanating for the first time from the White House. The latter production starred President Truman, who asked the public to "(1) use no meat on Tuesdays; (2) use no poultry or eggs on Thursday; (3) save a slice of bread every day."[4] The public was not impressed, and even the White House staff was upset by the committee's "namby-pamby program."[5] The committee failed, however, to agree upon anything more appealing.

Moral suasion was unsuccessful: the food situation did not improve, and prices continued to rise. The situation seemed to be critical. Even by the end of September, Truman began to consider calling a special session of Congress. He told his staff that if the food problem was not solved, Italy and France might yield to communism. The result would be that "we'll just have to get ready for war."[6] The president's sense of frustration rose as the situation went unresolved. He needed help, and no one seemed to be supplying it, not even exact information on Europe's needs. By the middle of October he burst out, "I'm not a superman, like my predecessor; I can't do everything myself."[7] Most of his staff and cabinet members had been urging him to call a special session. As Special Counsel Clark Clifford pointed out, it would at least be useful in building a record for the 1948 elections. Truman responded by asking his staff to work out a timetable for calling Congress into session. He was, however, in no hurry to deal again with the nettlesome Eightieth Congress.

On October 23 the president announced that he was calling a special session for November 17, 1947. He would ask Congress to deal with prices, which had increased 23 percent since the middle of 1946, chiefly during the past three months. Also on the agenda would be the question of helping Europe, Japan, and Korea deal with their serious shortages of food and fuel. (Clifford had suggested that a blunt statement also be made about Russia; Truman fended this off, saying, "I'm not ready to declare war yet.")[8] Meanwhile, the president urged his staff to prepare a program, even though he was pessimistic that Congress would act. As he told his aides, his concern was to do whatever he could to get the job done, not to be demagogic. Truman was depressed by the situation in Congress and by the division within his administration on what to recommend. As he wrote his sister on November 14, he was trying "to face the situation from a national and an international standpoint and not from a partisan political one," even if he had "to take all sorts of abuse from liars and demagogues."[9]

Truman went before Congress on November 17 to request funds to tide Europe, Japan, and Korea over the winter. He also asked for authorizations to deal with inflation. These included controls on credit, commodities, exports, and rents, as well as stand-by programs for rationing and for price and wage ceilings. Knowing that he was likely to get nothing, he asked for everything in order to show that he had tried to cope with inflation. Congress voted funds for overseas relief in December. The legislators could not, however, agree either among themselves or with Truman about how to deal with inflation. Beyond extending the government's power to control exports and the allocation of transportation equipment and facilities, they only authorized the promotion of domestic food-conservation practices and of increased agricultural production abroad. Congress did not deserve all of the blame, for key cabinet members—Clinton Anderson of Agriculture, Averell Harriman of Commerce, and John Snyder of the Treasury— failed to support the president's full program. Moreover, it did not help that Truman had called rationing and price controls "a police state approach" in his news conference of October 16.

The president nevertheless received considerable credit for being the champion of the consumer in combating the rising cost of living. Prices continued to rise, however, as mirrored in the government's Consumer Price Index—from 66.9 in 1947 to 72.1 in 1948. Thereafter, it leveled off, dipping to 71.4 in 1949 and returning to 72.1 only in 1950. Enactment of Truman's program might have been useful, but it was not essential. What largely came to the rescue, both in terms of supply and inflation, was that grain crops in Argentina and Australia exceeded expectations, as did the American winter-wheat harvest. Starvation was staved off in Europe, and inflation was checked in American food markets by autumn 1948.

If Truman had gotten little of the domestic legislation that he sincerely believed was necessary in 1947, he had been creating an image as the people's champion. This would come into sharper focus during 1948, when the chief product of the relations between president and Congress would be political dividends, not legislation. Aware of the situation, Truman played the game for all it was worth in portraying himself as the idealistic, compassionate leader. This began in his State of the Union message of January 7, 1948, in which he called upon Congress to join him in concentrating "not upon party but upon the country; not upon things which divide us but upon those which bind us together." He emphasized the need to protect human rights. His second legislative aim was to develop human resources through appropriate programs relating to health, education, Social Security, and housing. The third objective was the conservation and development of natural resources, and the fourth was the strengthening of the nation's economic system through promoting growth and protecting agriculture, labor, and business. His fifth goal was the authorization of further efforts to achieve world peace and security. He also made a special plea for the control of inflation.

Despite the president's request for expanded domestic programs, the estimate of federal expenditures in his budget message of January 12, 1948, was some $39.7 billion, only about $2 billion more than a year earlier. He believed that the government could spend this much and still have a surplus at the end of fiscal year 1949, because receipts for the year were estimated at almost $44.5 billion. The results would be disappointing, largely because of congressional insistence on cutting income, estate, and gift taxes by $5 billion. On April 2 Truman disapproved this third attempt by the Eightieth Congress to reduce taxes, saying that it exhibited "a reckless disregard for the soundness of our economy and the finances of our Government." This time the legislators were able to override his veto, spurred on, undoubtedly, by election considerations. The tax cut did not, as Truman had feared, contribute to a new round of inflation. Neither did it, as the congressional leadership had anticipated, increase purchasing power and investments in fiscal year 1949, largely because state and local governments boosted their taxes. Consequently, not only was American economic growth stymied in 1949, which contributed to a recession, but federal receipts also declined to less than $38.3 billion, set against expenditures of some $40 billion. At that, Truman and the legislators were at odds on what was appropriated.

Congress generally ignored the president's requests for new domestic programs, partly to provide the tax cut and partly for fear of excessive costs if such programs were initiated. (Truman's view was that economic growth would generate the funds to cover the later expanding costs of his recommended new programs.)

The president, relying heavily on the work of his Council of Economic Advisers, expounded upon the policy of growth in his Economic Report to Congress of January 14, 1948. With proper development of human and natural resources, stability of prices, and promotion of better economic and technological practices, the United States economy should grow. Improved education and health programs would make for a more-productive work force, and expanded social benefits would cushion those who needed it and supply extra purchasing power. An appropriate policy on natural resources would foster, Truman asserted, development of the nation's resources as well as conservation for future needs. And better relations between labor and management would reduce the disruption of production and income, just as an agricultural-security program would allow farmers to contribute to an increase in America's production and purchasing power. Selective governmental controls would smooth over the rough spots in the economy, and fiscal responsibility on the part of both the private sector and the government would restrain inflation. In short, the systematic pursuit of economic growth would make America's future rosy, by providing increased incomes, work, and federal revenues as well as a balanced budget. He warned, however, that "the attainment of our objectives will depend upon the best efforts of industry, agriculture, and labor, working with sympathetic understanding of one another's problems and of the common good."

Truman never made a better statement of his guiding economic policy, one that, in effect, he followed throughout his presidency. For him the policy worked reasonably well. He was, of course, the beneficiary of many things that enhanced his chances for success. Among these were new technologies and better management practices, spurred by the war; abundant natural resources; revitalized domestic and vast new overseas markets; a better-trained labor force; and a resurgence of American entrepreneurship. Still required, nevertheless, was national leadership that could see the relationships among these post–World War II elements and could manage them well. In this respect, the administration and, especially, the president himself were at least adequate. Never mind that Truman did not get all that he wanted or that he was not always clear-sighted. He got enough of what was needed, and he was perceptive enough to use it satisfactorily. If the engines of prosperity were later to go out of gear, that would be the problem of successor administrations. And it should be noted that the Eisenhower and Kennedy administrations, allowing for some adjustment and idiosyncrasies, generally followed Truman's larger economic policies (which in turn were a skillful reshaping of Franklin D. Roosevelt's policies).

This is not to say that Harry Truman was right on everything that he requested. Whether right or wrong, in 1948—even more than in 1947—he pressed ahead vigorously in asking for what he believed America needed. If he could garner anything of what he wanted from Congress, fine; if not, he would build a record that could serve him well in the November elections. Truman used special messages well in 1947 and 1948 in following this strategy, especially messages he sent to Congress when he signed bills that he deemed inadequate. For example, on June 30, 1947, he made it plain that the Housing and Rent Control Act would work hardships against many renters and would contribute to inflation, because it permitted rent increases, removed rent control in many instances, and weakened the protections against unfair evictions. Exploiting the issue, he also reiterated the need for federal action to supply cheap new rental housing and to promote private investment in the construction of housing, as proposed in the Taft-Ellender-Wagner bill. On February 23, 1948, the president, in a special message, again hammered at the need for better rent control and "more housing at lower cost."

His persistence paid off in part: in March a reluctant Congress extended rent control for another year and empowered the government to deal with illegal evictions. This enabled Truman to make the point, upon signing the bill, that if Congress would facilitate the building of hundreds of thousands of inexpensive housing units, the need for rent control would be eliminated. The leadership of the House blocked the Taft-Ellender-Wagner bill, and instead, Congress passed legislation to increase the amount of credit available for home purchases, especially by veterans. Truman signed the act, but stingingly pointed out that the law fell far short of needs. At the special session called later that summer, he once again demanded congressional action on the housing bill. Congress again blocked consideration of the Taft-Ellender-Wagner bill, but it did enact legislation to encourage further private development of housing. Truman's constant pressure thus resulted in more congressional action than otherwise would have been taken on housing. If by failing to provide for public rental housing and farm housing it fell short of what he had demanded, it nevertheless contributed to the president's portrayal of himself as being the tribune of the people.

Truman had less success with Congress in other areas of domestic policy. In a special message to Congress on May 19, 1947, he unveiled the details of his plan for improving the nation's health. He requested additional public-health services, especially for mothers and children; further federal support for medical research and education; more hospitals and physicians; and an insurance program that would allow people to pay their medical costs and to make up for their loss of earnings during times of illness. The reaction from certain quarters was ferocious. Insurance and pharmaceutical companies joined with the American Medical Association in conducting an intensive and expensive campaign against Truman's "socialized medicine" program. Undaunted, he sustained the pressure for a larger governmental role in matters relating to health. The leading vehicle for this in 1948 was a well-publicized comprehensive study of how to improve America's health. The report of this study, *The Nation's Health—A Ten Year Plan*, was released in September, just in time for the opening of the presidential election campaign. Not surprisingly, the study documented the need for the program that the president had recommended in 1947.

The administration used a similar approach in the area of education. The president had appointed the Commission on Higher Education, which made its report in December 1947. This was only part of his effort to provide various federal subsidies to educational institutions on all levels. As in the case of his health program, Truman often pressed Congress for action, and the legislators refused to respond, partly to keep federal spending down and partly for fear of governmental intervention in the schools. His congressional opponents had plenty of allies. Some public educators believed that Truman's proposals would largely benefit private schools, and some private-school educators thought that federal assistance would lead to the dominance of public institutions. Some persons in both areas feared federal dictation. Many Americans thought the Truman program would entail federal support for religious institutions, and others believed that it would increase secularism in education. As was the case with the administration's health program, the issues would only emerge in 1947 and 1948; but action would not be taken then or, indeed, during the entire Truman presidency. Except for the GI Bill, significant federal programs dealing with education and health were to lie well in the future.

Truman used much the same tactics, with much the same results, in dealing with a variety of other issues. Once again in 1948, vetoes and pocket vetoes formed a prominent part of the increasingly stormy dialogue between the president and Congress. Truman vetoed forty-three bills. The major measures that he vetoed included legislation to reduce income taxes; to exempt certain common carriers from antitrust laws; to make loyalty investigations of members of the Atomic Energy Commission (AEC); to exclude, in two different bills, groups from Social Security coverage; to sell certain Indian lands; and to transfer the Employment Service out of the Department of Labor. Congress attempted to override these vetoes in all cases except one—that pertaining to Indian lands—and succeeded in all except for the one relating to the investigation of AEC members. Again Truman was losing, and badly, in the legislative arena, although in doing so, he was gaining additional opportunities to portray himself as the people's president.

Two other areas of legislation deserve special consideration in discussing the interaction between Truman and the Eightieth Congress. One concerns civil rights; the other, agriculture. Truman, who believed in legal equality if not social equality, was perturbed by the racial tensions that led to lynchings and other assaults on blacks during the postwar period. This was a continuation of racial clashes that had occurred during World War II as black and white Americans increasingly confronted one another as a result of military service and expanded job opportunities. The situation was aggravated by violent incidents affecting other minority groups, including Indians, Japanese-Americans, Jews, and Mexican-Americans. Furthermore, many Americans took seriously the official wartime promises of freedom from oppression; therefore, the leaders of minority groups exploited such statements in their efforts to gain a greater measure of equality, opportunity, and protection. Truman's initial response was to support the continuance of the Fair Employment Practices Committee, but he lost this fight in 1946. In formulating other social programs, he kept in mind the favorable effect they would have on minority groups. The president endorsed legislation that Congress passed in 1946 to establish the Indian Claims Commission, which was to act on the financial grievances of Indians. By July 1946, in an unprecedented move, he had appointed blacks to the governorship of the Virgin Islands and to the Customs Court and a native of Puerto Rico as governor of that island. These were the first steps in modern times to accelerate the appointment of members of racial minorities to significant federal positions.

Truman's interest intensified as reports of violence against racial minorities, especially blacks, became common in 1946. Mounting pressures, from minority-group leaders and concerned whites, to do something about the violence honed his concern. There was little that he could do legally, however, except to have the Justice Department investigate such crimes in the slender hope that grounds for federal prosecution might be found. The president also put his assistant for minority affairs, David K. Niles, on the problem. What Niles came up with was the idea of forming a commission to make a comprehensive study of civil-rights problems in the United States. By September 1946 it was clear that this stopgap would be acceptable to most concerned parties. On December 5 Truman created the President's Committee on Civil Rights to recommend ways "to safeguard the civil rights of the people." He named worthies from various walks of life to the committee, appointing as its chairman the president of General Electric, Charles E. Wilson. On October 29, 1947, the committee presented its report, entitled *To Secure These Rights*, to the president. This volume contained thirty-five recommendations for federal, state, and local action to achieve freedom and equality in the United States. In brief, the committee urged the passing of legislation to deal with mob violence; to prevent infringement of civil rights; to extend full and equal rights of citizenship to all Americans; and to eliminate discrimination and segregation in accommodations, education, employment, housing, and public service. *To Secure These Rights* was widely read and discussed. It became at least, as Truman wrote in 1949, "a charter of human rights for our time."[10]

The president would use the volume not only as a text to lecture the nation on civil rights but also as a basis for demanding legislative action. In general terms, he had already taken all of this up with Congress in his 1947 and 1948 State of the Union messages. There was slight reaction from the lords of Capitol Hill. In 1947 Congress only passed legislation to allow Puerto Ricans to elect their own governor. Action in the executive branch was weightier, though not extensive. It was confined largely to initiating the Justice Department's policy of filing amicus curiae briefs in support of legal challenges to discrimination and segregation. The importance of this tactic was first seen in the Supreme Court's decision in *Shelley* v. *Kraemer* (1948) that judges could not use their powers to enforce racially restrictive housing covenants.

By February 2, 1948, Truman was ready to challenge the legislators directly on civil rights. It was then that he sent the first presidential message on this subject to Congress. Using the theme of the Founding Fathers that "all men are created equal," he cited "examples—flagrant examples—of discrimination which are utterly contrary to our ideals." This "serious gap between our ideals and some of our practices," he declared, "must be closed." In his ten-point "minimum program," he requested abolition of the poll tax; a permanent committee on fair employment practices and a commission on civil rights; federal protection against lynching; a civil-rights division in the Justice Department; home rule for the District of Columbia and presidential voting rights for its residents; strong civil-rights statutes; statehood for Alaska and Hawaii and more self-government for other territories; outlawing of segregated facilities in interstate commerce; elimination of inequities in naturalization laws; and settlement of the wartime evacuation claims of Japanese-Americans. Truman also announced that the government would act to remove discrimination in federal employment and the armed forces. He left no doubt that all this should be done partly because of its own intrinsic merit and partly to set a good example for a world "faced with the choice of freedom or enslavement."

Truman's civil-rights message put Congress and the Democratic party in an uproar. Threats of filibusters and other dilatory legislative tactics led him to say on March 11 that the administration would not press for action on civil rights during the current session of Congress, implying that this might jeopardize consideration of more-pressing legislation. Southern politicians responded strongly, too, as threats of secession from the Democratic party were often heard. The administration postponed acting on eliminating discrimination in federal employment and the armed forces. The president had obviously sidetracked his civil-rights program, but he would not recant on it. As he told members of his cabinet and the Democratic National Committee on March 12, "I stand on what I said; I have no changes to make."[11]

Black leaders pressured Truman to take substantial action. Labor leader A. Philip Randolph testified before Congress in March that he would urge young men to refuse to serve in the armed forces unless segregation was abolished in the military. Many black Americans found this idea to be a rallying point for exerting pressure, especially as the administration was exhorting Congress to reinstate the draft. The administration continued to stall on civil rights, partly to wait for the adjournment of Congress and partly to get Truman nominated for president. The adjournment of Congress in June marked no loss for either the president or for minority groups, because the legislators had largely ignored Truman's civil-rights program. If Truman was not yet considered a significant champion of America's minorities, the ostensible interest of congressional Republicans in civil rights had been discredited.

The Democratic National Convention in July was also a trial for the president. In order not to offend white delegates from the South unnecessarily, the White House draft of the platform resolution on civil rights was weaker than Truman wanted. Ultraliberals at the convention, led by Mayor Hubert H. Humphrey of Minneapolis, fought successfully on the floor to strengthen the resolution. Thus they made Truman appear to be a reluctant lion in the cause of civil rights. He won the nomination, nevertheless, and had a stronger plank upon which to campaign. Now that Congress and the convention were out of the way, the president could set aside his reserve and try to redeem his promises.

On July 26 Truman signed Executive Orders 9980 and 9981. E.O. 9980 established the Fair Employment Board, to combat discrimination in the hiring, retention, and promotion of civil-service employees. It was far from a grand success, but it slowly got results, and it laid the basis for further progress during later administrations. E.O. 9981 was more dramatic and more successful. It created the Committee on Equality of Treatment and Opportunity in the Armed Services. By the time Truman left office, the work of this committee would lead to substantial racial integration in the military and to fairer procedures for promotion and training. Much of black America agreed with the *Chicago Defender* that the executive orders were "unprecedented since the time of Lincoln"; the newspaper declared that the people would not "permit Mr. Truman to be crucified on a cross of racial bigotry."[12] During the 1948 campaign the president would remind Americans of the promise implicit in this editorial.

Agriculture is the other area that deserves special attention. Like his presidential predecessors, Truman had often mouthed generalizations about how farmers would be treated fairly. Indeed, farmers did well in the immediate postwar period, largely because of the high demand for farm products at home and abroad and partly because of the continuance of favorable wartime price supports. The supports were to lapse in 1948, however, and agricultural surpluses were developing because of the international recovery of other sources of supply. The Department of Agriculture, under Clinton Anderson, had been a vigorous defender of farm interests, even when its actions contradicted other administration policies, such as price controls and overseas food relief. Despite his oft-stated confidence in Anderson, Truman had to press him to give full support to presidential policies.

Secretary Anderson took seriously his tribuneship for farmers. He had supported high federal guarantees—at least 90 percent of parity—for many agricultural products; but he had qualms about the policy. As he wrote to John R. Steelman in December 1946, "under certain conditions, and for certain commodities, this support can serve to prevent the development of production patterns in line with peacetime needs." This was already a problem in regard to some products, such as potatoes, which were highly subsidized and were still producing surpluses. If demand should fall off, the situation would worsen. A way must be found, without hurting farmers, to hold down both surplus production and the payment of federal subsidies. The nation's program of agri-

cultural price supports must "be given prompt and thorough consideration by the Congress," Anderson declared.[13] The legislators were slow
in responding, largely because they could not agree among themselves
on a new national farm policy. Each senator and representative seemed
to have his own farm program, reflecting the atomization of the
American farm community. By June 1947 it was clear to Anderson that
the administration could expect little from Congress. Out of frustration,
he wrote that perhaps in 1948 the farm vote could remove from Capitol
Hill those who "slashed at the farm programs."[14]

Farm policy was one of the great topics for discussion in 1947 both
in Congress and in the administration. Based on its understanding that
former peacetime federal farm programs had not worked well, the
Department of Agriculture devised what it considered to be a realistic
program. This included mandatory price supports only for storable
products and at a reasonable level, say 75 percent of parity. The
department should have discretionary authority regarding price supports for perishable commodities. It should also be able to cause changes
in production from surplus crops to other crops that were more in
demand, as well as to provide consumer subsidies to increase the
consumption of certain crops. All this was by way of seeking to balance
supply and demand, to reduce demands on the Treasury, and to
maintain a decent income for farmers. It sounded reasonable, except to
large numbers of farmers and legislators. All the talk and study during
1947 produced no consensus on farm policy.

Congress had to act in 1948, when federal price-support legislation
would lapse. Moreover, market returns were dropping in 1948, with
forecasts of more-serious price declines for 1949. Farmers were beginning to get nervous. Predictably, this would mean the planting of larger
crops to compensate for lower unit prices; and this would result in even-
larger surpluses, even-smaller prices, and increased payments of federal
subsidies. The administration and Congress did agree on the passage of
the Foreign Assistance Act in 1948, which, among other things, would
promote the sale of some farm products abroad. This would not,
however, solve much of America's agricultural problem. The House and
Senate were in serious disagreement as to what to do. Although the
upper chamber was considerably attuned to the thinking of the Department of Agriculture, the representatives were split among those from
the South, who wanted high price supports and strict production and
marketing controls; those from the Middle West, who found lower
supports and lesser controls acceptable; and those from elsewhere, who
were mixed in their views.

After much seesawing and amending, the Senate Agriculture Committee approved a long-range plan, sponsored by George Aiken of Vermont. Aiken's bill in essence proposed a sliding scale of support between 72 and 90 percent of parity for major crops, having those that were in greatest supply qualify for the smallest level of supports. The bill also authorized the secretary of agriculture to impose production controls to deal with serious surpluses and, on a discretionary basis, to support other crops. The House was the bastion of stronger farm price supports, and its bill, sponsored by Congressman Clifford Hope of Kansas, provided for 90 percent of parity supports for basic agricultural commodities, with flexible supports for certain other crops.

By June the pitch of battle was ferocious as farm and other interested organizations, Republicans, Democrats, the House, and the Senate were at odds with themselves and with each other. The Truman administration supported Aiken's bill, but most Democrats in the House and Senate backed Hope's bill. Out was the idea of consumer subsidies; in was 90 percent support for tobacco, regardless of the support levels for other crops. As chairman of the House Agriculture Committee, Hope refused to allow hearings on Aiken's bill. In retaliation, Aiken sent Hope's bill to the floor of the Senate, where he immediately gutted it by substituting the language of his own measure. The two bills were sent to a conference committee, which soon became deadlocked. Things became increasingly tense as the adjournment of Congress approached, preliminary to the beginning of the national party conventions. At almost the last moment, on June 19, the Republican conferees compromised so that their party and the Eightieth Congress would be able to claim that they had aided agriculture. The result was to combine the measures so that the Hope bill would be in effect until 1950, when the provisions of the Aiken bill would come into effect. The House and the Senate hastily approved this peculiar marriage, and on July 3 President Truman signed into law the Hope-Aiken Act.

As Truman publicly observed in approving the new law, it did "not provide the basic declaration of long-range agricultural policy which is needed to round out the present farm program." He pointed out that Congress had failed to strengthen the soil-conservation program; to supply consumer subsidies; to appropriate enough funds for marketing research; and to provide for the economical storage of surplus commodities. "In the field of agriculture, as in so many others, most of the business of the 80th Congress was left unfinished." What the president did not indicate, for it was yet unclear, was that the legislators had left out money for constructing federal grain-storage bins. This would outrage many farmers who could not qualify for price supports if their surplus crops were not stored in such bins. After this legislative failure became plain, Truman the presidential nominee would gladly call attention to it. This would make a telling blow against Republican campaign efforts in 1948.

As pertains to domestic legislation, Truman was generally right in saying that "most of the business of the 80th Congress was left unfinished." The Republican Congress had often trumpeted how it would put things right for the nation. The legislators had, however, little major domestic legislation to show for their efforts during 1947 and 1948. There were the establishment of the Commission on the Organization of the Executive Branch (the Hoover Commission) and the Taft-Hartley, Hope-Aiken, and income-tax-reduction measures. The Hoover Commission and the Taft-Hartley Act can be viewed as important actions; but the first was a bipartisan effort, and the new labor law was so controversial that Congress and the Republicans probably won less credit for it than Truman did in opposing it and later using it effectively. As for the new farm law, the Aiken part of it was promising, but few persons believed that it would remain on the books long enough to be implemented. Moreover, the Hope-Aiken Act came out of such controversial circumstances that the Republicans received little credit for it. The few citizens who received significant benefits from the income-tax reduction greeted it joyously. Most Americans did not stand to benefit much from it, so they were receptive to the president's criticism that the tax reduction would unbalance the budget, contribute to inflation (even though it did not), and fail to foster economic growth. In regard to the labor and tax legislation, the Republican members of Congress put themselves in the position where Truman could portray them as the errand boys for well-to-do interests. On lesser domestic legislation, the Republican Congress also too often appeared to be acting for special-interest groups (even though usually with substantial Democratic support), an impression that Truman exploited with relish.

Then there was the reaction of Congress to other domestic legislation that the president had requested. There was little chance that the Eightieth Congress would pass any of it, at least in the form that Truman wanted. It makes little difference whether the reasons in each instance were good, bad, or otherwise. What is significant is that Truman could lambaste the Republican Congress for failing to address numerous large problems, whether they concerned the budget, monopoly, Social Security, education, housing, inflation, health, natural resources, or civil rights. Moreover, he had seemed reasonable not only in his requests but also in allowing the legislators considerable scope in formulating appropriate responses. Never mind that Congress fell short of accomplishment partly because of disagreements between its Democratic members and the administration. The Republicans, however often they were divided on the issues, were in the majority. Just as they sought credit for legislative actions, so they could not avoid the blame. This was especially true as Truman—in his legislative requests and presidential commentaries—became increasingly successful in setting the standards by which much of the public would judge the Republican Congress. In short, the legislators had given him little of what he had requested on domestic matters. They had, however, handed him potent weapons for appealing to the voters in 1948. The Eightieth Congress's record on foreign and military affairs would be different, but Truman would exploit that well, too, for he had initiated most of what the Congress had done.

6

★ ★ ★ ★ ★

THE COLD WAR COMES

It was ironical, in view of the events of 1947 and 1948, that Truman accepted Secretary of State James Byrnes's resignation the day after he outlined a Byrnesian foreign policy in his 1947 State of the Union address. The president's January 6 message was conciliatory, as public opinion still seemed to dictate. He indicated that the nation would rely substantially on negotiation in its foreign policy, because "the basic interests of [America and Russia] lie in the early making of a peace under which the peoples of all countries may return . . . to the essential tasks of production and reconstruction. The major concern of each of us should be the promotion of collective security, not the advancement of individual security." The president stressed that the United States would uphold the principles underlying the United Nations, would continue to engage in world relief, and would seek international economic cooperation. The armed forces would be reduced to the minimum level essential for national defense and the fulfillment of obligations abroad.

Truman's choice to implement foreign policy was the illustrious World War II army chief of staff, George C. Marshall, who had rendered valiant if unsuccessful service in 1946 in negotiating between the Nationalist and Communist forces in China. Marshall would be a very different secretary of state from Byrnes. No less would the general be an advocate of peace. He would be, however, less prepared to negotiate with the Russians and more likely to rely on his departmental bureaucracy. He would also be the president's faithful servant, not his competitor. In short, Marshall would usually be less important in setting policy than in carrying it out. Policy, during his days at the State Department, would be arrived at collegially, not by secretarial *force de main*.

While the guard was changing at the State Department, Truman was giving serious attention to military policy. Although the president was determined to keep down the size of the armed forces, he had plans to enhance their effectiveness. The War and Navy departments were restive because of the tight budgets imposed on them. Navy Secretary James Forrestal, for example, wrote to a friend in January that "the country simply cannot stand continuance of the heavy budget . . . , but with the present state of the world I for one do not want to see the economy attained at the expense of our ability to move, and move fast."[1] Faced with Truman's insistence upon a smaller budget and with the considerable sympathy that Congress had with that goal, the military services usually took what they could get in 1947 without much protest. The government pared the personnel strength of the armed forces to 1,583,000 this year, from 3,030,000 in 1946. It would remain roughly at this level until 1950. Compared to the strength level of some 335,000 in 1939, this was still a substantial military force, and one that was far better equipped.

In trying to enhance the military effectiveness of the United States, Truman sought not only to unify the armed forces but also to add supplementary services, a program that had been under consideration since 1945. Finally, on January 16, 1947, the secretaries of war and the navy reported agreement on a plan for unification, which was submitted to Congress in February. The resultant National Security Act of July established the Departments of the Army, the Navy, and—a new service—the Air Force, each of which was headed by a secretary and all of which were supervised by the secretary of defense. The Joint Chiefs of Staff, which consisted of the uniformed heads of the three services, would be responsible to the secretary of defense. This legislation also created the National Security Council, to advise the president on strategical matters; the National Security Resources Board, to deal with key supply questions; and the Central Intelligence Agency. The establishment of these bodies would contribute considerably to the institutionalization of the presidency and to its concern with world events. As these agencies had to rely on the chief executive for their existence, so he turned to them increasingly for information and advice.

Only with difficulty was the hope realized that unification of the armed forces would lead to better definition and coordination of military policies and missions. This required much presidential pressure, a great deal of effort by the first secretary of defense, Forrestal, and a reorganization in 1949, which gave the secretary substantially more authority. The effectiveness of the National Security Council depended upon its membership, which varied during Truman's presidency. It did, nevertheless, increase the exchange of information and ideas among top White House, military, foreign-policy, and intelligence officials. The National Security Resources Board never worked as well as it was intended to work in preparing the nation to have the resources needed for military contingencies. It was, however, usually deemed to be better than nothing. The Central Intelligence Agency (CIA) became the *primus inter pares* of United States intelligence agencies, but it was seldom central except in controversy. The CIA's effectiveness was often questioned, and it courted criticism by sometimes overstepping the boundaries of its missions. Shrouded in secrecy, it was largely immune from legislative oversight.

Truman's other great concern with respect to the military was changing the basis for recruiting it. Since 1945 he had wanted to replace the draft with a program of universal military training. The president had in mind a national defense force consisting of small standing military services, the National Guard and organized reserves, and a general reserve of those who had received universal training. The proposed program would obligate all able-bodied young men to undergo a year of military training as well as to acquire additional education. They would not belong to any branch of military service unless this was required by Congress. To Truman, the chief advantages of universal training were that the United States could thus keep its active military services and, therefore militarism, small; have a large reserve available for active duty in case of emergency; and make training more rewarding for those involved. The program's opponents argued that conscription by any other name was still conscription; that the general reserve would not be as ready for service, certainly in regard to specialties, if called upon—as Truman had suggested; and that universal training, given its basic mission, could not avoid being militaristic, especially as the regular services would have responsibilities in connection with it.

The president made no progress in Congress with his universal-training proposal in 1945 and 1946, and the military services offered only mixed support. In November 1946 he appointed an advisory commission to study the issue. He gave the members of the commission a good idea of what he wanted on December 20, as he talked about "giving our young people a background in the disciplinary approach of getting along with one another, informing them of their physical makeup, and what it means to take care of this Temple which God gave us." They would gain a sense of responsibility for and to the Republic "as Madison and Hamilton and Jefferson sold it in the first place." Even though, according to the polls, there was substantial public support for universal training, majority sentiment in Congress was opposed to it. When Truman decided not to request extension of the Selective Service Act in 1947, he did it partly to economize. He was also taking a calculated risk that the lapsing of the draft would encourage support for universal training. The elimination of selective service did fire some additional enthusiasm for the proposal in the Pentagon and on Capitol Hill, but not enough to make for its success. Universal training never became more than a highly publicized, fuzzy-headed side show in the Washington circus. To the end of his presidency, Truman would continue to request the establishment of the program. Whatever chance of enactment it had, however, died when selective service was reinstituted in 1948. Truman never got his heart's delight, which, supposedly for a pittance, would have provided the United States with an effective military reserve, a more-responsible citizenry, and healthy minds in healthy bodies, without any risk of increasing militarism.

In terms of foreign policy, Truman was more successful with the Eightieth Congress. This foreign policy was, however, different from what he had enunciated in January 1947. The president hoped that the Russians would become satisfied with their gains and would act more discreetly in the future. He also hoped that Marshall and other foreign-affairs officials would find ways to negotiate more successfully with the Soviets and that the United Nations would somehow be able to work miracles. Truman was alert, however, to the probability that the USSR would not change its aggressive approach. Indeed, lacking any adviser who would urge patience with the Russians, he was vulnerable to interpreting adverse international situations in the worst possible light. This was reinforced by his own tendency to assume the character of Captain Harry of Battery D when confronted with bad news, which discouraged those who might have viewed affairs moderately. As a consequence, Truman was like an atom that was ready to be split by a neutron. The world would not have long to wait for the atom-splitting that would substantially alter the course of United States foreign policy.

Truman's neutron was the situation in Greece. That country's monarchist government had been restored under a regency after German forces had left in 1944. But it encountered great difficulty in reestablishing its authority and in restoring King George II, partly because of chaotic conditions and partly because of left-wing efforts to gain power. Possessing men, material, and money as a result of World War II, Greek Communists needed little encouragement from Moscow to oppose the government. The inability of other Greek leaders to cooperate in solving their nation's problems contributed to the situation. The British, who were supporting the monarchist government, asked Washington to share their burden in Greece in 1945. America's answer was to supply some economic assistance and to press the Greek government to hold popular elections. The Left boycotted the elections of March 1946, which led to an overwhelming victory for monarchist elements. Fighting soon broke out between Communist and royalist forces, and the government developed a program of repression against dissidents. The situation was further complicated by the Greek Communists' tactic of using Albania and Yugoslavia as staging areas from which to launch attacks.

After a favorable plebiscite in September, George II returned to Greece, which spurred hope that the government would adopt a more-moderate policy. To encourage this, the United States in December sent a mission, headed by former Price Administrator Paul Porter, to study the economic situation. The Americans were becoming increasingly disturbed by conditions in Greece, especially by the possibility that Russia's influence would extend to that country. As the State Department advised Ambassador Lincoln MacVeagh in October, the situation could lead to an "early major crisis which may be a deciding factor in [the] future orientation of Near and Middle Eastern countries. It is of importance to US security that Greece remain independent and in charge of her own affairs, and we are prepared to take suitable measures to support [the] territorial and political integrity [of] Greece."[2] Soviet pressures on Turkey were also alarming, for if Turkey and Greece were to capitulate to communism, Russia would have easy access to the Middle East. To stymie this in Greece, the British mission should be to supply arms; the American mission, to provide economic assistance. The State Department further indicated that it expected the Greeks to form a broadly conceived coalition government.

The situation worsened in Greece, as fighting approached the proportions of a civil war. In January 1947 United States representatives joined in a movement to force the ineffectual government of Constantine Tsaldaris out of office. A new, broader-based government, headed by Dimitrios Maximos, took office. Reports from United States officials were increasingly alarming, however, especially about external Communist threats. Immediate assistance from the United States was urged. On February 20, Ambassador MacVeagh, speaking for himself, Paul Porter, and State Department observer Mark Ethridge, telegraphed Washington: "Situation here so critical that no time should be lost in applying any remedial measures . . . full collapse . . . might take several months. However, deteriorating morale both of civil servants and armed forces, as well as of general public, owing to inadequate incomes, fear of growing banditry, lack of confidence in Government, and exploitation by international communists, creates possibility of much more rapid dénouement."[3]

Undersecretary Dean Acheson and others in the State Department moved rapidly in urging action. Secretary Marshall, on Friday February 21, directed Acheson to initiate steps to send economic and military aid to Greece. Later that day the British expressed grave concern over the Greek situation and Soviet pressures on Turkey. What was disappointing was Foreign Minister Ernest Bevin's declaration that his financially straitened government could no longer provide significant help to either Greece or Turkey. The United States must, Bevin urged, assume the British burden. The British decision hastened the implementation of the new United States policy as well as increasing its dimensions. Over the weekend, consequently, State Department officials worked feverishly to gather information on what should and could be done. Liaison was maintained with the White House and with the army and the navy.

On February 24 Marshall conferred with Truman, Secretary of War Patterson, and Secretary of the Navy Forrestal; and conversations continued among their aides for much of the rest of the day. The question was raised about going to the UN, but it was agreed that the international organization probably could not act quickly enough. The experts and the senior bureaucrats wanted action, not caution. United, they easily won Truman and Marshall over. George Kennan's concept of containment merely justified the change in policy. As White House Aide George Elsey later observed, "Fine, this is exactly what our foreign policy is, the way we're going."[4]

Steps were soon taken to convince congressional leaders that the United States had to act to keep Russia out of Greece and Turkey. On February 27 there was a meeting at the White House with the chiefs of both parties in the House and Senate. Acheson took the lead, saying that a Soviet breakthrough in Greece and Turkey would leave the way open for expansion in western Europe, the Middle East, and even Africa. Action, and action soon, was required, and only America could supply it. Marshall backed up his undersecretary, asserting that "the choice is between acting with energy or losing by default."[5] Senator Arthur Vandenberg agreed that the situation was dangerous. As the key legislative leader, he responded to Truman, "Mr. President, if you will say that to the Congress and the country, I will support you and I believe that most of its members will do the same."[6]

For days on end, officials in the White House and the Departments of State, the Navy, and War were consumed with what the president should tell Congress. The matter was also discussed in the cabinet and again with legislative leaders. Finally, Truman decided to accept the State Department's draft of what he should say, which was less combative toward Russia than what Presidential Counselor Clark Clifford had suggested, but did not, as Forrestal's aide, Marx Leva, suggested, "face up to the full implications of giving [as the draft stated] 'support to free peoples' everywhere."[7] The goals of the State Department's draft were clear, however: to win congressional approval and public support for bolstering Greek and Turkish independence, while keeping down costs and not provoking an aggressive Soviet response.

The president delivered his message to Congress on March 12. He emphasized that Greece and Turkey were in danger of having totalitarian regimes imposed upon them "by direct or indirect aggression, [which would] undermine the foundations of international peace and hence the security of the United States." Therefore, "it must be the policy of the United States to support free peoples who are resisting attempted subjugation by armed minorities or by outside pressure." Truman added that this support should come "primarily through economic and financial aid." If the United States should fail to act, it could adversely affect not only Greece and Turkey but also their neighbors. He asked Congress, consequently, to appropriate $400 million for assistance to Greece and Turkey and to approve the detailing of United States civilian and military personnel to conduct supervisory, training, and reconstruction tasks.

The announcement of this program, which was popularly called the Truman Doctrine, marked a clear change in United States foreign policy. As Truman's assistant press secretary, Eben Ayers, commented, this was "the end of appeasement of Russia."[8] The president had not directly referred to Russia in his address, but it was clear whom he had in mind. After Truman's speech, a Soviet official in Greece asked Mark Ethridge, "What does this mean, Mr. Ethridge?" He replied, "It means you can't do it." "I understand that kind of language," the Russian countered.[9] The new policy was implemented speedily. When Ethridge, Porter, and MacVeagh had requested United States help for Greece, they had thought that the United States had about five weeks in which to do something. The administration amazed them, and probably itself, by acting in three weeks.

Congress did not act as rapidly as had the administration, but it did work quickly by its standards. Few legislators were pleased with spending more money, and many feared that this was just the beginning. There were those who resorted to the old saw about pulling British chestnuts out of the fire. Others were critical of the Greek and Turkish governments, fearful of the possibility of war with Russia, or apprehensive about the rise of United States imperialism. Still others had alternative plans, such as lending the money. Yet legislative approval was never in doubt despite reservations, especially among the Republican majority. Senate Republican Leader Robert A. Taft wrote: "I don't like the Greek-Turkish proposition, but I do recognize that perhaps we should maintain the *status quo* until we can reach some peace accommodation with Russia. I don't like to appear to be backing down."[10] In speaking about Republicans, Democratic Congressman Carl Vinson of Georgia said to James Forrestal: "They don't like Russia, they don't like communism, but still they don't want to do anything to stop it. But they are all put on the spot now and they all have come clean."[11]

The situation was, of course, more complicated than that. The opinion polls showed substantial public support for aid to Greece and Turkey. Vandenberg was as good as his word to Truman as he masterfully guided the legislation through the Senate. New York's Governor Thomas E. Dewey was only one of the many other prominent Republicans who gave timely endorsement to the Truman Doctrine. Moreover, there were many influential Democratic supporters in Congress, such as Senator Tom Connally and House Minority Leader Sam Rayburn. Rayburn mirrored the thinking of many members of Congress when he told the House: "People who love liberty and cry for a fair chance want us to . . . lead the world. . . . If we do not accept our responsibility, if we do not move forward and extend a helping hand to people who need and want help, who are democracies or want to be, who do not want to be smothered by communism, if we do not, I repeat, assume our place, God help us; God help this world."[12] Reluctant to take a chance that Rayburn, Vandenberg, and the president were wrong, the House passed the $400 million aid package by a vote of 287 to 107; and the Senate, 67 to 23. Truman signed the legislation on May 22.

Although the announcement of the Truman Doctrine in March had boosted morale in Athens and Ankara, it would take time for the new policy to show concrete results. In June the president appointed a former Republican governor of Nebraska, Dwight P. Griswold, to administer the program in Greece, which pleased many congressional Republicans. Griswold quickly became involved in Greek politics, forcing major changes in that country's government and policies during his fifteen-month sojourn. His mission was not without its troubles, because of his high-handedness and his many conflicts with the State

Department. Griswold's work had, however, led to much stabilization of Greek affairs by the time he resigned in September 1948. Turkey was an easier situation, not being confronted by insurrection or as bad an economic crisis. By 1948 it, too, was thought to be out of serious danger. By 1950 the Truman administration considered Greece and Turkey to be bulwarks of the international anti-Communist alliance.

The Truman Doctrine represented a major reorientation of United States foreign policy, and this was widely recognized. In endorsing it, Alfred M. Landon, the 1936 Republican presidential nominee, declared, "We are in European power politics up to our necks, and in it to stay."[13] America's alternate delegate to the UN, Adlai E. Stevenson, asserted: "We are on a new tack. . . . we propose through the 'Truman Doctrine' to intervene, unilaterally if necessary, at the request of the aggrieved, to support the principles of the United Nations Charter."[14] The gates were open for massive United States involvement abroad and for requests for assistance from other countries. Most Americans, according to public-opinion polls, believed that Russia was expansionist and authoritarian, and in ways that jeopardized the vital interests of the United States. Moreover, it seemed clear that many countries were vulnerable to Communist influence and even aggression. Many leaders abroad, especially in western Europe, saw the situation in the same way. Europe had not recovered from the devastation of World War II. Generally, it was not producing enough to meet its own needs, much less to contribute to the world's economic health. Moreover, European nations did not have the strength to defend themselves from foreign attack, prospectively from the Soviet Union. More important in 1947, there was the growing possibility that Communists, particularly in France and Italy, might be successful in appealing to voters in a time of economic crisis. There were also apprehensions that communism might expand into Asia, Africa, and even Latin America. These fears were not without foundation, given events in China and Korea and signs of Communist assertiveness and espionage elsewhere. There was also abundant evidence, even proclamations from Moscow, that Russia was willing to exploit weaknesses abroad. Genuine negotiation had become the victim of Western apprehensions and Marxist activity as the world quickly broke down into hostility between Communist and non-Communist elements. The Truman Doctrine was dramatic confirmation of this, the first of several.

In 1945 and 1946 the United States had contributed substantially to meet the emergency economic needs of other countries through UN-RRA, various other relief endeavors, grants, and loans. As we have seen, the United States also mounted another large food relief program in 1947. These would not be enough to accomplish international economic reconstruction, a goal that was not only intrinsically vital but also appeared to be essential to warding off the dangers of communism. Only the United States had the resources to speed up reconstruction, and the Truman Doctrine signaled that the cry for assistance against communism was the most likely way to release these resources. America's prospective allies were not shy in raising the cry, and Washington was increasingly intent on listening for it.

After World War II some European leaders were deeply concerned not only with meeting their reconstruction needs but also with the challenge of security. This was not new, for one could trace the concern for European security back to Henry of Navarre or, recently, to the proposed Anglo-French Declaration of Union in 1940. Winston Churchill boosted the idea of federated European action on common problems when he called for a United States of Europe in September 1946. In 1946 and 1947, European leaders occasionally met to discuss the possibility of federation. One result of this was the Treaty of Dunkirk in March 1947, whose intention was to foster better economic and military relationships between the British and the French. The persisting problem of reconstruction and the growing fear of communism gave immediacy to these talks. At stake were the political status quo in Europe and the salvaging of western-European influence abroad. The Truman Doctrine gave hope for American assistance in achieving these.

During the discussions of the Truman Doctrine, Army Chief of Staff Dwight D. Eisenhower had raised the question of providing funds to countries other than Greece and Turkey. It did not seem politic to link this to the Greek-Turkish aid program. Nevertheless, by March 1947 the Departments of State, Navy, and War were working on a comprehensive reconstruction program for Europe, and the cabinet discussed it on occasion. Meanwhile, the meeting of the Conference of Foreign Ministers in Moscow in March and April yielded no useful results, as Secretary of State Marshall saw it. He believed that Russia had resolved to halt progress toward reconstruction in Europe in order to make it a fertile area for the growth of communism. Other administration leaders, including the president, agreed with Marshall, which spurred further interest in a European aid program. Truman had asked Undersecretary of State Dean Acheson to stand in for him in making a major foreign-policy speech in Cleveland, Mississippi, on May 8. When the undersecretary suggested that the topic be economic reconstruction, Truman readily agreed. Acheson's address emphasized the need for large-scale United States financing to make Europe and Asia self-supporting and thus to promote democratic institutions, human dignity, freedom, and

United States security. Moreover, his speech alerted some to the fact that a major sequel to the Truman Doctrine was in the offing.

George Marshall would initiate that sequel at Harvard University on June 5. His talk there was based on a great deal of thought and consideration in high government circles, but Marshall himself determined the form and emphasis of his comments. He proposed massive United States aid to Europe in a struggle against "hunger, poverty, desperation, and chaos. Its purpose should be the revival of a working economy in the world so as to permit the emergence of political and social conditions in which free institutions can exist." Any European government was welcome to participate. If the program was to work, Secretary Marshall declared, Europeans would have to provide the initiative and jointly to design the program. America's role "should consist of friendly aid in the drafting of a European program and of later support of such a program so far as it may be practical for us to do so."[15] Thus the Marshall Plan was born. And it was well timed, coming shortly after Congress in May had voted $350 million for world-wide emergency relief and a week after a pro-Communist government had come to power in Hungary through a coup d'état.

The White House and the State Department had made little effort to prepare the press and foreign diplomats for Marshall's speech, largely because no one except the secretary knew exactly what he intended to say. Therefore, it was President Truman's comments on Senator Taft's criticism of heavy spending abroad that made headlines in the United States. Foreign journalists did even less well by Marshall, except for Leonard Miall of the British Broadcasting Corporation, who devoted most of his evening program to the secretary's talk, and Malcolm Muggeridge of the *London Daily Telegram*, whom Dean Acheson had briefed. By luck, Foreign Minister Bevin heard Miall's broadcast. He immediately recognized the importance of Marshall's address, supposedly saying either, "What an occasion!" "My God!" or "This is manna from heaven!"[16] The next morning, Bevin telephoned French Foreign Minister Georges Bidault, to suggest that they and their Soviet counterpart—since Marshall had not excluded the Russians—meet soon to discuss taking up the offer of the American secretary of state.

Bevin, Bidault, and Molotov met on June 27 in Paris. The Russian viewed the Marshall Plan as a prime example of American imperialism and rejected the principle of cooperation. On July 2, after receiving a wire from Moscow, Molotov delivered some maledictions and announced that Russia was withdrawing. As Bevin later told Acheson, "the withdrawal of the Russians made operations much more simple."[17] It did not only this but much more. As James Forrestal said,

"The great objective that Marshall had was to ascertain whether cooperation with Russia was possible or not, and to show to both the world and our country that every effort had been made on our part to secure such cooperation so that we should have the support of public opinion in whatever policy we found it necessary to adopt thereafter."[18] In this, Marshall's strategy worked, for public-opinion polls in the United States and Europe usually gave heavy support to his economic-aid program. Marshall, of course, took a tremendous risk. If the Soviet representatives had remained in the discussions of the Marshall Plan, they could have seriously impeded them or, more likely, torpedoed any hope of significant congressional appropriations, given the anti-Communist fervor on Capitol Hill. It appears that by withdrawing, the Kremlin blundered in terms either of sacrificing some foreign aid or of wrecking the Marshall Plan.

On July 3 Bevin and Bidault invited twenty-two European nations to name delegates to consider a cooperative plan of recovery. Five eastern-European countries declined, and Czechoslovakia later withdrew after pressure from Moscow. On July 12 the representatives of sixteen nations assembled in Paris. They came from Austria, Belgium, Denmark, France, Great Britain, Greece, Iceland, Ireland, Italy, Luxembourg, the Netherlands, Norway, Portugal, Sweden, Switzerland, and Turkey. Not accidentally, on that same day, Russia negotiated trade and aid agreements with its eastern-European satellite states, which later came to be called the Molotov Plan. These agreements had the effect of further reducing trade between eastern and western Europe, so the Iron Curtain was drawn tighter. Meanwhile, in Paris, the delegates set in motion the assessment of the needs and resources of the European nations in the Marshall Plan. One representative later asserted that "everybody cheated like hell in Paris, everybody."[19] Nevertheless, actions taken by the United States and other participating states ultimately yielded an acceptably high level of information and cooperation. The group that had been charged by the Paris conference to study European resources and needs reported in September. Outlining a four-year program of reconstruction, this Committee of European Economic Cooperation estimated the cost at $22.3 billion. The report also indicated that Germany must be involved in the program, which gratified most American observers who believed that this was essential for European recovery.

Through a variety of instrumentalities, the members of the Truman administration were meanwhile working to elicit congressional and public support for the Marshall Plan. They had able Republican allies in Senator Vandenberg; Congressman Christian A. Herter of Massachusetts; John Foster Dulles, Secretary Marshall's GOP adviser; and Henry L. Stimson, who headed the Citizens Committee for the Marshall Plan. The selling of the plan was plainly a bipartisan matter, and its identification with the soldier–secretary of state, instead of with the president, reinforced this. This was obvious in Herbert Hoover's comment to Senator Vandenberg in December that the former president did not want to be characterized "as opposing General Marshall [when,] like you, I think his hands on the major issue ought to be upheld."[20] Of course, the Marshall Plan did not have to be justified from scratch, because part of the campaign for its approval had already been won in the debates over the Truman Doctrine and the emergency-relief programs. The Russians also contributed effectively by sustaining their campaigns of invective and menace; European leaders did likewise by intelligently expressing their urgent concerns regarding reconstruction. Most striking was the high degree of agreement among informed Americans in viewing the situation. The Central Intelligence Agency reported to Truman on September 26 that "the greatest danger to the security of the United States is the possibility of economic collapse in western Europe and the consequent accession to power of Communist elements."[21] Vandenberg held that without something like the Marshall Plan, "independent governments, whatever their character otherwise, will disappear from Western Europe; that aggressive communism will be spurred throughout the world; and that our concept of free men, free government and a relatively free international economy will come up against accumulated hazards which can put our own, precious 'American way of life' in the greatest, kindred hazard since Pearl Harbor."[22]

The preliminary planning, publicity, and discussion had been finished by December. Then, on the nineteenth, Truman asked Congress to authorize the appropriation of $17 billion for the period from 1948 to 1952, beginning with $6.8 billion for the first fifteen months of the European recovery program. The justifications for the Marshall Plan were by now familiar. It would, as the president put it, "contribute to world peace and [American] security by assisting in the recovery of sixteen countries which, like the United States, are devoted to the preservation of free institutions and enduring peace among nations." He also reported that the Council of Economic Advisers considered the program to be "well within our productive capacity and need not produce a dangerous strain on our economy." Despite occasional acrimony on Capitol Hill, Congress moved expeditiously. Indeed, the final vote was overwhelmingly in favor of the Marshall Plan—329 to 74 in the House and 69 to 17 in the Senate. Truman signed the Foreign Assistance Act into law on April 3, 1948. The legislation was, he said, "a striking manifestation of the fact that a bipartisan foreign policy can lead to effective action."

Truman did well to emphasize Republican cooperation. Until early 1947, bipartisanship had been largely concerned with the development of the UN and the European peace treaties. By the time of the approval of the Marshall Plan, it had moved into a variety of areas, primarily because administration figures and legislative leaders, especially Vandenberg, had developed very similar views of the world. House Speaker Joseph W. Martin, Jr., wrote: "Whether one liked it or not, events of the previous decade had made the United States the leader of the non-Communist nations. The country could not, if it wished, isolate itself from a world suddenly drawn close together. We had to carry the burden of leadership, costly as it was."[23] The result was a wholesale restructuring of United States foreign policy during the Republican Eightieth Congress, which moved from approval of loans and grants for emergency relief to a large assistance program for Greece and Turkey and then to a very expensive, complex program of economic reconstruction for non-Communist Europe. The goals in all this were mixed. To say that the humanitarian and democratic concerns voiced by United States leaders were largely camouflage is ungenerous and incorrect, for a broad streak of idealism permeated the discussions of these programs. To say that American interest in developing export and investment opportunities and access to vital resources was minor is also wide of the mark. And there was a deep concern for the nation's security, because Communist expansion was widely interpreted in America as being something that could spark a third world war. Moreover, there was repugnance for the things that Americans so often associated with communism and Russia, especially atheism, repression, and violence. Many things motivated United States officials to act in a way that would be consonant with their country's pragmatic tradition: these ranged from the noble to the selfish. It is impossible to determine the priority of American motives, for they shifted with changing circumstances. What is important is that the actions they spurred had profound consequences.

Dirk Stikker, the Netherlands' foreign minister, later stated that "Churchill's words won the war, Marshall's words won the peace."[24] This is true in the sense that the Marshall Plan greatly accelerated efforts by and cooperation among non-Communist European nations to achieve economic reconstruction. Speed was important. After Congress had approved the Marshall Plan, Truman moved quickly to implement it. He appointed Paul G. Hoffman, a Republican industrialist, to head the Economic Cooperation Administration. This was a wise move, for it maintained bipartisanship in the European recovery program; also, Hoffman proved to be a very able administrator. The president gave him highly effective support, because he believed that the program had to succeed. As Truman dramatically told the Gridiron Club in 1948, "God Almighty, on two different occasions has appointed us to do a job. This time we must do it."[25]

The strengthening of the economies, not to mention the polities, of non-Communist Europe proceeded at different rates and in different ways in various countries. There is no doubt, however, that during the life span of the Economic Cooperation Administration—from 1948 to 1951—the more than $13 billion spent by the United States (as well as American advice and pressure) had a substantial impact. The economies of all of the participating European states were reinvigorated, thanks to their new buying power. Living standards were raised. Technologies were improved, as often were management, financial, planning, and personnel patterns. Moreover, the Europeans, with American encouragement, took steps to rationalize their economic relationships—for example, through the European Payments Union of 1950 and the European Coal and Steel Community of 1952. This, incidentally, was the sparking point for the later development of the European Common Market.

Yet it all had its problems. R. C. Mowat has written that the Truman Doctrine marked "the end of the *Pax Britannica,* and the establishment instead of the *Pax Americana* over what was coming to be known as the 'Free World.'"[26] There is truth in this, and the Marshall Plan was a key factor. Non-Communist Europe had to listen to its American guarantors, and to a considerable extent, it had to follow their lead. This seemed, however, a small price to pay for preserving so much of the status quo in Europe. Also, the conditions laid down by Washington for the Marshall Plan were relatively few, while the benefits for European leaders and peoples were many. Western Europe gained the strength that it needed in order to resist communism and a resurgence of Fascist movements. This was substantially based on the Marshall Plan's success in achieving its other basic purposes, the reestablishment of non-Communist Europe as a generally stable and prosperous economic area and the promotion of democracy and human freedoms.

While United States leaders were fashioning the Truman Doctrine and the Marshall Plan to insulate Europe from Communist expansion, similar things were happening elsewhere. Occupation authorities worked to shore up the economies of Germany and Japan and to introduce democracy in those places. United States assistance continued to flow into Nationalist China. The UN approved a United States trusteeship over various islands in the Pacific. The United States and the Philippines in 1947 concluded an agreement on the maintenance of American military bases there. The Truman administration also attempted unsuccessfully to bolster the defenses of the Americas under the terms of a World War II mutual-defense agreement. Failing this, the government acted to establish a mutual-assistance pact for the Western Hemisphere. In September 1947 President Truman and Senator Vandenberg traveled to Rio de Janeiro to participate in a conference that led to the signing of the inter-American treaty of Reciprocal Assistance. This so-called Rio Treaty was the first of four regional mutual-assistance pacts that the United States would sign and help to finance in order to foster cooperation among its allies in building defenses against common enemies. The three later agreements would be the North Atlantic Treaty, the Southeast Asia Treaty, and the Baghdad Pact.

All of this developed in the context of steadily deteriorating Soviet-American relations. Negotiations, whether in the Council of Foreign Ministers, the UN, or elsewhere, seemed to be fruitless. As Truman said to the American Society of Newspaper Editors on April 17, 1947, about the Russians, "We tried going along with them as far as we possibly could, trying to please them. There is no way to please them." Continued conflict in Greece; disagreements over the administration of Berlin and Korea and of peace treaties with Austria, Germany, and Japan; Soviet encroachments in Czechoslovakia and Hungary; and troubles elsewhere appeared to provide proof of this. Yet there was no appreciable fear of war in informed United States circles in 1947. Gen. Dwight D. Eisenhower reflected this attitude when he said in April, according to Secretary Forrestal, "the Russians would not initiate a war, short of stupidity or blunder, short of five years."[27] The tinder for hostilities was often available, however. After the Italian Peace Treaty became effective in September, Marshal Tito announced that Yugoslavia would occupy Trieste. President Truman's response was immediate and sharp: "Tell the son of a bitch he'll have to shoot his way in."[28] Tito did not force the issue.

It was in 1947 that the USSR revived its international instrument for agitation and propaganda under the name of the Communist Information Bureau. The United States also stepped up its efforts. The Labor and War departments worked hard to strengthen non-Communist unions in Europe, using American labor leaders to good effect. Cultural exchanges between the United States and other countries were accelerated. Additional use was made of the United States Information Service, although some Americans criticized it as being milksoppy for following Secretary Marshall's orders that it state the factual truth. The Voice of

America was created to carry the nation's story by radio throughout the world. In October, Gen. Lucius Clay laid plans "to attack communism and the police state before the German people, whereas in the past we have confined our efforts to presenting the advantages of democracy."[29] Despite discouragement from Secretary of the Army Kenneth Royall, who worried about State Department reaction, the United States military governor in Germany soon eased his propaganda program into operation.

The Russians had become more truculent by fall. In October, Stalin told the Politburo that communism could not live with capitalism. Molotov followed that up in November with a vehement attack on the United States, saying that the latter should not rely on the atomic bomb, which, he said, was no longer a secret. Americans were optimistic, however. On November 7 Marshall told the cabinet that the Communist tide had been stemmed, although that could lead to some desperate Soviet initiative during the winter. The CIA confirmed to Truman a week later that the Communist position in western Europe had deteriorated. "This process, which apparently began with the announcement of the 'Truman Doctrine,' has been accelerated by Soviet countermeasures." The CIA considered the Communist Information Bureau to be chiefly responsible. "The Cominform, with its clear identification of Communist parties as agents of the Kremlin, its proscription of the non-Communist Left, and its threat to the best hope of European recovery, sacrificed whatever political prospects the Communist parties yet had."[30] This had been borne out in recent elections in Denmark, France, Italy, and Norway. Although there were grounds for optimism with respect to Europe, prospects seemed to be less satisfactory elsewhere, especially in Asia.

United States leaders were concerned with affairs in Asia, but they were not sure what to do about them. Although the situation was far from satisfactory in Korea—divided as it was into rather exclusive American and Soviet zones of occupation—few Americans wanted to spend more money there. The United Nations agreed to supervise elections in Korea for the establishment of a national government, after which United States and Russian forces could withdraw. The Soviets refused to cooperate, so the elections were held only in the American area in May 1948. This led to the founding there of the Republic of Korea under Syngman Rhee; a People's Republic had already been created in North Korea. Timing their withdrawal for the end of 1948, United States officials worked to establish a viable economy in South Korea and to develop a constabulary force. Japan seemed to be stable under the leadership of General MacArthur, and the Truman administration worked to ensure the success of the newly independent Philippines. The United States was disturbed by the unrest in much of the rest of Asia, but it was largely content to let the Dutch handle affairs in the East Indies; the French, in Indo China; and the British, in Burma, India, and Malaya.

United States debates about the Far East chiefly concerned China. Truman was not interested in giving substantial aid to that country, seeing the faltering Nationalist government as a poor investment. Others, however, especially in Congress and among the military, saw the Nationalists as a potentially effective bulwark against communism. The result of the debates was an unsatisfactory compromise, which reflected the fact that bipartisan agreement on foreign policy did not extend to China. Several hundred million dollars were funneled into China. After Chinese Communist forces conquered the country in 1949, the administration was bitterly criticized for "losing" China, although it was clear that only massive American assistance, going far beyond what any American advocated, could have given the Nationalists even a chance of survival on the mainland.

Military issues were strenuously discussed in 1948. America's military leaders had fairly well accepted Truman's low budget for fiscal year 1948; but they resisted the president's proposal in 1948 of an equally low budget for fiscal year 1949. They believed that they lacked the resources that were needed in order to meet any significant call for emergency military action. Manpower, ships, and airplanes all seemed to be fully committed in their present assignments. Moreover, most of the generals and admirals remained unconvinced by administration arguments that atomic weaponry could win a full-scale war. Defense Secretary Forrestal would obey his commander in chief's fiscal orders, but he never ceased trying to persuade Truman that the military needed more money if the United States was to play power politics successfully. Forrestal's subordinates occasionally went further, lobbying Congress and the public for more funds.

Truman was taking a risk, for his authorization of military strength was below that proposed by Congress. He was gambling that his military program, if efficiently managed, would meet all needs. This way he might balance the budget and force the authorization of universal training. He was also taking a chance that his economic-assistance programs abroad would discourage Soviet aggression and would help to reconstruct foreign nations so that they could man their own defenses. That Truman was lucky in his gamble should not obscure the fact that there were serious deficiencies in United States military strength from 1946 until well into the Korean War. Had there been the need for large-scale deployment of military power on an emergency basis, the nation could not have met it. Furthermore, the United States was falling behind in the acquisition of new equipment. The National Guard and the Organized Reserve were small and unknown quantities. Few, too, were the World War II veterans who would rush to take up the colors; the motto of many of them was that the government would have "to burn the woods and rake the ashes" to find them.

The navy offered a panacea: namely, that given enough ships and men, it could police the world. Few accepted this, not even Forrestal, although he wanted to increase naval strength. The air force made similar claims for itself, and with more impact, which led to repeated conflicts within the Pentagon and between the administration and Congress in 1948. At issue was the air force's demand for seventy bomber groups, instead of the budgeted fifty-five. To have satisfied the air force would have meant stripping the army and navy of resources, for Congress would have allowed the air force to grow only in the way that Paul would have been paid through the robbing of Peter. Truman resisted the aggrandizement of the air force because he was determined to maintain a rough parity among the three services.

The president had to go to great lengths to restrain the growth of the military. By April 1948 each service was lobbying strenuously for itself, and such efforts paid off, at least for the air force. Congress increased the authorized manpower strengths by fifty-three thousand for the air force and by eight thousand for the army; the air force was allowed sixty-six bomber groups. Truman and Forrestal, however, kept substantial control of the money involved and how it would be spent. Budgetary legerdemain kept expenditures within the bounds that were acceptable to the cost-conscious president, largely by prolonging the period over which new equipment would be procured. In May, Truman brought in his budget director, James E. Webb, to whittle down what Congress had appropriated and to suggest a lid on military expenditures of $15 billion per year. This was in line with the president's view, supported by Secretary Marshall, "that we are preparing for peace and not for war."[31] Despite the many pressures on him, Truman was not going to stand for a runaway military budget. The $15 billion lid was to remain administration policy until the middle of 1950.

The pressures on Truman to expand United States military power grew in response to deteriorating world conditions. Russia apparently had reassessed its policies after seeing the effects of the Truman Doctrine and the progress made toward implementing the Marshall Plan. In December 1947 the CIA reported that "the Communists, under Soviet direction, have launched a concerted campaign of disorders, strikes, and sabotage in France and Italy. . . . The Soviet Government appears to be intensifying its propaganda and penetration efforts in the Far and Middle East."[32] This was just the first of many such alarming reports from various sources. There were signs that warfare had intensified in Greece. Truman said that the demise in February 1948 of what was left of Western-style democracy in Czechoslovakia "has sent a shock throughout the civilized world." Finland seemed to be in danger of going the way of Czechoslovakia. Truman's response came in his March 17 "Threat to the Freedom of Europe" message to Congress, in which he called for prompt action on the Marshall Plan, authorization of universal training, and the restoration of selective service. Congress soon passed the Marshall Plan and, in June, reinstituted the draft. Also, at Truman's later urging, military appropriations were increased, although they remained under the administration's lid. It was all very clever. The president had shown his tough side to the Russians, his reliability to America's prospective allies; and he had also given a sop to the military and found a cheap source of military manpower.

The war of nerves that had broken out between East and West saw other responses. By March 1948 the Russians used the veto twenty-one times in the UN Security Council in order to block action. Washington's reaction had been to rely on an ad interim committee of the General Assembly, which was veto-proof, to handle emergency problems. Nevertheless, the veto had made the UN largely into a debating society on most key issues. Most of its useful work would be done through its specialized arms. The Truman administration was supportive of these appendages, particularly of their efforts to facilitate trade, as was the case with the UN's International Trade Organization and the concord of twenty-three nations, in October 1947, on the General Agreement on Tariffs and Trade, which lowered barriers to world commerce. In June 1948, Congress grudgingly augmented this by extending for a year the Trade Agreements Act, which was the basis for tariff-reciprocity and most-favored-nation program of the United States. Without the war of nerves, this beneficial legislation might have lapsed.

Western Europe wanted to go beyond the Marshall Plan in its response to the war of nerves. Many of Europe's leaders were spurred on by the fact that since 1939 the Soviet Union had, through annexations and infiltration, gained control of some 390,000 square miles of territory and 90 million non-Russian people. There were also the problems of almost 5 million men whom Russia had under arms; the fighting in Greece; Soviet pressures on Finland, Norway, and Turkey for concessions; continued sharp East-West disagreements on Austrian and German occupation policies; and high-paced Communist political campaigns in France and Italy. Western European countries were also well aware of their economic and military weaknesses. The fruits of the Marshall Plan could not come too quickly for them. Meanwhile, they tried to rally together on their own. In January 1948 British Foreign Minister Bevin declared that Europeans would have to take the initiative in providing better protection for themselves. Representatives of Belgium, Britain, France, Luxembourg, and the Netherlands, additionally prompted by the February coup in Czechoslovakia, met in Brussels in March to prepare a mutual-defense treaty. This so-called Western Union could be no match for Soviet power. It was, however, an important step forward toward the collective defense of non-Communist Europe.

Americans were interested in this from the beginning. Bevin kept Marshall fully informed; indeed, Bevin pressed in March for United States involvement in developing plans for Atlantic and Mediterranean security systems based on the Western Union. Canadian Prime Minister Louis Saint-Laurent effectively backed Bevin, saying that free nations might "soon find it necessary to consult together on how best to establish . . . a security league."[33] Americans did not rush in through the Western Union door. Caution was the watchword, given the amount of money that would be involved and the traditional United States opposition to permanent alliances. The Truman administration's position was to demand solid evidence that the Western Union countries were helping themselves before he would recommend that the United States bind itself to their defense. Of course, the administration did encourage the expansion of the Western Union to include other European nations and Canada.

Meanwhile, the United States had other concerns. Latin American countries were pressing for assistance, especially after the Marshall Plan had been proposed. In 1948 Truman would only ask Congress to add $500 million to the Export-Import Bank's lending authority for development in Latin America. The chief reason for this relative indifference was obvious: there were too many claims on the resources of the United States, and priorities had to be set. Latin America was not in great peril. As the United States ambassador to Brazil, Herschel Johnson, asserted in 1948, it was like "a case of smallpox in Europe competing with a common cold in Latin America."[34]

More pressing was the question of Palestine. In fashioning a policy for this troubled land, Truman had to walk a thin line because of the many interests involved. He hoped that the United Nations could resolve the fate of Palestine so that his administration could avoid serious criticism from the Arabs, the British, and the Jews as well as provocation of the Russians. Yet the president was prepared to take action, if necessary, and he was highly sympathetic to the establishment of a national home for the Jews. He knew that Anglo-American relations would not be ruptured whatever he did; he believed that the Soviets were more likely to get involved in the situation if the United States did not support the Jews; and he was willing to anger the Arabs, despite the attractiveness of their oil resources to energy-hungry America. Moreover, American Jews kept him constantly aware of their keen interest in creating a Jewish state. It is impossible to say, however, that their threats of electoral action swayed him, given his frequent angry outbursts about their pressures. As an example, there is Eben Ayers's report of Truman's reaction in December 1947 "that when election comes around they will say that we've done nothing for them recently."[35] Probably more important was the president's deep moral concern, which was supported by American public opinion in various polls.

In November 1947 the UN General Assembly voted in principle in favor of partitioning Palestine into Jewish and Arab areas. The British announced that they would leave Palestine on May 15, 1948; so action on partitioning had to be taken quickly. This was no small matter, for not only did Arabs and Jews increase their jockeying for position, but the UN also failed to mobilize a force to uphold the terms of partition. The Truman administration turned out to be divided. The president promised Chaim Weizmann, the grand old man of Zionism, that he would be faithful to the UN resolution. Yet elements in the Defense and the State departments worked to prevent partition in order to pacify the Arabs and to prevent civil war in Palestine. Reflecting the State Department's waywardness, on March 19 the United States ambassador to the UN, Warren R. Austin, announced a new policy toward Palestine—a temporary joint trusteeship by Britain, France, and the United States. There was an uproar in the White House. Truman wrote in his diary: "This morning I find that the State Dept. has reversed my Palestine policy. The first I know about it is what I see in the papers! Isn't that hell? I'm now in the position of a liar and a double crosser."[36] After much discussion within the administration, he told the press on March 25 that the United States proposed that there be a trusteeship not "as a substitute for the partition plan but as an effort to fill the vacuum." This was the best he could do to repair the damage done by the State Department. The UN returned to work out a Palestine policy, but without success.

Events took care of themselves, as it turned out. A Jewish state was proclaimed in Palestine on May 14. Seeking to beat Russia to the punch in establishing the godfathership of the new nation, Truman announced United States recognition of Israel ten minutes after its birth. On the next day, Arab forces invaded Israel, and on the following day, Truman promised to work for aid to the new state. The UN soon negotiated a truce, but it was an uneasy one that was broken before the end of the year. Starting in 1948, the question of Israel became a thorn in the world's flesh, for Jews and Arabs could not agree on the state's boundaries or on the settlement of dozens of related questions. Moreover, the United States became the guarantor, though often an uneasy one, of Israel. In retrospect, it is not clear whether the State Department's efforts in favor of a temporary trusteeship would have been as satisfactory as the president's policy. Plainly, Jews received what they had long sought and been promised—a national home; Truman benefited from their political support in 1948; relations between the United States and the Arab nations suffered over the decades; and Arabs received a considerable stimulus toward modernization and unity, however fragile that might be. It is impossible to say, however, whether the situation offered Russia and the United States any greater opportunity for disagreement than they would otherwise have had or that the American oil problems and financial burdens connected with Arab-Jewish disputes would not have developed anyway. The questions were never clear-cut; so it would be foolish to expect that the answers would be.

While the crisis in Palestine was coming to a head during the spring of 1948, affairs in Europe seemed less critical. Communist attempts to seize power at the polls had been beaten back in Italy in April. In May the CIA reported that as a consequence, Communists had lost prestige in western Europe and apparently would abstain from fomenting strikes and other disorders. Certainly, Soviet initiatives had subsided in Germany and Greece. The CIA's report of June 17 to the president went as far as to declare that Russia was "genuinely interested in exploring the possibility of easing the tension between the USSR and the West."[37] As a matter of fact, the United States was caught off guard by Russia's next move.

In reaction to British, French, and United States talks about creating a central administration for western Germany, the Soviets in late March tightened restrictions on highway and railway traffic into Berlin. This situation eased after the Western Allies bridled; but on June 24, the Russians stopped all ground traffic into the city from the west. The Blockade of Berlin had begun, and the Western Powers were unsure what to do about it, especially as it was discovered that their right to have access to Berlin had never been documented. The choices confronting the United States, Britain, and France seemed to be to show determination to fight their way into Berlin, to abandon it, or to find some middle ground. The American military governor, Gen. Lucius Clay, advised Washington of his conviction "that a determined movement of convoys with troop protection would reach Berlin and that such a showing might well prevent rather than build up Soviet pressures which could lead to war."[38] The Pentagon vetoed this move as being too dangerous. Neither it nor the CIA nor the National Security Council nor any other official body, however, knew what to do. It was left to the president to decide, which he did on June 28. Then he declared, as Secretary Forrestal paraphrased him, "we were going to stay period," although as to how to do this, Truman indicated that "we would have to deal with the situation as it developed."[39] The answer would be not so much military or diplomatic as technological and organizational. The approach was particularly American, one literally of flying over the problem, which the Pentagon soon recommended.

On June 30 Secretary Marshall told the press about the nation's policy, as settled by Truman, which was to supply Berlin by aircraft. The dramatic United States, British, and French air lift was the means by which the blockade was cracked and the crisis resolved, although it took time. Other things would be considered, and they would have their effect too. For example, negotiations with the Russians were initiated; United States forces in Europe were reinforced; more encouragement was given to developing western-European defenses; and attention was given to supporting Yugoslavia in its growing disagreements with the USSR. If the Soviet leadership thought that the United States, Britain, and France would back off from the crisis in Berlin, they were very much mistaken.

It appeared that Russia wanted to split the Western Powers and to force the renegotiation of the four-power control of Germany in order to block the development of a West German state that would be aligned with the United States, Britain, and France. Indeed, the blockade of Berlin worked contrary to what the Russians wanted, because it further unified western-European countries and made them more reliant upon the United States. It also accelerated the establishment of a West German government in 1949, and the crisis spurred the United States to increase the number of its military personnel from 1,446,000 on June 30, 1948, to 1,615,360 a year later. Furthermore, the United States began to apply carrot-and-stick tactics to force Denmark, Norway, and Sweden to align themselves with other western-European powers. Washington would later bring similar pressures to bear on Ireland, although, as with Sweden, unsuccessfully.

Meanwhile negotiations among the military governors in Berlin over the blockade bogged down. In August 1948 the United States, British, and French ambassadors held discussion in Moscow with Stalin and Molotov. These started out promisingly, but they soon took an ugly turn as the Soviet leadership demanded that the Western Powers recognize that they could stay in Berlin only on Russian sufferance. In September the negotiations were transferred back to the military governors in Berlin; these negotiations failed, because the Russians insisted upon their right to use the air corridors to the city, and this enabled them to harass the air lift. The three Western Powers refused to retreat in the face of such harassment. The Soviets soon turned to their traditional ally, winter, for assistance. Despite bad weather and some disastrous crashes, however, the air lift was able to supply Berlin throughout the winter. There were additional Russian-inspired provocations in the city to test the ability of the Western Allies to maintain order without fomenting insurrection. It was to be a difficult winter in and over Berlin. Occasionally, the British and the French got edgy about American toughness in negotiating with the Russians, but basically the three allies, along with the Berliners, stuck together in dealing with their common foe, even though the crisis was not resolved until well into 1949.

Even before the imposition of the blockade in Berlin, the Senate had acted to encourage consideration of United States participation in a permanent military alliance. Senator Vandenberg had become alarmed that Russia would use its veto on the Security Council to block UN peacekeeping efforts. Therefore, he sponsored a resolution recommending that the government develop regional collective self-defense arrangements, as recognized in Article 51 of the UN Charter. On June 11, 1948, this resolution came before the Senate, where Vandenberg pointed out that it would promote "individual and collective self-defense against armed aggression within the Charter and outside the veto."[40] After striking out any reference to American military aid (on Senator Claude Pepper's motion), the Senate overwhelmingly adopted the resolution. This was in line with public opinion, which registered no less than 65 percent approval of an alliance with western Europe, according to Gallup polls taken between April and November.

The Vandenberg Resolution gave the green light to the administration to explore collective-security arrangements with Canada and the countries in the Western Union. In addition, the blockade of Berlin spurred United States and western-European interest in an alliance. Truman used the Vandenberg Resolution as the basis for arranging talks among concerned nations in Washington, beginning in July. Work on a mutual-defense treaty for the North Atlantic nations continued into the fall, but was recessed for the elections in the United States. The principles of such a regional security arrangement were well agreed upon before the talks resumed in earnest in December. The North Atlantic Treaty was yet to be born, but its gestation was well under way. The reasons were not hard to see. The growing tensions of the Cold War and the fear that the United States might be left to face the Soviet menace without allies had sparked American interest. In western Europe there were similar motivations. A collective defense appeared to be the answer, one that all parties could afford and one that could discourage a Russian military push to the west.

There were, of course, other results of the mounting war of nerves between East and West. There were times when war seemed imminent. For example, the Berlin crisis became so tense that on September 13 Truman wrote in his diary, "Forrestal, Bradley, Vandenberg (the Gen., not the Senator!), Symington brief me on bases, bombs, Moscow, Leningrad, etc. I have a terrible feeling afterward that we are very close to war."[41] The military took advantage of such alarms by pressing for more funds. In the Pentagon, there was talk of a $23 billion military budget for fiscal year 1950. The Joint Chiefs of Staff and Secretary Forrestal, under pressure from Truman, scaled it down, first to $18.5 billion and then to $16.9 billion. The president was adamant on a maximum of $14.4 billion. He was, as Forrestal put it, "determined not to spend more than we take in in taxes."[42] Truman would win this battle with the Pentagon, for he never let anyone forget who was the commander in chief.

The concern over internal security also mounted in 1948. Congressional committees were increasingly zealous in their inquiries into alleged subversive activities in governmental and even private sectors. The Federal Bureau of Investigation was pressing for more authority, indeed, for sole authority to deal with subversive activities. The Justice Department revised its World War II index of dangerous and potentially dangerous individuals, as well as its plans for detaining them in time of emergency. On March 30, Rear-Adm. Sidney W. Souers, the executive secretary of the National Security Council (NSC), recommended the development of a "coordinated program (to include legislation if necessary) designed to suppress the communist menace in the United States." He added that after doing this, America should "cooperate closely with governments which have already taken such action and encourage other governments to take like action."[43] The NSC and the White House deferred consideration of this until after the elections. Congressional interest in antisubversive measures was also on the rise.

One bill considered was HR 4482, which would "bar un-American parties from the election ballot." The administration's position on this was clever, perhaps too clever. It avowed "complete sympathy, of course, with the desire that no subversive or disloyal person should be permitted to hold an office of honor, trust or profit in the Government," but it held that the measure would encounter legal problems because of the due-process and bill-of-attainder clauses in the Constitution.[44] Such an equivocal opinion merely contributed to delaying the enactment of antisubversive legislation until Truman's second term.

There was no doubt that the pressure for action was mounting. At the polls, public opinion reflected a high interest in questions of internal security. Testimony about subversive infiltration of the government, which former Communists gave before the House Un-American Activities Committee, accelerated the Red-scare psychology. The president tried to play down the congressional hearings. At his news conference of August 5 he declared that they "are doing irreparable harm to certain people, seriously impairing the morale of Federal employees, and undermining public confidence in the Government." Yet, two weeks later, he conceded to the press that the Justice Department was working on a measure dealing with loyalty and espionage, but one that would not violate the Bill of Rights, which he believed the congressional hearings had done. As for Republican presidential nominee Thomas E. Dewey's suggestion that it was urgent to get Communists out of Washington, Truman told the press on September 2, "I think Mr. Dewey's intention is to eliminate the Democrats from Government, not the Communists." The president would find it less easy to be witty about such things during his second term.

There had been many excursions and alarms in 1948. Indeed, the year would end on another note of concern after the Hungarian government arrested Joseph Cardinal Mindszenty, which infuriated Catholics all over the world. Yet, the administration had achieved most of its foreign-policy goals during the year. The economic and political security of western Europe was improving; Israel seemed to be satisfactorily established; the Soviet bluff had been called in Berlin; and the bases were being laid for the emergence of a Western-oriented German state. Nevertheless, the nationalists were continuing to lose ground in China, and instability was rife in the Arab Middle East. Germany was split from east to west; and Korea, from north to south. There was still unrest in Latin America and, especially, in Southeast Asia.

The Cold War had begun in earnest in 1947 and 1948, and it had long-term consequences for the United States and for the world. The United States had decided to act like a global power, which was seen in its implementation of the Truman Doctrine and the Marshall Plan, the Berlin Air Lift, the recognition of Israel, and the laying of the bases for the North Atlantic Treaty. The unification of United States armed forces and the establishment of the CIA and the NSC were also beginnings for the use of power in ways that were far from traditional in the United States. Schooled by the exigencies of the Great Depression and World War II and alarmed by postwar Communist aggrandizement, few Americans argued against the many unprecedented actions taken by the Truman administration. In fact, most citizens who were polled were relieved, because they were convinced of the need for such actions.

7

★ ★ ★ ★ ★

PERSONALITY: PRESIDENT AND POLITICIAN

It was during 1947 and 1948 that Harry S. Truman emerged as a leader in his own right, as far as the public was concerned. By then he had acquired enough knowledge and self-confidence to be the president instead of the acting president. He had also structured the White House staff and the cabinet to suit him and his style of operation. Certainly, by 1948 he had cast off his earlier image as a well-intentioned but sometimes baffled caretaker, who too often relied for advice and decisions on agency heads and White House staff members. If Truman did not seem to be Superman, he no longer appeared to be the Clark Kent of American government.

Truman was a man of many dimensions. He was a passable pianist, and he was a voracious reader. He loved to play poker and be one of the boys, which scandalized some Americans. He swam a bit and briskly walked a lot for exercise. He was also very sentimental, especially about his family, to whom he was very close and toward whom—at least in regard to his wife, Bess, and his daughter, Margaret—he was very protective. Although he often told his wife and daughter about his work, they played little more part in his administration than did weekend guests who influenced their host to behave himself in their presence.

Truman thought and acted on the basis of several phases of his personality. There were in fact many Trumans: Little Harry, who could, as he had from childhood, please almost anyone when it suited him; Truman the Politician, who could, thanks to his training in the tough

Missouri school of politics, compete aggressively for place and power; Captain Harry of Battery D, the tough, direct, decisive, yet playful fellow, who had found ways to prove his manliness in military service during World War I; Truman the President, who could consciously restrain the other sides of his personality in order to act the statesman; and Dirty Harry, who could both get mad and get even. These, and perhaps other, roles Truman played singly or in some combination during his presidency.

Truman was thrifty; perhaps this was a legacy from his childhood. He rarely gave away the gifts that he received as president. Food was retained for use in the White House; it was not given to the staff or to charitable institutions. Occasionally, he treated his visitors and staff to drinks, but not to bottles. A White House usher commented in 1948, "The President must have enough liquor to last him the remainder of his life."[1] The public did not notice that Truman was left-handed. He seemed to have a constitution of iron. Yet he had to wear trifocal glasses, occasionally he carried a cane, and he worried about his age, writing in 1948 that "the head at 64 doesn't work as well as it did at 24."[2] Once in a while he was unwell; but as Truman the President and certainly as Captain Harry, he might pass it off, saying it was "nothing that about so much bourbon wouldn't cure."[3] There was also a streak of the humorist in Truman. He liked to exchange stories with members of his entourage, not all of which were suitable for mixed company. One concerned his naval aide, Rear Adm. James H. Foskett, about whom Truman passed on the story, "Who's got the biggest p---- in the navy?" The answer was, "The naval aide's wife."[4] Another example of Truman's humor, more presidential this time, appeared in his talk for Washington's Gridiron Club in December 1947. Then he spoke of fantasy appointments, one of which was a secretary of reaction, whom the president wanted so that he could "abolish flying machines and tell me how to restore oxcarts, our boats and sailing ships. What a load he can take off my mind if he'll put the atom back together so it can't be broken up."[5]

There was much more to Truman's make-up, testimonies to which are legion. His kindliness when people needed it has often been noted, as have been his courage, decisiveness, honesty, and, at least by 1947, self-confidence. He was superb at delegating authority and at backing up his subordinates when they acted on his instructions. He was very much concerned with choosing right, as he saw it, as against wrong in making his decisions, even when politics were at stake. He worked effectively with his staff, the cabinet, and the National Security Council. He endeavored to differentiate among his presidential, political, and personal actions; his trouble was that he expected others to do likewise.

He sought a variety of views before coming to official decisions, and he seriously weighed these ideas; his problem here was that this variety did not encompass all worthwhile views. He was noted for his simplicity of thought and style, although the difficulty with this was that complexities were often eliminated when they should have been considered. None of these problem areas was peculiar to Truman as president, but his immersion in historical knowledge as a way to guide his decisions perhaps was. There were two problems with this: one was that his reading of history was often uncritical and idiosyncratic; the other was that too often he substituted his knowledge of history for philosophy, which is just as perilous as substituting one's knowledge of philosophy for history. Whatever his flaws, Truman did try to take the long view. He saw himself as the champion of right, as indicated by his reading of history. This meant that he often felt compelled to pursue peace, democracy, justice, prosperity, and the people's interests more as absolutes to be fought for than as goals to be bargained for. It was difficult for him to accept that they could be defined differently and assigned different priorities by other people.

By any definition, Truman's job was big. It was made steadily larger by the nation's expanding agenda of domestic and international goals. As president, Truman was at the center of all the pulling and hauling involved in the management of governmental affairs. Just the mechanics of his job were awesome, because the government had grown so large and the presidency so important. During a typical week, he had to meet with the press, legislative leadership, the cabinet, and various other official groups, as well as daily with his staff. There were countless meetings with individual aides, agency heads and their deputies, senators and representatives, state and local officials, party leaders, foreign statesmen, and prominent citizens. There were appointments to office to be made; an immense amount of correspondence to be read and answered; speeches and statements to be given; and endless documents to be reviewed, approved, and signed. There were many official functions to be attended: these ranged from being present at state dinners to the bestowing of military decorations to the hailing of Boy Scouts and civic leaders. There were publicity puffs on behalf of good works such as the March of Dimes, the Red Cross, fire prevention, and traffic safety. And there was the time consumed in preparing for all this and often in traveling. There were also the endless irritations: to mention a few, leaks to the press; insubordinate, attention-demanding, or inadequate appointees; and squabbles among agencies and aides. The pressure was enormous, and the president's time was at a premium.

Staff was often the key to what Truman did, whether one speaks of White House aides or of officials of executive agencies. Questions of staff vexed Truman during his first two years in office; but by 1947, things began to come together. The president had no significant problem with his appointments, correspondence, and press secretaries—respectively, Matthew Connelly, William Hassett, and Charles Ross—or with his chief executive clerk, Maurice Latta or Latta's successor in 1948, William Hopkins. By 1946 Clark Clifford as special counsel and John Steelman as assistant to the president had proved their mettle; by 1947 they were well ensconced in their positions as the ranking White House aides. Roughly speaking, Steelman handled domestic matters, particularly of an economic nature, and Clifford dealt with military and foreign-policy concerns, although either could wind up with surprise assignments. Truman used both of them as troubleshooters, idea men, researchers, speech consultants, critics, and what have you. Indeed they were so successful that the president came to rely less and less on specialized aides. Small groups of generalists had developed around Clifford and Steelman by 1947 to support their operations, both of whom borrowed freely from the talents of other White House aides, even such specialists as David K. Niles on minority affairs and Donald S. Dawson on personnel matters.

By 1947 Truman was also relying heavily on the Bureau of the Budget, directed by James E. Webb, especially to screen legislative as well as budgetary proposals. According to Charles Murphy, the bureau "came to be, in a sense, an extension of the White House staff."[6] There were also the military aides, but here the story was a less-happy one. Truman's friend Harry Vaughan would serve as military aide throughout his presidency. As a reservist, General Vaughan was not on especially good terms with the army, and he looked like "an unmade bed" or, although he drank little, "as if he had a perpetual hangover."[7] He was a generous, amiable man, and his role was chiefly to serve as a presidential confidant and as master of ceremonies for Captain Harry's court. His indiscretions were legion, so he was a lightning rod to attract criticism aimed at the White House. The naval aide's office seemed to be equipped with a revolving door during Truman's first term, as Clifford replaced James K. Vardaman, Jr., and was in turn succeeded by a navy regular, Admiral Foskett. The president became dissatisfied with Foskett; so another regular, Adm. Robert L. Dennison, took Foskett's place in 1948. Along with Adm. Sidney Souers, the executive secretary of the National Security Council, Dennison rendered important service as an adviser. The air force aide, Gen. Robert Landry, played a lesser role.

Truman's chief of staff, Admiral Leahy, who was advancing in age, became steadily less significant and retired in 1949.

By 1947 the White House staff had become a mix of specialists and generalists. It was to be a remarkably stable group at least until 1950, when Clifford left and Ross died, and even until 1953, considering how many White House aides remained on to the end of the Truman presidency. The basic mix and organization, though never static, remained; and it gave a special character to the Truman White House, as did the unusual reliance on the Bureau of the Budget. The White House staff and the bureau served the president effectively, partly because they usually worked well together and partly because Truman listened to them and encouraged full discussion. Nevertheless, it was clear that he was the boss, the person on whose desk "the buck stops." For all their influence, they were advisers, not executives or policy makers.

There was also further development in the leadership of the cabinet, upon which Truman relied much more than had Roosevelt and Hoover. There had been a great deal of shuffling of cabinet and other key appointments in 1946 and 1947 as the president had sought to form an administration of his own. By early 1947, except for George C. Marshall, who was just coming in as secretary of state, the cabinet did not seem to be impressive. W. Averell Harriman appeared to be an unknown quantity at the Commerce Department; Lewis B. Schwellenbach, at Labor, seemed to lack initiative; Clinton P. Anderson, at the Department of Agriculture, was often considered to be out of tune with administration policies; and many persons believed that Julius A. Krug was mediocre at Interior. Postmaster General Robert E. Hannegan, Treasury Secretary John W. Snyder, Attorney General Tom C. Clark, Secretary of War Robert P. Patterson, and Secretary of the Navy James V. Forrestal were generally considered to be adequate, but little more. In addition, the general tenor of the cabinet, and indeed of most of the administration, seemed to be conservative, which vexed the New Deal wing of the Democratic party.

President Truman assessed the cabinet differently, although he would make changes in due course. He believed that the executive agencies usually were operating well enough, his key test being whether their chiefs were loyal and able men who would effectively respond to his goals. He expected the undersecretaries and assistant secretaries to make up for the deficiencies of their bosses. On the whole, they did this well, whether it was, for example, Dean G. Acheson in the State Department, Charles F. Brannan in Agriculture, Oscar Chapman in the Interior Department, Jesse Donaldson in the Post Office, David A. Morse in Labor, or David K. E. Bruce in Commerce. Truman was highly satisfied with several of his cabinet members, sometimes assessing them more favorably than did the press or the public. Snyder was a very effective administrator; he was also loyal and candid. This Missourian would stay at his post to the end of Truman's presidency, earning his chief's praise for being "able, efficient and right in his handling of the money matters of the government." Another Missourian, Hannegan, gave the president all that he wanted in terms of political support and loyalty. Clark became increasingly well respected as attorney general; he won Truman's accolade for doing an "excellent job." Truman believed that Harriman was "great," but that assessment had to be for his general contributions, because he was not at Commerce long enough to earn such a description there. Truman never came to grips with Forrestal, whose reputation nevertheless rose, especially after he took on the punishing job in 1947 as America's first secretary of defense. The president greatly admired Marshall, who was held in awe by almost all Americans while he was secretary of state. Truman respected Patterson, as did most observers, even though Patterson was not another Stimson. Patterson left federal service in 1947 with the coming of the new defense organization. The president would bide his time with Schwellenbach, Anderson, and Krug.

The composition of the cabinet continued to change after Marshall joined it. Unlike the early Truman cabinet, however, it was more a matter of evolution than of shake-ups. Postmaster General Hannegan resigned in November 1947, largely for reasons of health. Because Truman had decided to dispense with the tradition of having the chairman of the party's National Committee also serve as postmaster general, this gave him two key positions to fill. He named Senator J. Howard McGrath to be chairman of the Democratic National Committee and sixty-two-year-old Jesse Donaldson, a career official, to be postmaster general. With good reason, Truman would later call Donaldson "the best we've had." In April 1948 the president sent Averell Harriman to serve as his principal agent abroad in connection with the European Recovery Program. Charles Sawyer, a sixty-one-year-old attorney from Ohio, succeeded Harriman as secretary of commerce. Truman later dubbed him "the top in that position." This may not have been true, but Sawyer was effective in running his department and in keeping businessmen satisfied with his sympathetic attitude toward them. In May, Clinton Anderson resigned to run for the Senate. The president commented that Anderson had quit when "the going became rough." Yet one can sympathize with Anderson, for he had tried hard in his job and had built a basis of support among farmers for Truman in the 1948 election. Assistant Secretary Charles F. Brannan took Anderson's place as secretary of agriculture. Although Brannan was controversial, he was an excellent administrator and won a reputation for having unusual integrity. The last change in 1948 came in the secretaryship of labor, with the death in June of Lewis Schwellenbach. Truman had trouble in replacing the reclusive but loyal Schwellenbach, because no one was eager to assume his portfolio under the double onus of the Taft-Hartley Act and a president who seemed to be doomed to lose in the November election. Finally, in August, the forty-seven-year-old former governor of Massachusetts, Maurice J. Tobin, accepted the post. Tobin was politically adept in dealing with unions, Congress, and his party; he also used his assistants well in running the Labor Department. What seemed to impress Truman most about Tobin was, however, that he took the secretaryship "when everyone thought I'd be out in November 1948."[8]

The Truman cabinet was well shaped by 1948. Of the 1947 and 1948 appointees, Brannan, Donaldson, Sawyer, and Tobin would join Snyder in serving until the end of Truman's presidency. They varied in age, background, and political coloration. This was, however, an asset to an administration that had to appeal to many different constituencies. If none of them was a great statesman, they all possessed loyalty, courage, and ability, the three qualities that the president admired most. During Truman's second term, he would acquire a new secretary of state in 1949 (Dean Acheson) and a new secretary of the interior in 1950 (Oscar Chapman), both of whom remained to the end of the administration. Again, loyalty, courage, and ability characterized these men. They are usually ranked among the best who have held their offices. The secretaryship of the Defense Department would be a turnstile after Forrestal left, seriously ill, in March 1949. Truman thought that Louis A. Johnson was a disaster in the position; George C. Marshall, however distinguished, could only give a year to the job; and Robert A. Lovett was considered able and loyal. After Tom Clark left in 1949, the attorney generalship deteriorated, as we shall see, under J. Howard McGrath, until the president brought in James P. McGranery to head the Justice Department in 1952. McGranery had only enough time as attorney general to restore some respect to the office.

Truman's appointees had many things in common, most importantly their view of the world. Although they disagreed a bit on what to do about it, they did agree with the president in viewing the Soviet Union as a menace to world peace and on the need to contain Russian expansionism. Given their backgrounds, this is not surprising. Most of them had seen military service, and all had had substantial records of governmental service. All had been touched by Woodrow Wilson's vow to "make the world safe for democracy" and by Franklin D. Roosevelt's artful embroidery on that theme. All were full of America's greatness in winning its share of World War II, and all believed that the United States was the world's best hope for peace, prosperity, and democracy. They had been appalled by the failure of Western democracies to stop the rise of aggressive, authoritarian powers after World War I. No more Munichs for these men, who thought they knew what to do to prevent such disasters. They had seen what government could do when it mobilized the nation, first to combat depression and then to win World War II. They were willing, if necessary, to mobilize again. They might disagree about how to achieve prosperity, but they were generally agreed on how to deal with the Soviets. Required was a strong foreign policy, backed up by enough military strength to convince possible enemies that the United States was willing to fight for peace and democracy.

These men and their kind in other positions of leadership across the country were not naturally bellicose. Neither were they willing to ignore a gauntlet thrown down by a foe. They had become accustomed to wielding power, sensitive to the idealistic lyrics written by Wilson and Roosevelt, and keenly aware of their nation's strength and potential as well as of events abroad. The leaders of the Truman era were unlikely to retreat to the attitudes of earlier generations of Americans. A new Rome had emerged during their lifetimes, and they were its centurions and consuls. Their prime motive was to protect their nation from foreign threats, which now seemed much more dangerous because of rapid technological developments and because American interests stretched out over the world. The United States also had the means to meet foreign threats and to expand its interests abroad. And the opportunity was there, because World War II had left only the United States and Russia in the position to vie for world leadership. America's leaders believed that the country could not afford to ignore an aggressor's challenge. Truman wrote in April 1948 in the draft of an undelivered speech: "We are a peaceful nation. But we must be prepared for trouble if it comes. Twice in a generation brave allies have kept the barbarian from our borders. It can't happen that way again. . . . Our friends the Russkies understand only one language—how many divisions have you—actual or potential."[9] In short, by 1948 Truman and the men around him believed that the United States had to be strong enough—economically, politically, and socially—to see that the free world's barricades were manned against the barbarians.

Truman had no doubt that he could provide a government that would understand this situation and could act to meet it. This would be a strong factor in his decision to seek election in 1948. Yet he had mixed feelings about the presidency. He liked the status that it gave to his family, and he took joy in many aspects of his job. His complaints were, nevertheless, frequent: he often fulminated against foreign leaders, Republicans, recalcitrant or incompetent Democrats, labor leaders, industrialists, Congress, and the press. He disliked being in crowds and being constantly under personal scrutiny, two of the common conditions of presidential life. Equally irritating was his confinement to "the great white jail," as he often called the White House. Moreover, he had to deal too often with political prima donnas and the highly ambitious. In November 1947 he wrote to his sister that "a man in his right mind would never want to be President if he knew what it entails." He confided to his diary three months later that "it's hell to be the Chief of State!"[10] Then there were the embarrassments that the press seemed to be so fond of. A minor scandal in 1947 about the speculative investments of White House physician Dr. Wallace H. Graham led Press Secretary Charles Ross to observe, "You can guard yourself against the wiles of your enemies but not the stupidity of your friends."[11] There were plenty of other embarrassments, including Truman's continued relations with the Pendergasts; his commutation of the mail-fraud sentence of former Mayor James M. Curley of Boston; the constant hullabaloo among many Protestants over Washington's closer relations with the Vatican; and the incessant criticism, for architectural and financial reasons, of Truman's decision to add a balcony to the White House. Little wonder the president thought that he was a national scapegoat. He wrote to his brother, Vivian, in March 1948: "One day you do things you think are for the welfare of the country and the next you are up against a complete reversal of feeling because something else that is right doesn't please. I think the proper thing to do, and the thing I have been doing, is to do what I think is right and let them all go to hell."[12]

Despite his often-expressed reservations about his job, Truman did not shrink from assuming the burden of running for a second term. He never precisely analyzed his motives, but the clues are abundant: he had foreign and domestic programs that he wanted to see through; he felt a responsibility to his party and his supporters; he had political scores to settle; he had little confidence in his would-be successors (which may have been a smoke screen for ambition); and he wanted to show that he could win, despite the doubts about that eventuality even in his own party. In short, as he said, he "was not brought up to run from a fight."[13] The president dodged every public attempt during 1947 and well into 1948 to smoke him out on his plans in regard to the election. Yet, early in 1947, at Clark Clifford's instigation, an informal strategy board was formed to funnel good ideas to Truman. This group consisted of some of the administration's younger and more-liberal officials, including Federal Security Administrator Oscar Ewing, and coordinator; Ewing's aide, Don Kingsley; Clifford's colleague, Charles Murphy; Leon H. Keyserling; Charles F. Brannan; David A. Morse; Assistant Secretary of the Interior C. Girard Davidson; Wayne Coy of the Federal Communications Commission; and occasionally others. Meeting every other Monday night, this group worked effectively to find issues, tactics, and targets for Truman in preparation for the 1948 campaign. They also served as a source of support for him on immediate issues, most notably integration of the armed services, the veto of the Taft-Hartley Act, and the recognition of Israel.

Other aides to the president and the Democratic National Committee early began to make plans for Truman's 1948 campaign. One memorandum in the summer of 1947 contained the suggestion that until the national convention the president should speak *"not as a candidate for election,* but as the representative of the whole people."[14] Truman generally followed this advice. After this time the political suggestions from administration figures and Democratic leaders came pouring in at an increasing pace. These included Clark Clifford's famous forty-three-page memorandum of November 19, 1947, which correctly predicted that Governor Thomas E. Dewey of New York would be the Republican nominee and that Henry A. Wallace would also run for president. What Clifford missed was that Truman's civil-rights program would lead to the presidential candidacy of Governor J. Strom Thurmond of South Carolina on a States' rights ticket.

In December 1947, by selecting Senator J. Howard McGrath to be chairman of the Democratic National Committee, Truman gave a strong clue to his intentions for 1948. Certainly, the senator made little secret of the fact that he was working for Truman's election. On a radio forum program in February 1948, McGrath slipped up by saying that he was going to elect Truman. When pressed, McGrath retreated, indicating that this was only a hunch. The president's response, in his February 5 news conference, was that it "was a good hunch." It was, of course, more than that, because Truman's aides had for some time been preparing for the campaign. On March 8 McGrath announced Truman's candidacy for the Democratic presidential nomination.

The president had many things going in his favor. Substantially more Americans identified themselves as Democrats than as Republicans. As chief executive, he controlled vast resources, including patronage, budgetary support, and unparalleled publicity. Truman also had a small army of people, on and off the payroll, who were willing to work for his election out of fear, favor, habit, or personal liking. He also had the ardent support of the Democratic National Committee's apparatus, which worked effectively for him. Then there were the Republicans, who were far from united in their efforts to contest the 1948 elections. Although they controlled Congress, almost every week their actions on Capitol Hill revealed the serious differences between them and their party's prospective nominee, Governor Dewey.

Truman's political liabilities were equally great. He had not shown signs of being charismatic. His voice was flat and nasal, his prepared texts were often stilted, and his gestures were limited to chopping hand motions, which were not always appropriate to what he was saying. He did not look the statesman, and he did not have the offsetting appeal of youth. When he did things that the public approved of, other persons received much of the credit; when he did things that the people disapproved of, he usually received the full blame. No wonder that between March 1947 and March 1948 the public's approval of his performance, as indicated in the Gallup poll, dropped from 60 to 35 percent. And Truman could count on little fair cooperation from a Congress that was controlled by the opposition party. Commenting on the increasingly political motivations of his fellow Republicans, Senator Vandenberg wrote in November 1947 that "the world is full of tragedy; but there is no tragedy greater than that we have to have a presidential election next year."[15] Truman agreed, writing testily in his diary in January 1948: "Congress meets—Too bad too. They'll do nothing but wrangle, pull phony investigations and generally upset the affairs of the Nation."[16]

One of the major challenges facing the president for 1948 was the splintering of his party on both the Left and the Right. Numerous Democratic liberals were criticizing his domestic policies, and some were questioning his foreign policy. To their way of thinking, Truman was not only an unworthy successor to Franklin D. Roosevelt, but he had also surrounded himself with conservative and even mediocre people. After the Democratic rout in the 1946 elections, liberal dissenters organized along new lines. First, in December 1946, came the formation of the Progressive Citizens of America (PCA), many of whose members favored third-party action under Henry Wallace's leadership. In January 1947, other Democrats, who were more committed, organized the Americans for Democratic Action (ADA), which was disposed to find someone other than Truman to lead their party in 1948, in particular, Gen. Dwight D. Eisenhower.

In 1947 there was much talk within the administration of how to deal with Wallace. Most Democrats were furious with him in April, when he was overseas and charged the administration with bellicosity toward Russia and with undercutting the United Nations. There were proposals that Wallace be denied a passport, which Truman opposed. Adviser Stephen T. Early suggested that Wallace's mystic letters be publicized, in order to discredit Wallace, a tactic that Truman vetoed. As talk of a Wallace third-party ticket rose, FBI Director J. Edgar Hoover began reporting to Harry Vaughan on Wallace, the PCA, and their Communist connections. Hoover also reported on the ADA's romance with Eisenhower. Whatever was discussed in governmental circles, Wallace was not discouraged. On December 29, 1947, he declared his independent candidacy. In February 1948, with the PCA's support, Senator Glen Taylor of Idaho announced that he would be Wallace's running mate, and the die was cast. The Communist party later gave its endorsement to the Wallace-Taylor ticket. The Wallace movement started out with high hopes, but by spring it was evident that its birth had marked its highest point in appeal. The significance of Wallace's candidacy was not that he might have been elected. It was, instead, that by making appeals for an understanding with Russia, racial fair play, advanced social-welfare programs, and nationalization of monopolies, the former vice-president could influence public thought and torpedo Truman's presidential campaign. This was based on the theory that it would be better for ultraliberal leaders to have a Republican administration that would surely fail and cause a sharp popular swing to the left than to have a Truman administration that might not fail.

Wallace was not, however, Truman's only competitor for Democratic votes in 1948. Wallace's emphasis on civil rights reinforced the sense of urgency that was being felt within the White House to act on the matter. In pressing the issue of civil rights, Truman evoked more anger among southern white Democrats than he had anticipated. Letters of protest poured into the White House; southern congressmen denounced Truman's civil-rights initiatives; southern governors talked about secession from the party; and even administration loyalists were disturbed. In February, five southern governors, led by J. Strom Thurmond of South Carolina, warned Democratic National Committee Chairman J. Howard McGrath that "the South was no longer in the bag."[17] All this led the administration to defer action on civil rights until after the Democratic National Convention in July. Clearly, the president was walking a political tightrope between the Wallace movement and many southern whites on civil rights. Truman was counting not only on his civil-rights program to offset Wallace's appeals among black and liberal Democrats but also on party loyalty and his other programs to save the South for him.

There was another complication, however: many liberal Democrats, especially in the ADA, viewed Truman as a liability. They set out to find another leader for their party, one who might be acceptable to all Democrats, including blacks and southern whites. General Eisenhower was their man, although blacks became noticeably cool towards him after he testified in April in favor of continuing segregation in the army. Nevertheless, he was still almost everybody's favorite for president, as many Republicans and Democrats tried to persuade him to accept the nomination of their respective parties. Among the Democrats this was carried to absurd lengths, as ADA liberals, southern white supremacists, labor leaders, and urban bosses sought to recruit as their nominee the very popular but politically unidentified war hero (who had never even voted). Truman's reaction was understandably prickly. "Jim Roosevelt, Jake Arvey, A.D.A. and Frank Hague are for Eisenhower. Doublecrossers all," he wrote just before the Democratic convention.[18] The general politely discouraged those who courted him, but the president never forgave him for not having, at an early date and definitely, removed himself from consideration. Yet Eisenhower's dilatoriness contributed to Truman's nomination. By the time that Eisenhower disavowed any interest in becoming president—only a few days before the Democratic Convention opened in July—it was too late for a majority of the delegates to agree on any nominee other than Truman.

In preparation for the convention, Truman's aides and the staff of the Democratic National Committee had done effective work in publicizing him and in lining up delegate support. The president himself had made what, in his opening speech on June 4, he called a "nonpartisan, bipartisan trip . . . to see the people as they are." In two weeks he delivered formal addresses in Chicago, Omaha, Butte, Seattle, Berkeley, and Los Angeles, in addition to informal remarks in sixteen states from Pennsylvania to Oregon. This trip was a preview of his general-election campaign, one that showed a new-model Truman, a personable and hard-hitting campaigner. His frequent tactic of speaking extemporaneously or from notes worked more effectively than his delivery of formal speeches. It persuaded his staff of what he had learned from his senatorial campaigns: he could reach audiences best by being just plain Harry. Instead of a dry analysis of legislation, who would not prefer to hear a comment such as the one that Truman made in Nebraska on June 6, after receiving a gift of spurs: "These spurs are wonderful. When I get them on, I can take the Congress to town. Give them a trial, just as soon as I get back to Washington."

Meanwhile, the Republicans had been battling fiercely to decide on their presidential standard-bearer. The nomination was highly coveted, for it seemed sure that 1948 would be a Republican year, assuming that Eisenhower did not run for the Democrats. Since he had declined to wage a contest for the G.O.P. nomination, most Republicans correctly assumed that he would also reject the Democrats. Governor Dewey, Senator Taft, and Minnesota's former Governor Harold E. Stassen, among others, therefore entered the lists. The Republican National Convention met in Philadelphia, beginning on June 20. The Dewey team's deft hard work outshone the efforts of his opponents; so the delegates nominated the New Yorker for president on the third ballot. Later the convention ratified Dewey's choice for a running mate, Governor Earl Warren of California. The platform on which they would run was relatively liberal in its proposals and moderate in its criticism of the Democrats. Plainly, the document was at variance with the record and rhetoric of the Republican Eightieth Congress.

Truman and his advisers quickly saw the significance of this. When, at his July 1 news conference, the president was asked about the Republican vice-presidential nominee, he replied, "I like Governor Warren." He added, "I don't have anything against Governor Dewey, except that I am going to beat him in this coming campaign." Already by June 29, Truman's staff had recommended that Congress be the primary campaign target, instead of the moderate G.O.P. national ticket. Their memorandum asserted: "This election can only be won by bold and daring steps, calculated to reverse the powerful trend now running against us. The boldest and most popular step the President could possibly take would be to call a special session of Congress early in August." This would point up "the rotten record" of the Eightieth Congress and the "reactionary" Republicans in it. "It would show the President *in action on Capitol Hill,* fighting for the people. . . . It would force Dewey and Warren to defend the actions of Congress, and make them accept the Congress as a basic issue." It would also divide the Republican party on a variety of issues.[19] Truman soon put his imprimatur on this plan, although some members of his administration opposed it. As he later told his staff, the Republican platform was "the most cynical and asininely hypocritical document you ever read." In a special session, either Congress would live up to the Republican party's liberal platform promises because he forced them to do so, or they would be shown up as renegers. It would be a case of saying, as Truman put it, "Now, you s--- o- b------ come on and do your g-- d------."[20]

Before Truman could implement his plan, he still had to win the Democratic presidential nomination. The national convention convened, also in Philadelphia, on July 12. With Eisenhower out of contention, anti-Truman liberals made a few unsuccessful attempts to find someone to contest Truman's nomination. They also failed to modify the platform that had been dictated by the White House, except in their winning a floor fight and forcing the adoption of a more-liberal plank on civil rights. This irritated Truman and infuriated the southern delegates, but the new plank was consonant with what the president favored. The southerners, in turn, tried to change the platform, but without success. They spent their political capital on backing Senator Richard B. Russell of Georgia for the presidential nomination. This was chiefly a matter of show, because, by July 14, Truman had cornered enough delegates to win, with 947½ votes to 263 for Russell. The southern delegates refused, however, to make Truman's nomination unanimous. Then the convention turned to the task of choosing a vice-presidential nominee, although it was clear that the delegates would accept whomever the president designated. Truman had not given much thought to the question. Just before the convention, he had had Clark Clifford sound out William O. Douglas, who responded that it would be inappropriate for a justice of the Supreme Court to accept the nomination. Several factions urged the president to choose the Senate minority leader, seventy-year-old Alben W. Barkley. Truman procrastinated, probably because he had been nettled by the Kentuckian's forlorn bid for the presidential nomination; but finally, he gave his nod to the well-liked senator, and the convention gave Barkley the nomination, though by then he viewed it as a "warmed over biscuit."[21]

The convention had been marked by a defeatist attitude. Yet, one Democrat, Harry S. Truman, believed that the party could win the election, or so he said to his fellow Democrats and Americans—those who were still awake at 2 in the morning of July 15, when he delivered his acceptance address. It was a long and rousing speech, from his declaration that "Senator Barkley and I will win this election and make these Republicans like it—don't you forget that!" to his assertion that "the country can't afford another Republican Congress." It was an energetic recitation of all the marvelous things he believed the Democrats had done for America and of the things he thought the Eightieth Congress had done "*to* the people, and not *for* them." Truman pointed out the good things that the 1948 Republican platform espoused but that the Republican Congress had failed to do. Well, he was going to give them a chance to do those things. "I am therefore calling this Congress back into session July 26th. . . . I am going to . . . ask them to pass laws to halt rising prices, to meet the housing crisis—which they are saying they are for in their platform." And this was just the beginning of his list. Truman predicted that the Republicans were "going to try to dodge their responsibility . . . . but I am here to say that Senator Barkley and I are not going to let them get away with it." The president's acceptance speech was an appropriate prelude to the campaign that was to follow, and the reaction from most Democrats was enthusiastic.

When Truman appeared before Congress at the opening of the special session, his political stock could only rise. On July 17 the hastily constructed States Rights party had nominated a national ticket of Governors J. Strom Thurmond of South Carolina and Fielding Wright of Mississippi. These Dixiecrats were not, however, drawing anywhere near the amount of support that they had anticipated. Moreover, the public-opinion polls were showing a steady decline in voter support for Henry Wallace and his Progressive party. Neither Dewey nor Truman had increased his popularity as a result of the Republican and Democratic nominating conventions. They stood at roughly 48 and 37 percent approval levels, respectively, in the June and late-July Gallup polls. It was significant that the president's support had not declined, despite the fact that his party had lost its left and right wings. In a sense, he had gained, for he had impressed upon the country that he intended to be a fighting political leader. Yet this was only a beginning; he had a long way to go before he would convince anyone that he could win.

Truman's handling of the special session of Congress was his first offensive ploy. As he had promised he would, he asked Congress on July 27 to act to stop inflation and to alleviate the housing shortage. "We cannot afford to wait for the next Congress to act." He also requested federal aid to education, an increase in minimum wage and in Social Security benefits, authorization to accept more displaced persons, a loan for the UN building, financing of public power projects, salary raises for civil-service employees, and enactment of his civil-rights program. If the president was not asking for something for everybody, he was asking for something for most Americans. Congress met for only about two weeks. From Truman's standpoint, its record was dismal. Congress passed some bank and consumer controls, but they fell far short of what he had requested in order to check inflation. The Housing Act was little more than a gesture. The legislators responded fully only on the loan for the UN building in New York. On everything else, they failed to act. When asked, at his August 12 news conference, to assess the special session, Truman said, "it was a kind of a poor result that we got." One reporter asked him, "Would you say it was a 'do-nothing' session, Mr. President?" He replied, "I would say it was entirely a 'do-nothing' session. I think that's a good name for the 80th Congress." Thus the lyrical refrain for his campaign was born.

Truman's presidential campaign began on September 6, when he visited Michigan for a day to court organized labor. He did not take to the road in earnest until he spoke in Pittsburgh on September 17. From then on his campaign continued, with only a few short breaks, as he gave several speeches daily. His performances were chiefly informal talks from the rear platform of his private railroad car, the "Ferdinand Magellan." These were interspersed with formal addresses, which were often broadcast over the radio. He also supervised the other aspects of his campaign—letters, statements, coordination of the work of the Democratic National Committee, and the synchronization of his and Senator Barkley's efforts. Truman had Clark Clifford, George Elsey, Matthew Connelly, and Charles Ross with him, as advisers and to help with arrangements, speeches, communications, and public relations. Donald Dawson was the president's chief advance man, arranging for voter turnouts in connection with Truman's appearances. Other White House staff members remained in Washington to handle routine affairs of state and to feed queries and material to the campaign train.

The president spoke in twenty-eight states, concentrating on the Middle West. He was in Ohio so often that its citizens must have thought that the White House had been relocated there. This concentration paid off, for on election day Truman carried Ohio and most of the states in the Middle West. During his campaign, he emphasized issues of interest to farmers, labor, and consumers, occasionally giving attention to the concerns of city dwellers and black Americans. There were, however, two overarching issues, both of which concerned the president. As he pictured it, the campaign boiled down to Truman—the world-class champion of peace, prosperity, democracy, and the people—fighting against special interests at home and authoritarianism abroad. It was also Truman—the man of experience and concern who got down to brass tacks—against a bland, generalizing Thomas E. Dewey and, worse yet, the reactionary Republican leadership of the Eightieth Congress. There was no need to campaign against Wallace or Thurmond, for they would be done in by their extremism and their associates.

Not all Democrats were enthusiastic about Truman's campaign. Eben Ayers noted in his diary on October 6 about attitudes in the White House: "There is much confusion and taut nerves, due to the political campaign and the belief that the President is going to be defeated. There are few optimists in the place."[22] Truman never faltered, however, in his conviction that he had a chance to win the election. He wrote to his sister on October 5: "It will be the greatest campaign any President ever made. Win, lose, or draw, people will know where I stand and a record will be made for future action by the Democratic Party."[23] His enthusiasm and diligence influenced the staffs of the White House and the

Democratic National Committee to work hard for him. Three cabinet members—Attorney General Tom Clark, Secretary of Agriculture Charles Brannan, and Labor Secretary Maurice Tobin—also stumped effectively for the president. Undersecretary of the Interior Oscar Chapman devoted much time to the campaign, and Louis Johnson put the party's finances in good shape. Although many Democratic officeholders held themselves at arm's length from their party's presidential nominee, others—for example, House Minority Leader Sam Rayburn and Indiana's former Governor Henry Schricker—gave him good support. Senator Barkley pitched into the campaign, and labor made great efforts on Truman's behalf. Then, too, as the president loyally backed most other Democratic candidates, many of them came to reciprocate.

What Truman was standing on in his campaign were the many programs that he had recommended to Congress and that had been encapsulated in the 1948 Democratic platform. There were the foreign-policy and military issues, universal training, foreign aid, Israel, peace, and, above all, checking communism. The domestic issues that were involved affected all Americans: these included inflation, housing, federal aid to education, health care, higher minimum wage and Social-Security benefits, flood control, public power, civil rights, labor, conservation, agriculture, and regulation of business, among others. As he had been since 1945, Truman was proposing no less than that the federal government guarantee a fairer distribution of what America had to offer. The economy could afford it, because under his leadership the economy would grow. The economy could also afford to finance whatever was needed in order to protect the nation's way of life from foreign aggressors. Indeed, the United States economy, people, and government could not afford to do otherwise than to promote prosperity at home and to defend it abroad, because the two were intertwined.

The president got his political messages across pithily. For example, on September 6 in Grand Rapids, Michigan, he described his administration as believing "in the welfare of the whole people and not just in the welfare of the real estate lobbies and a few other great lobbies." It was also on that same day, in Flint, that he first used the phrase, " 'do-nothing' 80th Congress." This he would often repeat, sometimes prefacing it with "good-for-nothing," in order to force the Republicans on the defensive. In his speeches, Truman was often masterful at working in complimentary local references, some humor, and a bit of folksiness. Most important, however, was his combativeness in defense of his administration and in his attacks on the Republican Congress. He gathered vitality as the campaign proceeded. The more he campaigned, the more people turned out to see him, and the more they went away impressed with his vigor, decisiveness, and dedication. He was not afraid of hyperbole, and his little homilies frequently struck home. "Remember that the reactionary of today is a shrewd man," Truman said in Detroit on September 6. "He is a man with a calculating machine where his heart ought to be." Or in Rock Island, Illinois, on September 18: "You know the issues in this campaign are not hard to define. The issue is the people against the special interests." Or in Elyria, Ohio, on October 26: "I am on a campaign to tell the American people the truth about the issues in this election. They are not getting the truth from the Republican candidate, who is trying to pretend that there aren't any issues." Or in St. Louis, on October 30: "If you will vote for yourselves, you will vote the straight Democratic ticket, and everything will be safe for the world, and for Missouri, and for the United States. Now, don't forget that. Just do a little thinking."

Increasingly during the campaign, public attention focused on Truman. Governor Dewey usually contented himself with indulging in generalities, in portraying himself as the able, impeccable, and unflappable statesman who would win and then set everything to rights. It is not surprising that he became considered "the little man on the wedding cake" in contrast to Truman's "Give 'em hell, Harry" image. And Dewey's strategy was intentional. After all, he was leading comfortably in the public-opinion polls, and he had the support of most of the nation's press. Moreover, he did not want to split his party, which was divided on many issues, or to drive off prospective independent and Democratic supporters. Dewey had been too bellicose in 1944, and he did not intend to make that mistake again. Showing confidence and imperturbability should do the trick. When you are ahead, why take the risk of offending people? Let Truman do that with his attacks. And let him work his head off doing it. This is why Dewey campaigned less than the president did. It was enough for the New Yorker to stick to the high ground, to indicate that in his administration, things would be different and better.

Dewey also counted upon victory because of the split in Truman's party. Wallace and Thurmond were running vigorous campaigns, and given their issues and Democratic antecedents, they could take votes only away from the president. Just as Truman did better than Dewey had anticipated, Wallace and Thurmond did less well. Thurmond was hampered by the opposition of most of the press and by his campaign's slender financial resources. Moreover, his extremism in criticizing Truman's civil-rights program and governmental centralization went further than the majority of white southerners could tolerate. Wallace, though he campaigned more extensively than Thurmond did, could not rally mass support with the civil-rights cause or seem to outbid the president on other domestic issues. Nor was Wallace able to switch the emphasis of the campaign to foreign policy, on which too many Americans believed he was cozy with Stalin.

Wallace lost strength as the weeks went by, and Thurmond and Dewey did not increase theirs. Truman was the one who got stronger in the polls during the campaign. Dewey planned to glide to victory, based on his early large campaign lead; and the pollsters and pundits generally agreed that he would do so. Increasingly, though, Truman's campaign workers came to believe that he had a chance, which spurred on their efforts all the more. As for the president, he believed, unlike Dewey, that the campaign would affect a substantial number of voters, especially workers, farmers, and blacks; and he acted accordingly in order to reach them. Truman's victory was a surprise to most Americans. He wound up with 24,179,345 votes, well over Dewey's 21,991,291; the difference between the nominees of the two major parties was almost as much as Thurmond's 1,176,125 and Wallace's 1,157,326 combined. Truman did even better in the Electoral College, receiving 303 votes to 189 for Dewey and 39 for Thurmond, who captured four southern states. The president won most of the states that he had campaigned in, although he lost Michigan, New York, and Pennsylvania, despite strenuous efforts. Moreover, a Democratic Congress was elected. The one discouraging note was that the percentage of eligible voters—53—going to the polls was, despite the excitement of the 1948 campaign, the lowest since 48.9 percent had turned out in 1924.

Eben Ayers wrote of Truman's election what many Americans thought: "It seemed unbelievable to us, much as we had hoped for it."[24] In retrospect it is not so unbelievable. Roosevelt had built a coalition of Democratic voters that only a disaster could have dismantled rapidly, and Truman was no bringer of disaster. He had found ways to appeal to most of the New Deal voters as well as regular Democrats. What he had not done was to reverse the erosion of the coalition's strength, which had been going on since 1938. This failure would have serious ramifications. The president would find it hard to follow up his election victory with legislative successes, and his party would find it impossible to stave off defeat in 1952. Yet, Truman's election was a personal triumph, for he had come from behind to win, and he was more responsible for his victory than successful presidential nominees usually are. The question was, What could he make out of this victory during his second term?

8

★ ★ ★ ★ ★

THE FAIR DEAL

The 1948 election campaign had exhausted Truman and his aides. After the exhilaration and the cheers that came when it was clear that the president had won another term, they could best celebrate by going to Key West for two weeks of recuperation. Truman needed it badly, and he knew that his staff did too. Relaxation aimed at regeneration was the rule for the fortnight between November 7 and 21. As Clark Clifford put it, "I don't know how the Government ran during that time";[1] but it did, because there were no crises, and Congress was not in session. The executive agencies and their heads, most of whom had done little or no campaigning, coped with the ordinary affairs of state.

Indeed, the regeneration went on for the rest of 1948. The president said little that was newsworthy in his press conferences and public statements. He asked all of his cabinet members to stay on, and there were no significant changes in the White House staff. Moreover, it was clear that his domestic program had been established during his first term, and few surprises were anticipated in his foreign and military policies. The administration's goals were still economic growth and reform at home and the promotion of peace, democracy, and economic stability abroad. Truman did want to refine this program. So the word went out from Key West that he wanted a reappraisal of the state of the nation. Executive agencies, including the Council of Economic Advisers, were soon working on their contributions to the president's January 1949 State of the Union, budget, economic, and inaugural addresses.

This was the key work of the administration and the White House during the last six weeks of 1948.

This work reflected the fact that the presidency, under Harry Truman, was becoming as much an institutionalized as a personal office. Frank Pace, Jr., who served as budget director and secretary of the army, later declared—though with some exaggeration—that Truman "created the institution of the presidency."[2] This meant that Truman had contributed greatly to refining the structure of government and to delegating substantial responsibility for formulating proposals for programs. This was done not just through the use of old-line federal agencies but also through his increasing use of the Bureau of the Budget, the Council of Economic Advisers, the National Security Council, the White House staff, and ad hoc commissions to give him the ideas and information upon which to make decisions. In this way he—and many of the other federal officials involved—hoped that decisions and implementation of them would be based more on fiscal and administrative criteria than on political and personal bases.

Although the composition of this institutionalization would change during later administrations, they all would follow Truman's lead in having the president serve as chairman of the boards that ran the executive branch. This contrasted with Franklin Roosevelt's personal involvement in or Calvin Coolidge's relative remoteness from the various phases of governmental management. Institutionalization applied not only to the president but also to the heads of executive agencies, thanks in part to the reforming efforts of the Hoover Commission. Because the federal government had gotten too big and of concern to too many elements, it could not be operated by a collection of satraps who owed homage to the sovereign overlord in the White House. Truman believed that the federal government, from top to bottom, owed it to the people to tighten its structure and to pay more attention to the principles of economy, efficiency, and effectiveness.

Congress could, of course, thwart the best-laid plans of any presidency, whether these were personal or institutional. Truman believed that this had happened too often during his first term. He was confident, however, that matters would improve with the Eighty-first Congress. The Democrats would hold the Senate by a majority of 54 to 42 and the House by 263 to 171. Moreover, in his most-optimistic moments, Truman could hope that many of the congressional Democrats would feel beholden to him for their elections and that others would have been chastened by the results of the 1948 election. The president was also prepared to use a wide variety of techniques to muster legislative majorities for his program. Among these would be patronage, recognition, various entitlements, persuasion, cajolery, intimidation, and appeals to loyalty, patriotism, and whatever else came to mind. Truman would also try to rely heavily on the Democratic leadership on Capitol Hill, Vice-President Alben Barkley, Senate Majority Leader Scott Lucas, Speaker Sam Rayburn, and House Majority Leader John W. McCormack.

Unfortunately for Truman, his tactics seldom worked well in influencing Congress on domestic matters. His generosity in not punishing Dixiecrat defectors in Congress did little good. Indeed, it allowed them often to frustrate the administration because they had retained their positions of power in the congressional hierarchy. It is true that Rayburn placed Truman supporters in vacancies on key House committees, but there were not enough of them, nor were they senior enough to prevail often. The loading of important House and Senate committees with a disproportionate number of Democrats did little to increase backing for the president; but it did give Republicans more reason to complain and to oppose him. Barkley, Rayburn, and McCormack, if not Lucas, were uncommonly loyal to Truman, but their tactics were not sufficiently effective to make any great difference. Congress was beyond the control of the White House. There were usually enough Democratic and Republican conservatives, as well as recalcitrants, in Congress to block administration proposals on domestic issues and to cause major battles occasionally even on foreign policy. And this coalition was well organized, especially in the Senate. Senator Paul H. Douglas wrote: "Its members always showed up for roll calls, and its power was occasionally openly flaunted, as when Harry F. Byrd and Robert A. Taft sat together on the floor checking the list of Senators and sending out for the absent or the few recalcitrants."[3] Whatever Truman and his allies in Congress did was usually deemed to be wrong. When they were moderate, it was taken as a sign of weakness; when they were bold, it was taken as an attack. They had neither the weapons nor the ability to turn the president's narrow 1948 election victory into substantial legislative success. The congressional Democrats were at least as badly split as they had been in the Eightieth Congress, and the most conservative of them usually were in control of committees. The Republicans would prove to be less amenable to agreeing with the administration than they had been before; they may have lost in 1948, but they were planning to win again soon.

All this was far from clear when Truman appeared before a joint session of Congress to deliver his State of the Union message on January 5, 1949. Confident, even buoyant, he began with the news that "the state of the Union is good." He then gave, as his program for 1949, those key proposals that his administration had developed beginning in 1945, contending that the results of the 1948 election indicated that the people supported them. He added that "every segment of our population and every individual has a right to expect from our Government a fair deal," thereby giving a name to his program. Two days later, the president sent his Economic Report to Congress, to detail his Fair Deal proposals. Inflation, though currently quiescent, was still a threat, he declared. This would require a budgetary surplus and a reduction of the national debt, which in turn would dictate higher taxes, primarily on corporate profits and estates, and increased contributions to Social Security. Also important were continued regulation of bank and consumer credit and, as a new wrinkle, federal promotion of production in certain critical areas, such as steel, which could otherwise present bottlenecks to economic growth. Truman wanted the continuance of rent and export controls and the authority to impose, when needed, selective controls on prices, wages, and allocations of materials. To meet the effects of inflation, he requested substantial increases in the minimum wage and in old-age and survivors' insurance benefits. He was vitally concerned with stimulating economic growth and a fairer distribution of its proceeds. Hence, he recommended the development of natural resources; new farm legislation; better housing legislation; the extension of reciprocal tariffs; federal aid to education; national health-care program; and the coverage of more workers under federal benefit programs. Truman had already made clear in his State of the Union message that he wanted civil-rights legislation and repeal of the Taft-Hartley Act.

In his Budget Message to Congress of January 10, the president got down to the dollars and cents of what his proposals would cost. Although he was keenly concerned for the nation's social and economic development, he was not a spendthrift. Truman wanted a budget surplus in fiscal year 1950. He pointed out, however, that there would be a deficit of $873 million if Congress did not enact his proposed taxes. Plainly, he was offering a trade-off to the congressional conservatives. Enact his Fair Deal program, including $4 billion in tax increases, and the results would be not only greater prosperity and needed reforms but also a balanced budget, reduction of the $252 billion national debt, and restraint of inflation. What Truman failed to realize was that most congressional conservatives were less interested in a balanced budget, cutting the debt, and controlling inflation than in stopping his proposed reforms and his tax increases. In any event, to make his budget more attractive to Congress, he had also kept increases for social and military programs down and had made signifcant cuts in federal programs relating to international affairs, transportation and communications, agriculture, and veterans. Of course, any number of things could occur to make a mockery of the president's carefully wrought budget estimates. Not the least of these would be a large military-aid program, which he would allude to in his Inaugural Address of January 20.

Not all of Truman's requests were controversial, particularly his proposals relating to the management of the federal government. In October, Congress voted more pay to recruit and retain people in the most-responsible federal executive positions, and it passed the Classification Act, which reformed the salary structure for much of the civil service. More important, and enacted earlier, in June, was the Reorganization Act, which was an upshot of the work of the Hoover Commission. This legislation provided that the House or the Senate, when it received a plan from the president in regard to reorganizing a part of the executive branch, would have to reject it within sixty days, or it would stand approved. This would expedite the consideration of such plans over the years, and more often than not, Congress approved them. Some of the approved reorganization plans did generate controversial results, but there is no doubt that most of them fostered economy, effectiveness, and efficiency in the operation of the federal government. A related effort, aimed at governmental reform, was the Budget and Accounting Procedures Act of 1950, which was hailed as the most significant law that had been passed in this area in almost thirty years. It contributed to more-responsible and more-efficient ways of using federal funds and of administering the government.

It was Truman's Fair Deal program, however, that was at the center of attention and dispute in 1949 and 1950. The civil-rights part of the program quickly came to the fore, and it is a prime example of the problems that the administration encountered. After his 1948 victory at the polls, Truman wrote, "We shall win that civil rights battle just as we won the election."[4] The president moved quickly to rally public opinion and his forces in Congress in order to enact his civil-rights requests of February 2, 1948. There were also promising gestures from the White House, such as the ending of racial segregation at the Washington National Airport by 1949 and the banning of the color line at Truman's inauguration. More important, in January the House of Representatives adopted a rule allowing the chairmen of originating committees to force measures out onto the floor for action after they had been stuck in the Rules Committee for twenty-one days. This would be important in getting action in the House on numerous Fair Deal bills, including those of interest to blacks and other Americans from minority groups.

Unfortunately for the administration, in 1951 the Rules Committee regained its power to obstruct legislation.

The key to the passage of civil-rights legislation in 1949 and 1950 was restricting of filibusters in the Senate. Under Senate Rule 22 of 1917, debate could be closed by a two-thirds vote of those senators present. This made the closing of debate hard enough, but in 1948, President of the Senate Arthur Vandenberg ruled that this cloture provision did not apply to motions to consider legislation, which vitiated Rule 22. In early 1949 the Democratic Senate leadership, under Scott Lucas of Illinois, was inept in responding to a generous Republican move to apply Rule 22 to any motion or measure. Lucas's failure allowed southern senators to filibuster against altering cloture. At Truman's behest, Senator Lucas and Minority Leader William F. Knowland then offered a petition, signed by thirty-three senators, to shut off debate on the motion to overturn Vandenberg's resolution. Vice-President Barkley, presiding over the Senate, ruled favorably on the petition on March 10. Senators Vandenberg and Richard Russell led the fight to challenge Barkley's ruling, which the Senate voted to reverse. Worse yet, on March 17 the Senate adopted a resolution that in order to apply cloture to motions, it was necessary to have a two-thirds vote of all senators, not just of those who were present. The effect of this was to make it almost impossible to stop filibusters; it was a crushing blow to the administration and to advocates of civil rights.

Discouraged though the administration was, it continued to press its civil-rights program in Congress. Such legislation had been introduced in the House and Senate by April 1949, encompassing anti-poll-tax, antilynching, antidiscrimination-in-interstate-commerce, voting-rights, and Fair Employment Practices Commission measures, among others. Despite strenuous efforts and a high degree of public support, the administration failed to gain enactment of any key civil-rights measures. The power of the coalition of conservative Democrats and Republicans was too much for the administration to defeat unless it wanted to jeopardize all legislation by courting continuous filibusters, which even most of the liberal legislators would not have tolerated. Thus, the Truman administration's civil-rights victories in Congress were few and minor.

Truman stepped up the appointment of blacks to significant federal positions, including some that the Senate had to confirm, most notably that of William H. Hastie to the Third Circuit Court of Appeals in 1949. Yet the total number of blacks who held high appointments was only ninety-four by the end of the Truman administration. Other legislative successes in civil rights were meager. In October 1949 the president signed a bill providing for construction of a hospital in Albuquerque that would integrate medical facilities for Indians and non-Indians. That same month he vetoed a bill guaranteeing Social Security and other federal benefits to the Indians of Arizona and New Mexico, because it would have transferred authority over Indian water rights and inheritances from the tribes and from federal courts to state courts. Congress removed this offending provision by April 1950, and Truman signed this legislation as part of the Navajo-Hopi Rehabilitation Act. In July, Congress enacted legislation that conferred on the people of Guam local self-government and United States citizenship and that allowed Puerto Ricans to reorganize from territorial to commonwealth status, which was done in 1952. Each of these measures was important in its particular jurisdiction, but they were minor parts of Truman's civil-rights program.

The biggest advances in civil rights during 1949 and 1950 came in terms of administrative and judicial action, and these did not move as effectively as they had been intended to move. The Fair Employment Board (FEB), which was established in 1948 to give minorities equal treatment in federal hiring—moved at a leisurely pace. This was partly because of the board's conservatism, impeding civil-service rules, and inadequate funding. Moreover, few positions opened up in federal employment before the Korean War, although afterward the gains were significant. No one questioned that things were better with the FEB than they had been without it. It was a matter of the door's being opened slowly to increased recruitment, retention, and promotion of minority personnel. There was also the problem of Truman's loyalty-security program, which moved at cross-purposes with his fair-employment system. In short, those who pushed hard to take advantage of the FEB procedures might be viewed askance by the government's loyalty boards. This led to the firing of only a few minority civil servants, but it evidently gave pause to many in testing their rights. After all, too many members of loyalty boards were quick to see a connection between civil-rights activism and disloyalty. If the president saw that his two programs might be in conflict, he never showed it; his aides also disagreed on the issue. The result was that the administration never moved the FEB into high gear or coped with the problem of the loyalty boards and minorities.

More impressive were the efforts of the President's Committee on Equality of Treatment and Opportunity in the Armed Services, which was also created in 1948. Popularly called the Fahy Committee after its chairman, former Solicitor General Charles H. Fahy, this group worked diligently to integrate the military services. Truman fully supported the

Fahy Committee; in January 1949 he told the committee and the military secretaries that he wanted "concrete results—that's what I'm after—not publicity on it." He promised "to knock somebody's ears down," if necessary, to secure that.[5] Even before the Fahy Committee met in 1949, the air force had made some significant steps toward integration and toward eliminating strength quotas for minorities. It cooperated with the committee, as the navy and the marines usually did. The army was the spoiler, which was important because it contained more minority personnel than did the other services. It tried maneuver after maneuver to evade both the letter and the spirit of the president's program, but by January 1950 the Fahy Committee had forced the army to agree to go the way of its fellow services.

The army's agreement was not enough, however. As the Fahy Committee's executive secretary, E. W. Kenworthy, concluded in July, "the army intends to do as little as possible towards implementing the policy which it adopted and published."[6] The Korean War was what made the army live up to its word. Flooded with black recruits then and hindered by the inefficiency of segregation, army generals began to integrate, first at home, then in Korea, and finally in the bastion of hold-out, the European commands. By the end of the Truman administration, the air force, the army, and the navy were largely integrated racially, and opportunities for equal treatment had been very much enhanced; but more remained to be accomplished. This included increasing the number of minority officers, fully integrating military facilities, and applying the principles of Truman's E.O. 9981 to the National Guard and reserve components. The greatest battles had been won, however, thanks to the persistence of Truman and civil-rights groups.

This and more, of course, took place in the context of the times. It was during the Truman period that civil-rights groups, especially black and Jewish ones, became better organized, more vocal, and better coordinated than ever before. And they had a good deal of support from labor, liberal, and religious organizations. This influenced Truman to make civil rights part of his program and often to let the nation know how important it was. Moreover, he had a good deal of company: several members of his administration—for example, Attorney General Tom Clark and Interior Undersecretary Oscar Chapman—were forthright in their feelings and actions on behalf of civil rights. The results were widespread, although hardly revolutionary, as advocates of civil rights challenged discrimination and segregation in the courts, in administrative offices, and in legislative chambers. By 1952 eleven states and twenty cities had fair-employment laws, nineteen states had laws banning some form of racial discrimination, and only five states retained the poll tax.

The civil-rights movement was even affecting the citadel of segregation, housing. The Truman administration increased its efforts after 1948 to open more public housing to blacks, most of it on an unsegregated basis. The president acted in 1949/50 to bring the Housing and Home Finance Administration and the Veterans Administration together on policies to stop supporting restrictive covenants in housing covered by federal home-mortgage insurance. In 1952 this was extended to the Federal Housing Administration. These were only beginnings; it would take continued pressure on the agencies involved in order to make the policies effective. Moreover, realtors and their clients often circumvented the regulations. The essential problem was better housing, however; and in this respect the administration did not do well. Its urban-renewal program too often meant black removal, for there were usually fewer dwelling units available in the new public housing than there had been in the slums that this housing replaced.

More notable progress was made in the courts. Counsel for minority groups continued to have scattered successes in trials and appeals, although these were usually limited in their applicability. In 1950, however, the Supreme Court decided three very important cases involving civil rights, in each of which the Justice Department aided blacks by filing amicus curiae briefs. All three decisions were unanimous and were announced on June 5, which strengthened their impact. In *Henderson* v. *U.S.*, the court held that segregation on railway dining cars was illegal under the Interstate Commerce Act. The other two cases were decided on the basis of the equal-protection clause of the Fourteenth Amendment. In *McLaurin* v. *Oklahoma State Regents*, the justices ruled that a black student could not be physically separated from other students within the University of Oklahoma. In *Sweatt* v. *Painter*, the court declared that a separate black law school in Texas was not equal to the University of Texas Law School, to which the petitioner must therefore be admitted. The Supreme Court had not yet found cause, though it had been urged to do so by Attorney General Clark, to overturn the separate-but-equal doctrine of *Plessy* v. *Ferguson* (1896). The court was coming very close, however, and it had made clear that it was not likely to tolerate the segregation of public facilities. As Thurgood Marshall, the chief counsel for the National Association for the Advancement of Colored People, asserted after the three decisions had been announced, ''The complete destruction of all enforced segregation is now in sight.''[7]

There was much more to the Fair Deal program than civil rights (and a good deal of it was of interest to minorities). The president put up a good front regarding all of his legislative program at the beginning. Yet toward the end of February 1949 he showed irritation with congressional resistance. In his major Jefferson-Jackson Day address on the twenty-fourth, he declared: "The special interests are fighting us just as if they had never heard of November the 2nd. . . . They are again trying to frighten the people with the old, wornout bugaboo that socialism is taking over Washington." Truman suggested: "I may even get on the train again and make another tour around the country . . . to tell the people how their Government is getting along." This is a threat that he did not carry out, even though Congress responded poorly.

On March 30 he signed the Housing and Rent Control Act, which extended and strengthened rent controls until June 30, 1950. This was only the lesser part of the housing program that Truman wanted. Counting on considerable support from Republicans and southern Democrats, he continued to press Congress for authorization to add 810,000 public-housing units, basically apartments, over a period of six years to the 170,000 units already built under 1937 legislation. The president faced stiff opposition from real-estate interests. His aides also irritated Senator Robert Taft, who was the spearhead of Republican support for public housing, by giving him only one hour to study the administration's bill before it was introduced. The result was that Taft proposed his own plan. By March 1949, however, the differences had been smoothed over, and Taft worked hard for the administration's bill. The measure sailed through the Senate, despite various maneuvers by the opposition. Truman exerted great pressure on the House to follow suit, as did labor, civil-rights, and consumer groups and interested Republicans. The real-estate lobby worked hard to defeat the bill, and their allies in the House tried to split northern and southern supporters by amending the bill to prohibit racial discrimination in public housing. As the Senate had already done, the House rejected this ploy, for it was plain that the amendment, however worthy, would cause the defeat of the housing bill. Soon afterwards, the House passed the bill, and Truman approved it on July 15. The Housing Act was hardly the far-reaching legislation that its proponents hailed it as being in 1949. Only 156,000 units were started under it by 1952, and only 356,000 units had been built by 1964. Also, much of this housing was too cheaply constructed, and little attention was given to making the environment of the housing projects attractive or to helping their inhabitants to make the most of their new homes. Public housing was decidedly a mixed blessing.

President Truman resorted to special messages in his efforts to prod Congress into acting on his Fair Deal program. One of these messages, that of April 22, concerned his request for a federal health-care program, which encompassed health insurance; the expansion of medical, dental, and nursing schools; the construction of additional medical facilities; and the facilitation of medical research. Truman felt strongly about his health-care program. He wrote to a Kansas City physician in September: "Where a man getting $2,400.00 a year has to pay $500.00 for prenatal care and then an additional hospital bill on top of that there is something wrong with the system. . . . I am going to try and remedy it."[8] He did try. The American Medical Association (AMA) conducted a strenuous campaign against "socialized medicine," because of its fears that the government would dictate to doctors and that, as Senator Paul H. Douglas tersely said, "more rivals would reduce fees."[9] Federal Security Administrator Oscar Ewing spearheaded the campaign for Truman's program, but he could not match the efforts of the AMA. Ewing persuaded a reluctant president to seek a more-limited program in 1951, which also failed of success. All that Congress did was to increase the government's funding of hospital construction.

By May 1949 Truman was out of sorts with Congress: he was disappointed with Senate Majority Leader Scott Lucas, and he believed that conservative congressional Republicans and southern Democrats had coalesced to block his Fair Deal program. By May 24 he had agreed with the Democratic leadership on Capitol Hill to surrender some of his program. When Lucas leaked this news to the press, the president was furious with him for, in effect, encouraging Truman's foes in Congress. His frustration was further fueled by the Senate's refusal to confirm his crony Mon Wallgren, a former governor of Washington, as chairman of the National Security Resources Board (NSRB) and by a congressional investigation of the Atomic Energy Commission (AEC), which was aimed at forcing the resignation of liberal David E. Lilienthal as chairman of the AEC. At Wallgren's request, Truman withdrew his nomination in May. The investigation of the AEC dragged on, although Lilienthal had the president's full support. Charges that Lilienthal had violated the law and had seriously mismanaged the AEC were not substantiated. He had had enough of conservative congressional criticism, however, and he finally resigned, effective February 1950.

It was in May 1949 that labor issues were joined, when the House voted down the administration's attempt to repeal the Taft-Hartley Act. Truman vowed to fight on for repeal, although it was clear by June that the Senate was not interested in taking action. Also, before the end of the session, serious labor disruptions had occurred; these diminished the chances for repeal even more. John L. Lewis's United Mine Workers led off the turmoil. The demand for coal had declined, and producers sought to reduce employee benefits in order to compensate. Lewis retaliated in June by declaring a week-long vacation for coal miners, to be followed by a week of work and another week of vacation. Then he instituted a three-day work week. Senator Taft was caught with an uncharacteristic grin on his face upon hearing of Lewis's action. Soon afterward, the Senate rebuffed efforts to repeal or alter the Taft-Hartley Act.

Many Americans were appalled by Lewis's audacity. And the situation would worsen, as a coal strike broke out and lasted from September 19 to November 9. In January 1950 wildcat strikes broke out in the coal fields; and by February, coal supplies were such that Truman felt compelled to resort to use of the Taft-Hartley machinery. After his fact-finding board had reported that the strike was endangering the nation's welfare, the president directed the attorney general to seek an injunction. Lewis ordered the miners back to work, but they did not respond. Therefore, the government sought a contempt citation against Lewis and the UMW, which the court in March refused to grant for lack of evidence. Truman immediately asked Congress for authority to seize the mines. This was not to the liking of either the miners or the owners, so they quickly agreed on a new contract. This was to be Lewis's last major strike and victory.

The imbroglio in the coal industry was only one of such that confronted Truman in 1949/50. In July 1949 a sticky impasse developed in the steel industry; it led to a strike, which contributed to a national recession. The steel dispute was not settled until November, after a great deal of work had been done by the administration. That fall, the aluminum industry was struck. Tricky negotiations between the Bell System and telephone workers consumed much of 1950. Moreover, trouble began to brew on the railroads in 1949, and in June 1950, five of them were struck. This led the president to seize the Chicago, Rock Island, and Pacific Railroad in July in a test of strength. The situation had gotten out of hand by August, however; therefore he seized all of the nation's railways in order to forestall strikes. The disputes between labor and management were not settled until May 1952, when the government returned the railways to private control. These were only the major labor troubles during the Eighty-first Congress. If there had been any chance for repeal of the Taft-Hartley Act during Truman's second term, industrial disputes had killed it after the spring of 1949.

These disputes put Truman and his chief negotiator, John R. Steelman, to great tests. There were times when the president was tempted to cry out against labor or management. He controlled himself, however, because he knew that antagonizing them with rhetoric would not hasten the settlement of industrial disputes, and it certainly would not enhance the chances for enactment of the Fair Deal program. Perhaps this strategy worked with the Eighty-first Congress, because it did not leave the administration empty-handed with regard to legislation that was of interest to labor. In October 1949 the legislators increased the minimum wage from forty to seventy-five cents an hour, expanded the number of employees covered by it, and strengthened safeguards against oppressive child labor. On October 26 Truman could rightly call this "a major victory in our fight to promote the general welfare of the people of the United States." He followed this up in 1950 by pressing for legislation to extend and increase unemployment insurance and Social Security benefits. Congress did not change the unemployment-insurance program. In August, Congress did, however, double old-age and survivors benefits, include 10 million more Americans under the Social Security program, and improve the provisions regarding children and the disabled. Both of these acts were a boon to labor and minority groups.

Truman had grandiose ideas about the development of natural resources. One problem was that he was not clear as to what these ideas involved; another was that whatever he proposed faced spirited opposition. On April 13, 1949, he asked Congress to establish a Columbia Valley Administration, patterned much after the controversial Tennessee Valley Authority. This was intended to be the first of many such regional planning measures centered on the development of water resources. What the president got instead was a record number of dams authorized for the West under the Flood Control Act of 1950, which, although it was acceptable to his administration, was not what he had envisioned. To the end of his presidency, Truman would continue to promote the idea of comprehensive, planned valley projects, but without success. Such legislation was never even reported out of committee in Congress. Mistakenly, Truman had taken his 1948 election victory in ten of the eleven western states as a mandate for valley projects. What happened was that the proposal of multifaceted projects gave rise to opposition from many sources across the country. As it turned out, those Americans who favored federal development of water resources in combination with economic and social planning constituted a small group indeed compared with those who were skeptical about one or more facets of such a program. A majority of those who asked who would profit from and who would control comprehensive valley projects came up with answers that were unsatisfactory to themselves. At the root of the opposition was the fear not only of faraway Washington but also of a fairly autonomous valley authority that would control too much and be insensitive to local interests. As a way to develop natural resources and the West, scattered federal dams were acceptable to the administration and to most of the opponents of valley projects. The dams were, however, anathema to conservationists, who saw them as destructive of the environment, and to others, who saw them as a federal subsidy to private interests who would profit from the distribution of their products. Thus, new impetus was given to the long struggle between conservationists and developmentalists.

In short, the Truman administration never consistently or cogently defined its energy policies, however keenly and comprehensively aware it was that there was an energy crisis in the offing. It achieved some notable things; for example, more generating capacity and transmission lines, as well as the electrification of almost all farms by 1953. Often enough, federal power policies, regardless of the form of energy involved, were subordinated to political concerns, because organized labor usually sided with the developmentalists, who not only offered juicy job opportunities but also were frequently powerful Democrats. Moreover, in most federal offices all the way up to the White House, the great god of economic growth—for the sake of prosperity and national security—counted for more than the often-local gods of conservationists. Then, too, pertinent federal agencies often worked at cross-purposes. Not being able to find a solid majority on what should be done, Truman endeavored to satisfy everyone, with predictably confusing results.

Personality also contributed to Truman's ambivalence on energy questions. He had resisted Secretary Harold L. Ickes's initiatives to develop a national policy, partly because he viewed it as a grab for power by the Interior Department and partly because of his apprehension of those whom he considered to be glib talkers in that agency. Spokesmen for other agencies concerned with energy, such as the Agriculture Department and the Army Corps of Engineers, encouraged the president's suspicions of the Interior Department, as did members of Congress who represented special resource interests. Truman was more comfortable with Interior Secretaries Julius Krug and Oscar Chapman, because they were more attuned than Ickes had been to the administration's policy of economic growth and its security concerns.

Some of Truman's appointments mirrored the interaction between personality and politics. In 1949 he nominated the veteran regulationist Leland Olds for another term as chairman of the Federal Power Commission (FPC), but conservatives and energy interests in the Senate blocked Olds's confirmation. Senator Robert S. Kerr of Oklahoma was one of the leaders in the fight to defeat Olds, which was not surprising, given Kerr's interests in natural gas and Olds's crucial position in having the FPC retain jurisdiction over the price of that commodity. Kerr tried to reverse the FPC's position through legislation. This bothered Truman, but in a rare advance commitment, he agreed to sign Kerr's natural-gas bill, if it passed and if certain improvements were made in it. This seemed a natural thing to do politically, for Kerr was a charmer and on crucial issues he usually supported the president. Moreover, Speaker Sam Rayburn, who was as friendly to natural-gas and oil interests as he was to Truman, fully backed the Oklahoma senator. Congress passed Kerr's bill in April 1950, by which time it had come under a great deal of criticism as being special-interest legislation sponsored by a senator who was financially interested in it. Truman was becoming more and more disturbed, and he called his key aides together to discuss whether he should stick to his promise to Kerr and Rayburn or whether he should veto the bill in the public interest. Eben Ayers wrote of his chief, ''I have never seen him more clearly troubled over a decision.''[10] When the president consulted Rayburn about his dilemma, Rayburn told him that it would take more than a veto of Kerr's bill to affect their relationship. That was enough for Truman. He directed his staff to prepare a veto message, which was sent to Congress on April 15, where it was sustained.

This was not the end of the matter, for in 1950 Truman appointed Mon Wallgren as chairman of the FPC. In 1951 the commission reversed its position on regulating the price of natural gas, and strangely enough, soon afterward the president's crony resigned his position. Truman, in his news conference of July 19, indicated that he did not see an anomaly between the FPC's reversal and his 1950 veto of the Kerr bill. This led to the questions of how clearly Truman understood issues relating to power and whether his comfort with men like Rayburn and Kerr had not led him to contradict his program. In this case, there was a happy ending for the avowedly regulationist administration, not that it deserved it. Consumer advocates, alarmed at the prospect of rapidly rising prices for natural gas, successfully carried the matter to the Supreme Court. The Court's decision compelled the FPC to reverse its own decision again and to resume its jurisdiction over the sales and pricing of natural gas to interstate pipeline companies.

Whatever the reasons and whatever the energy resource, the administration failed to devise a comprehensive policy for natural resources. The Interior Department's attempts to formulate and to administer such a policy were frustrated; the White House's initiative to deal broadly with the question—the establishment of the National

Security Resources Board in 1947—did not succeed; and congressional efforts—for example, by Senator Joseph C. O'Mahoney of Wyoming—to create a federal department of natural resources failed. Truman's problem was not a lack of concern for establishing a policy, one that would be fair and perceptive in both conserving and developing natural resources. His failure was that he could neither reconcile the many conflicting interests that were operating in the governmental and private sectors nor find a policy that he could stick to regardless of the opposition. The coming of the Korean War would change the drift of the nation's policies on resources, but it would not solve the problems connected with them.

Plainly, after his election in 1948, Truman had been too optimistic about what he could accomplish with Congress. He had gotten little of what he had requested in 1949, and even this basically amounted only to amendments to New Deal measures. It was also nip and tuck whether Congress would be as cooperative in 1950 on domestic matters. His use of persuasion, patronage and other favors, and appeals to party loyalty and the public interest had seldom been effective. The president's disappointment with Congress increased as the legislative branch proved, from his standpoint, to be almost constantly wayward. He eschewed campaigning over the country for public support; instead, he had decided by June 1949 to keep Congress in session as long as possible and to exert more personal pressure on the legislators. It meant grueling long days of work for him; it also meant a great deal of frustration, although in public he held out hope that Congress would eventually come around. Truman tried to relieve the strain by taking more short vacations. By April 1950 he was trying to curtail his schedule of appointments, complaining, "I just can't take it any more."[11]

In May 1949 Truman had decided to reduce the elements in his program that he would emphasize. Even he recognized that he had asked for more than he could reasonably expect. One of the most important cutbacks concerned the president's request for a tax increase in order to avoid a federal deficit. The opposition of the conservative Democratic-Republican coalition to surrendering the tax cuts achieved in 1948 was such that Truman had to rule out a tax increase in July. This was hard for him to swallow, and he became increasingly upset by the government's inability to balance the budget. During his October 20 news conference, he declared that he could not do "it without the cooperation of the other branches of the Government. There is nobody in the world, I am sure, who believes in economy more than I do. Nobody puts it into effect more effectively than I do." When asked if he was unhappy about deficit financing, he replied excitedly, "Who isn't unhappy about it? Who isn't unhappy about it? But it was brought about through no fault of the President.''

Truman's perturbation is understandable. Thanks to the 1948 tax cut, the federal deficit for fiscal year 1949 was $1,811 million, which was three times as much as he had earlier estimated. The estimate for fiscal year 1950, which he gave in January of that year, was even worse—a deficit of $5,534 million, which was more than six times what he had estimated a year earlier. His economies and those of Congress just could not match the decline in federal revenues resulting from the tax cuts. Complicating matters, of course, was the arrival of a recession in 1949. Unemployment had increased to 6.4 percent by July, and it grew to 7.6 percent in February 1950 before falling to 5.2 percent in June. The gross national product fell from $267 billion during the last quarter of 1948 to some $257 billion during the final quarter of 1949 before it began to rise again in 1950. Not surprisingly, gross private domestic investment declined by almost 28 percent in 1949, compared with 1948, before picking up again in 1950.

The result was a fiscal stand-off between Capitol Hill and the White House. It was clear to members of Congress that 1949 was no time to increase taxes. Just as plainly, Truman understood that it was no time to reduce the overall level of federal expenditures. The deficit would have to widen, as neither side would give way. About all that Truman was left with was the Hoover-like tactic of emphasizing the basic soundness of the economy. In his Midyear Economic Report of July 11, 1949, he said: ''The United States economy is the strongest and most productive the world has ever known. . . . We are now in a transition period, in which we must work toward conditions that will promote a more stable and enduring growth in production, employment, and purchasing power.''

Understandably, by 1949 Truman was relying more heavily on his Council of Economic Advisers (CEA), given that the majority of its members believed in economic growth. A report of the CEA later summed it up thus: ''In mid-1949, when pessimism threatened the business community, the Council of Economic Advisers maintained its confidence in the fundamental strength of the economic outlook. We recommended against drastic revisions in public policy to counteract the 'depression' which some thought was on the way.''[12] For political as well as economic reasons, this is what the president had wanted to hear. His reliance on the CEA increased after the dissenter on the council, Edwin G. Nourse, resigned in October. It increased even more after the prime champion of economic growth, Leon Keyserling, took Nourse's place as chairman in 1950. Soon Keyserling was a frequent participant in sessions of the cabinet and of the National Security Council, an unusual status for a CEA chairman.

Economic growth was now an integral part of administration policy, partly for its own attraction but also partly because national security became increasingly important with the coming of the Korean War in 1950. It is small wonder that there would be less concern about such things as conservation, business regulation, and social reforms. The gospel was that economic growth would lead to more jobs and higher wages, just as it would better enable the United States to defend itself. In order to achieve these things, other matters would have to give way. Although the Truman administration was the heir to the New Deal, its leaders came to believe that they could rely on a new prosperity to achieve the essential goals of valid Rooseveltian programs. The Truman presidency would represent a transition to the modern American state, just as the Eisenhower presidency would. The reasons were somewhat different, because the Eisenhower administration was the heir to Hoover's New Day of trickle-down prosperity and voluntary social action. Nevertheless, the basic mix of the two postwar administrations was not all that different, because both of them represented a commingling of the basic precepts of the New Day and the New Deal, a hooking up of the locomotive of prosperity to the day coaches of social welfare. And there seemed to be plenty of room to add Pullman accommodations for the *nouveaux riches*. Of course, the Truman administration would talk more about social welfare; the Eisenhower administration, more about free enterprise, and sincerely so. They would also talk a lot about liberalism and conservatism, without anyone's being very sure by then what those labels meant. The fact of the matter was that the Truman administration could not do without capitalistic growth to finance its goals, any more than the Eisenhower administration could do away with earlier social reforms and still sustain stability.

This did not mean that Truman had an easy time in achieving what he did accomplish. One index of this was his heavy reliance on his veto power. During the first session of the Eighty-first Congress, he vetoed thirty measures, which almost matched his earlier peak of thirty-three during the second session of the Seventy-ninth Congress. Most of his vetoes in 1949 pertained to the relief of individuals, cities, and businesses; and the rest were far from important or controversial on the national level. Congress succeeded in its sole attempt during 1949 to override a presidential veto, and that was of a private bill. During the second session of the Eighty-first Congress in 1950, Truman vetoed his record number of bills for any one session—forty. Again, most of these were private relief bills, but there were some outstanding exceptions.

Congress tried five times, twice successfully, to override the president's vetoes. One case, that of the Internal Security Act, will be dealt with later. The other case in which Congress overrode Truman concerned an increase in veterans benefits, to which the legislators would have been politically sensitive, just as the president was budgetarily sensitive. One of his vetoes that succeeded concerned amendments to the Nationality Act of 1940. This Truman had vetoed with regret, for the new legislation would have repealed the denial of citizenship to Asian immigrants. Unfortunately, it would also have categorically withheld or withdrawn citizenship from those of foreign birth who had belonged to so-called subversive organizations. His regret grew as Congress later passed the objectionable part of this legislation, over a veto, although it failed during his administration to enact again the section on Asian citizenship. The president's other important vetoes during 1950 concerned Senator Kerr's Natural Gas bill; legislation to reduce the political rights of civil servants and to open the way for congressional committees to obtain executive-branch records; and a bill to weaken the Federal Trade Commission's power to determine illegal price discrimination.

This last veto showed Truman's concern for antitrust issues. The administration had serious problems in containing monopolistic tendencies in a rapidly changing and expanding economy, although it tried hard. The government's efforts were bolstered by the Antimerger Amendment of 1950, which was championed by Senator Estes Kefauver of Tennessee and, especially, by Congressman Emanuel Celler of New York. Throughout his administration, Truman had staunchly though unsuccessfully supported antitrust legislation, just as he had vetoed several bills that would have whittled down the government's power to deal with monopolistic practices. He went out of his way to encourage Celler in formulating strong antimonopoly legislation. After long hours of debate and maneuvering in committee and on the floor, Congress finally passed the Celler-Kefauver bill in December 1950. This act forbade companies to buy the assets of their competitors. Thus a large loophole in the Clayton Antitrust Act of 1914 was plugged.

The Celler-Kefauver measure was possibly the most important antitrust legislation enacted during the seventy years since the passage of the Clayton Antitrust Act. Yet, as Congressman Celler commented, "this public law provided only one approach," which meant that the efforts of antimonopolists over the years had only been "partially rewarded."[13] As president, Truman did use other approaches in order to foster small business and to maintain competitiveness in trade. Among them were the administration's provisions for the wider distribution among businessmen of federal surplus property, contracts, subcontracts, loans, subsidies, and informational and instructional services. Through reorganizations and appointments, Truman generally increased the efficiency of federal regulatory commissions in coping with economic concentration. He also encouraged the Justice Department to take appropriate legal action, and he participated in creating the Small Defense Plants Administration to take care of the interests of small businesses during the Korean War. The president did all of these things not only because of his own experience as a small entrepreneur but also because of his convictions that economic concentration was inherently bad for society and that the promotion of small business was essential to the success of his policy of economic growth. Small business thrived during the Truman presidency, as the number of business concerns jumped from 1,909,000 to about 2,667,000 between 1945 and 1953, the largest proportionate increase since the 1870s; and the rate of business failures was the lowest recorded for any eight-year period in United States history. Yet the administration failed to reduce the level of the concentration of economic power in big business. The economic opportunities of the time and the government's policies that enhanced the growth of small business did the same for large business. As in so many other areas, the government found itself working at cross-purposes.

In this, Congress would contribute mightily. Congressman Richard Bolling of Missouri observed, "The conservatives in the Eighty-first Congress did not have the strength to undo the New Deal, but they could block Harry Truman's Fair Deal."[14] There was more to the story, however. Just as Democrats composed an important part of the conservative bloc, so liberals occasionally posed insuperable obstacles for the administration's legislative program. A prime example was Truman's proposal for federal aid to education. Early in 1949 the prospects for its enactment seemed good. Most southern legislators favored the legislation, and Robert A. Taft, the Senate's Republican leader, backed it. The measure offered per-pupil grants to the states; the states, if they so chose, could allot some of these funds even to parochial schools for textbooks and bus service. Unlike earlier proposals, the bill seemed to have something for everybody. The Cold War also served to soften the opposition. Illustrative of this was the testimony before Congress of Benjamin Fine, the influential education editor of the *New York Times*, that "perhaps education's greatest contribution to the national welfare at the moment is protection against the invasion of subversive ideologies."[15] All went well in the Senate, except for one matter. The National Association for the Advancement of Colored People tried to amend the bill to deny federal aid to states with segregated schools, but this move was defeated. It was, it seems, a matter of priorities. Senator

Hubert Humphrey of Minnesota pompously declared: "As much as I detest segregation, I love education more."[16] On May 5 the Senate passed the bill.

It was in the House that more trouble occurred. The appropriate education subcommittee, with North Carolina's Graham A. Barden serving as chairman, eliminated the provisions for equal allotment of funds to black and to white schools and for funds to parochial schools. Catholics fulminated, and civil-rights advocates shifted over to the opposition as a result. Francis Cardinal Spellman of New York called Barden a "new apostle of bigotry"; and when Eleanor Roosevelt defended Barden, Spellman attacked her as well. John Lesinski, chairman of the House Education and Labor Committee, promised that Barden's bill, which reeked of "bigotry and racial prejudice," would not be reported.[17] In 1949, with ample support from Majority Leader John McCormack and other Catholic Democrats, Lesinski was as good as his word. The situation did not improve in 1950 or during the rest of Truman's presidency. Moreover, if Congress would not act on federal aid to elementary and secondary schools, Truman could not hope to secure assistance for higher education, which was of less interest to the voters and to most members of Congress. It all pointed up the fragility of the Fair Deal coalition in Congress. A majority of the members of the House and the Senate could usually accept this or that part of Truman's Fair Deal program, but they could not stick together if the measure included something else that a significant number of them did not like. Whether so-called liberals or conservatives, the senators and representatives of Truman's time were masters of opposition, not of compromise, on domestic legislation. The conservative coalition of Democrats and Republicans was, to be sure, a potent force in blocking the Fair Deal; but it would not have been so successful if the liberals had been more adept at making concessions.

Another aspect of the frustration of the Fair Deal had little to do with who was liberal and who was conservative. Instead it boiled down to an institutional clash between the administration and Capitol Hill. Agricultural policy is a good example of something that was caught on the horns of this conflict. With the return of a Democratic Congress in 1949, machinery was set in motion to replace the Hope-Aiken Act of 1948. Congressional Democrats were eager to make changes, a rush to action that was spurred by a declining farm market in 1949. There was considerable variety in the positions taken by interested parties in congressional hearings and debates. Some wanted to refine the 1948 legislation, but far more wanted firmer price supports, and many demanded higher supports. There was also the attempt of Agriculture

Secretary Charles F. Brannan to take a fresh approach to the farm situation. In April 1949 he proposed making payments to farmers to bring their incomes up to stated levels while allowing agricultural products to find their own price levels in the free market. What he was requesting, in short, were federal subsidies to keep farm income high and consumer prices low. This was the essence of the Brannan Plan, which represented the most imaginative official approach to farm legislation in the two generations since 1933.

In detail, what Brannan proposed was to substitute an income-support standard for the parity formula, so that the government could make direct payments to farmers for perishable products when their prices fell significantly below parity. These products, which involved most farmers, would then be sold to consumers for whatever prices they could fetch. Other commodities would be supported at levels that the secretary determined to be fair. The government would give income supports only to family-sized farms and ranches, not to large commercial operations. The Brannan Plan was designed to guarantee that farm families would have adequate incomes, to reduce the temptation to produce surpluses, and to assure consumers that they would benefit from the lower prices that any surpluses would bring. Moreover, it was intended to eliminate special arrangements for politically powerful agricultural groups and hefty payments to large commercial operations. It would also help to save the family farm by shoring up its financial basis. And the secretary of agriculture estimated that all this could be accomplished at no more cost than had previously been attached to federal farm programs.

The Brannan Plan gave the nation an outstanding opportunity to stabilize traditional American agriculture. Even more than the 1948 Hope-Aiken Act, though, the Brannan Plan was politically unfeasible. Although it was an administration measure, it had not been fully discussed in all reaches of the Department of Agriculture, much less with farm and congressional leaders. The plan was alarming to a variety of interests. The growers of nonperishable crops, such as tobacco, would become second-class citizens under the Brannan Plan, and large commercial operations would be cut loose completely from the federal treasury. The bugbear of increased federal control of agriculture reared its head, and objections arose that the government would in effect be subsidizing food prices for consumers. There were also cries that the plan would eventually cost too much and that it provided no incentive for farmers to improve their operations. It is not surprising that Brannan was attacked both by the defenders of the Hope-Aiken Act and by those who wanted to return to the comfortable earlier New Deal formulas. Nor is it surprising that of the major farm organizations, only the Farmers Union, with which Brannan had close political ties, backed his plan.

Some Democratic congressmen nevertheless saw the Brannan Plan as a way to cement the alliance among labor, small farmers, consumers, and minority groups that had been instrumental in Truman's 1948 election victory. Consequently, in June 1949 the House Agriculture Committee approved a farm bill that incorporated many of the plan's features. In July some southern Democrats revolted, however, and they were quickly joined by Republicans and numerous other Democrats after various farm elements sharply criticized the Brannan Plan. On July 13 the House voted down its committee's bill. After this, and because of Senator Clinton P. Anderson's failure to support the proposals of his successor as agriculture secretary, the plan had no chance in the Senate. Congress soon took matters into its own hands and, in October, passed the Agricultural Act of 1949, which Truman approved without enthusiasm. The legislation provided for flexible price supports, but at higher levels, with extremely favorable stipulations for the most powerful blocs of producers of such commodities as cotton, tobacco, and wheat. Congress had played it safe with a patchwork measure that satisfied most farmers; but it was a compromise that was based more on politics than on economics, one that could do little to resolve long-range agricultural problems. Brannan and Truman prepared for a new fight in 1950, hoping to use declining farm prices to get legislative approval of part of the secretary's program. The administration's plans to make the Brannan Plan a major issue in the 1950 elections were thwarted by the coming of the Korean War, which brought prosperity to most farmers and focused the nation's attention on other issues.

Truman's Fair Deal had little chance of being enacted, for the deck was stacked against it. Faced with the lack of a solid liberal consensus among the public and members of Congress, the president set out to accomplish too much, with the result that he accomplished little. He did not, moreover, have enough tools to work with in order to persuade, reward, or threaten. And his plurality in 1948 was such that few representatives and senators believed that they owed him anything. Too often, those who supported him on one issue would be either lukewarm or in opposition on another. Truman could usually count on support from Speaker Rayburn and Majority Leader McCormack, but they often gave it gingerly because of the nature of their own constituencies and the conservatism of most committee chairmen in the House. Vice-President Barkley was in much the same position in the Senate, and Majority Leader Lucas and Majority Whip Francis J. Myers were often reluctant to use their influence in support of the administration's program. At one point in 1950, Truman exploded, saying that Lucas and Myers "do not have the guts of a gnat."[18]

In addition, too many members of Congress spoke for special interests. One example was the powerful Richard Russell, whom the president sarcastically called "the great Georgia Senator, representative of the National Chamber of Commerce, the Coca Cola Company etc."[19] Then, too, many of the denizens of Capitol Hill were genuinely independent. Truman complicated this problem by the great difficulty he had in reconciling himself to independence on the part of those who otherwise gave him considerable support—for example, Senator J. William Fulbright of Arkansas and his freshman colleagues Clinton P. Anderson of New Mexico, Paul H. Douglas of Illinois, and Estes Kefauver of Tennessee. Truman's critical attitude toward them thrust them off on even-more-independent courses. Truman's greatest ire was saved, though, for the most-senior members of Congress. He believed that the Twenty-second Amendment should have limited senators and representatives to twelve years of service, which "would prevent the focilization [sic] of the key Committees." He thought that the chairmen of the appropriations committees were "aged and decrepit men, who if they think at all think of the time Champ Clark was Speaker." Truman added that "there are old time Senators who even make Louis XIV of France and George I of England look like shining liberals." A limit on the years of congressional service would, he declared, "help cure senility and seniority—both terrible legislative diseases."[20]

The president was understandably frustrated with the Eighty-first Congress. In a speech on November 8, 1949, he said that "trying to make the 81st Congress perform is and has been worse than cussing the 80th." Truman heralded the end of the 1949 session by writing in his diary: "81st Congress quits after one hell of a session. The disappointed Republicans tried every strategy to ruin the session. Even the 'good' ones joined the Dixiecrats . . . to defeat a program." He added, "They failed."[21] Perhaps, but the president knew that he was in for serious trouble when many Republican legislators hooted and Democrats smirked when, in his State of the Union message of January 4, 1950, he insisted on the enactment of the Fair Deal. By May 1950 he was in a bitter mood when he talked to his news conference about congressional obstructionists who should be removed from office. He hoped to carry the country against them in the 1950 elections. Indeed, he made an initial sally against them during May in a railway tour of thirteen states. His trip seemed to have no significant political effect. By the time of the 1950 congressional campaigns, the issues were substantially different because of the war in Korea. The election results were not what Truman had hoped for. If the Fair Deal had little chance in the Eighty-first Congress, it was doomed in the Eighty-second.

There was, of course, more to the presidency than battles with Congress over programs. Staffing the administration was challenging. As already observed, there was a larger, though still token, number of blacks appointed to office. This was also true for women, as evidenced by the designations of veteran politicians Georgia Neese Clark as treasurer of the United States and India Edwards as executive director of the Democratic National Committee, socialite Perle Mesta as minister to Luxembourg, and seasoned official Anna Rosenberg, a Hungarian immigrant, as assistant secretary of defense. Truman had troubles with some of his appointments: for example, the Senate's rejection of Mon Wallgren and Leland Olds as chairmen, respectively, of the NSRB and the FPC, and the hounding of David Lilienthal from the chairmanship of the AEC. The president had much else to complain about. In February 1949 he told the directors of the Mutual Broadcasting System that it was difficult to get good people into government because of the pay and because they were subject to so much public abuse. And this was before McCarthyism got rolling. Then, members of Truman's party did not always cooperate. In June 1949 he complained that those who had been recommended for federal appointments by the New York City Democratic organization were, in Eben Ayers's words, "crooks and thugs." The president soon added that the nominees for the Court of Appeals in the District of Columbia were "scalawags."[22]

Yet Truman was usually successful in getting whom he wanted for his major appointments in 1949 and 1950. A prime example was Dean Acheson, who replaced George C. Marshall after the latter resigned as secretary of state in 1949. After James Forrestal left the secretaryship of defense for reasons of health that year, Truman nominated former Assistant Secretary of War Louis Johnson to succeed him. Soon Army Secretary Royall and Navy Secretary Sullivan departed. They were replaced, respectively, by Assistant Defense Secretary Gordon Gray and a seasoned public figure, Francis P. Matthews, both of whom were considered to be a notch above their predecessors. Better yet, in 1950, were Thomas K. Finletter, who took Stuart Symington's place as secretary of the air force, and George Marshall, who replaced Secretary of Defense Johnson. This same year, Budget Director Frank Pace, Jr., succeeded Gray at the Army Department. The Defense Department, therefore, underwent two shake-ups in 1949 and 1950.

There were two vacancies on the Supreme Court in 1949. Truman gave the first to Attorney General Tom Clark and the second to his old Senate friend Judge Sherman Minton. This would result in the Supreme

THE PRESIDENCY OF HARRY S. TRUMAN

Court's becoming a Truman Court, one that would usually uphold as constitutional whatever the executive branch and Congress did. Clark's nomination to the Court led to other high-level appointments. For attorney general, Truman chose the chairman of the Democratic National Committee, Senator J. Howard McGrath, who was to be a strong supporter of minority rights and the Fair Deal program at the Justice Department. McGrath's appointment marked the loss, however, of one of the president's most-ardent supporters in the Senate. Furthermore, McGrath's slowness in investigating charges of corruption would lead to his departure under fire from the attorney generalship in 1952. Truman named William M. Boyle, Jr., one of his former senatorial assistants and then executive vice-chairman of the Democratic National Committee, to replace McGrath as chairman of the committee in 1949. The president came to consider him as a perfect fit in the job, largely because Boyle did exactly what Truman wanted and did it well.

Two other major changes in 1949/50 came with the resignations of Interior Secretary Julius Krug and of Clark Clifford, the special counsel to the president. Krug's place was taken by Undersecretary Oscar Chapman, a stalwart Truman supporter who had been a senior officer in the Interior Department since 1933. Charles Murphy, a veteran congressional aide who had been on the White House staff since 1947, succeeded Clifford. Murphy would be effective as Truman's new righthand man, although he handled his work more as a committee chairman than as the star attraction among presidential aides. During the rest of his presidency, Truman would often consult with Clifford the private citizen, so Clifford was gone but not lost.

One of the problems that dogged Truman during his second term was what was increasingly called "the mess in Washington." Signs of this had been seen earlier in the public's interest in the indiscretions of White House physician Wallace Graham and, especially, of military aide Harry Vaughan. Truman had not been sensitive enough or else he had been too loyal to his friends, which marred the integrity of his administration. The year 1949 was a big one for Vaughan hunters. He was severely criticized for accepting a decoration from Juan Perón's Argentina, although he was only one of many other United States officers and officials who did so. Aggravating the situation was Truman's public response on February 22 to General Vaughan's antagonists that "any SOB who thinks he can cause" me to discharge someone "by some smart aleck statement over the air or in the paper, he has got another think coming."

More important was the news in June about people who claimed to be able to procure government contracts for their clients for a 5 percent commission. The Senate began to make investigations, and soon Vaughan's name surfaced in connection with the "5 percenters." After Vaughan explained to the White House staff that his involvement was innocent, Truman assured him that everybody was on his side. It soon turned out that Vaughan had accepted several supposedly experimental-model deep-freeze units as a courtesy, keeping one for himself and distributing the others to the White House lunchroom, Truman's home in Independence, Chief Justice Vinson, Treasury Secretary Snyder, Appointments Secretary Matthew Connelly, and Federal Reserve Board Governor Jake Vardaman. On August 1 the White House staff decided against issuing any public statement by Vaughan, because, as Eben Ayers said, "it would raise the devil." The heat of the Senate investigation was such by August 13 that this decision was reversed, and the White House issued a statement concerning the distribution of the deep-freeze units. What the statement did not deal with was the record of visits by James V. Hunt—allegedly a key figure among the "5 percenters"—to Vaughan, John R. Steelman, and Wallace Graham, which the rest of the White House staff had interpreted as showing, according to Ayers, "nothing wrong, though possibly unethical."[23] The Senate investigators did not find General Vaughan culpable of anything. His judgment was seriously questioned, however, as was the president's for keeping him on the staff. It is astonishing that Truman and his military aide never realized the harm that Vaughan's activities did to the administration by flawing its integrity, although other White House aides were sensitive to it.

The president found it convenient to chalk the criticisms of Vaughan up to character flaws in members of Congress and especially of the press. Truman had not been favorably impressed with the Fourth Estate during his first term, and he was downright cranky with the press during most of 1949 and 1950. Indeed, no single group irritated him more, because of its frequent criticism of the administration. Among his many fulminations against the press was this declaration in his diary in 1949: "[Drew] Pearson's no good. He, Fulton Lewis and Walter Winchell . . . are pathological liars par excellence."[24] Lest one think that the president was vexed only by the more-flamboyant and extreme journalists, keep in mind that his other targets included such elite figures as Arthur H. Sulzberger, David Lawrence, Doris Fleeson, Marquis Childs, and the Alsop brothers, whom Truman termed the "Sop sisters."[25] He even wrote a letter, which he did not send, to Walter Lippmann, the grand sage of press analysts, saying that he would do better work in a latrine than in an ivory tower. The hypersensitive Truman summed up his view of the press in a confidential note in 1950: "When newspapers stick to news and advertising they are excellent public servants. When they editorialize and let liars write editorials for them they are prostitutes of the public mind."[26] His antagonism neither escaped the press nor fostered good relations with it. And if anything, he would be even crankier with journalists during his last two years in office.

Truman suffered much frustration and vexation on domestic matters during 1949 and 1950. Yet, even with all that, it is plain that he had more success with the Eighty-first Congress than he had had with the two preceding congresses or would have with the Eighty-second Congress. The administration's legislative successes were not as far-reaching as they were hailed as being at the time, but they were not insignificant. Certainly, he had reason to take pride in the passage of the housing, minimum-wage, Social Security, and antimerger legislation, as well as the several economy and efficiency measures. What stung the president, his administration, and indeed the public were his losses. Little if any legislative success had been achieved on the administration's proposals regarding agriculture, civil rights, education, health care, labor, resource development, and taxes. In short, Congress had blocked the Fair Deal measures, those most identified with Truman, in part because he had not established priorities. Yet, by its own terms, what the administration would be most successful at were foreign and military affairs. Its activities there would be intrinsically important as well as play a great role in determining what could be achieved on the domestic front.

9

★ ★ ★ ★ ★

RAISING THE STAKES

The Truman administration's success with military and foreign-policy programs during the Eighty-first Congress reflected the persistence of the East-West war of nerves. The president made clear his foreign and military policies in his major addresses of January 1949. The nation's foreign policy, he said in his January 5 State of the Union message, was "to encourage free states and free peoples throughout the world, to aid the suffering and afflicted in foreign lands, and to strengthen democratic nations against aggression." Therefore, in his Budget Message to Congress on January 10, Truman asked for continuance of the European recovery program and aid to Greece, Turkey, Korea, and China, as well as consideration of military assistance to North Atlantic Treaty nations. He requested only enough for national defense to keep the armed forces roughly at their current strengths and to increase reserve forces by 17 percent. Despite serious international tensions, he did not see the need to rearm the United States significantly, although he was eager to help America's allies do so.

The president devoted his Inaugural Address of January 20 largely to foreign policy. He contrasted democracy with the "false philosophy" of communism, which holds that "man is so weak and inadequate that he is unable to govern himself, and therefore requires the rule of strong masters." He declared that "Democracy is based on the conviction that man has the moral and intellectual capacity, as well as the inalienable right, to govern himself with reason and justice." In the struggle between the two systems, he said, the "initiative is ours," because the

United States was striving for freedom, peace, prosperity, and justice. America's major courses of action to promote this work were, first, continued backing of the United Nations and, second, continued support for world economic recovery and the expansion of trade. Third, he requested expansion of collective defense arrangements, particularly among North Atlantic countries, in order to deter aggression. Fourth, he asserted, "we must embark on a bold new program for making the benefits of our scientific advances and industrial progress available for the improvement and growth of underdeveloped areas." This Point IV program, as it would come to be known, was intended to help the world's poorer countries to help themselves.

Truman's legislative requests on foreign policy sprang from his perception of the international scene. He was largely successful in securing congressional approval of his foreign-policy programs, because the legislators were more likely to share his views of the world than of the nation's needs. Repeatedly, Republicans and conservative Democrats, who opposed the president on domestic programs, would essentially go along with him on matters of foreign policy. Relations with Russia, as had been true since 1945, were at the core of the situation. The Soviets showed no sign of wanting to negotiate important differences with the West or of letting up on their pressure or propaganda. Given Communist activities and the secrecy that enshrouded the Kremlin, it was easy for Americans to ascribe all manner of evil to the Russian leadership. However much the United States was open to criticism during the Truman presidency, one must recognize that Soviet leaders refused to meet their American counterparts anywhere close to half way. If Americans were sometimes arrogant, unwise, and even delusional in their exercise of power, it is also arrogant, unwise, and delusional to suggest that they should have been much more understanding of the Russians than the Soviets were of Americans.

Even before 1949, negotiations between the United States and the USSR had become confined to minor, though pressing, issues. Negotiations on broader issues had been abandoned, thanks to Russian intransigence and an American sense of frustration. Truman summed up a widespread American view of the Soviet leadership when, on October 13, 1949, he told his news conference: "I don't think ethics has anything to do with communism. I know the Communists have no ethics." In speaking to newspaper editors on April 20, 1950, he asserted that Communists "systematically" used "deceit, distortion, and lies." The predominant conclusions in the United States were that communism was evil and monolithic and that one had to use strong measures in dealing with it. It was no accident that a military man, Gen. Walter

Bedell Smith, had been sent to Moscow as the United States ambassador in 1946 and that he was replaced in 1949 by Adm. Alan G. Kirk. Nor was it accidental that Truman refused to meet with Joseph Stalin unless Stalin would come to the United States; unless the president could set the stage for it, he did not intend to act in a drama of negotiation with the Soviet leader.

The Council of Foreign Ministers still met, but their negotiations had become fruitless exercises. Whatever small hopes the new secretary of state, Dean Acheson, might have had for using negotiation to crack the Russo-American stalemate would vanish during 1949. It was obvious that there could be no agreement on the futures of Germany and Korea. Separate governments, divided by the thirty-eighth parallel, had developed in Korea. There would be a similar situation in Germany in 1949 with the merger of the United States, British, and French zones of occupation into the Federal Republic of Germany and the emergence of the People's Republic of Germany in the Russian zone. That year the Soviets blocked agreement on a peace treaty with Austria. Nationalist forces in China were being routed, and Communist strength seemed to be on the rise in other parts of Asia, including Indonesia, the Philippines, Malaya, French Indo China, and Hyderabad in India. There was Communist agitation in Africa and South America, and Communist propaganda was appearing almost everywhere. The Russians seemed to be in full control in eastern Europe, except in Yugoslavia. Soviet adventurism was also continuing in Iran, and other parts of the Middle East appeared to be threatened. Although the United States exaggerated and misinterpreted much Communist activity, including ascribing it all to the Kremlin, the overall situation left abundant cause for alarm in Washington and the capitals of other non-Communist countries.

The most-immediate problem for the United States and its European friends was the continuance of the Soviet blockade of Berlin. By spring 1949 in was clear that the Western nations were not going either to leave Berlin or to give substantial concessions to Moscow on German questions. For example, despite the blockade, the Americans, British, French, and Germans forged ahead in establishing a West German government. By April the Soviet Union was indicating that it was about ready to lift the blockade, because it was no longer serving any purpose; by May the Russians had ended their restrictions on transportation and communications between Berlin and West Germany in exchange for a promise by its erstwhile Western Allies to discuss German issues. The analysis at this time by the American military governor, Gen. Lucius Clay, is interesting. He believed that the lifting of the blockade signified "a complete change in Soviet tactics to win Germany." The Russians would accept the new West German state, he argued, which they would try to convert into "a buffer state which if we tended to lessen our present efforts they could exploit by promises and other means." This meant that the West had to "continue with the type and kind of effort which has been so disastrous to communism in Europe during the past two years."[1]

Whether or not Clay's urging was needed, the Truman administration pressed forward with plans to cement West Germany to the Western alliance. In the meeting of the Council of Foreign Ministers in Paris during May and June 1949, Russia and the Western Allies were not able to agree as to how talks on Germany should proceed. Indeed, this was to be the last of such meetings, thus symbolizing the collapse of any hope for East-West negotiation of broad issues during the Truman administration. The Russians were now on the defensive in Germany, and the United States, Britain, and France were unwilling to grant concessions that would again allow the Soviets to veto developments in West Germany. The only choice that the Western Allies offered to the USSR was for its occupation zone to merge with the rest of Germany under the new Bonn Constitution, or to remain separate. As for Berlin, access rights to the city never were settled. One of the favorite pastimes of the Russians over the years would be to test the resolve of the Americans, British, and French to keep Berlin open to the West.

Events in Germany constituted just one item that reinforced the United States view that the Soviets were dangerous, untrustworthy, and incorrigible. The trial and conviction of Hungary's Joseph Cardinal Mindszenty on trumped-up charges in 1949 was another, one that led American Catholics to take a stiffer stand against anything that smacked of communism. During this year there was also the trial of Alger Hiss for perjury in connection with allegations that he had passed on secrets to the Russians. His trial made the year's most alarming news—the Soviet detonation of an atomic bomb—all the more ominous to most Americans. This not only contributed to heightening the nation's Red scare; it also spurred the administration and Congress to reassess the defense policies of the United States in 1949 and 1950. The result would lend support to the expansion of the nation's armed forces and of military aid abroad. Another important consequence was Truman's order, early in 1950, to the Atomic Energy Commission to continue working on nuclear weaponry, including the hydrogen bomb. The United States may have lost its monopoly of the atomic bomb, but it did not intend to lose its edge over the Russians in such devices. The horrifying nuclear-weapons race was on. The Americans had developed and tested the hydrogen bomb by November 1952, but it would not be long before the Soviets would follow suit. By then, however, the United States had begun work on atomic-powered submarines and aircraft, as well as on guided missiles.

One bit of good news in 1949, from Washington's standpoint, was the opening of a chink in the iron curtain. In 1948 Marshal Tito indicated that Yugoslavia would pursue its destinies independently of Moscow's wishes. Although initially suspicious, the Western Powers soon moved to encourage the split. As British Foreign Minister Ernest Bevin said, "Tito may be a scoundrel, but he's our scoundrel."[2] Trade relations between Yugoslavia and the West were resumed, and the United States did not oppose that independent Communist country's membership on the UN Security Council, although Russia fought it fiercely. More important was Truman's answer to a question at his December 22 news conference about whether America would oppose aggression aimed at Yugoslavia. "We are opposed to aggression against any country," he said, "no matter where situated." In 1950, on the president's motion, Congress gingerly extended famine relief to Tito's domain. The relationship between the two nations would have its ups and downs, but what was encouraging to many Americans was that one Communist country had detached itself from the Soviet sphere.

Events in China more than offset developments in Yugoslavia in bolstering American fears of Moscow and in spurring differences in policy. By November 1948 the success of Chinese Communist forces was such that the Central Intelligence Agency advised Truman: "The situation in China has deteriorated to the point where its stabilization by the Nationalist Government is considered to be out of the question."[3] In 1949 the president worked to scale down United States assistance to Nationalist China, and by April the navy was arranging for the evacuation of American citizens from China. Criticism of the administration grew, particularly from Republicans, for not giving stronger support to the Nationalists and for not following a bipartisan policy on China. Hints of conspiracy and Communist influence in government became common. The White House stood firm on its policy, however. Its intelligence sources indicated that additional aid to Nationalist China would be costly but ineffective, and it might lead to war for the United States.

Opponents of the administration interpreted the situation differently, and the debate over China occupied much of Washington's time during 1949 and 1950. Senator Arthur Vandenberg stated the Republican case in August 1949, when he wrote: "I think we virtually 'sold China down the river' at Yalta and Potsdam and in our subsequent official demands for coalition [between the Nationalists and] Communists. . . . We must *not* surrender the Far East to the Soviets."[4] As for what should be done, Herbert Hoover summed it up in December, after the Communist victory in mainland China. The United States "must continue to recognize and support the Nationalist Government," even extending its protection to Formosa, Japan, and the Philippines in order to maintain "a wall against Communism in the Pacific." The United States should also prevent Chinese diplomatic outposts from becoming "nests of Communist conspiracies," oppose Communist Chinese membership on the UN Security Council, and hope for a free China as "at least a symbol of resistance in South Eastern Asia."[5] It would be along these lines that debate on China would be conducted during the rest of the Truman administration.

The administration suffered much from the attacks of its opponents on the China question. Truman never conceded that he had not done everything possible to stabilize China, and he continued to follow policies that he considered to be dictated by his intelligence sources. After the fall of the Nationalists in December 1949, the administration granted some economic aid to Formosa, but it refused to offer defense assistance. And the government, in order carefully to avoid letting incidents involving Americans in Communist China get out of hand, ordered United States banks and citizens out of China and did not respond beyond issuing protests against the mistreatment of Americans. The administration went as far as to indicate that it was willing to deal with Communist China as it was with Yugoslavia, but Peking rejected this overture. Washington refused to recognize the new government and blocked its admission to the United Nations. The signing of a treaty of alliance by Russia and China guaranteed that the enmity between Peking and Washington would be of long duration.

While the Chinese Communists were entering the final stages of conquering their Nationalist foes, the policy of the United States toward the Soviet Union developed further. Part of this was rhetorical, as was exemplified by the heightened toughness of the president's statements. On April 6, 1949, Truman spoke to the new Democratic members of Congress. He declared that he did not again want to make the decision to use the atomic bomb, "but if it has to be made for the welfare of the United States, and the democracies of the world are at stake, I wouldn't hesitate to make it again." Truman occasionally showed flashes of optimism, indicating that the world was moving toward peace, however slowly. The way to promote this, he believed, was to show potential aggressors that America and its allies were strong. He said to the Veterans of Foreign Wars on August 22: "We are not arming ourselves and our friends to start a fight with anybody. We are building defenses so that we won't have to fight." Yet he wanted more than defenses. "I am sincerely hoping that eventually that war of nerves will end up in surrender," he told his September 1 news conference, "and that we will have peace in the world." When asked what he meant by "end up in surrender," he shot back: "Just what I said. I can't make it any plainer." In short, what Truman and most of his fellow citizens wanted was for the Russians to act according to an American scenario. It was plain that the "war of nerves" was working, though not with the results that the Soviets wanted. Instead of responding by giving concessions, the Americans and their European friends were contributing to the escalation of international tensions.

In 1949 the best example of this was the development of the North Atlantic Treaty, which marked the addition of the military containment of communism in western Europe to the policy of economic containment that was represented by the Marshall Plan. After all, if western-European nations could cooperate to achieve economic stability, there was no reason why they could not band together to improve their defenses. The principles for the North Atlantic Treaty and the probability of American participation in and funding for it had emerged in 1948. After the 1948 elections in the United States, the prospective signatories resumed their discussion of the treaty. Work on the treaty moved along rapidly, and its text was published on March 18, 1949. The document was signed in Washington on April 4 by representatives of Belgium, Britain, Canada, Denmark, France, Iceland, Italy, Luxembourg, the Netherlands, Norway, Portugal, and the United States.

The heart of the North Atlantic Treaty was the pledge of the signatory nations that an armed attack against any of them would be met by assistance from all of them in repelling the aggression. All agreed, too, to increase their ability to resist attack by means of individual and collective endeavors. There were also vows to foster economic development and the peaceful settlement of disputes, as well as to promote democracy, personal liberty, and the rule of law. In short, the treaty was more than a defense alliance. It was also an instrument to foster European cooperation in tackling a broad range of economic, political, and social problems. Among the European signatories, the treaty would take on life in promoting international economic agreements of great importance. These included, most immediately, the European Payments Union of 1950, to facilitate currency exchange and international payments, and the Coal and Steel Community of 1952, which evolved into the European Common Market.

Ratification of the North Atlantic Treaty came quickly, with Canada acting first on May 3 and Denmark, France, Italy, and Portugal last on

August 24. The Senate of the United States ratified the treaty, eight-two to thirteen, on July 21. The size of the majority and the speed with which it acted reflected the Senate's concern for shoring up western Europe's and, by extension, America's defenses against Russia. On July 25 President Truman hailed the Senate's action, saying, "This treaty is an historic step toward a world of peace, a free world, free from fear." "But," he cautioned, "it is only one step." This was true, for additional steps had to be taken to breathe life into the North Atlantic Treaty. Nevertheless the treaty was of signal importance historically, for its ratification meant that the United States had reversed its traditional policy of not entering into entangling peacetime alliances.

The North Atlantic alliance was to be entangling for America well beyond the commitments specified in the treaty. Scarcely had the document been ratified when Truman asked Congress to authorize funds to improve the defenses of America's allies, not only in Europe but elsewhere as well. For this the president requested $1.4 billion. This was much more controversial than the treaty itself. Words were open to interpretation, but cash and military equipment were tangible commitments: once given, they could not be recalled or reinterpreted. Moreover, as some opponents of the treaty had pointed out—Senator Robert Taft, for example—the Russians would probably respond by accelerating the war of nerves. If war did not seem likely as a consequence, progress toward peace was even less likely.

Fear of the Soviet response was not, however, a significant factor in the opposition to Truman's request for large-scale military aid to America's allies. Several other reasons came into play. Some of the treaty's supporters, such as Democratic Senator Paul Douglas, were alarmed by the size of the president's request, especially because there was no guarantee that the recipients of the aid would contribute their fair share of defense burdens. Senator Vandenberg had been a key leader in the movement to ratify the North Atlantic Treaty, but even he had reservations. He wrote to his wife after the treaty had been ratified: "How will it all work out? At best, it's a calculated risk." What most worried him was that "we are going to have a God-awful time with the implementing arms bill a little later." It turned out to be more "God-awful" and sooner than Vandenberg had imagined. Truman and the State Department did not take the trouble to consult very much with Congress. The result was that the president's proposal for arms assistance asked for too much, too soon, and with too little consultation. Vandenberg responded immediately. On July 25 he wrote: "I served blunt notice today that I simply would not support the present bill. It's almost unbelievable in its grant of unlimited power to the Chief

Executive. It would permit the President to sell, lease or give away anything we've got at any time to any country in any way he wishes. It would virtually make him the number one war lord of the earth."[6] Vandenberg was not alone in his views. There were plenty of Democratic and Republican senators who believed that Truman was asking for unlimited authority in connection with the North Atlantic Treaty arms-assistance program. It seemed to them, too, that he was being cavalier about bipartisanship and consultation with Congress in this matter. They intended to teach the president a lesson.

Why the administration's rush? Largely, it was because America's European allies and some elements in Washington wanted the North Atlantic Treaty to be backed up quickly with something substantial. This wish was based in part on the widespread conviction in western Europe that America's nuclear monopoly would not last long and that steps therefore had to be taken to bolster traditional defenses. There was also the worry, which the Truman administration shared, that after the end of the Berlin Blockade the Soviets would try something else to test the West. Truman and Secretary of State Acheson took the Senate's ratification of the North Atlantic Treaty as evidence that the Congress would follow through unhesitatingly in appropriating funds for military aid. They miscalculated. By failing to make key Democratic and Republican congressmen partners in taking the next step, the administration had unnecessarily courted trouble.

The House began hearings on the military-aid bill on July 28. The administration's witnesses—Acheson, Defense Secretary Johnson, Averell Harriman, George Marshall, and Omar Bradley, chairman of the Joint Chiefs of Staff—presented a solid front. They were, however, subjected to a steady stream of fire. Matters were even worse in the Senate, where Vandenberg rallied a majority of the members of the Foreign Relations and Military Affairs committees to his side. The senator did not want to defeat the measure, but he demanded that serious consideration be given to the level of funding, consultation with allies in formulating a plan of mutual aid, and limiting the president's authority in distributing military assistance. Vandenberg concluded that the "bill has got to be rewritten if any bill is to pass" during 1949. Confronted with strong opposition, the administration presented a new bill on August 5. There was no change in the amount of funds requested, but where the money would go was specified. The secretary of defense and the Joint Chiefs of Staff were also to be given roles in deciding what would be transferred from United States military stocks; checks were placed on transfers of money; and the bill conformed a bit more to the provisions of the North Atlantic Treaty. Although Vandenberg publicly complimented Acheson on the new measure, he exulted to Walter Lippmann, "We have killed the 'war lord bill.' "[7] Acheson was pleased that what President Truman wanted most, the $1.4 billion in military aid, seemed to have been saved.

Yet the struggle was far from over. The administration's critics, including Vandenberg, fought to reduce the level of funding and to increase the use of the treaty's planning procedures in shaping the military-assistance program. On August 16 the House voted to cut the authorization in half. With Vandenberg's guidance, the Senate on September 22 agreed to reduce the funds to $1 billion and to enhance the use of treaty processes in using the money. The military-assistance measure now went to a conference committee, but it went there unattended by Vandenberg, who returned to Michigan for much-needed medical attention. Indeed his efforts during the difficult battle over military assistance were his last in the Senate. Dying of cancer, he would not return to Capitol Hill except for a few brief visits before his death in 1951. Although the administration would not recognize it in 1949, they would miss Vandenberg sorely, for on this bill, as on so many others, it was he who had made it palatable to Congress. Truman and Acheson would have needed him in order to secure final approval of the revised military-assistance bill, except that the Russians came to the rescue. With Truman's announcement on September 23 that the Soviets had detonated an atomic bomb, the House-Senate conference committee readily agreed to accept the upper chamber's version of the military-assistance bill. The two houses soon concurred. The president signed the Mutual Defense Assistance Act on October 6. Thus, the next great step had been taken to make America's system of defense and alliance more effective. Truman also saw the measure as a way to allow the other North Atlantic nations to protect themselves from potential aggression and to develop their economies further. He suggested, too, that the growing strength of the United States and its allies would encourage the Soviet Union to negotiate its differences with the West.

The Mutual Defense Assistance Act of 1949 would be just one of many efforts to bolster the defenses of America and its allies throughout the world. For more than a generation, dollars, equipment, and military personnel would pour abroad in the cause of containing Communist expansion. To a considerable extent the military-aid programs served this purpose; but they served others purposes as well. They made a substantial contribution to the growth of technology, industry, and jobs. Abroad, the military-aid programs sometimes had similar effects in addition to strengthening the staying power of ruling elites. In some countries outside of Europe, moreover, American military assistance was significantly used to restrain popular challenges to existing regimes. It often gave United States leaders the power to direct what they—despite their talk of democracy—believed should happen in foreign countries for the best interests of the United States. Only occasionally did the recipients of United States military aid seriously disagree with Washington on international strategy, for fear of losing the Yankee bounty. Furthermore, the defenses erected outside of Europe were sometimes not enough to deter Communist initiatives, whereas they contributed to internal corruption and repression and constituted a steady drain on the American Treasury.

The problem for the next generation would not be so much with the basic United States strategy as with its implementation. There had been criticisms voiced during the structuring of America's aid and alliance policy, even by several of the program's architects. Some of these reservations were answered in the formulation of agreements, treaties, and legislation; but many were not, and for fairly clear reasons. One, the threats from Moscow and soon from Peking seemed to be too over-powering to permit a more-searching consideration of Washington's tactics. Two, United States leaders often trusted too much in their own abilities and good intentions to believe that serious excesses would occur. Three, they did not fully perceive the nature of the power that they held, the changes that had occurred in the world even since 1939, and what the future might bring. In other words, they believed that reason and their stronger allies would hold Washington in rein; that the thought of the pre–World War II period, when many of their percep-tions of the world were formed, was still largely valid; and that they could absorb new lessons, even though relevant ideas and data would accumulate more rapidly than ever before. And four, United States leaders were slow to understand that people elsewhere often did not think like they did, or even like each other on many issues.

This is not to say that the Russians or anyone else were any more perspicacious in formulating and pursuing their goals. In two qualities, Americans were notably deficient: these were patience and skepticism in reacting to new developments. Herbert Hoover, for one, often called for patience; but he, along with most other United States leaders, apparently defined it as a quality that lasted only for months instead of years. No one called for skepticism; that would have been un-American. Yet a healthy dose of it might have kept United States officials from overestimating their ability to solve problems quickly. Optimism, not skepticism, was the reigning American style. As Harry Truman told his news conference of May 4, 1950, he did not think that the situation with Russia was ''nearly so bad as it was in the first half of 1946. I think it is improving. Maybe I am an optimist, but I have to be, to be President of the United States."

By 1949 the consideration of extending anti-Communist defenses had become a constant pursuit of United States officials. Attention was being given to initiating the rearmament of Germany and Japan. Stronger ties were being sought with the Vatican, which seemed ideologically to be America's staunchest ally. The Truman administration encouraged economic cooperation between those two traditional antagonists, France and Germany. In order to bolster the monetary underpinning of anti-Communist economies, the decision was made in 1949 to have the United States dollar replace British sterling as the linchpin of world finance. There were those who pressed the administration to establish strong ties with Francisco Franco's Spain. Truman bridled against this when, in 1949, former Postmaster General James A. Farley, Francis Cardinal Spellman, and Senator Patrick McCarran sought to have a United States ambassador appointed to Madrid. Indeed, the president told his staff, "I think McCarren [sic] has been reached"; the president thought that Franco was as bad as Hitler and Mussolini.[8] By 1950, however, Congress had extended a loan to Spain, over Truman's opposition, and soon the president felt constrained to appoint an ambassador. By 1952, negotiations would begin for the establishment of United States naval bases in Spain.

There was also American concern for defeating Communist influences in labor unions abroad as well as at home. In 1950 William Benton of Connecticut, one of Dean Acheson's few strong supporters in the Senate, guided legislation through Congress, which provided that in purchasing material for foreign-assistance programs, preference be given to industries in which union leaders were not Communists. The Department of Labor, which would have strong backing from American unions, strove to establish the non-Communist International Confederation of Free Trade Unions. The Labor Department was dissatisfied with the flagging efforts of General MacArthur's headquarters in making trade unions "the mass vehicle for democracy in Japan [instead of] the spearhead of Communism," as Assistant Secretary John W. Gibson wrote in a secret report in 1949. The department assigned one of its aides to the Diet in Tokyo, so as to gain legislation that would pattern Japanese labor practices after the best in the United States. The Labor Department also devised propaganda tactics that would, without "making martyrs out of them," essentially eliminate Communists as an influence in Japan.[9] All of this fitted in well with the efforts of the Truman administration, as Assistant Secretary of Labor Philip M. Kaiser wrote, to develop "constructive bulwarks against Communism in Europe and in other parts of the world."[10]

Everything was complicated by the defeat of the Nationalist government in China in 1949. As a result of the Communist victory in mainland China, the Truman administration came under serious and long-lasting attack at home and seemed to be dithering in reassessing its policies in East Asia. Critics, largely Republicans, would have a field day in charging that the Communists had won in China because of the administration's policies. Such an allegation could not be rebutted easily in front of a large home audience that, since 1937, had been persuaded of the importance, integrity, and courage of the Chinese Nationalist regime. Many Americans thought that the Truman administration had been incredibly inept and perhaps had been influenced by American Communists and fellow travelers. Fortifying this were charges that the administration had been too much concerned with European affairs. Senator Robert A. Taft, for example, had said as early as 1948 that "the Far East is ultimately even more important to our future peace than is Europe."[11] Yet it is ironical that the critics of the administration's China policies rarely showed a willingness to be as generous in supporting anti-Communist forces in Asia as they were in aiding America's European allies. It is little wonder that the administration's leaders suspected the motives if not the intelligence of their critics on Asian matters.

Taft and others had no solution to the Chinese riddle. They did insist, however, that the United States yield no more ground in Asia, although they were seldom helpful in suggesting how this could be accomplished. The issue worried the administration, too, for it did not want Communist influence to spread in Asia. Yet this threat had been growing, as had purely nationalistic movements, since 1945, in Burma, French Indochina, Indonesia, Korea, Malaya, the Philippines, and parts of India. To provide substantial assistance to such areas was, however, beyond the capacity of the United States. The CIA had advised the president, as early as November 1948, that "action to protect US security interests in the Far East will for some time have to be confined largely to the peripheral areas."[12] In 1949 the Joint Chiefs of Staff (JCS) and General MacArthur described the American defensive perimeter in the Pacific as excluding Taiwan and the mainland of Asia. In January 1950 President Truman and Secretary of State Acheson separately reiterated this, as did Gen. Omar Bradley, chairman of the JCS, almost on the eve of the Korean War. It is little wonder that the administration's opponents would engage in a saturnalia of criticism soon afterwards.

The administration had endeavored to deal with its security interests in Asia in 1949 and 1950. On January 1, 1949, after the UN had reported that a lawful government had been created in the United States occupation zone, Truman extended diplomatic recognition to the new Republic of Korea. The government followed this up by providing economic and military aid to Korea, although it was far below the level of assistance supplied to western Europe, and Congress was slow in approving it. It is understandable that the administration did not take seriously the outcries from Capitol Hill for aid to East Asia, even more so when the congressional appropriations for China were rather paltry—$75 million in 1949.

Japan seemed secure under United States occupation. Yet the occupation was expensive, and by 1949, officials in Washington were considering the negotiation of a peace treaty with, as well as rearming, Japan. The Philippines were designated to receive aid under the Mutual Defense Assistance Act, which bolstered the regime there, as well as American security and trade interests. In the Netherlands East Indies, the Dutch had not been able to restore their authority, and this had led to the establishment of the Republic of Indonesia. The United States quickly extended recognition to the new nation in 1949 and granted a $100 million loan in 1950 in the hope that friendly relations would be established with President Achmed Sukarno's government, which followed an independent course. Burma isolated itself to a considerable extent from the rest of the world. As for India, its government under Jawaharlal Nehru was seldom unfriendly to the United States, Russia, or China. The Truman administration, instead of counting itself fortunate in this situation, felt aggrieved that India was not a bastion of Western interests in Asia. Truman was particularly disturbed by India's slowness to settle its dispute over Kashmir with Pakistan, which unsurprisingly became increasingly friendly toward America. By 1950 the president believed that Prime Minister Nehru was a "very subtle international crook."[13] Truman would not leave office feeling any better toward the Indian leader, who was fashioning an independent course for his nation. That was enough to earn Nehru a very hot place in Captain Harry's inferno.

The revolution against the French in Indochina was proceeding with some success, so much so that France granted a measure of governmental autonomy there. In 1949 and 1950, France established the states of Vietnam, Cambodia, and Laos, all as members of the Paris-dominated French Union. This did not stop the activities of Ho Chi Minh's rebel army, which was receiving aid from Russia and China. The establishment of Vietnam, Cambodia, and Laos did, however, lead the United States to add Indochina to its list of recipients of aid, in the hope that the transfer of authority to the new governments would be accelerated and that they would be effective in resisting insurgent forces. In May 1950 Truman approved the granting of $10 million worth of military assistance. The president's naval aide, Admiral Dennison, said that Truman believed that Indochina was a lost cause. If so, it raises the question as to why aid was extended. One can assume that it was to gratify the French and potential critics in Congress as well as to give credibility to United States security efforts elsewhere.

Developments in East Asia, especially the fall of the Nationalist Chinese government in December 1949, led to an intensive reassessment of United States policy. At the end of the year, the National Security Council (NSC) advised the president that the United States should meet apparent Communist threats by promoting stability and self-sufficiency in Asia and by the development of military strength in selected Asian countries. These were big words, but the NSC knew that the resources to back them up were limited. Consequently, it recommended that the United States (1) encourage the formation of mutual-aid associations of non-Communist Asian states, which America could later assist, if requested; (2) support "within our means" their resistance to external or internal Communist threats; and (3) encourage economic growth and trade liberalization, though without "assuming responsibility for the economic welfare and development of that continent." The NSC also urged the consideration of a peace treaty with Japan; assistance to Korea; continued recognition of the Chinese Nationalists, while exploiting rifts in the Communist world, including China, keeping it from obtaining strategic materials and equipment from abroad, and preventing, "through diplomatic and economic means," Communist China from taking over Taiwan. The NSC also recommended that the United States strengthen its position in Japan, the Ryukyus, and the Philippines; encourage the development of non-Communist native leadership in Indochina and the support of the Sukarno regime in Indonesia; use the British Commonwealth of Nations to collaborate in joint policies in Asia; and accelerate American propaganda efforts.[14] It was an ambitious program. The question was, Would it work?

The administration would also reconsider America's position vis-à-vis its Pacific dependencies, partly as a result of the Cold War. Alaska and Hawaii seldom presented problems, but Truman pressed Congress, unsuccessfully during his presidency, to admit them as states in order to bind them closer to the United States. This was related to the movement within the administration to grant greater rights to the smaller United States dependencies in the Pacific. In September 1945, Interior Secretary Harold Ickes proposed placing these areas under civilian jurisdiction under the authority of his department. The subject was referred for joint consideration to the War, State, Navy, and Interior departments, which failed to agree on a course of action. After touring the Pacific in 1947, Julius Krug, Ickes's successor, was highly critical of the paucity of individual rights on American–held islands under military governors. This was a condition, he told Truman, "which we would not tolerate on the mainland and would probably criticize if it existed under a foreign regime." Krug called for local self-government, civilian administration, and increased individual rights in United States dependencies, former Japanese mandates under the League of Nations, and even on American-occupied Okinawa, which might "serve as a spearhead of our way of life."[15]

In response to Krug, Truman directed the secretaries of war, state, the navy, and the interior to present him with an appropriate plan. All were agreed that something should be done. It was largely in the spirit, however, of what Secretary of State George Marshall said about Micronesia in 1947: "We must observe certain forms, but we must have . . . almost complete liberty of action."[16] There seemed to be a consensus in the government that there should be civil government and some rights for the inhabitants of Guam, Samoa, and the former Japanese mandates, the Trust Territory of the Pacific. Decision was delayed because of "obstruction to orderly planning," according to one presidential aide.[17] This situation revolved around questions—raised chiefly by the navy—as to when to implement civilian administration, how to maintain military security, and whether officers in the armed services should be civil governors.

As a consequence, it was not until 1949 that, at President Truman's insistence, the administration proposed organic legislation for congressional consideration and began to transfer the islands to civil administration. In 1950 and 1951 Guam, Samoa, and the Trust Territory came under civilian rule. Congress also extended some of the provisions of the Bill of Rights to the Guamanians; but the Samoans opposed such legislation for themselves, because it failed to protect their social and landholding institutions, questions that were not resolved until 1960. Yet the Guamanians and the Samoans enjoyed some self-government and rights, while the people of the Trust Territory only experienced the substitution of a civil governor for a military governor (and not even that on Eniwetok Atoll). Moreover, the navy continued to exercise considerable authority, controlling access to Guam and the Trust Territory through a stringent program of entry clearances. In the Trust Territory, on the initiative of the CIA, Saipan and Tinian were transferred back to the navy just before Truman left office in 1953. The fruits of change in the American Pacific were even more mixed, for the bright promise of civil rule, where it existed, was never fully achieved. The island peoples continued to be highly dependent upon the largess and dictates of Washington.

The Middle East also continued to be of concern to America in 1949 and 1950. Although Turkey had become a strong ally, the situation was otherwise unstable as new nations sought to establish themselves in the Middle East and as outside forces vied for influence throughout the area. Oil was a great attraction, as were the strategic possibilities of the region in serving as a bridge connecting Asia, Africa, and Europe. United States policy was to support existing regimes and to persuade them not to strike out against the administration's client state, Israel. It would be a difficult policy to pursue, given the weaknesses of many existing governments and the complications arising from the many sharply conflicting interests in the area. The United States rejected the alternative of ignoring developments there. This could only have led to increased violence in the Middle East, further Russian involvement, and greater endangerment of Israel; it could also have resulted in stopping the flow of oil to America and its allies as well as to restricting their markets and investment opportunities in the region. It is easy, in retrospect, to suggest that the actions of the Truman administration had troublesome consequences. Yet, in Washington's view at that time, any other policy would have been worse for American and even for Middle Eastern interests.

Therefore, during Truman's second term, the United States heightened its technical and military assistance to key Middle Eastern states, especially Israel and oil-rich Saudi Arabia. Lebanon was cultivated, for it seemed to be the model of what American leaders hoped would develop elsewhere in the region. There were also attempts to be even-handed between Arabs and Israelis. Symbolically, this was seen in Truman's announcement of January 31, 1949, that de jure recognition had been extended to Transjordania and Israel. Four days earlier he had asked Congress to contribute to a UN fund for the relief of Arab refugees from Palestine, partly out of concern for their plight and partly to placate the Arab states. Congress soon responded with an appropriation of $16 million. In 1950 the president requested and received an additional appropriation of more than $27 million for the UN's Palestinian refugee relief fund. The United States also encouraged the making of agreements between Israel and its neighbors, but this was a difficult task. None of the parties, including Israel, was prepared to make the necessary concessions to ensure peace in the area. Until the Egyptian-Israeli agreements that were encouraged by the Carter administration more than a quarter of a century later, this situation was not to change significantly.

Iran was a special case, as it had been since 1945. Increasingly, America had given military and economic aid to support the regime of the young shah, Reza Pahlavi. His government did respond, though shakily. Plainly at stake, given Soviet pressures and unrest in Iran, were the country's independence and the imperial regime's existence. America's interest in Iran and Reza Pahlavi was also clear. It appeared that only the shah could keep Russia out of Iran; a Russian-dominated Iran would form a strategic wedge between the Indian subcontinent and the Middle East, as well as provide an advanced base for Soviet aggrandizement in Africa; and the United States and its allies could not afford to lose Iranian oil and trading opportunities. There did not seem to be any acceptable alternative to backing the shah, a policy that appeared to be working out satisfactorily. If by 1950, from the Truman administration's viewpoint, things were not secure in the Middle East, at least they had not gotten out of hand.

The administration had its failures, of course. Congress was less responsive to the administration's requests for the United States to join with other nations in attacking problems other than military ones. In 1949 and 1950 Truman again asked Congress to authorize United States membership in the International Trade Organization (ITO) in order to establish and implement a code for world trade. Congress, spurred by economic interests that were fearful lest such an operation would adversely affect American trade, would have no part of the ITO. Another bit of legislative intransigence disturbed and even horrified many Americans. This concerned the refusal of the Senate Foreign Relations Committee to report out the UN convention outlawing genocide. Given the events of World War II and the slaughters that had occurred since then, it seemed inconceivable that the Senate would refuse to act, but refuse it did.

Considering the Truman administration's increasing concern over events in faraway places, it is surprising how its interest in Latin America dwindled after the signing of the Rio Pact of 1947. It was not just a matter of taking its neighbors in the Western Hemisphere for granted, although this was part of it. It also involved, as in the question of making a loan to Mexico's state-operated oil industry, United States resistance to supporting state enterprises instead of capitalistic ones; and as in the case of Brazil and several other Latin American countries, the fact that they were presenting Washington with unnecessarily extravagant shopping lists. The Communist threat to Latin America just was not great enough to encourage Washington to take much interest in its neighbors to the south. Moreover, there were serious Yankee suspicions about the reliability of many Latin American governments. As the CIA put it in October 1949, "A general state of political instability continues to be adverse to US interests in Hemisphere solidarity."[18] Although these attitudes would change a bit as a result of the Korean War, which, for example, led to the granting of the long-pending loan to Mexico, it was only a bit. Ironically, the biggest change in United States foreign policy was in regard to Argentina, and it came on the eve of the Korean War. The Truman administration had been unsympathetic to Argentina, thanks to Buenos Aires' lack of cooperation with the United States during World War II and the excesses of the postwar regime of Juan Perón. Many Americans came to believe, however, that Peronist Argentina, an increasingly valuable trading partner, could contribute to the grand coalition against communism. A quid pro quo arrangement was worked out so that by June 1950 Perón's government ratified the Rio Pact, and the Export-Import Bank extended a loan to Argentina. The lesson seemed obvious: the United States was getting less fastidious about the politics of its allies. Yet during the rest of the Truman presidency, Latin America would only occasionally share the bounty of the colossus of the North.

One new program of the administration did raise hopes in Latin America and elsewhere for more United States assistance. This was the Point IV, or Technical Assistance, Program unveiled in Harry Truman's 1949 Inaugural Address. The idea came from Ben Hardy, a public-affairs employee in the State Department. Hardy had not been able to persuade the department to accept his idea of exporting American technical knowledge to underdeveloped countries. He took his thought to George M. Elsey, who was coordinating the preparation of Truman's Inaugural Address. This idea is important, thought Elsey, and he discussed the idea with his boss, Clark Clifford, who in turn took it to the president, who accepted it. Thus Point IV, the most imaginative of the foreign-policy ideas of the Truman administration, was born. The new secretary of state, Dean Acheson, had the surprise of first hearing about it when Truman gave his address. Acheson's reaction was rather negative, as were those of many other State Department worthies, who did not see their organization as an action agency. Internecine battles took place within the administration for months after Truman enunciated the Point IV program. So it was not until June 24 that he asked Congress to authorize it in order to promote technical, scientific, managerial, and economic self-help programs in underdeveloped countries. He hoped that other technically advanced nations and the UN would launch similar efforts. The president requested a modest appropriation of $45

million from Congress, so that America could "move quickly to bring
. . . the promise of a better future through the democratic way of life."

Congress did not move quickly in considering Truman's proposal,
in part because the administration was not united in pressing for it. As
Dean Acheson later wrote laconically, "The State Department was slow
in realizing the importance of Point Four."[19] There were some enthusi-
asts, such as Henry G. Gomperts, an aide to Labor Secretary Maurice
Tobin, who declared that the program was "the most Christian and
enlightened example of the brotherhood of man we have seen in
centuries."[20] Few members of Congress were enthusiastic, however;
Point IV seemed too idealistic to many and an unnecessary expense to
others. Not surprisingly, Point IV wended its way but slowly through
Congress. It finally emerged as a part of the Foreign Economic Assistance Act of 1950, the chief purpose of which was to continue a variety of
other aid programs.

Truman signed this authorization on June 5, 1950, but the battle was
not over. Congress cut the funds for Point IV to $10 million, largely
because the program was not deemed to have any military value.
Alarmed, the president met with key senators and enlisted the assistance of Speaker Rayburn, writing him on August 25 that "I can
conceive of no more tragic blunder than to throw away this opportunity
of doing so much to strengthen the cause of freedom at such little cost."
Truman's intervention worked, as Congress finally appropriated $34.5
million. Unfortunately, Truman entrusted the administration of the
Technical Assistance Program to the State Department, which was slow
in implementing it. The program finally did get under way, however,
under the direction of Henry G. Bennett of the Oklahoma Agricultural
and Mechanical College. It faced many perils, despite the plaudits that
its work earned. Bennett died in an airplane crash in late 1951; the State
Department was feeble in its support; business and many foreign
governments were slow to cooperate; and Congress often sought to
restrict the program's funds, although by fiscal year 1953 they had
grown to $155 million. Point IV was a bright idea whose full potential for
cooperation among peoples was never reached, although components
of the program surfaced again in the Kennedy administration's Peace
Corps.

Other things were developing, however, that were more in tune
with the American fear of Communist aggrandizement and military
strength. Despite the efforts of President Truman and many members of
Congress to restrain defense expenditures, pressure grew to increase
them. Truman might put a tight lid on defense spending, and Senator
Taft, for example, might work hard to reduce military appropriations.

Nevertheless, there were many in the Pentagon and on Capitol Hill who would argue for increasing America's defense budget. Their arguments were usually clear. Each turn of the screw in the Cold War further justified the development of United States military power. It was all well and good to expand the defense capabilities of western-European countries, they contended, but inevitably this would require the commitment of additional American military personnel and equipment. Moreover, with the Communist victory on the mainland of China, they asked, was not the further deployment of the navy indicated? When the Russians shot down a United States plane, as happened in April 1950, did not this demonstrate the need for a stronger air force? As America's security concerns were girdling the globe, how could the nation meet its obligations with military forces that seemed scarcely adequate in 1948? It is not surprising, therefore, that the pressure was building for larger defense forces. Indeed a measure—however vexing—of Truman's impact in alerting the nation to what he perceived as the international Communist menace was that so many Americans questioned his policy of restraining the growth of the country's military forces.

Truman, in 1949 and 1950, yielded some ground. Given domestic pressures and world events, he could scarcely ignore all the cries of distress from the Pentagon and Congress. Therefore, although the president had requested about $10.3 billion for national defense for fiscal year 1949, the government wound up spending some $11.9 billion. He asked for $12.3 billion in new military appropriations for fiscal year 1950, but expenditures totaled about $12.4 billion. Trying to keep a tight rein on defense spending, Truman requested even less for fiscal year 1951— about $11.4 billion. The rub was, however, that the leaner his military budgets were, the more the proponents of a larger defense program worked to overthrow the administration's fiscal restraints.

Truman's considerable success in limiting military expenditures until the summer of 1950 was partly attributable to the support given to the policy by the Bureau of the Budget, under James Webb and later under Frank Pace, and by the new defense secretary, Louis Johnson. Also of assistance was legislation of August 1949 that strengthened the authority of the secretary of defense over the Departments of the Air Force, Army, and Navy. The administration also hoped that it would tighten control of the service departments by the replacement, in 1949, of Secretary Sullivan by Matthews at navy and of Royall by Gordon Gray at army; and in 1950, of Gray by Pace at army and of Stuart Symington by Thomas K. Finletter at the air force. Yet these appointments created problems of their own. Matthews turned out to be something of an advocate of preventive war; Gray was an unenthusiastic team player; Finletter was an ardent, though clever, advocate of a stronger air force; and Pace had not been long in his job before the Korean War broke out and a new era began.

Although Louis Johnson was quite successful in pursuing military economy, there were difficulties with his administration of the Defense Department. Truman's military aide, Gen. Harry Vaughan, said that Johnson was "the only bull I know who carries his own china shop around with him";[21] and for once, Vaughan was right. Secretary Johnson particularly involved the president in personnel controversies in the Defense Department. For example, matters got out of hand with Chief of Naval Operations Louis Denfeld, who, in a glare of publicity, was dimissed from his post for not cooperating fully in the defense unification program. Truman was also irritated by Johnson's opposition to the nomination of Thomas K. Finletter to be secretary of the air force in 1950. Indeed, Johnson threatened to resign, but the president's reaction was that he would appoint Finletter and that Johnson could quit if he wanted to.

There was a plethora of other issues connected with defense policies. Truman, thanks largely to his long service in the National Guard, entertained the illusion that reserve forces were a significant part of United States defenses. And there was abundant political support for this notion, because the National Guard had a strong lobby in Washington. The Selective Service System emerged as another strong lobby, with the reinstitution of conscription in 1948; and a rational case could be made for it as long as Americans were convinced of the need for a strong military force. Gen. Lewis B. Hershey, director of the Selective Service System, said in justifying his agency's work: "Recruiting cannot insure the armed forces sufficient numbers of acceptable men to maintain their authorized strengths."[22] This was true enough, as was his contention that the draft was vital to speedy mobilization (although some Americans had doubts as to how important this was in the age of the atomic bomb). Another factor in the nation's defense equation was United States assistance in developing the armed forces of its allies. Overall, the draft and foreign military assistance, if not the development of reserve forces, seemed to be reasonable and relatively inexpensive ways to maintain the defenses of the free world. There was, however, the growing question, if the threat was so grave, of whether more American military personnel, munitions, and equipment were needed in order to have an effective and reliable defense.

This question was at the heart of the occasional intransigence of the navy and the air force in regard to United States defense policy. It was not new in 1949 and 1950, for it had been a serious issue since the

Truman administration had begun to implement unification of and economy in the armed forces. The air force would not abandon its campaign to increase the number of its bomber groups and of its advanced-design long-range aircraft, such as the B-36 and the B-50. The navy saw this campaign as a threat to the use of ships as the nation's first line of defense and offense. Moreover, the senior service feared that the air force would take over naval and marine air components. Both services supported their positions not only by boasting of the superior potential of their equipment but also by denigrating each other. Perhaps more important was that the two services, along with the army, cried with alarm about the growing strength of Communist military forces. Secretary Stuart Symington usually stayed in line. On the eve of his departure from the air force on April 18, 1950, however, he could not resist the opportunity to assist his service. He asserted in a speech in San Francisco that the United States had no adequate defense against nuclear attack. Symington ringingly declared: "What is the advantage of a balanced budget if we—and what is more important our children—end up in the concentration camps of slave states."[23] This seemed to reflect the peculiar psychology—to paraphrase Henry Stimson's observation about the navy—that sometimes led the air force to retreat from logic into a distant world where Daedalus was god, Billy Mitchell his prophet, and the United States Air Force the only true church.

Even more strikingly, the navy went off on its own tangent. This came out in 1949 in what the press labeled as the revolt of the admirals. Capt. John G. Crommelin, who was attached to the Joint Chiefs of Staff, was the lead-off officer in this. He issued a press release on September 10, complaining that both the navy's morale and its offensive power were being destroyed. Secretary Matthews disciplined Crommelin by denying him promotion to deputy chief of naval personnel and transferring him from the JCS. In October, in appearances before the House Armed Services Committee, Chief of Naval Operations Denfeld criticized Defense Secretary Johnson for violating the spirit of the Unification Act, and Admirals Arthur W. Radford and Ralph A. Ofstie condemned air-force plans as being unsound and morally offensive. These and other incidents led to Denfeld's ouster and the reassignment of several other high-ranking naval officers. As such, these incidents marked the high point in a long chain of events that reflected the bitterness between the navy and the air force.

Funding was, of course, central to the internecine warfare that had broken out in the Pentagon. The economy program was bothersome enough, but the navy was sorely vexed when Congress increased the air force's allocations by $615 million above the president's budget recommendations for fiscal year 1950, although Truman impounded the funds. It was additionally disturbing when Finletter was appointed as secretary of the air force in 1950, for he was a strong advocate of increasing his service's budget. This not only kept the navy stirred up, but it also put Finletter on a collision course with Defense Secretary Johnson, who the new air-force secretary believed "was engaged in the economies of the armed services to an unnecessary degree."[24] Matters were further complicated by Johnson's tendency toward high-handedness. Yet, whatever Truman's favorable personal thoughts about Finletter, the president was determined to keep defense expenditures low. As he told the press on June 22, 1950, when asked about the continuing legislative pressure for a seventy-group air force, "We have given the Air Force all the groups for which the budget can meet the expense. . . . It doesn't make any difference how many groups are authorized [by Congress]."

All this was true. Moreover, the president had established a delicate balance in the management of the Pentagon by the spring of 1950. Johnson would do his bidding budgetarily. Yet, in Finletter, the air force had a secretary who could keep the advocates of air power happy; the navy, in Matthews, had one who could discipline the most-rambunctious admirals and yet please the others; and the army, in Pace, had a civilian head who would do what Truman wanted and yet seem amenable to advice from the generals. There were, however, undercurrents that could bring great changes in defense matters. For one, congressional advocates of larger appropriations for the air force might grow powerful enough to upset the balance that Truman had achieved. For another, some development on the international scene could create overwhelming sentiment to scrap Truman's plans. And for yet another, forces were gathering in the administration that could alter the president's military policies.

This last undercurrent became important by 1950, leading to the issuance of NSC 68. This policy document was the result of extensive deliberation by the National Security Council. Moreover, NSC 68 would become the blueprint for the long-term military policy of the United States. The NSC's staff, in March 1949, had circulated a paper urging larger military expenditures, strengthening the defenses of the Western world, and heightening propaganda efforts, among other measures. Opposition from the State Department, especially from Charles E. Bohlen and George F. Kennan, led this document to be dropped from the NSC's agenda on the grounds that the political and economic containment of Russia would work. Moreover, with Louis Johnson at the Defense Department, there continued to be great resistance to any policy that contemplated greater military appropriations. Nevertheless, many Americans had become increasingly nervous as a result of the Berlin Blockade, the Soviet possession of the atomic bomb, and the Communist victory in China; and there were no signs by 1950 that tensions were relaxing. There were also important shifts in personnel. Bohlen and Kennan departed from their positions early in 1950, and Leon Keyserling, the new chairman of the Council of Economic Advisers, saw defense spending as a way to spur economic growth. Furthermore, Charles Murphy, Clark Clifford's successor as counsel to the president, was ready to encourage ideas on a heightened United States military posture, which he and Clifford shared.

It was a delicate situation for Truman. He believed in the concept of having a lid on defense spending, but he had lost confidence in Keyserling's predecessor, Edwin G. Nourse, had become irritated with Defense Secretary Johnson, and was increasingly out of touch with James E. Webb after Webb had left the budget directorship to become undersecretary of state. Moreover, the more-defense-minded secretary of state, Dean Acheson, skillfully cultivated the president and often outmaneuvered his cabinet rival, Louis Johnson. Responding to Acheson's alarms, the Russian possession of the atomic bomb, and the problems in the Pentagon, Truman established an ad hoc State-Defense committee on January 31, 1950, to review the United States military situation. This committee reported in April. It made such a case for a build-up of United States military efforts that, despite Secretary Johnson's foot dragging, the top leadership of the Departments of Defense and State concurred in the report. Moreover, Charles Murphy was greatly impressed, and he recommended to Truman that the NSC take up the report. This was done by the NSC, which allowed Leon Keyserling into its ranks so that he had the opportunity to impress upon its members that increased defense spending would not hurt the economy. Out of these deliberations came NSC 68.

This document indicated that current United States policies could not meet the military, political, and socioeconomic challenges of the Soviet Union. NSC 68 also dismissed negotiation, isolationism, and preventive war as solutions to the war of nerves between Communist and free-world nations. No, the answer was "a more rapid build-up of political, economic, and military strength and thereby of confidence in the free world than is now contemplated." In the military realm this called for more-adequate defensive forces and the power to counterattack successfully if need be. This, in turn, required a "substantial increase" in military expenditures and assistance, some additional foreign economic aid, and the further development of intelligence, internal-security, civil-defense, propaganda, and covert- and psychological-warfare operations. The NSC concluded that the "program will be costly" but that the United States could afford it. Moreover, it "might not result in a real decrease in the standard of living, for the economic effects of the program might be to increase the gross national product by more than the amount being absorbed for additional military and foreign assistance purposes."[25] Acheson and company were not ones to dillydally, and the NSC had adopted the policy statement before the end of April had passed. Influenced by the flow of events and, especially, by expert advice, President Truman approved NSC 68.

Nothing came of NSC 68 immediately, however. The new policy needed additional discussion in administration circles, and its conclusions had to be sold to Congress and the public. It was, after all, a crash program, one that could substantially change American society. The coming of the Korean War would make it easier to implement the provisions of NSC 68. There was, however, a major problem with the catalyst of the conflict in Korea. If the Truman administration had concluded that the United States had cut back military expenditures too far, what they proposed preparing for in NSC 68 was a war that would be rather different from the one in Korea. No one had thought in terms of a small war! Nevertheless, Korea was used as the pretext for preparing for the possibility of a large war, with the hope that it would also prepare the free world for small wars too. As Army Secretary Frank Pace, Jr., put it later, "We didn't realize" after World War II that America's "international leadership was very likely to bring us into contact with problems we hadn't faced before. Whenever a war comes you've always cut back too far. Nobody is ever going to be ready for *any* kind of war . . . . once one come[s] you almost inevitably overorganize yourself for it."[26] This was true during the Korean War, and no small reason for it was the hold that NSC 68 had laid on United States policy makers.

It is not surprising that if the government became more agitated in conducting the Cold War by 1950, there would be those who would become increasingly interested in tightening up internal security. Similar fears fed both concerns. The internal-security situation had been touchy enough before 1949/50. The president's loyalty-security program of 1947, the heightened investigative efforts of federal agencies, and the inquisitorial activities of several congressional committees had not only responded to American fears of subversion but, in turn, had also reinforced them. By 1949 there were pressures from within the administration, particularly from the NSC and the Justice Department, to increase the government's internal-security efforts. Truman both resisted and encouraged these. On the one hand, he was concerned with demonstrating that his administration was maintaining the security of the state; on the other hand, he worried that hysteria over internal security might disrupt governmental operations and injure innocent people. Thus he could, at his news conference of March 3, 1949, call the leaders of the American Communist party "traitors" and, on June 9, declare that no one should be employed as a college instructor "who believes in the destruction of our form of government." On June 16 he could, however, indicate to the press that he opposed loyalty oaths for teachers, that the nation was going through a hysterical crisis like that of the time of the Alien and Sedition Acts of 1798. But more than just words was involved. The president fully supported the Justice Department's prosecution of top Communist leaders for violating legislation, such as the Smith Act of 1940, which was much like the old Sedition Act. Moreover, the work of his loyalty-security program increased. By March 1952, 20,733 federal employees had been investigated, of whom only 384 were discharged, although 2,490 left the government before the government had reviewed their cases.

The explosion of an atomic bomb by the Soviets and the fall of the Nationalists in China in 1949 increased American security concerns. Many Republicans raised the question of how these could have happened except through subversion. For them, this question seemed to be answered in January 1950. Then, former official Alger Hiss was convicted of perjury in denying that he had passed secrets to the Soviets; it was revealed that British scientist Klaus Fuchs had confessed that he had given atomic secrets to Russia; and there was the trial of Judith Coplon for stealing FBI documents. After Hiss had been convicted, Dean Acheson's comment that, out of Christian principles of friendship, "I do not intend to turn my back on Alger Hiss"[27] added fuel to the fire. Right-wing critics of the administration contended that this was conclusive evidence that the secretary of state (and hence the administration) was soft on communism. For the rest of Acheson's years in office, his antagonists would be unrelenting, which was ironical, for there were few who were so resolute in their opposition to communism as was Dean Acheson.

Some members of Congress exploited the issue of subversion to the hilt, most conspicuously a first-term Republican senator from Wisconsin, Joseph R. McCarthy. On February 9, 1950, in Wheeling, West Virginia, McCarthy charged that 205 members of the Communist party were employed by the State Department. The next day, in Salt Lake City, he declared that the number was 57, and the day after that he sent a telegram to the president, repeating his charges and demanding that something be done about the situation. On February 20 McCarthy announced in the Senate that he could document that 81 employees of the State Department were loyalty risks. The administration issued denials. Moreover, Truman's spokesmen in the Senate repeatedly demanded proof from McCarthy, who proved himself to be a master of evasion as well as of innuendo. Yet, many Americans took favorable notice of the Wisconsin senator's accusations.

Truman's first impulse was to answer McCarthy's telegram of February 11 by writing to tell him that never before had he "heard of a Senator trying to discredit his own Government before the world. . . . Your telegram . . . shows conclusively that you are not even fit to have a hand in the operation of the Government."²⁸ The president did not send this, contenting himself with public denials of the senator's charges. By March 30 Truman shifted to the tactic of trying to link McCarthy to Russia. He said to the press: "The greatest asset that the Kremlin has is Senator McCarthy," because McCarthy was trying to resurrect isolationism and, in order to do so, was "perfectly willing to sabotage the bipartisan foreign policy of the United States." By mid April, Truman was stressing the importance of maintaining and even expanding bipartisanship in foreign policy in an effort to recruit liberal and moderate Republicans in the administration's movement to isolate McCarthy. Truman's hope for support from fair-minded Republican senators was dashed by the timidity of most of them in the face of the aggressive tactics that were being used by McCarthy and his growing band of eager GOP followers.

Joseph McCarthy pushed ahead, making charges helter-skelter in the ever-brightening national limelight; while those whom he accused had no legal recourse available to them except to face him in a Senate hearing room, where he would be the grand inquisitor. This was no time for the administration to ease up on its internal-security activities, even if, as evidence of the time indicates, some White House aides considered doing so. McCarthy was winning the battle of the headlines, for no one could keep up with his bewildering number of charges or match him at innuendo. A subcommittee of the Senate Foreign Relations Committee, under the leadership of the conservative Democratic senator from Maryland, Millard E. Tydings, did try to investigate McCarthy's accusations. The White House viewed this as promising, for if Truman and Tydings agreed on any one thing, it was that McCarthy was a threat to the nation and to themselves.

Truman met with Tydings on April 28 to plan the discrediting of McCarthy by demonstrating that McCarthy had incomplete, outdated, garbled, and even stolen information. Senator Tydings was nervous about the undertaking, probably because he was better acquainted with his colleague from Wisconsin and was up for reelection that November. The White House staff was more optimistic, as reflected in Assistant Press Secretary Eben Ayers's comment that McCarthy "has already been pretty well discredited through failure to prove his accusations."[29] What Ayers overlooked was that what many Americans wanted were guarantees of the loyalty of officials in a time of crisis, not a finding that McCarthy's charges had not been proven. There was also a serious procedural problem in having the Foreign Relations Committee carry out the investigation: namely, that the president would not breach what he considered executive privilege by giving personnel files to the committee. Thus, Truman instructed the Loyalty Review Board to prepare a report, based on its review of the appropriate files, for the committee's use; later he allowed the subcommittee to inspect pertinent files that had been earlier examined by congressional committees. This was a boon to McCarthy, however, for it enabled him to declare that the subcommittee had not had full access to the files and therefore to infer that the administration had something to conceal. In order to ward off what Truman and the Justice Department regarded as being the greater evil—full congressional access to the government's investigative files— they had played into McCarthy's hands. The Tydings subcommittee cleared those in the State Department whom McCarthy had accused of having subversive links, and the Foreign Relations Committee adopted the subcommittee's report by a vote of nine-to-two. In July, Vice-President Barkley's ruling that the report could be filed without objection was challenged. The Senate rejected the challenge, but by a vote of only forty-five to thirty-seven. This showed that McCarthyism was a force to be reckoned with in the upper chamber. How much of a force, few could have predicted at that time.

The president meanwhile considered other ways to blunt McCarthyism. In 1948 and 1949 Truman's staff had been interested in having him ask Congress to create a blue-ribbon commission to probe the problem of loyalty in the federal government. The idea was raised again in May 1950, but Truman was unenthusiastic, despite Senator Tydings's and the White House staff's support of it. The president was optimistic that his and the Tydings subcommittee's refutations of McCarthy and his associates would succeed. To further this end, on June 27, the president gave a major address about the need to protect individual rights under the rule of law. His speech was too general to be interpreted as an attack on McCarthyism, and the news then of hostilities in Korea overshadowed his speech anyway. Truman's misreading of the internal-security problem as something that had been created solely by others, as something that he could handle with generalizations and routine political maneuvers, was confirmed the next day. Then he told his staff that he was "all hipped up over this abuse of power by men in public office." He added, "I sit and shiver at the thought of what could happen with some demagogue in this office I hold."[30]

The president could shiver for other reasons. In addition to McCarthy, there were those in Congress, both Democrats and Republicans, who sought harsh legislative solutions to problems of internal security. Such legislation had been proposed during the past several years. The administration, however, along with the Democratic leadership in Congress, had succeeded in defusing it. They would not succeed in doing so in 1950. As with other domestic policy and even foreign and military affairs, the coming of war in Korea would mark a major dividing point on questions of loyalty and security.

10

★ ★ ★ ★ ★

THE FOCUS SHIFTS

The outbreak of hostilities in Korea in June 1950 was a turning point both in the Truman presidency and in recent United States history. The general outlines of NSC 68 had been approved, but the policy had not yet been scheduled for implementation because of President Truman's reservations about its cost. It was the Korean War that would shift United States interest from developing Europe's defenses against Soviet aggrandizement to meeting Communist challenges everywhere. This was to be done, not within the confines of limited budgets, but on the basis of massive spending for military purposes at home and abroad. Accompanying this would be less concern for attacking domestic social problems and greater partisanship in all matters. The dreams of 1945—peace and prosperity—would now be largely pursued through war and preparations for war. This did not come about suddenly, for the United States had been approaching it step by step. What the war in Korea represented was the peak of American insecurity, of unity in regard to the danger of communism and of disagreement on how to deal with it. At last, the Cold War had become a hot war, and it seemed evident that more-militant policies were needed.

Korea was an outstanding test of United States foreign and military policy during the two decades after World War II. It was a surprising test, for no one anticipated that such a test would come on that distant peninsula. Americans could get agitated about China, but few considered Korea either important or a danger point. The Truman administration's exclusion of Taiwan from America's defense perimeter caused considerable debate, but Korea's exclusion passed almost unremarked. The United States had its policy toward Korea, and Washington assumed that it would work. This policy was to supply just enough economic and military aid to Western-oriented Christian President Syngman Rhee to establish a state in South Korea that could discourage Communist infiltration and agitation. Americans did not believe that the new Republic of Korea would be a target of invasion, partly because of the United Nations' role in its establishment, partly because of America's interest in it, and partly because South Korea did not seem to be worth taking. Indeed, the National Security Council consequently had paid little attention to Korea for more than a year before the clash of arms there.

Few Americans saw war coming anywhere during that spring of 1950; it appeared that the status quo would hold. Some dissenters anticipated a Communist Chinese attempt to conquer Taiwan, and a few—for example, Senator Millard Tydings—thought that the United States and Russia would come to blows. President Truman, mirroring the majority sentiment, answered Tydings's concern at his May 4 news conference, saying: "I think he is unduly alarmed. I think the situation now is not nearly so bad as it was in the first half of 1946. I think it is improving." This view was generally supported by military and intelligence officers. Moreover, with the possibility of the implementation of NSC 68 at hand, Truman's military advisers were not interested in piecemeal advances in funding that were occasioned by home-grown war scares. Indeed, in May the Joint Chiefs of Staff opposed a State Department proposal to increase military assistance to South Korea by $6 million, but Truman overruled them. One person, Herbert Hoover, was alarmed (perhaps he did not know about NSC 68): he thought that the military had gone soft on the Cold War. As the former president put it on June 12 to one of Gen. Douglas MacArthur's aides, "Have our top military officers gone crazy or gone cowards?"[1]

There were, of course, problems in Korea. For a year, North Korean military units had been crossing the border, as had South Korean patrols. This was generally interpreted as being one of the facets of the Cold War that one had to live with. Americans did not become interested in these crossings until after they had become more frequent, about June 18, and after there was word of extensive North Korean troop movements near the border. On June 24 the United States ambassador in Seoul, John Muccio, reported an all-out offensive from the north. Secretary of State Dean Acheson relayed the information to President Truman, who was in Independence and who approved of asking the UN Security Council to call for a cease-fire. Meanwhile, the news from Korea was becoming more and more disturbing. The troops of the Peoples Republic of Korea were outmanning, outgunning, and outmaneuvering those of South Korea. On June 25 Truman decided to return to Washington to meet with his top advisers that evening.

On the afternoon of the twenty-fifth the UN Security Council met to declare a breach of the peace and to order a cessation of hostilities and a withdrawal of the North Koreans to their side of the thirty-eighth parallel. The resolution carried, nine to nothing, with Yugoslavia abstaining and the Russian delegate boycotting the meeting because of the participation of the Nationalist Chinese representative. This last action is important, because it casts serious doubt on the then almost-universal American assumption that the Russians had motivated the North Korean attack. It is true that the Soviet Union had built up North Korean military strength, that there were Russian military advisers in North Korea, and that the Soviets would assist the North Koreans during the war; but there is no significant evidence that Moscow called for the attack, one for which the fervently nationalistic North Korean leaders were eager. If it is true that the attack was solely or largely a North Korean irredentist venture, it explains why the United States assumption that all that South Korea needed was a modicum of assistance was wrong. It shows that the joke circulating in the Pentagon during the early weeks of the war was unintentionally profound: Louis Johnson said that we could lick the Russians, but he didn't say anything about the North Koreans. In short, the Communist world was not as monolithic, as controlled by Moscow, as most Americans assumed then and for many years to come.

Harry Truman arrived in Washington at 7:15 P.M. on June 25, and Secretaries Acheson and Johnson met him. They drove to Blair House to have dinner with the service secretaries, the JCS, and other senior officials from the State and Defense departments. Truman's sense of crisis and action was strong, so he was open to a full and frank assessment of the situation in Korea. Everybody favored resisting the North Korean aggression, because it was seen as a Russian-inspired test of United States resolve. How to resist was another question, for no one was eager to commit American ground forces. The president authorized the supplying of South Korean forces with additional equipment, the evacuation of United States dependents from Korea, the dispatch of an American survey team to assess the military situation, and the sending of the Seventh Fleet to the Straits of Formosa. On June 26 Truman publicly warned that the United States was taking the aggression in Korea seriously. He added, "Wilful disregard of the obligation to keep the peace cannot be tolerated by nations that support the United Nations Charter.''

The situation in Korea worsened, and Truman had to make additional decisions, which he announced on June 27 after meeting with congressional leaders. One, he directed United States air and naval units to support South Korean forces; two, he ordered the Seventh Fleet to stop any attack on or from Taiwan; three, the government would furnish additional military aid to the Philippines and to Indochina; and, four, the United States would ask the Security Council to request members of the UN to assist South Korea in repelling aggression and in restoring order. This last the Security Council did, though it was again boycotted by Russia.

Endorsements began to come in soon, even from Republicans. Governor Dewey voiced his agreement with Truman's actions, saying that all Americans should back them. Senator Taft, although he was careful to note that the president had not consulted Congress, also offered his support. The 1936 Republican presidential nominee, Alfred M. Landon, indicated that he, too, wished that Truman would have consulted Congress. Nevertheless, he well summed up Truman's position as ''Look—we have tried everything to get along with you people— now you are looking for trouble and we are going to act.'' For this, Landon applauded ''the raw courage of the President.''[2] There were problems, however. It seemed difficult to get Defense Secretary Johnson to move quickly enough and to stop talking so much. Truman observed, ''If this keeps up, we're going to have a new secretary of defense.''[3] Another sign of trouble came when special emissary John Foster Dulles, after his return from Japan, talked to Truman on July 1. Dulles declared that General MacArthur should be recalled because of the poor coordination in his headquarters and because of the timidity of his staff, a view that was hardly confined to Dulles. The president said that he could not relieve the general because of the political repercussions that this would lead to at home.

Actually, whatever MacArthur's failings were otherwise, he had done what the president had wanted during the early days of the war. The general started the flow of military equipment to South Korean forces, facilitated the evacuation of United States civilians, and sent a first-class team of officers to appraise the situation in Korea. Indeed, on June 29 MacArthur went to the peninsula, where he was appalled by the inability of South Korean soldiers to resist the invading North Koreans. MacArthur nevertheless advised Washington that United States naval and air support would be enough to stem the Communist tide and that, contrary to instructions, he had authorized bombing missions north of the thirty-eighth parallel.

Truman and his advisers had hoped to avoid sending United States ground forces to Korea, although Dulles and American diplomats in Moscow urged that this be done. Not only did the administration want to hold down costs and casualties; it also wanted to avoid provoking the Russians and the Chinese to enter the conflict. That could, after all, have meant the beginning of World War III and disaster for all involved. Nevertheless, the administration was resolved by June 27 to keep the Republic of Korea from falling, which would represent a grand victory for Russia and its allies and could encourage them to engage in aggression elsewhere in the world. The administration did not seriously consider any alternative to protecting South Korea, although it feared that substantial United States involvement there might lead to a Soviet invasion of western Europe.

By June 29, word from Moscow that the Soviet Union would not enter the conflict encouraged optimism in Washington. Secretary of State Acheson indicated his approval of bombing North Korea and, if necessary, of using ground forces. Defense Secretary Johnson and the JCS accepted the idea of creating a United States beachhead in Korea, though only for the purpose of evacuating Americans. Consequently, President Truman authorized MacArthur to send troops to secure port and air-base facilities in South Korea, to schedule bombings in the north, but to initiate no action close to the Chinese and Russian borders. MacArthur, meanwhile, had changed his mind about committing United States ground forces to battle. He asked that a regimental combat team be dispatched to Korea immediately and, as soon as possible thereafter, two divisions. This request reached Truman at 5 A.M. on June 30. Although the president did not want to make a decision immediately, he did so when Secretary of the Army Frank Pace, Jr., told him that MacArthur believed that the situation did not permit of delay. Truman then authorized the use of a regimental combat team. At 8:30 A.M. he met with his major military and foreign-policy advisers to consider sending two American divisions and accepting Nationalist China's offer of two divisions. It was agreed to send all United States troops that were needed, but Dean Acheson successfully opposed the introduction of the Nationalist Chinese, because that might provoke the Chinese Communists to attack either Korea or Taiwan. The JCS supported him, indicating that it would be a poor use of United States transport to ship Nationalist troops, in whose ability they had little faith anyway. (Moreover, it could have been said that Syngman Rhee did not want any Chinese in Korea, for fear they would not leave.)

Thus the die was cast. Believing that the non-Communist world might be confronted by the start of the Kremlin's attack by force, the administration had decided, in implementing its containment policy, to use force in Korea. The administration would soon prepare to do likewise elsewhere, if called upon to do so. Truman had not, however, cast restraint to the winds. This was shown in his diary entry of June 30: "Must be careful not to cause a general Asiatic war. Russia is figuring on an attack in the Black Sea and toward the Persian Gulf."[4] Truman would continue to be guided by the conviction that the Soviet Union had to be kept out of the Korean War in order to prevent the conflict from developing into a third world war.

Authorizing United States troops to fight in Korea was one thing; making the decision effective was another. Early in the war, United States air and naval forces helped to slow down the North Korean attack, but they could not stop it. Despite their effectiveness, they were under strength. The army was in worse condition. MacArthur had no regimental combat team on hand, the closest one being in Hawaii. The best he could do immediately was to send a makeshift infantry battalion into combat. All that this Task Force Smith, as it was called, could do was to engage in delaying actions while other American units trickled into Korea and set up defensive positions against the enemy. Plainly, the Americans were playing against time, hoping that they could muster enough troops in Korea to stop the North Koreans from occupying the entire peninsula. Unit after unit, under strength or brought up to minimum strength by cannibalizing other outfits, joined the struggle. First came the Twenty-fourth Division, whose commander, Maj. Gen. William F. Dean, was captured in combat on July 21. Then came the Twenty-fifth and the First cavalry divisions. Efforts were undertaken to make South Korean troops, now down to five divisions, more effective in battle. Sea and air units of some other members of the UN arrived. Still, the North Koreans advanced. Taejon fell on July 20 and Chinju on July 29. The United States commander in Korea, Lt. Gen. Walton H. Walker, declared: "There will be no more retreating! . . . We are going to win!"[5] By August 2, with the arrival of the Second Division, the Fifth Regimental Combat Team, the First Provisional Marine Brigade, and the British Twenty-seventh Brigade, Walker had the strength to give meaning to his words. The UN troops soon were able to establish the Pusan perimeter, a small boxlike area in southeastern Korea of some 3,500 square miles. This marked the end of the advance of the North Korean Army. From this enlarged beachhead, Walker's forces would hold the enemy at bay until MacArthur put into effect a plan to counterattack.

While Walker's men were fighting in Korea, the president had problems of his own in Washington. Pressure was being created on Truman from Congress and within his administration to seek congressional authorization of what he had done. He charged Dean Acheson with preparing a report on this matter. On July 3 the secretary of state recommended that the president should report to a joint session of Congress on the situation, but for his authority to act in Korea, he should rely on his constitutional position as commander in chief. Truman decided not to approach Congress, which had just recessed for a week. He believed that most senators and representatives were satisfied with his actions and that a tardy request for a resolution would probably stir up much unnecessary debate. He was probably correct at the time; but there is much to be said for the argument that in late June he should have asked for a congressional resolution granting him authority. This probably would have been granted quickly, and it would have muted the oft-repeated later charges that he had not sufficiently consulted Congress, that the conflict in Korea was Mr. Truman's war. Although minor at the time, it was enough of a worry that he decided on July 17 to deliver an address to a joint session of Congress, which would be carried by the radio and television networks. In this speech of July 19, Truman meticulously outlined the causes of the conflict and the steps that had been taken to deal with it. The president declared that the situation not only called for supplying the men and material needed for victory in Korea but also for developing the military strength of the United States and its allies.

One of the administration's objectives was to ensure that the United Nations be involved in the prosecution of the Korean conflict in fact as well as in principle. On July 7 the Security Council voted to designate a commander for UN forces in Korea and to authorize them to fight under the UN flag. Truman named General MacArthur to be commander of these forces, at the Security Council's request. By July 19 Australia, Great Britain, Canada, France, the Netherlands, and New Zealand had dispatched men and equipment to Korea. Nine other countries had already sent or were sending military forces by the end of 1950, and fifteen others were contributing to civilian relief in Korea. Many Americans were not impressed with these efforts, however. The Truman administration consequently drew repeated fire from its domestic critics for the huge share of the burden that the United States carried in Korea and for the price that the nation paid in giving assistance to those who did participate.

The administration tried, for example, to secure Latin American support for the war in Korea, but it received little beyond endorsements of the UN's actions. Only Colombia made a significant military contribution. What the United States offered in return for their assistance was never enough as far as the Latin Americans were concerned, and this was usually hedged with restrictions, which they often believed were insulting. Most Latin American countries had supported the United States during World War II, but they had received few benefits as a result. While the United States had given Europe and even parts of Asia substantial aid, little had been given to Latin America. Brazil is a good example. From 1946 to 1949 the Export-Import Bank extended $105 million in loans to Brazil, which was urged to seek private investments. Undeterred, in 1949 Brazil requested $100 million annually for the next six years. What it received for 1949 was $14.5 million, a reminder about past loans, and the advice that Brazil was benefiting from purchases stimulated by Marshall Plan aid elsewhere. In 1950 the situation was complicated by Brazil's unfavorable reaction to the $125 million loan granted to Argentina, a country that had not helped the United States. With the coming of the Korean War, Washington pressed Brazil for troops and approved a $25 million loan. Brazil was not impressed, and the two nations began negotiations to arrange something more. Indeed, there was talk of providing $350 million in loans and of giving Brazil two cruisers that it had requested. The cruisers were transferred, but the edge was taken off this by the United States' bargain sale of two cruisers to Argentina. Relations became delicate as negotiations continued. The upshot was that the United States lent little more to Brazil, which in turn never did send fighting forces to Korea.

Much the same thing happened in the relations between the United States and most other Latin American nations during the Korean War. These countries were vexed by what they considered to be Uncle Sam's high-handedness in telling them what to do and its tight-fistedness in helping them do it. The Truman administration was irritated, too, by what it considered the selfishness of so many of its neighbors to the south when the United States was carrying so many burdens. The nation, as the administration saw it, could only carry so many relief clients, and Latin America was neither among the most needy nor among the most deserving. Moreover, of all areas it should be as eager as the United States to thwart the international menace of communism. Plainly, Washington was not receiving the message that Latin America was sending to it: if it wanted cooperation, it would have to pay for it; if it wanted respect, it would have to be more sensitive to Latin American aspirations. The Truman administration was unprepared to do either of these things. The result was that Latin America gave the United States little cooperation and respect and that Washington grumbled unreasonably about it. In short, the United States believed that it could not get along without Latin America, and it could not get along with Latin America. It chose a dithering middle way, which did neither itself nor Latin America much good in the long run.

There were questions as to what sort of conflict Korea represented. President Truman declared, in his news conference of June 29, "We are not at war." It was a case of the nation, as a member of the UN, "going to the relief of the Korean Republic to suppress a bandit raid." When a reporter asked if it would be correct to term it "a police action under the United Nations?" Truman agreed, which hence became the official name of the war. This labeling had the advantage of pointing up that this was a UN action, not the result of a declaration of war by the United States. All this was good and fine, but the Korean conflict was a war in every way for the United States, except that it was being fought under the auspices of the UN at Truman's request. It is, therefore, little wonder that Senator Taft's charge that this was Truman's war became increasingly effective as time passed. Yet the president acted within his constitutional rights in asking the Security Council to deal with aggression in Korea, just as the Security Council acted legally in doing what it did. Nor is there any legal question that Truman could respond in the way that he did to the Security Council's call for assistance in Korea. After all, the Senate had ratified the Charter of the UN, which legitimized the process; and Truman, as commander in chief, had the constitutional power to respond to the Security Council's call. And Congress, in effect, gave the president what he requested in order to meet the challenge in Korea. The real question was whether it was politic for Truman not to ask for a congressional resolution authorizing his actions. He had calculated the odds and had concluded that it was best not to risk lengthy congressional debate when rapid action seemed so clearly to be needed. If the conflict in Korea had been ended successfully in a matter of months, Truman's calculation of the odds would have been correct; but the war stretched out for more than three years, and his administration consequently was to pay a heavy political price.

Questions also arose about using the atomic bomb and pushing beyond the thirty-eighth parallel to conquer North Korea. The president was not publicly forthcoming on these initially, refusing to comment on the first and saying no on the second. Both courses of action were discussed in the highest circles, however, and neither was ruled out. The administration was clearly trying to keep its freedom of action to meet situations as they developed, although without unduly alarming Americans. Nevertheless, a scare emerged across the country, during the summer of 1950, that the United States might be on the verge of undergoing an atomic attack by the Soviet Union. Truman strove to counteract this by making frequent optimistic statements about confining the conflict to Korea and winning there.

Meanwhile, the administration began to mobilize the country for war. Draft calls were accelerated, and some National Guard and reserve units were called to duty. In July, August, and September, Truman asked Congress for a variety of war-related pieces of legislation. In addition to funds for the prosecution of the Korean War, his requests also concerned allocations for atomic research, propaganda, foreign military assistance, Point IV, and civilian defense, as well as higher taxes. Congress generally proved to be responsive. In July, Truman also proposed measures to boost war production, which led to the Defense Production Act. He intentionally eschewed asking for stand-by price, rationing, and wage controls in order to expedite the passage of this legislation. Ironically, many members of Congress showed more interest in authorizing controls than in facilitating war production. Therefore, on August 18 the president felt compelled to communicate his concern that Congress might deliver the cart instead of the horse. Early in September, Congress responded by passing the Defense Production Act, which supplied incentives to business to increase defense production, gave war orders top priority, reduced the production of civilian goods, and authorized the stabilization of prices and wages.

The Defense Production Act was the domestic cornerstone of Truman's war policy. On September 9 he took to radio and television to explain what the legislation meant. It meant no less than doubling defense expenditures by the United States in one year, from $15 billion to $30 billion, and probably even more later. It also meant sacrifices in terms of higher taxes, harder work, fewer civilian commodities, wage and price restraints, consumer-credit restrictions, and, by implication, fewer new social programs. Yet it was all in a just cause, to "convince the Communist leaders that aggression will not pay." And the act would have the advantage of creating additional jobs. Truman also announced that within the administration, responsibilities had been assigned to carry out the purposes of the new law.

This governmental activity was impressive, but there were serious problems to be considered. As the Council of Economic Advisers reported in late September, these things were being done "in the face of a situation changing so rapidly that it has been hard to stand upon firm ground in recommending new policies."[6] The gross national product, employment, prices, profits, and wages had risen. The increases in the first two categories were gratifying; but the rises in prices, profits, and wages were alarming, because of the specter of inflation and the fact that increased civilian purchases could lead to shortages. There was disagreement within the administration and Congress on what policies to adopt. Congress gave the president the higher taxes that he wanted, but it also created loopholes for evading the payment of them. There were those, such as Stuart Symington of the National Security Resources Board and Senator J. William Fulbright, who wanted stricter controls of prices and incomes. Truman feared, however, that the country was not ready for them; he believed that higher taxes and credit restrictions would be more effective in restraining inflation. The discussion of these and other issues would be complicated by the unanswerable questions of how long the war would last and how much it would cost.

If there was no significant disagreement on greatly expanding the defense strength of the United States and military assistance to its allies, there was resistance, especially from the Defense Department, to substantially enlarging the economy. The fear was that an artificially expanding economy might put everything out of joint. Truman accepted the urging of the Council of Economic Advisers for further economic growth, a policy that the administration followed with great success until the last stages of the war. The result was a large increase in productivity (with relatively few civilian shortages); the virtual elimination of unemployment; generally increased income; and a rise in federal revenues that almost paid for the cost of the war. There was, however, another problem that alarmed the former small businessman and antimonopolistic senator who was now the president. As Truman put it, this was the "danger to free competitive enterprise" of a war acceleration of economic concentration. On September 28, he ordered fourteen major federal agencies to use their power to combat this, though "without impairing the defense effort."[7] The resultant efforts were generally successful, especially the administration's work to favor subcontractors in the defense industry.

The Korean conflict also offered opportunities for stepping up the implementation of United States foreign policy as it had been developing since 1947. The pervasiveness of the desire within the Truman administration to do this was demonstrated in a secret letter, written in January 1951, by Assistant Labor Secretary Philip M. Kaiser to Secretary Maurice J. Tobin: "A primary objective of United States foreign policy is to mobilize and gird ourselves and our allies to meet the threat of military aggression. A second objective, which is essential to achieving the first, is to strengthen our bonds with other democratic nations so that they may be in a position both physically and psychologically to assist us in meeting the threat of communist aggression." From this communication, much can be drawn about the thinking of the administration and even of the American people at the time. It was commonly believed that there was a serious threat of aggression from a monolithic communism. The United States was the leader of the non-Communist nations, which, with proper treatment, would become America's handmaidens in the struggle against communism. Kaiser's letter also reflected the interest of the Labor Department—an interest that was shared by many federal agencies—to play a role in shaping and implementing United States foreign policy. For Kaiser and Tobin, this was based on their conclusion that organized labor internationally "is the chief target for communist aggression" and that the department was vital to the creation and support of "sound and democratic labor movements."[8]

The Central Intelligence Agency supported the fear of a Kremlin-directed threat to the non-Communist world. In August 1950 this organization reported to Truman that Russia, after tying up most combat-ready American forces in Korea, was using the UN to try to discredit the United States for intervening in a civil war on that peninsula. The Soviets were also developing aggressive threats toward Indochina, Taiwan, and Yugoslavia. Moreover, Europe was in danger, which meant that the North Atlantic Treaty countries would have to develop a more-effective defense. This would, according to the CIA, "require great US initiative and pressure, a more closely integrated common effort under the NAT, and a determined campaign to lift European morale from its present apathy."[9] Neither the president nor the NSC needed convincing. The CIA's assessment merely confirmed their line of thought, and they were getting plenty of western-European support for it. Truman, on August 1, had already asked Congress for a supplemental foreign-aid appropriation of $4 billion, $3.5 billion of which was intended for the North Atlantic area. Congress granted him this in September. In late summer, officials from the State and Defense departments accelerated negotiations to integrate and increase the defenses of the North Atlantic Treaty nations. Agreement was arrived at by December. At the request of the representatives of the treaty nations, on December 18 Truman also named Gen. Dwight D. Eisenhower to assume the task of putting the O in NATO as Supreme Allied Commander in Europe.

Other bits and pieces of the stepped-up containment program fell into place. In late June, additional funds were provided for the defense of Indochina, and a United States military mission was dispatched there. More important, the United States accelerated its drives to prepare peace treaties with Austria, Germany, and Japan. There was little hope in Washington that the World War II allies would conclude a peace treaty with Austria, and none that one would be agreed upon for Germany. Nevertheless, the United States raised the issue, partly to demonstrate Russia's intransigence and partly to encourage the development of Austria's and Germany's confidence in the United States. Also significant was America's attempt to facilitate Germany's acceptance into the economy, the political life, and even the defense activities of western Europe. France was the sticking point in giving the new German republic a part to play in NATO. Finally, in December, the NATO countries agreed to it in principle. This was, however, only a compromise on paper, for six years would pass before it became a fact. Indeed, because of new disagreements and of shortages of weapons, the creation of an effective western-European defense would take longer than was anticipated during the flush of optimism that occurred by the end of 1950.

There were many other American efforts in 1950 to meet the perceived world-wide Communist threat. These included attempts to pressure Ireland to join NATO, which failed; to improve relations with India, Pakistan, Afghanistan, Ceylon, and Nepal; to strengthen Yugoslavia's independence of Russia by granting a loan and by giving foodstuffs; to tighten trade restrictions between the East and the West; and to spur the implementation of the Point IV program. Consideration was also given to entering into new military alliances. Clearly, NSC 68, which Truman had approved bit by bit in 1950, was being implemented. It was also plain that it had taken the coming of war in Korea to gain congressional and even full presidential support for this global defense effort. This even applied to matters that Truman found uncomfortable, such as closer relations with Argentina and Spain.

The Korean War also served to raise internal-security questions to a new high. Increasingly, there were those, especially Republicans, in Congress and over the country who were looking for scapegoats. This explains the crescendo of demands for the resignation of Dean Acheson, who was charged with being responsible for the Korean War and for harboring Communists in the State Department. Truman stood by his secretary of state, and with good reason, for no one could have been more diligent in the service of the president than was Acheson. Others were not so lucky. Congress denied Sumner T. Pike the chairmanship of the Atomic Energy Commission in 1950, apparently because he was too liberal; and bipartisan criticism of Edward U. Condon for being soft on communism forced him out of office as director of the Bureau of Standards in 1951.

The president took as the chief threat the movement to enact a harsh comprehensive internal-security bill. This type of legislation had been under consideration since the Eightieth Congress, and just before the Korean War it fell short of the number of votes needed in order to pass it. The war gave the measure new life. The internal-security bill would make Communist activity illegal, would require Communist organizations to register with the government, and would discourage those who were thought to sympathize with communism. Truman charged Senate Majority Leader Scott Lucas with keeping the measure from coming up on the floor of the upper chamber, but Lucas failed to do so. A group of liberal senators, including Paul H. Douglas of Illinois, Hubert H. Humphrey of Minnesota, and Herbert H. Lehman of New York, aggravated the situation by offering an alternative measure. They proposed the authorization of compulsory detention of suspected persons, on the motion of the attorney general, in time of emergency, with habeas corpus provisions for their release when justified. This, they believed, would be better than denying Communists and fellow travelers freedom of expression and otherwise penalizing them. Although the Senate defeated this substitute, Democratic Senator Patrick McCarran of Nevada later combined it with the internal-security bill, but without the safeguard of habeas corpus.

Meanwhile, in August, Truman lectured Congress on the legislation. He pointed out that although the Bill of Rights did not prevent the nation from protecting itself against subversion, neither did the need to protect the republic counter the constitutional obligation to safeguard individual rights. Existing law, he declared, permitted Americans to deal effectively with internal threats to the security of the state. In an attempt to sidetrack the internal-security bill, the president recommended tightening laws concerning espionage, the registration of foreign agents, the security of military installations, and the detention of deportable aliens. Truman's tactics of delay and substitution failed. In September the House adopted McCarran's internal-security bill, and only seven members of the Senate voted against it. The reason for the measure's success early in the Korean War was plain. As Paul Douglas admitted in his autobiography, "To oppose the bill would mean being labeled pro-Communist."[10]

Harry Truman had the courage to oppose the McCarran Act; and on September 22 he sent a blistering veto message to Congress. Not only would the clumsiness of the measure waste the government's time in trying to carry it out, he asserted, but the new law would also "greatly weaken our liberties and give aid and comfort to those who would destroy us." The president had the satisfaction of receiving mail that was overwhelmingly opposed to the act. Fired by the hysteria of the times, however, the House and the Senate overrode his veto, 286 to 48 and 57 to 10, respectively. Truman also had the consolation of seeing what he had said about the legislation come true. The Internal Security Act of 1950 proved largely to be unworkable, and the judiciary later held that much of it was unconstitutional. The measure was effective in one way, however, in that for several years it contributed to muting dissent in America. Nor would it mark the culmination of heavy-handed legislative attempts to deal with internal security. Yet to come were the McCarran-Walter Immigration Act of 1952, the Communist Control Act of 1954, and the heightened inquisitorial activities of several congressional committees, all of which was highlighted by the emergence of Senator Joseph McCarthy as America's Torquemada until the Senate censured him in December 1954.

The president meanwhile had to deal with insubordination at the highest levels of the management of the war. Almost simultaneously, Truman had difficulties with Defense Secretary Louis Johnson, Navy Secretary Francis Matthews, and UN Commander Douglas MacArthur. The core of the problem was that they were speaking out too often in opposition to policy. Truman was already irritated with Johnson for picking fights with Dean Acheson and for his slowness to act. The president, as he told his July 6 news conference, got the secretary of defense to agree that Johnson himself, the service secretaries, and the JCS would "devote all their time to their job over there, instead of making speeches." Nevertheless, the gulf between Truman and Johnson widened. Averell Harriman told the president that Johnson had congratulated Senator Taft for demanding Dean Acheson's resignation and that Johnson had assured Harriman that he would see to it that the former secretary of commerce would be Acheson's successor. Stories also reached Truman that Johnson had presidential ambitions, even if he had to run as a Republican.

General MacArthur complicated matters by sending a message to the national encampment of the Veterans of Foreign Wars, suggesting that they adopt a more-aggressive military policy. On August 26 Truman ordered MacArthur to withdraw his message, but the press got hold of it anyway. The president wrote in his diary, "MacArthur is acting up, as is the Secretary of Defense."[11] Almost simultaneously, Secretary Matthews gave a speech in Boston, calling for preventive war against Russia. Truman reprimanded him; and like MacArthur, the navy secretary was contrite. In fact, Matthews offered his resignation, which the president refused, although he had to accept it almost a year later, after the secretary's continued transgressions. As though Truman had not had enough embarrassment, he added to it himself. After Congressman Gordon L. McDonough of California demanded that the marines be represented on the JCS, the president replied on August 29: "For your information the Marine Corps is the Navy's police force and as long as I am President that is what it will remain. They have a propaganda machine that is almost equal to Stalin's." Howls of outrage were heard throughout the land, and Truman felt compelled to apologize to the marines on September 6, for what he called his "unfortunate choice of language."

By the time that Truman had made his apology to the marines, he had also decided to ask Secretary Johnson to resign. He did not act on this decision until September 11. Then he told his secretary of defense that Democratic members of Congress wanted him discharged because they feared that his retention would weaken their chances for reelection in November. This was at least an exaggeration, because Truman's real reasons were Johnson's conflicts with other officials, his verbal indiscretions, his chuminess with Republicans, and his slowness in conforming to new policies during a war. Even after their discussion, Johnson procrastinated, and after the cabinet meeting of September 12 Truman had to compel the secretary of defense to sign a prepared letter of resignation. The president had already arranged with Gen. George C. Marshall to serve as Johnson's successor. This required special legislation of approval, for generals were barred from serving in high Defense Department positions. Congress enacted the measure quickly, and the Senate confirmed Marshall's appointment as secretary of defense on September 20. Truman thus resolved the Johnson situation. Moreover, he was able to keep the MacArthur and Matthews matters from boiling over until separate times in 1951.

Meanwhile a major turn in the war in Korea was beginning. MacArthur had convinced his superiors in Washington of the need for a bold counteroffensive move. Essential to it, in his eyes, was a massive amphibious assault at Inchon, which lay well up the western coast of Korea, close to Seoul and even to the thirty-eighth parallel. The idea was to surprise North Korean forces and to outflank them while General Walker's troops were launching counteroffensives from the Pusan perimeter. The operation, which began on September 15, worked brilliantly. The situation of the North Koreans resembled a rout by September 30, as they had lost Seoul and still occupied only one-quarter of South Korea. By October 19 the UN forces had pushed the North Koreans to their own boundaries in the west and almost one hundred miles beyond them in the east. The Inchon counteroffensive showed MacArthur at his best as a master of audacious maneuver, meticulous planning, and superb execution. It also reflected great credit on the United States, South Korean, and other UN air, ground, and naval forces. And Walton Walker emerged as an outstanding tactician, especially because his troops had to play their vital role considerably under strength. If what happened later showed MacArthur at his worst, it should not obscure the fact that the recovery of South Korea in 1950 was an outstanding episode in United States military history.

As early as July there were serious discussions in high places as to whether UN forces should cross the thirty-eighth parallel. South Korea's President Rhee urged such a step as a way to bring order to Korea and to unify it (under his control, of course), and many American officials agreed with him. Secretary of State Acheson opposed it for being at least premature. On July 31, however, Pentagon planners recommended crossing the border between South and North Korea. This recommendation was based on the assumptions that UN forces were strong enough to invade North Korea, that Russia would not undertake military action, and that President Truman, Congress, and the UN would support this action. Dean Acheson later gave this as an example of a military recommendation "premised upon the meticulous statement of assumptions that as often as not are quite contrary to the facts and yet control the conclusions."[12]

The next step came on September 1, when the NSC interpreted the UN's June 27 resolution as authorizing military operations north of the thirty-eighth parallel. After the Inchon operation, opinion in the upper reaches of the Truman administration was unanimous about crossing the parallel and unifying Korea. The JCS, on September 27, directed MacArthur to file an appropriate plan of operations. This he did the next day, although he also protested having the JCS retain final approval of his actions. The JCS additionally instructed MacArthur not to violate Chinese or Soviet borders and not to employ any but Korean forces in the provinces adjacent to China and Russia. Moreover, MacArthur was directed that if he should encounter Chinese or Soviet forces, his actions should be only defensive, and Washington should be notified. In fairness to MacArthur, the details of the JCS's instructions on this point were not completely clear.

President Truman quickly approved MacArthur's plan of operations. Unfortunately for all in the future, Defense Secretary Marshall telegraphed MacArthur that "we want you to feel unhampered tactically and strategically to proceed north of the 38th parallel."[13] MacArthur's interpretation of this as giving him a free hand in North Korea was fortified by a resolution of the UN General Assembly on October 7, which endorsed the creation of a united, democratic, and independent

Korea by UN forces. On October 9 MacArthur used this resolution to reiterate his demand for the surrender of North Korea, the alternative being the enforcement of the UN's will by military action. The general probably went too far, but the ambiguity of the UN resolution, as well as of his instructions from Washington, lent itself somewhat to his interpretation.

One high-ranking United States official, Air Force Secretary Thomas K. Finletter, said in 1972 that he did not remember what his position was on crossing the border, although other evidence does not indicate that there was any dissent in high circles of the administration. Finletter did conclude, however, that crossing the thirty-eighth parallel was "a ghastly miscalculation," "a disaster," and a distortion of the defensive nature of the UN operation.[14] And a disaster is what it was— not only the decision to cross the parallel but also MacArthur's plan of operations and the way in which he carried it out. The plan was to use his X Corps to capture Wonsan by sea on the east and then to link up with Walton Walker's northward-driving Eighth Army along the Wonsan-Pyongyang road. This plan was fraught with difficulties, which included overloading transportation to move the X Corps from the west to undertake an amphibious landing at Wonsan; the bifurcation of command of the X Corps and the Eighth Army; MacArthur's exercise of command from Tokyo, which was seven hundred miles away; the leaving of a vacuum between the two prongs of the attack; and the obstruction of supplies to Walker's army while the X Corps was being moved. Some eyebrows were raised, and there was grumbling in the Eighth Army, but no more. This was MacArthur's plan, after all, and boldness and the unexpected were his stock in trade. Moreover, the plan had had to be thrown together on short notice.

MacArthur set his plan in motion after he had called for the surrender of North Korean forces on October 1. He assumed that the weather, the Chinese, and the Russians would be restrained, that his forces would master the unfamiliar terrain, and that fortune would smile on his enterprise. Much would happen before it became clear that fortune was fickle in Korea. It is easy to assume, however, that another plan would have worked. For example, many Americans later declared that victory would have been won if the UN forces had stopped at a line running roughly from Wonsan to the North Korean capital of Pyongyang. The flaw in this thinking is obvious. With relative impunity, North Korean troops could have harassed the Wonsan-Pyongyang line, and they would have had abundant supplies and possibly "volunteer" forces from China and Russia. There is also no reason to think that this plan would have soothed the Chinese or that it would not have been taken by them as a sign of weakness, thus leading to their intervention anyway. Of course, UN forces could have more easily defended the Wonsan-Pyongyang line, given its relative narrowness and closeness to supply sources. There is no reason to assume, however, that the onset of winter weather and the introduction of huge numbers of experienced and well-disciplined Chinese troops would not have compelled the UN forces to retreat, with consequences equivalent to what actually happened until 1953. To a large extent, the die had been cast with Truman's decision to intervene in Korea. American optimism that it would be a short war obscured what everyone should have known in June 1950: namely, that war is a serious enterprise and should not be entered into lightly, especially with powerful enemies waiting in the wings. Given this, the United States should have been prepared for a protracted military undertaking or sought to have negotiated a restoration of the status quo ante bellum in October or contented itself in June with merely condemning the aggression in Korea.

The situation was a Hobson's choice to begin with. It seemed that if the administration had only condemned the invasion of South Korea, aggression might have been encouraged elsewhere in the world. Optimism about the nation's strength and impatience with the enemy ruled, however, and the United States decided to intervene in Korea. What Americans did not understand was that once they were committed to defend South Korea, they would probably have to fight until the enemy was prepared to conclude a peace. It made no difference whether Washington settled for the thirty-eighth parallel, a Wonsan-Pyongyang line, a line farther north, or the Manchurian-Russian border. The initiative was in the enemy's hands, and that enemy would seem to be inscrutable. Secretary of the Army Frank Pace, Jr., who became disappointed with the consequences of the Korean War, later said: "I don't believe that it was possible to accommodate with the Communist world at that time."[15] Thus, the question was how to cope with the Communist leadership: should we do more, or should we do less? No one in Washington had a satisfactory answer, and this was just as true with respect to the Korean War as anything else. In Korea, if one were to have stopped short of total victory during the fall of 1950, that would have left the enemy with the potential to continue fighting. This is the major reason for the decision to go beyond the thirty-eighth parallel, then beyond the Wonsan-Pyongyang line, and then to Korea's northern border. The nagging question was, What if the Russians or the Communist Chinese or both should enter the conflict? How could the fighting then stop short of becoming World War III?

Truman and most of the men around him were sensitive to this. Early in October he decided that it would be useful to meet with MacArthur in order to establish their accord on what was being done in the Far East. It seems fair to say that the president also wanted, at one and the same time, to demonstrate his confidence in MacArthur, to show him who was the boss, to benefit politically from association with the hero of Inchon, and to gain information. Truman decided to hold the conference on Wake Island on October 15, so that the general would not have to be away from his post too long. Among those present were the president, MacArthur, Army Secretary Pace, JCS Chairman Omar Bradley, Pacific Fleet Commander Arthur W. Radford, presidential aide W. Averell Harriman, and Assistant Secretary of State Dean Rusk. The meeting did not get off to a good start. Truman was irritated not only because MacArthur was slow to come to greet him but also because MacArthur arrived without a tie and wearing a soiled, rumpled cap. (Later on, Truman would exaggerate this incident.) The two men then chatted privately for an hour. The general apologized for the VFW incident, implied that he would conform to policy regarding Taiwan, and assured the president that the war in Korea was all but won and that there was little chance that the Chinese Communists would intervene.

By the time of the general conference, there was cordiality all around. Indeed MacArthur was treated as an oracle, and he responded accordingly. He said to the president and his party: "I believe that formal resistance will end throughout North and South Korea by Thanksgiving. . . . I hope the United Nations will hold elections by the first of the year. Nothing is gained by military occupation. . . . No commander in the history of war has ever had more complete and adequate support from all agencies in Washington than I have." When Truman asked what the chances were for intervention by the Chinese or the Russians, the general answered, reflecting one of America's many intelligence-gathering failures, "Very little." The Chinese had troops but no air force; the Soviets had air strength in the area but no troops; and coordination between them would be "flimsy. . . . We are the best." If the Chinese did intervene, MacArthur estimated that they could maintain no more than sixty thousand soldiers in Korea, which the UN forces could contain or defeat handily. He then urged the negotiation of a peace treaty with Japan and the creation of a Pacific equivalent of NATO.

Then the conversation turned to Indochina. MacArthur could not comprehend why the French "do not clean it up." Admiral Radford warmed to this subject, declaring: "We probably have more chance of assisting in Indo-China than anywhere else. We must stiffen the backbone of the French." Harriman contributed: "The French must change their attitude relative to Indo-China." By now the Captain Harry in Truman was ready to emerge. "We have," he said, "been working on the French in connection with Indo-China for years without success. . . . This is the most discouraging thing we face. . . . If the French Prime Minister comes to see me, he is going to hear some very plain talk. . . . If you don't want him to hear that kind of talk, you had better keep him away from me." Although much of this was just talk, it did reflect the willingness of Americans in the two decades after World War II to jump in where others were cautious in treading. The long-term results in the case of Indochina would be catastrophic. The conference ended with a return to the question of Korea. The group dismissed Indian Prime Minister Nehru's statesmanlike suggestion to place Indian and Pakistani troops as a buffer along Korea's borders with China and Russia. MacArthur's plan was "to put South Korean troops up there" as a way of supporting the government of the Republic of Korea. The president agreed strongly with this position.[16] Truman and MacArthur had spent less than three hours together, but the president left Wake Island believing that they were in complete accord.

If Truman had doubted MacArthur before the Wake Island meeting, he did not at its conclusion. UN forces were advancing rapidly in Korea; and no one expected Communist Chinese intervention, despite Foreign Minister Chou En-lai's warning on October 3 to the Indian ambassador that if United States troops were to cross the thirty-eighth parallel, China would enter the conflict. This was backed up by Chinese radio broadcasts announcing the same thing. No one in Washington or Tokyo took these threats seriously. MacArthur's optimistic analysis apparently had reinforced the Americans-in-Wonderland attitude. What had impressed Truman was the general's statement that the war would be over by Thanksgiving. Even if no one was going to hold MacArthur to a strict time schedule, this news was striking, coming from the liberator of the Southwest Pacific, the shogun of Japan, the hero of Inchon, and, now, the oracle of Wake Island.

Things did not work out MacArthur's way, for he was wrong on too many counts. The president was wrong, too, in his new belief in the UN commander. Indeed, in his news conference of October 19, Truman got carried away when asked if he and MacArthur were in agreement on Taiwan. Bristling, he deplored the inability of some newspeople to "understand the ideas of two intellectually honest men when they meet." General MacArthur, he declared, "is a member of the Government of the United States. He is loyal to that government. He is loyal to the President. He is loyal to the President in his foreign policy, which I

. . . *wish* a lot of your papers were.'' Events would, however, soon test MacArthur's loyalty and, indeed, his credibility, in the president's mind.

Truman would suffer many trials soon after the Wake Island conference. There were the forthcoming congressional elections, and there was the entry of the Chinese Communists into the Korean War. Moreover, there was an attempt to assassinate the president. Nationalists in Puerto Rico had begun disturbances there, which had led to numerous casualties. On November 1, two Puerto Rican Nationalists assaulted Blair House, where Truman was living temporarily. White House police were able to thwart this effort, but in the process, a guard and an assailant were killed, and two other guards and another assailant were wounded. Although Truman was never directly in danger, he was shaken up by the affair and was disturbed by the further confinement of his movements thereafter. He wrote sarcastically in his diary, "It's hell to be President of the Greatest Most Powerful Nation on Earth.''[17] Some weeks later, when John Steelman presented the president with a photograph of the slain guard, Leslie Coffelt, Truman became tearful and speechless.

The president participated little in the 1950 election campaign. It seemed better to attend to official business; moreover, it was not a particularly edifying campaign. The Republicans made much of their allegations that the Democrats were being soft on communism. There were also the medical profession's all-out attack on the administration's health-care program and the revolt of many farm interests against the Brannan Plan. Then there were the consequences of Senator Estes Kefauver's investigation of organized crime, which had exposed links chiefly with Democratic politicians. There was also the impact of the news of the Chinese military intervention in Korea three days before the election. The results of all this at the polls badly hurt the administration's support in Congress. The Democrats were left with 234 members in the House and only 49 in the Senate, down from 263 and 54, respectively, two years earlier. Worse yet, it was largely Truman's supporters among the Democrats who had been the most vulnerable at the polls, and it was extremely antiadministration Republicans who had taken their places.

The greatest trial facing the Truman administration that fall was the Chinese intervention in Korea. The UN forces had crossed the thirty-eighth parallel on October 1, had advanced to Wonsan on the east by October 11, and by October 26 had cleared almost half of North Korea. This was not the fulfillment of MacArthur's planning that it seemed to be. It was the South Korean Third Division, racing northward, that had captured Wonsan by land, not the X Corps by sea, as planned. The unnecessary shifting of the X Corps to the east had kept that organization inactive and had choked transportation and supplies for the Eighth Army, thus hampering the latter's operations. The separation of commands between Walker's Eighth Army and MacArthur's X Corps remained, while some South Korean commands floated virtually free. Moreover, MacArthur changed his mind about the linking up of UN forces between the west and the east. Clearly, their successes now were born of North Korean weaknesses, not of the brilliance of MacArthur's command.

Indeed, events were outdistancing the UN commander's plans. On October 17 he set a new objective, a line forty to sixty miles south of the Chinese border. Before long he directed his generals to attack beyond this, although he had not effected a link up of UN forces across the neck of Korea. By October 24 it was plain that MacArthur was disregarding his instructions not to let any troops except South Koreans come close to the Manchurian border. Moreover, his forces were pressing rapidly forward over difficult terrain, far beyond their supply ports, on primitive roads, and over a broadening front. If the Chinese or the Russians were to appear in force, the only way that the UN forces could hold their own would be through engaging in massive aerial attacks across the border. And this was contrary, as MacArthur knew, to policy, because of the losses that the air force would have incurred and the possibility that such attacks would have ignited a third world war. In short, the headlong dash of UN forces to the border was poorly coordinated and ill-advised. The moment of truth came on October 26, when a South Korean regiment reached the Manchurian border. Then Chinese troops in the area attacked the regiment and all but destroyed it. Washington and Tokyo dismissed this and other UN encounters with Chinese forces within the next few days as being insignificant. United States officials in those two cities were, however, worried by what might be in the offing.

American leaders did not have long to wait. Russian MIG-15 airplanes appeared over the combat zone on October 31, and on the next day the front was enveloped in intensive fighting between Chinese and UN forces. UN troops had been halted and in some sectors even thrown back. MacArthur sought permission to conduct bombing along the Manchurian border, which he was granted as long as the raids did not violate Chinese territory. He continually pressed for authorization to carry the air war to Manchuria. Washington denied him this, but little else. MacArthur talked of a massive UN counteroffensive, while officials in Washington tried to calculate what the Chinese wanted, what they would do to get it, and how far MacArthur should be allowed to go in trying to stop them. The UN commander was of no great help, for his estimates of the situation often changed. He talked of absolute victory. Yet MacArthur kept the commands of the Eighth Army and the X Corps separate, and these forces were divided into seven columns that found themselves deep in rugged hostile country, along a broad front, and far from supply bases. Meanwhile, winter was fast approaching. Despite growing doubt in Washington, no one there was willing to disagree with the commander in the field. Not only were United States commanders in the field traditionally given great leeway, but this commander was Douglas MacArthur, who just might be able to achieve victory with one more offensive.

MacArthur set the date of his great offensive for November 24. Meanwhile, Truman, as had MacArthur, demanded that Chinese troops leave Korea, warning of serious consequences if they did not. The president also assured China and the world that UN forces would not attack China. These threats and reassurances had no effect; so Mac-Arthur launched his offensive as scheduled. Despite the UN commander's confident words at its beginning, the new offensive was a desperate gamble; and it was a gamble that he lost. The Chinese initiated a counterattack on November 25, and by November 28 the UN advance had turned into flight from the enemy. MacArthur called this an "entirely new war," which was being carried out by two hundred thousand enemy soldiers, largely Communist Chinese regulars.[18] On November 30 Truman declared to his news conference that despite the crisis, "the forces of the United Nations have no intention of abandoning their mission in Korea." Everything was being done to deal with this new aggression.

In a sense this was true. There was a constant round of meetings at the UN and in Washington, which led to no significant agreement or action. There was, however, another problem—MacArthur—who had become increasingly rash in his comments about his allies and the interpretation of his orders. After a meeting of the secretaries of state and defense and the JCS, on December 3, Assistant Army Chief of Staff Matthew B. Ridgway became irritated with the fruitless discussions. He pointedly asked Air Force Chief of Staff Hoyt Vandenberg: "Why don't the Joint Chiefs send orders to MacArthur and *tell* him what to do?" Vandenberg replied: "What good would that do? He wouldn't obey the orders. What *can* we do?" Ridgway exploded: "You can relieve any commander who won't obey orders, can't you?" Vandenberg looked at him in disbelief, and then walked away.[19] The commander in the field would remain MacArthur, the bringer of miracles, for a while longer; but no miracles occurred. By Christmas Day, after suffering great losses, the UN forces had been pushed back to the thirty-eighth parallel, with no end in sight to their retreat. Almost as discouraging was the death, on December 23, of Gen. Walton Walker, whom many considered the outstanding commander in the UN constellation. On December 25 General Ridgway arrived in the Far East to take Walker's place. MacArthur was wise enough or desperate enough to say to Ridgway: "The Eighth Army is yours, Matt. Do what you think best."[20]

Before Ridgway's appointment, December 1950 had been a busy time of soul-searching and decision making in Washington. Suggestions to seek a cease-fire were rejected. Proposals to pour in more United States troops were deemed to be unrealistic, because few trained soldiers would be available until March. Other UN members were not prepared to make any substantial new contributions, and the United States refused to strip its outposts elsewhere in the world. Nationalist Chinese troops were unacceptable, at least because their introduction into Korea would give the Communist Chinese new reasons for their intervention. Public opinion fluctuated in December. The Communist Chinese had so outraged many Americans that there was increased sentiment for using the atomic bomb. Indeed, the question was discussed seriously in the highest circles, both then and later, though the administration rejected the use of the atomic bomb as being unsuitable in the Korean War, immoral in a small country, and something that might ruin its effectiveness as a shield for Europe. By the middle of December, contrary public opinion arose as thousands of Americans wrote to Truman, demanding that American troops be brought home. This may have been related to word from Washington that the bomb might be used, which the president had sent out as a negotiating ploy.

When asked in his November 30 news conference if the UN arsenal against the Chinese Communists might include the atomic bomb, Truman said, "That includes every weapon that we have." When asked if he had considered using the atomic bomb, he answered, "There has always been active consideration of its use," although he added, "I don't want to see it used." This was front-page news, and the reaction was tremendous. Most important, allies of the United States were perturbed. The White House's clarification of Truman's remarks, that only the president could order the bomb's use and that no such order had been given, did not calm the storm. Prime Minister Clement Attlee rushed to Washington to voice Great Britain's alarm over Truman's bomb rattling, the possible extension of hostilities in the Far East, shortages of supplies, and the possible weakening of European defenses. The prime minister may have been, as the pundits said, a modest man who had much to be modest about; but his visit of December 4–8 put the president on the spot.

Truman had to reassure Attlee that there would be no use of the atomic bomb in panic, although he hedged on consulting with the British about its use; that hostilities would not be widened, and that negotiations for a Korean cease-fire would be considered, though there would be no withdrawal from Korea or admission of Communist China to the UN; that steps would be taken to combat shortages of supplies; and that NATO would be developed. Though neither the Americans nor the British may have been pleased with the results of the Truman-Attlee conference, it had cleared the air. The British had exchanged their continued support of the war in Korea, which they could hardly withdraw, for United States assurances regarding the atomic bomb, restraint in the Far East, supplies, and the strengthening of European defenses. It was a good swap for the British, and it made United States policies clearer, however irritating the process might be.

The problems between London and Washington also assisted the Americans in reaching some conclusions about the adverse turn of events in Korea. Everyone in the administration was aware of how bad the situation was. Truman put it this way on December 2: "General MacArthur is in serious trouble. . . . We must get him out of it, if we can. . . . It looks very bad."[21] The president was also in trouble. His allies were upset, the situation in Korea was alarming, and the country was disturbed. Policy did begin to take shape, however. On December 5 Truman directed that all speeches and statements made by federal officials relating to foreign and military policy had to be cleared by the State and Defense departments. Although MacArthur's continuing series of unauthorized comments to the press had spurred the formulation of this order, it was not aimed at him alone. On December 11 the NSC recommended the consideration of negotiations for a cease-fire in Korea. The president approved this recommendation. Truman also suffered his most-painful change of staff on December 5, when Charles Ross died unexpectedly at his desk. No one in the president's official family had been closer or more intelligently loyal to his chief. Ross's successor as press secretary was Joseph H. Short, Jr., of the Baltimore Sun. Short was no Ross, but he was loyal and diligent, perhaps too diligent, for he also died suddenly, in September 1952.

On December 1 Truman asked Congress for $16.8 billion extra for the current fiscal year in order to strengthen the armed forces and to finance the war in Korea. Although the reverses in Korea signaled the need for more funds, this was the occasion more than the reason for the president's request. Indeed, it was the administration's most important push to effect the policy contained in NSC 68. A large party of officials had been working on this for months. By November they had reached agreement on everything except the dollar amount. Truman's special counsel, Charles Murphy, decided that action had to be taken. He had reviewed many estimates of what was needed. Finally, to be on the safe side, Murphy recommended the largest amount he had seen. Despite Defense Secretary Marshall's irritation, the president accepted this figure. What it meant was that, after congressional approval, almost $42 billion would be appropriated for military purposes in fiscal year 1951, a far cry from Truman's earlier $14 billion lid. By January 6, 1951, Congress had passed and the president had approved the supplemental appropriation, which gave force to NSC 68 and the global character of America's defenses against communism.

Closely related to the administration's move to implement NSC 68 was the president's decision to declare a state of national emergency, which had been under consideration for some time. After sounding out congressional leaders, Truman declared a national emergency on December 16. He had taken to radio and television the night before to announce: "Our homes, our Nation, all the things we believe in, are in great danger. This danger has been created by the rulers of the Soviet Union." Truman declared that it was the country's policy to continue the fight for UN principles in Korea, to strengthen the defenses of free nations, to increase America's military might, and to expand the nation's economy and keep it stable. The crucial news was that armed forces of the United States, which numbered less than 1.5 million in June and about 2.5 million now, would soon rise to 3.5 million. This meant stepping up selective-service calls and activating two more National Guard divisions. Moreover, there would be at least a tripling of military production within a year, the continuance of credit controls, higher taxes, and a variety of federal actions to control prices and wages. To assist in this work, the president announced the creation of the Office of Defense Mobilization and the appointment of Charles E. Wilson of General Electric to head it. Truman also indicated that as commander in chief, he was calling the striking railway workers back to work. Think of all this, he concluded, "not as a sacrifice, but as an opportunity, an opportunity to defend the best kind of life that men have ever devised on this earth."

The next day the president issued Proclamation 2914, which declared the existence of a national emergency and thereby resurrected a number of special executive powers. On December 18 Truman asked Congress for emergency powers to reorganize the executive branch in order to foster defense mobilization and to permit the modification of defense contracts so as to facilitate production. In January 1951 Congress gave him the power to do the latter. It decided not to grant emergency reorganizational powers, however; so the president was compelled to do the best he could with the authority he already had. In January, Congress also approved Truman's requests for a hefty excess-profits tax and a civil-defense program.

In roughly six months, the United States had gone from peace to war. The transition had been relatively painless for most citizens, as wartime life would be, despite Truman's talk of sacrifice. Few Americans doubted the existence of the dangers of which he spoke. What many had come to doubt by the end of 1950 was the efficacy of the Truman administration's policies in dealing with communism. The roots of this stretched back to the dawn of the Cold War, and its flowering came after MacArthur's failure to contain the Chinese Communists in Korea. The results were an exaggerated example of the government's proposing and of dissenters' opposing, of the administration's asserting that it had the answers to the crisis and of the opposition's contending that the government was substantially incompetent. The situation was even more complicated: personality conflicts and ambitions entered in, as did increasing fears that the survival of American society was at stake; that the Communist monolith was smarter, tougher, and more aggressive; and that its agents were everywhere. Given all this, it is little wonder that by 1951 Truman's honeymoon with Congress in regard to Korea and to foreign and military policy would end and that his popularity with the American public would fall to a record low.

11

★ ★ ★ ★ ★

CONFLICT AT HOME
AND ABROAD

Everything was ready for what was to become known as the Great Debate on United States foreign policy. As early as November 1950, Senator Robert A. Taft, fresh from his reelection victory in Ohio, called for a reexamination of foreign policy. And there were growing currents of unrest in Congress and in the country as the situation in Korea deteriorated during that month and in December. Herbert Hoover kicked off the Great Debate. On December 20 the former president declared that non-Communist forces could not win in Korea or in a land war against Russia and that nuclear war was unthinkable now that the Soviet Union and the United States both possessed the atomic bomb. He asserted that the United States should emphasize the development of its air and naval forces in order to preserve the Western Hemisphere as the Gibraltar of Western Civilization and to retain control of the Atlantic and Pacific oceans. Moreover, European nations had to assume responsibility for their own defense. By following this policy, Hoover said, Americans could work to balance the nation's budget, combat inflation, feed the world's hungry, and yet refrain from appeasing communism.

Hoover's address, which was popularly called the Fortress America speech, became the touchstone for the Great Debate. On December 22 Secretary of State Dean Acheson indicated that Hoover had espoused a policy of retreat in the face of the enemy, which would have dreadful consequences for the world's freedom. President Truman declared in his December 28 news conference that "the country is not going back to isolationism. You can be sure of that." Others, such as the administration's special envoy, John Foster Dulles, tried to split the difference between the positions of Hoover and Truman. Still others, such as Joseph P. Kennedy, the former ambassador to Great Britain, demanded a reassessment of America's foreign policy. Indeed, Hoover and Kennedy worked in concert, with the former president stressing to his Democratic collaborator that the facts supported "fully that our task is to prevent commitment of American troops to Europe in any such situation as this." In other words, their reaction had been touched off not only by the reverses in Korea but also by the refusal of Europeans, at recent meetings in Brussels, to commit enough troops to their own defense.[1]

Senator Taft opened the congressional phase of the Great Debate on January 5, 1951. He believed that the Russians, despite their intransigence and aggressive tendencies, did not want another world war. Yet freedom was sufficiently at risk that the United States had to seek a way in which to win over men's minds against communism. The United States also needed superiority in air and naval forces in order to preserve freedom in non-Communist nations. As for troops, Taft agreed that the nation's commitments must be honored. He called for a congressional authorization before sending additional troops anywhere, with none being shipped to the North Atlantic Treaty Organization until America's allies showed that they could develop a workable land defense. Taft declared that this policy would keep down expenditures, restrain inflation, and reinforce liberty at home. Several Democratic and Republican senators challenged Taft's arguments. Why should Europe want to be defended by being bombed by Americans? Why should one assume that Russia did not want war in Europe? If war came in Europe, why should one assume that United States troops could not defend their allies there? Was not the Ohio senator's counsel one of weakness in the face of enemies who were shooting at American boys? As Tom Connally said, it is considered, at least in his state of Texas, "that when a person shoots at you, he is being unfriendly."[2]

Taft was not inflexible; he indicated that he would agree to having at least three United States divisions in Europe and that he was willing to discuss foreign policy with Truman or other appropriate administration leaders. This was considered as an overture to resuscitate bipartisanship, but many—with good reason—doubted Taft's ability in knowledge or temperament to become the new Vandenberg in matters of foreign policy. In addition, there was the Ohioan's contempt for Dean Acheson. The administration was, therefore, unwilling to try out the Senate's Republican leader. Failing this, it was left only with the choice of deemphasizing bipartisanship. It seemed, after all, that no other Republican senator—say Henry Cabot Lodge, Jr., of Massachusetts—

had the power or—say Kenneth S. Wherry of Nebraska—had the attitudes needed to make it effective. So, the Great Debate would continue. Wherry introduced a resolution on January 8, declaring that no troops should be sent to Europe in connection with NATO unless authorized by Congress. This became the key issue in the Great Debate during early 1951, one on which members of both parties would be divided.

President Truman's chickens were coming home to roost, although he would never admit it. His failure to seek congressional authorization of United States participation in the Korean conflict and to secure appropriate European contributions to NATO's activities left Congress freer than usual to criticize the administration. This covered a broad range of issues, including the conduct of the war in Korea, foreign aid, mobilization, and most of the administration's domestic programs. And Truman's critics did not have to be consistent over time in order to cast doubt on his administration's wisdom. For example, a Gallup poll released in August 1950 indicated that 68 percent of the respondents favored stopping Russian expansion in Asia and Europe; by January 1951, 66 percent of the respondents wanted the United States to pull out of Korea.

Of course, much of this reversal of support was tied into events in Korea. Gen. Matthew Ridgway had assumed command at Christmastime 1950, but he could not immediately turn affairs around in Korea. He had to discover what he had to fight with, he had to rekindle the fighting spirit of the United Nations forces, he had to establish a unified command for them, he had to devise strategies to halt the Chinese advance, and he had to cope with MacArthur's doubts that UN forces could remain in Korea unless they were to receive major reinforcements and unless they could bomb Communist China. All this was aggravated by the knowledge that the Chinese would launch a new offensive on New Year's Eve. Confident that the fortunes of the war could be reversed, General Ridgway applied himself unceasingly to achieving this end. The new Chinese offensive was predictably effective, and UN troops pulled back to positions deep inside South Korea, along a line where the Han River flows east and west. Ridgway's forces enjoyed mastery of the seas and the skies as well as superiority in armor. Without reinforcements of troops, however, these were not enough to turn the tide of battle against the numerically dominant foe. Ridgway had to rely upon his ability to shape his troops into an effective fighting force. This he did magnificently, confounding MacArthur and their masters in Washington. Far from being pushed back to the Pusan perimeter, as many predicted, Ridgway's forces held at the Han River line, some seventy-five miles from the thirty-eighth parallel and about one hundred and fifty miles from Pusan.

The fall back to the Han River line and the advance of the Chinese Communists to occupy a quarter of the land area of the Republic of Korea in January 1951 were disheartening to the administration and even more so to Congress and the American public. Ridgway was not likely to advertise that the stand along the Han River was a cause for optimism. Even he could not be sure that his attacks on the problems confronting him would soon succeed. His will, spirit, and ability did, however, rub off on his allies, lieutenants, and men. Moreover, Ridgway was determined to counterattack as soon as possible. On January 25 his forces moved forward, and by the end of February they had fought their way to a line just south of Seoul. The capital was recaptured on March 15, not to be relinquished again during the war. By April 22, UN forces had regained almost all of South Korea and held some of North Korea. MacArthur would claim credit for the advance, but it was actually attributable to Ridgway's planning and effort.

Ridgway's successes would only dampen the Great Debate, just as it would only give the administration an additional reason to pursue its policy. Truman reiterated this policy in his legislative requests in January 1951. The stakes were high, as the president knew, so he tried to be his most persuasive and objective. It was difficult, because, as he said after writing his State of the Union message of January 8: "It's not easy for me to be objective, you know. I'm a partisan fellow."[3] He was pleased with the result. He wrote in his diary on January 10: "Telegrams and letters are running 15 to 1 favorably. Never worked so hard on a speech. All say it showed effort. Hope it does some good."[4] The 1951 State of the Union address was the summary of a policy and the rationales for it that had been emerging for years. Truman told Congress that the nation and its political and economic institutions were healthy, indeed strong. And they needed to be, not only to thwart aggression in Korea, but also because the war there was "part of the attempt of the Russian Communist dictatorship to take over the world, step by step." If the free nations would act wisely, they could beat back the Soviet challenge.

The United States, Truman declared, "has a practical, realistic program of action for meeting this challenge." First, he proposed additional economic assistance, directed toward helping to build European defenses and developing economic strength elsewhere. Second, he requested further military assistance to improve the defenses of the free world, particularly in Europe because of its economic importance and its capability to contribute to its own protection. Third, although vowing that America would "not engage in appeasement," the president advocated working for "peaceful settlements in international disputes," both through the UN and directly with the Soviet Union. Fourth, in effect, was his call for the United States to "have strength as well as right on our side." This required having military forces about three-and-one-half million strong on active service. The task confronting Congress, he said, was to consider legislation to support all this. This included outlays for military purposes and foreign aid; facilitation of industrial and agricultural production; further stabilization of prices, rents, and wages; better housing for and training and use of defense workers; and a substantial boost in taxes. Although Truman slipped in some of his Fair Deal program under the rubric of defense, he also added some of it on its own merit. This included aid to education, health insurance, and better benefits for old-age and unemployment insurance; but it did not include civil rights or significant labor reform.

The president's Economic Report to Congress of January 12 supported much of what he had said in his State of the Union address. Unemployment, he reported, had dropped to 3.6 percent by the end of 1950. This was good news, but it posed problems, because increased national income meant higher demand and had led to a rise since June in retail and wholesale prices, respectively, of almost 6 and 11 percent. Happily, this was more than offset by increases during 1950 in farm income of some 10 percent; wages, of almost 16 percent; and business profits, of 46 percent. Many things could be inferred from this, of course. There was a need for more production, although it was up 7 percent in 1950 and was rising by an even-faster rate by the end of the year. There was room for higher taxes, and there was the danger of the nation's running short of workers. Credit was expanding too rapidly, thus contributing to inflation. In turn, inflation was causing workers to demand higher wages and business to set even-higher prices, which would lead to more inflation and could impede the growth of production. It is small wonder that Truman had wanted higher taxes and now wanted controls on credit, prices, rents, and wages.

In his Budget Message of January 15, 1951, the president requested expenditures of $71.6 billion for fiscal year 1952, as compared to the $42.4 billion he had asked for a year earlier. This increase dramatically mirrored the cost of the war in Korea and of having the United States become the defensive anchor of the non-Communist world. Another reflection of this was that the eventual cost of the obligational authority he asked for in order to start contracts in fiscal year 1952 was almost $94.5 billion, contrasted with almost $40.5 a year earlier. In both cases—appropriations and obligational authority—the financing of military and foreign-affairs items constituted the chief reason for the astounding increase, accounting for $120.8 billion of the $166 billion recommended for the coming fiscal year of 1952, compared to some $36 billion of almost $82.9 billion recommended a year earlier. Of the other major functions of the federal government, Truman asked for modest increases for natural resources, education, and general research. His requests for general government and for transportation and communications were almost exactly the same as a year before. The president requested less for everything else. He estimated a deficit of $16.5 billion for fiscal year 1952, unless Congress would follow his recommendation to increase taxes in order to balance the budget.

While Congress was debating what to do about the president's program, the administration struck out to do what it could do with the powers it already held. On January 17 Truman established a policy on national manpower mobilization, which was aimed at using whatever resources the government could muster to assure that military and production personnel requirements were met. This would lead to few significant changes. Indeed, there was one example of great confusion in the policy. This was the use of braceros—legal and illegal laborers from Mexico—which unions and blacks had been opposing in order to improve wages and conditions for American farm workers. In response to this opposition, the administration in June 1950 had created the Commission on Migratory Labor. The commission reported in April 1951, recommending increased penalties for using wetbacks (illegal Mexican laborers); the ultimate elimination of employing foreign labor; and the extension to farm workers of the minimum wage, collective bargaining, unemployment insurance, and assistance in housing, health, and education. These recommendations put the administration on a collision course with powerful political elements, particularly in the Southwest, that benefited from the use of Mexican labor. Indeed the administration could not emerge a winner, given the claimed needs for wartime manpower. In June, Congress enacted legislation authorizing negotiations with Mexico for the importation of braceros. Truman could only hope that the legislators would deal with other aspects of the farm-labor problem. All that came was an act in 1952 making it a felony to employ or harbor illegal immigrants, a provision that was seldom enforced.

In line with the administration's manpower policy, efforts were made to encourage the employment of minorities, women, and the handicapped, even to the extent of recruiting Puerto Ricans for work on the mainland. Especially noteworthy was the creation, in December 1951, of the President's Committee on Government Contract Compliance. The coming of the Korean War had led black leaders to demand the reestablishment of the Fair Employment Practices Committee of World War II. There were spasms of negotiation and study in the government, but action came slowly. It seemed that no sooner was the administration close to acting, than some emergency would sidetrack the issue. After all, what was the hurry? Employment opportunities were improving steadily. There were also those who feared that a new fair-employment initiative would offend powerful elements and that the administration therefore would lose more in Congress than it was already losing. It seemed clear that President Truman was the sticking point and that congressional support in 1951 for the war effort was his chief concern. As one black member of the administration, Assistant Selective Service Director Campbell C. Johnson, observed of Truman, "He has his head in the lion's mouth, and this is no time to tickle the lion."[5]

The president was dilatory in responding to continued pressures from black leaders. This was seen in the gradual issuance of seven executive orders between February and October 1951. These required eleven major federal agencies to stipulate that defense contracts and subcontracts could not discriminate against anyone on the basis of race, creed, color, or national origin. This was not enough for black leaders, because adequate enforcement provisions were lacking. Finally, on December 3, 1951, after Congress had adjourned for the year, Truman acted. Then he issued Executive Order 10308, creating the President's Committee on Government Contract Compliance (CGCC).

The CGCC was no FEPC. It only oversaw the work of executive agencies in requiring defense contractors and subcontractors not to engage in discriminatory hiring practices. It could recommend, but it could not enforce; it could hold hearings, but it could not subpoena; and it dealt only with defense contracts, not with a broader range of economic activities. Moreover, it was a small operation, having 10 employees, compared to 119 for Franklin Roosevelt's second FEPC. Yet the CGCC could and did publicize problems, partly because its members were diligent and included recognized black, business, Jewish, and labor leaders. The black *Pittsburgh Courier* was close to the truth in calling the committee a "half-a-loaf FEPC," the best Truman "could do under the circumstances."[6] If the CGCC's successes fell short of what was needed in order to combat discrimination in employment, at least it had some successes; it also signaled that the federal government had a fair-employment policy. And it was a policy that became permanent, as it was followed by President Eisenhower's Committee on Government Contracts, President Kennedy's Committee on Equal Employment Opportunity, and appropriate legislation during Lyndon Johnson's administration.

Policies regarding manpower mobilization and fair employment were only bits and pieces of the larger policies that the Truman administration pursued in 1951. Few of these bits and pieces were significant, but some were interesting because of their bearing on future situations. One of these was the work of the Materials Policy Commission, which Truman established, under the chairmanship of William S. Paley of the Columbia Broadcasting System, to make an appraisal of America's material resources and requirements. The report of the Paley Commission, issued in five volumes in June 1952, was a landmark effort. The commission called for a comprehensive energy policy. This was predicated on its conclusion that national and world economic growth would consume oil and natural gas at an alarming rate. In turn, this would lead to significant importation of oil and ultimately would require great United States reliance on coal, synthetic oil, hydroelectric power, and nuclear energy. Importation was something to be avoided, for fear that external sources be cut off; the rest demanded greater research efforts and the formulation of definite policies for their development and utilization. In short, the Paley Commission foresaw the energy crises of the 1970s and beyond, but it was to no avail. The Truman administration had neither influence nor time enough to get Congress to act.

The administration's efforts on energy seemed outstanding in comparison with those of its successors. In addition to the establishment of the Paley Commission, there was the creation, during the winter of 1950/51, of the Petroleum Administration for Defense and of an assistant secretaryship in the Interior Department to try to plan comprehensively in regard to resources and energy. Little of a long-range nature was to come from these efforts, given the pressures of the Korean War and a paucity of support in Congress. Truman also had a White House staff task force, and he tried to reinvigorate the National Security Resources Board on energy issues. NSRB Chairman Stuart Symington responded by proposing broader and long-range concerns for his agency, especially in order to prevent the eventual exhaustion of energy and other natural resources. This interest led essentially nowhere because of lack of support among other federal agencies and on Capitol Hill. Thus the president's dreams for the emergence of an effective energy policy would remain unfulfilled.

Truman's concern for the use of water spurred only slightly more response. In 1950 he had appointed the Water Resources Policy Commission, which issued its report in March 1951, stressing the need to pay attention to the development and use of America's water resources. The president was even less successful in this instance in stirring up interest among federal agencies. The best he could do with Congress was to exploit the occasion of serious floods in July in the Middle West. Congress responded by voting relief funds and appropriations for flood-control projects, which Truman hoped might eventuate in a comprehensively planned Missouri Valley Authority.

Seldom in 1951 did Congress gratify Truman by passing domestic legislation that he desired; but this did happen in October, in the case of an amendment to the Taft-Hartley Act. This eliminated the need for costly and potentially unsettling National Labor Relations Board elections in cases where employers and unions had already agreed on a union-shop contract. That Congress should be so enlightened was interesting, for the Labor Department was deciding to drop its crusade—as Truman had in effect done earlier in the year—to repeal the Taft-Hartley Act. Advisers to Undersecretary of Labor Michael J. Galvin had reported in November, when recommending a change of position: "Many of the men in government and labor who once fought to repeal the Law and restore the Wagner Act or something similar have now recognized that continued advocating of repeal is unfeasible, if not unwise."[7]

The president could not expect much from the Eighty-second Congress. His description of its predecessor, "the majority is made up of Republicans and recalcitrant Southern 'Democrats,'"[8] was even more true of the House and the Senate in 1951 and 1952. The new Senate majority leader and whip, Ernest W. McFarland of Arizona and Lyndon B. Johnson of Texas, were even less in tune with Truman's program than were Scott Lucas and Francis Myers, whom they had succeeded. What this meant was that the Fair Deal was dead in Congress and that the administration would have to fight almost every inch of the way for its mobilization, foreign, and military policies.

Truman pressed hard for increased taxes in order to keep down the size of the federal debt and to contain inflation. Congress took a leisurely approach in formulating its response. Many Republicans, especially Senator Taft, and some Democrats believed that if the tax increase were restrained, the administration would trim its requests for appropriations. The result would then constitute not only less of a burden on taxpayers but also less involvement abroad and more encouragement for America's allies to meet the cost of their own defense. The Revenue Act of 1951, passed in October, was the result of the interplay between the president and Congress. In it, Truman scored an important victory, for the act was designed to raise $5.5 billion in additional revenues, which was $2 billion more than the bill initially reported by the Senate Finance Committee would have raised. The president had persuaded Congress that he meant to spend what he had requested. As it was, there would be a deficit of $4 billion for fiscal year 1952, not of $10 billion, which Truman had worried about. Although the new law was a victory for the administration, it had some important flaws from the president's viewpoint. Not only did it perpetuate loopholes for tax avoidance, such as the 27.5 percent depletion allowance on oil and natural gas; it added others. Upon this base a major American industry of tax accountants and lawyers would be built, and the well-to-do would be able to reduce their share of tax payments.

Despite the struggles with Congress, 1951 and 1952 were not years in which the president often wielded his veto power. Perhaps this came from Truman's fears that Congress would too often override his vetoes. A case can also be made that the House and the Senate offended him legislatively far more often by failing to act on his recommendations than by passing unacceptable laws. In any event, in 1951 Truman applied vetoes or pocket vetoes to only thirteen acts. Eight of these were personal or corporate relief bills. Of the other five, his veto was overridden twice, both times on legislation of interest to veterans, which he considered to be raids on the federal treasury. His effective vetoes dealt with the segregation of schools for military dependents in the South; legislative involvement in transactions for land for defense purposes; and liberalization of pensions for widows of the veterans of nineteenth-century wars.

The big struggle between the White House and Congress, of course, was reflected in the Great Debate of 1951. This covered every aspect of United States foreign and military policy, not only on the size of the military, but also on where troops should be sent and how many, foreign economic and military aid, relations with allies, internal security, and mobilization policy. Everything was fair game, and the stakes were high. Truman repeatedly made his program clear. It was, simultaneously, to establish the territorial integrity of South Korea; to perfect America's defenses; to help develop the defenses and economies of non-Communist nations that wanted assistance; and to mobilize the resources of the United States in order to support these undertakings. He hoped that all of this could be done in ways that would foster the growth of democracy on a global basis; that it would eventually result in fruitful negotiations between East and West; and that it would ultimately lead to a significant degree of disarmament and international cooperation. In short, the president's aim was, as ever, a more prosperous, stable, and peaceful world.

What Truman's largely Republican critics disagreed with him on—and they were far from agreed among themselves on what should be done—was about how far America should go in doing these things. Regarding Korea, some wanted to carry the war to China, in support of Douglas MacArthur's position; others, like Senator William F. Knowland of California, wanted to reduce United States involvement on the peninsula and to let other nations, particularly Nationalist China, take a greater share of Korea's defense; and still others, like Herbert Hoover, gave signs of waiting for an opportune moment for Americans to leave Korea. All wanted to improve United States defenses, but they disagreed on what to emphasize, be it naval, air, or land forces. Few of the critics wanted to spend as much for defense for as long as did the president, and few of them agreed with the size of his requests for foreign economic or even military assistance. Moreover, they had serious reservations about the cost and the controls involved in Truman's plans for defense mobilization. The opposition also believed that allies of the United States, especially the NATO nations, could contribute more to their own and Korea's defense and could forgo trading with the enemy, Communist China. What it boiled down to was that Truman's critics feared that he would jeopardize the economy and even the nation's freedom in a strategically unsound quest for improving the defenses against communism. In the minds of his critics, the president was associated with a long retreat in the face of Communist aggression, and nothing he did would inspire them to have faith in him. Similarly, the bitterness of so much of their opposition did not lead him to have confidence in them. The only thing that the great majority of Americans could agree upon at this time was that there was a world-wide Communist menace, which the United States had to deal with.

So, the Great Debate continued, as it would to the end of the Truman presidency. The immediate issue early in 1951 was how many United States troops should be committed to Europe. At the beginning of February, Gen. Dwight D. Eisenhower assured key members of Congress that NATO's European members would supply most of the forces. This was far from being satisfactory, for, as Senator Knowland commented, "that might be anything from 51% up to 90%."[9] The administration's repeated assurances that western Europe would assume most of the burden for its own defense—and thus the defense of United States interests in Europe—only slightly reduced support for the Wherry resolution to have Congress control the number of troops committed to NATO. Defense Secretary George Marshall could talk about a maximum of six divisions being sent. Neither he nor the chairman of the Joint Chiefs of Staff, Omar Bradley, nor Secretary of

State Dean Acheson could, however, be pinned down to that figure as a ceiling. After all, they could not tell what the future would bring or exactly how United States troops would be deployed. Finally, in early April, the Senate adopted Resolution 99, a diluted version of the Wherry resolution, which did not completely satisfy anyone. Thereby the upper chamber declared that no more than four divisions of United States troops should be assigned to the defense of Europe "without further congressional approval"; that before sending these troops the JCS should certify that America's NATO allies were contributing fully to the common defense; and that consideration be given to using West German and Spanish military resources. On April 5 President Truman greeted this as "further evidence that the country stands firm in its support of the North Atlantic Treaty."

The administration could, of course, interpret Resolution 99 less favorably. Many governmental leaders were unhappy with the certification concept and with the provision for consultation with Congress. Nevertheless, the administration could live with Resolution 99, especially since the most important issue had been silenced. After all, the Senate had failed to define the basic requirement for European contributions to NATO forces. Some senators, like Democrat Paul H. Douglas of Illinois, who otherwise fully supported the administration's military policy, wanted this to be defined. They failed to press it, however, trusting in the good faith and ability of the government. Douglas later lamented this, writing: "France, the nation most immediately protected, never made an adequate contribution. . . . Great Britain felt so financially insecure that it cut its contribution. The smaller European nations have made inadequate additions. Just as they had depended on Great Britain before both the world wars, so now they depended on the United States."[10] Thus, the United States would pay disproportionately for the Truman administration's faith in its NATO allies. The United States paid 76 percent of NATO's cost in 1954, 71 percent as late as 1971, though only 56 percent by 1980.

Meanwhile, public confidence in President Truman was deteriorating. The Gallup poll reported in September 1950 that 43 percent of its respondents approved and 32 percent disapproved of how Truman was handling his job. By January 1951, 36 percent approved and 49 percent disapproved, and by March only 26 percent approved while 57 percent disapproved. The White House was concerned that, as Press Secretary Joseph Short put it, its "story" was "not reaching the American public." On March 30 Short met with several other presidential aides to initiate an effort by top officials to "carry the message of the Administration's policies and objectives to the 48 states."[11] Truman was already working with an editor of *Collier's* magazine, William Hillman, on a book about the president. This was just the beginning of the administration's accelerated efforts to explain itself to the people. These did not work, which explained much of Truman's increased testiness with the press during the rest of his term.

Truman and his administration did not lack for publicity. Indeed, in April 1951 this publicity would reach its peak in an event that would fuel the Great Debate to new vigor—namely, Truman's relief of Gen. Douglas MacArthur from his command in the Far East. MacArthur had never, even under Presidents Hoover and Roosevelt, been a humble subordinate. He had been guilty of insubordination, especially since the commencement of the Korean War, and his indiscretions had helped to earn him a back seat in the efforts to turn the conflict around since Christmas 1950. Consequently, MacArthur became more restive, knowing that he was only technically in command in the Far East. The House Republican leader, Joseph W. Martin, Jr., had been one of the administration's strongest critics. He contended that Chiang Kai-shek should be permitted to use his eight hundred thousand troops to attack mainland China in order to help achieve victory in Korea. Martin also persisted in asking whether the United States intended to win in Korea, suggesting that if it did not, the administration was guilty of murdering American boys there. The administration's answer was that it was seeking a limited war to bring China and North Korea to the negotiating table and to avoid igniting a third world war.

In March 1951 Martin sought support for his position from MacArthur, asking him to comment on his views about a second front in China. The general replied on March 20 that Martin's "view with respect to the utilization of the Chinese forces on Formosa is in conflict with neither logic nor [the American] tradition . . . of meeting force with maximum counterforce."[12] In the course of making his comments, the general also managed to cast aspersions on European diplomats as well as on the administration's policy in Korea. Martin did not know what to do with MacArthur's remarkably candid letter, which was not marked confidential. The Republican leader in the House later indicated that disagreement between two Democratic eminences helped him to decide. After Senator Tom Connally had said that there would be no war with Russia in 1951 while Speaker Sam Rayburn had warned that the possibility of a new world war confronted the United States, Martin released MacArthur's letter to the public on April 5.

Truman reacted swiftly. He wrote in his diary on April 5, "The situation with regard to the Far Eastern General has become a political one. MacArthur has made himself a center of controversy, publicly and privately."[13] On the next day the president reviewed his recent relations with MacArthur. He concluded: "This looks like the last straw. Rank insubordination."[14] Truman called in Dean Acheson, George Marshall, Averell Harriman, and Omar Bradley to discuss the situation. He already believed that MacArthur should be relieved of his command, but he did not tell his advisers this. They did not arrive at a conclusion on April 6, so the president asked them to meet with him again the next morning. After this meeting on April 7, Truman wrote in his diary, "It is the unanimous opinion of all that MacArthur be relieved."[15] He directed that the necessary orders be prepared. On April 9, these orders were dispatched, relieving MacArthur of all of his commands and appointing Ridgway to succeed him.

Why had Truman acted so decisively? Not only was he fed up with MacArthur for being unusually insubordinate and for entering the political arena, but the general's indiscretions also seemed to be part of a program to thwart the administration's plans to initiate cease-fire talks in Korea. Moreover, matters were brightening, for Ridgway's forces were continuing to advance in Korea. Truman thought that he was correct constitutionally and militarily in relieving MacArthur, and he believed that most Americans would see it his way. They did not, in part because his Republican critics were quick to exploit the situation. Soon after hearing of Truman's action, Congressman Martin telephoned MacArthur to ask if the general would address a joint session of Congress, which he agreed to do. Martin then got the endorsement of other House and Senate Republican leaders, who were outraged by MacArthur's dismissal. The Democratic congressional leaders had no choice but to concur in inviting the general to address Congress, which was a traditional honor conferred upon United States military eminences. Truman had already issued a press statement explaining that he had relieved MacArthur because the latter did not wholeheartedly support UN and administration policies in Korea, although the president took care to praise the general's past contributions. On April 11 Truman took to the radio to elaborate on United States policy and on the need to relieve MacArthur. Two days later he publicly indicated his pleasure that Congress had invited the general to address it. And why not? The White House mail so far had run almost two-to-one in support of Truman's action, and he fully expected that MacArthur would observe the amenities upon his return to the United States.

The tide would change quickly, however. On April 16 White House aide Eben Ayers noted the tremendous reaction to MacArthur's dismissal, much of which was "intemperate and hysterical."[16] The voluminous mail on the subject became increasingly hostile after April 13.

The widespread and continuing press commentary ran very much the same way. The Gallup poll showed that 66 percent of its respondents disapproved of Truman's action, while only 25 percent approved. At no time during his presidency did so many Americans express themselves so vigorously about an issue. The issue clearly was seen by most citizens as one of the strong general against the weak president in standing against Communist expansion. When MacArthur returned, he did not report to Truman, his commander in chief, as precedent and protocol demanded. And when the general spoke to Congress on April 19, he was, as in other public appearances that spring, cleverly contentious and identified himself with the president's critics. As Congressman Martin reported, when MacArthur finished addressing Congress, there was not ''a dry eye on the Republican side nor a dry seat on the Democratic. The theatrical effect was superb.''[17]

Truman had ordered his aides not to criticize MacArthur, and most of them obeyed. On John Steelman's recommendation, though, the president did direct George Elsey to let Anthony Leviero of the *New York Times* examine the documents relating to the Wake Island conference. Leviero summarized these in an article of April 21, which received much attention, although it did not do much to help Truman, who was sharply criticized for not having released the documents to all the media. But by generally playing down the MacArthur issue, the White House allowed it to lose its fire by summer, although it would contribute to keeping the Great Debate going. Congress continued to debate and to investigate, often with MacArthur's name being invoked. It seemed increasingly plain that the Great Debate was aimed less at reversing United States foreign and military policy in 1951 than at shifting power to Congress and turning things around at the polls in 1952.

Despite the Great Debate and the MacArthur episode, the Truman administration steadily went about the business of trying to implement its mobilization, foreign, and military policies. The administration had been at odds with itself as to how to spur economic mobilization and yet to restrain inflation. Alan Valentine, the director of the Economic Stabilization Administration, fought to go slow on controls, but he was losing out to Director Michael V. DiSalle of the Office of Price Stabilization. Valentine resigned in January 1951, and the administration soon called for the full imposition of price and wage controls. This was easier said than done. By March, organized labor had boycotted the federal mobilization committees; this led to the collapse of the Wage Stabilization Board, which had to be reorganized in April. The result was that labor succeeded in gaining concessions in formulating wage increases. Agriculture and business also became combative, which led to modifications in the government's price-control programs. Underlying this was constant infighting among the stabilizers, the interested federal agencies, and various congressional elements. Everyone had his own idea of how economic stabilization should work, so the administration's price and wage controls were never fully effective.

There was also the question of credit restraints, which in February, at Treasury Secretary John Snyder's insistence, the president asked his chief advisers to consider more seriously. Part of the problem here had been the Federal Reserve Board's (FRB) tendency—with substantial support from the nation's bankers—to become independent of political direction. In response to Truman's request, FRB Chairman Thomas B. McCabe, director of the Office of Defense Mobilization Charles E. Wilson, Chairman Leon Keyserling of the Council of Economic Advisers, and Assistant Secretary of the Treasury William McChesney Martin, Jr., formed a committee to deal with restraints on credit. In March the result of the committee's work—which might have been much different had Secretary Snyder not been ill—was that the FRB no longer had to support government bonds at par. From this point on, the "Fed" was free to do as it pleased. Although Assistant Secretary Martin became the chairman of the FRB that spring, he did not follow the wishes of the Treasury or, for that matter, of the CEA or the Commerce Department. He became the champion of keeping credit going in order to avoid an eventual recession, which appealed to Truman because of his disastrous post–World War I business experience. Cheap loans would fuel industrial expansion and consumer credit. Ultimately, the price would be paid, however, in spurts of inflation, increases in interest rates, and in higher taxes.

Yet the economy worked well during the Korean War. From the middle of 1950 to April 1953 the value of the gross national product increased from $275.4 billion to $364.2 billion, or by about 32 percent. The consumer price index rose from 71.2 to 79.7, or by 12 percent, with most of the rise appearing during the first nine months of the war. Unemployment dropped from 5.6 percent to 2.7 percent, by far the best record since World War II. Average hourly earnings in the area of manufacturing climbed steadily from 51.3 to 61 cents, or by some 19 percent, which was well ahead of inflation, without even counting the overtime pay of many Americans. Clearly, this was a time of prosperity. Even the rates on three-month treasury bills increased only from 1.2 to 2 percent, and private interest rates rose, but only slightly. It was a remarkable record.

It did not seem so remarkable to President Truman at the time. In 1951, to the Defense Production Act, he sought to add provisions to subsidize production, to increase various economic controls, to finance governmental construction and operation of defense plants, and to expand the guarantees of farm parity. Congress responded by adding only some incentives for production; moreover, this legislation weakened price controls by allowing higher price ceilings. In August, Truman asked Congress to reconsider and to grant him what he had requested, but his plea was in vain. One can understand Congress's reluctance to act, for inflation did not seem to be as threatening or production as low as the president said it was. Nevertheless, the new legislation did give the government additional powers to act to maintain and even expand defense production in order to meet pressing obligations to NATO and in Korea.

What Congress did and what the public thought were influenced by the course of the war in Korea. This was a factor that could do Truman little good, barring a quick and smashing victory over Communist forces. Ordinary advances by UN troops encouraged Americans to think that they did not need to do much more, while any reverse led to scathing criticism of the administration. UN forces continued to move forward until April 22, 1951, when the Chinese launched a spring offensive that pushed UN troops south of the thirty-eighth parallel. It was the last all-out effort by the Chinese to expel the UN armies from Korea, and it failed. On May 20, UN forces began their counteroffensive, which General Ridgway thought could have been pressed to the Yalu River. The orders were not given to do so. The price would have been too high, involving an estimated one hundred thousand casualties. Moreover, Ridgway observed: "Our prize would have been no more than many square miles of inhospitable real estate, much of it a-swarm with guerrillas for years to come. The enemy would have shortened his supply routes as we lengthened ours . . . . our battle line would have been stretched from 110 miles to 420 miles."[18] As the UN commander saw it, the American people were not prepared to support the size of forces needed to hold that long line, to risk a bloody war in Manchuria, or to remain indefinitely at war on the Asian mainland. Even MacArthur had not had a satisfactory answer. When Senator Lyndon B. Johnson asked him what would happen if the Chinese were forced back into Manchuria and refused to stop fighting, the general could only answer that he did not believe they would continue to fight.

In their spring 1951 counteroffensive, the UN forces only advanced to positions slightly beyond the thirty-eighth parallel. They had thus roughly achieved their original objective of expelling the invaders from South Korea. The rest of the war would seesaw around the boundary of the thirty-eighth parallel. It was a victory, but it was not the complete victory that many Americans wanted. By May the administration clearly had decided that a full victory in Korea would be too costly and that a political solution must be sought. The Communists responded on June 23, when the Soviet delegate to the UN, Jacob A. Malik, indicated that it was time to discuss a cease-fire and an armistice in Korea; and the Chinese Communists soon demonstrated that they were interested. By July 10 negotiations had begun in Kaesong, in Communist-held territory.

Everything looked hopeful for the termination of hostilities. This would, however, prove to be an illusion. Charges and countercharges with regard to incidents and bad faith marred and even interrupted the proceedings. More than two years were to pass before an agreement on the truce would be reached, by which time Truman had left the White House. By December 1951 the president was discouraged and thought the less that was said about the situation, the better. He said to his news conference off the record on December 13: "I do not want to be quoted on anything in regard to Korea. Now, this situation is exceedingly delicate and dangerous, and it is your situation as well as mine. . . . So keep still about Korea and the truce." Truman's pessimism was reflected in the White House mail, as the correspondence in the combined category of "End the War in Korea, Use the Atom Bomb, and Bring Troops Home" rose from 5,122 pieces received during the second week in December to 9,007 during the third week and to 20,072 during the fourth week, which was a record for any topic in 1951 except for the most-active week regarding MacArthur. Meanwhile, as the months passed, the administration hewed to the strategy of holding the line and keeping casualties to a minimum. It was, as it would be to the end in 1953, a frustrating war aimed at showing the Communist forces that they could not seize South Korea and that they would have to make peace.

Korea may have been the Truman administration's main focus abroad during 1951, but it was not the only one. Washington sought to develop its ties with its allies. One of the government's chief objectives was to secure French cooperation on a variety of issues, especially in a meeting during January between President Truman and Premier René Pleven. Truman and Pleven exchanged pledges of support for each other's objectives in Korea and Indochina. Pleven reiterated France's wish to achieve greater economic integration in Europe, the formation of a European army within NATO, and continued United States support and consultation on defense and economic matters. This meeting and discussions with President Vincent Auriol in March seemed to be amiable on the surface. What they disguised was the fact that the French were not agreed on what they wanted. It also became clear that many French leaders were, like Auriol, deeply suspicious of Germany's rearmament and, like Pleven, were more hopeful about accommodation with the Russians than were the Americans. Consequently, the Americans and the French never reached comfortable understandings during Truman's presidency. Indeed, the Americans saw the French as a divisive force that would delay German rearmament, scuttle the European Defense Community, underestimate Soviet hostility, and fail to do its part in East Asia. Yet out of the interplay between the United States and France would come enough French contributions eventually to achieve basic NATO objectives, the establishment of a West German defense force, discussions with Russia, and, especially, greater economic cooperation among western-European nations.

Again, in 1951, Truman made gestures indicating his administration's interest in world peace and its willingness to discuss reducing armaments. In March and November he announced that the United States, France, and Great Britain proposed using the UN inventory of the arms of military powers as a basis on which nations would make arrangements to reduce armaments. Although the president declared that Communist aggression had brought the world to a crisis point, the United States was willing to join with Russia and others to cut back on the burden of arms and to lessen the possibility of war. It was reported in November that upon hearing this, Andrei Y. Vishinsky, the Soviet delegate to the UN, laughed through the night and could not get to sleep.

Even less likely to bear fruit was Truman's message of July 7 to Russia, transmitting a congressional resolution expressing America's friendship and good will for all peoples and the deep desire of the United States to bring about peace. He added to this his hope that America's peace aims would be shared with the Soviet people, although he also chastised the Russian leadership for obstructing communication among peoples. The Kremlin could not have received this message cheerfully. It was not until a month later that Truman's message was released in the Soviet press, a delay that the president almost gleefully pointed out, along with past Russian obstructions to public communication. In reporting on this to Congress on August 20, he concluded that there was no reason to alter United States policy toward Russia. The Soviet Union might talk about peace, Truman said, but plainly it was not doing anything about it.

This was not the stuff out of which détente could be made. From the administration's point of view, United States gestures toward peace and disarmament only pointed up the intransigence of the Soviet Union, as did the stormy course of cease-fire negotiations in Korea. There was also fear in Washington that Moscow would try to exploit the occurrence of famine in India. The president was unhappy with Indian Prime Minister Jawaharlal Nehru for having complicated the settlement of the Kashmir question with Pakistan and for having given unsolicited advice on how to handle the Korean War. Clearly unable to make Nehru out, Truman wrote: "One Britisher calls him a 'political crook.' He's Britain's McCarthy maybe."[19] Nevertheless, Truman was not prepared to let India become vulnerable to Communist initiatives; therefore he consulted with Herbert Hoover on India's food crisis and asked Congress for famine relief in February. Congress acted in June, providing that up to 2 million tons of grain be sent to India on easy credit terms and authorizing the application of much of the interest that would accrue to the educational exchange programs between the two nations.

Iran presented a more difficult problem. Its relations with the West had deteriorated since 1947, partly because Iran had not received the assistance that it had expected. The British had also refused to make the concessions that Iran had demanded with respect to the operation of the Anglo-Iranian Oil Company. By January 1951 the nationalization of the company seemed to be in the offing, which strained relations with the United States as well as with Britain. In March the assassination of Iran's prime minister, Ali Razmara, seemed to spoil the last chance for accommodation. His successor, Mohammed Mossadegh, soon steered nationalization through the Iranian parliament. The Central Intelligence Agency saw in this situation a ripe opportunity for Communist exploitation; there was also the possibility that the West would be cut off from Iran's rich oil resources. The Truman administration sprang into action, requesting more military and technical assistance for Iran. Washington also pressed the British—though not very successfully—to make a better deal with Iran, and it negotiated with Mossadegh to create a more friendly climate. Not enough United States aid was forthcoming, the British were reluctant to act except to bring down Iran's government, and Mossadegh proved to be quixotic and mercurial. The year 1951 closed no better than it had opened, as far as Washington was concerned, with the Soviets perched on Iran's border, eagerly awaiting the next act in their neighbor's drama.

Iran in 1951 was just part of the Truman administration's concern to bolster anti-Communist defenses almost everywhere in the world. In January the National Security Council stressed the need to do so in Afghanistan, Ceylon, India, Nepal, and Pakistan through aid, propaganda, and the promotion of cooperative defense efforts. The United States stepped up its efforts to try to stop the shipment of contraband from Western nations to Communist China, but with little success. On May 24 Truman unveiled his requests to Congress for a massive program of mutual-security aid, primarily for Europe, but also with significant amounts to be allocated to Asia, Africa, and Latin America. This really was a continuation of United States programs of economic and military aid, except that the president was asking for proportionately more in military assistance and for administrative coordination of programs dealing with military and economic aid. As was the case with his other public statements on world affairs in 1951, he packaged his mutual-security requests in the rhetoric of crisis as he spoke of "a very real and terrible danger," "communist dreams of world conquest," and the Soviet "drums of war." What was needed was concerted action by free countries in order to meet Russia's economic, military, propaganda, and subversive challenges. The burden would be great for the United States, but the strengthening of free peoples around the globe would halt Communist aggrandizement. Congress took its time in acting, but finally, in October, Truman was able to approve the Mutual Security Act, although it provided for only $6.9 billion, or about four-fifths of what he had requested. Soon the Mutual Security Agency was created to administer the program. To show that he meant business, the president appointed the tough Cold War warrior W. Averell Harriman as its director.

Truman was unhappy with Congress's refusal to go all of the way with him on extending foreign aid, although in retrospect it is remarkable how far the legislators did go while many of them were scolding the administration about its foreign policies. He was also upset by the enactment of legislation that barred giving economic or financial assistance to countries that sold potential or actual war material to Russia and its allies. In June, Truman called upon Congress to modify this proviso in order to allow for essential trade without penalty between Communist and non-Communist nations. In a letter to a cousin, he fulminated about the proviso, largely because he believed it might "stop rearmament of Europe" and partly because of the galling fact that Missouri Senator James P. Kem had sponsored it.[20] The president was able to deal with the trade restriction by taking advantage of a legislative stipulation that exceptions could be made, although when he used these, he invited sharp criticism. Nevertheless, the whole business embarrassed the administration in foreign relations and did slow down European rearmament. There was also the exceptional case of Yugoslavia, which the administration wanted to use as an example of a Communist state that had broken with the Kremlin. The United States was providing Yugoslavia with economic assistance, so that it would be less vulnerable to Soviet pressures. The extension of this aid in November, under an exceptionary clause of the Mutual Security Act, was the occasion for another round of abuse of the administration by its many critics.

An important part of the foreign-economic program of the Truman administration was to continue the president's authority to make reciprocal trade agreements with other countries and to lower tariff rates. Although this had been a touchy issue since New Deal days— thanks to the continuing influence of high-tariff interest groups— Congress overwhelmingly extended the Trade Agreements Act in June 1951. Indeed, the legislators renewed it for two years. Thus, this legislation continued to be a vital part of United States foreign policy, and not just by reducing trade barriers through reciprocal agreements and unilateral tariff adjustments. The legislation also allowed the administration to take full advantage of most-favored-nation arrangements in its efforts to liberalize world trade. The overall effect was to encourage trade to be conducted on a more competitive and less restrictive basis. This substantially increased the growth of commerce among free-world nations, particularly on the part of the United States. The resulting economic interdependence was an important tie in keeping together the anti-Communist coalition of countries.

Meanwhile the administration was working hard in other ways to develop the world-wide anti-Communist alliance. A particular strategy had been devised for East Asia, which Truman announced in April 1951. The United States expected to keep its armed forces in the Ryukyu Islands and the Philippines. It was working on a peace treaty with Japan that would include a security arrangement, and it was forging mutual-security alliances with the Philippines, Australia, and New Zealand. Technically, this was meant to discourage Japanese aggression, but in actuality, the intent was to create defensive alliances against the Soviet Union. The security treaty among Australia, New Zealand, and the United States was drafted by July 1951, signed in September 1951, and went into force in April 1952. The ANZUS treaty was touted as the equivalent of the North Atlantic Treaty, but it was considerably less than that. Basically, it was a commitment among the three states to render military assistance in case of attack, to provide some coordination of military planning, and to exchange pertinent information. The two Pacific nations also assented to the conclusion of a peace treaty with Japan. The Filipino–United States pact was signed in August 1951 and went into force a year later. It tied the United States closer to protecting the young nation against foreign attack, and the Philippines were to aid America militarily when called upon to do so. The Filipinos also agreed to the Japanese treaty. In a sense these alliances would be the basis for the development of the Southeast Asia Treaty Organization in 1954. Washington rejected the larger treaty concept in 1951, however, because of the delicate relations then between non-Asian states and the former colonial areas.

Peace and security arrangements with Japan were crucial to United States strategy. John Foster Dulles, as consultant to the secretary of state, was the responsible party in working these out. Not only were his estimable powers as a negotiator used effectively, but his high standing in the Republican party reduced the likelihood that the Senate would obstruct the ratification of any agreements. By 1949 Washington had given up hope of coming to agreement with Moscow on a peace treaty with Japan. The outbreak of the Korean War and the intervention by China strengthened United States resolve to proceed with a treaty without Russian cooperation. These events also softened the resistance to a peace treaty on the part of non-Communist states. The United States believed that it could take the lead, because its arms had been largely responsible for defeating the Japanese Empire, because Japan had not been partitioned, and because the United States, through MacArthur, had guided the Japanese government during the postwar period.

Once President Truman had decided to conclude a peace treaty with Japan, the questions remained of what the treaty would include and how it would be achieved. Crucial to answering these questions was the matter of coping with the objections and fears of various interested parties. The Defense Department believed that a treaty would be premature; allies of the United States feared a resurgence of Japanese power; Communist China and Russia also feared this, as well as the United States forces that might remain in Japan; and many Japanese feared that they might lose their United States defense shield and also have an unpalatable treaty imposed upon them. The administration believed that it could ignore Communist objections, especially after the onset of the Korean conflict. General MacArthur devised a formula that placated both the Pentagon and the Japanese: namely, to negotiate a separate security treaty that would allow United States forces to stay in Japan as allies instead of as conquerors. Beyond this, there should be a peace treaty to declare an end to the war, and there should be separate treaties between Japan and various countries to settle other matters in dispute. The last part of the formula was to assure interested nations that the United States would guarantee their security, at least against China and Japan. This would have the advantage for the United States of offering opportunities to gain foreign bases and to receive military assistance, if needed. Truman agreed to MacArthur's formula in essence in September 1950, and the United States had begun to implement it by 1951.

The result, in 1951, was a Japanese-American security pact, providing not only for United States protection of Japan but also for American military forces and bases in Japan. There was also a multilateral peace treaty with Japan, which had no punitive or reparations provisions. Interested nations were given the right to work out agreements dealing with whatever claims they had against Japan. Many of Japan's former enemies opposed or had serious reservations about the peace-making process. They were kept informed, but they were seldom heeded. Indeed, the Japanese had more to say about the process and the substance of the peace treaty than did most of its former enemies. Communist countries and those nations—for example, Burma and India—that did not want to march in the train of the proposed global Pax Americana had no choice but to accept the results.

The conference on the Japanese treaty was held in San Francisco in September 1951. The Americans controlled the proceedings, and they had enough votes from among the delegates to ram through the treaty that they wanted. In effect, the Russians who were in attendance were treated to some of their own medicine. The result of the treaty was that Japan could return to the society of nations with little cost in penalties or in maintaining its security. The United States appeared to benefit hugely by using the treaty to forge a series of links in its anti-Communist alliance system. Australia, New Zealand, and the Philippines gained wanted security pacts with the United States. The payoff to South Korea and Taiwan for behaving themselves on the Japanese treaty was considerable in terms of the military and economic assistance that they received. The British and the French got substantial aid, as well as United States support for their holding operations in Southeast Asia. Even India, despite its disagreements with the United States, received assistance, as did Thailand. Everything involved in the Japanese peace and security treaties seemed to be a master stroke in the American effort to bolster the military and economic defenses of East Asia and the Pacific.

If Harry Truman in 1951 seemed to be more bellicose and more zealous in developing the defenses of non-Communist nations, it was partly because he thought that tensions with Russia were increasing. British, French, and Indian leaders, among others, worried about United States rigidity. They counseled greater patience and even suggested increasing efforts to explore the possibility of détente with the Soviet Union. The president and his chief advisers could not, however, see any encouragement for this from the Kremlin. Furthermore, the administration's critics at home were objecting that Truman and company were not being tough enough in dealing with the Communist menace. Because the United States was paying most of the cost of the common defense, it intended to have its own way. Americans were not going to go hat in hand to the Russians, not with the war in Korea flaming on, the mounting reports of repression in Communist countries, and the continuation of Soviet-inspired propaganda, espionage, and other hostile actions. To be sure, there was talk of peace from Moscow; but there was no sign of acting on it, except for the negotiations in Korea, which had degenerated into exchanges of vituperation between the Communist and UN representatives.

What seemed the most-saddening proof of Truman's suspicions of the Kremlin was the Russian explosion in 1951 of a second atomic bomb. Nuclear weaponry had been of great concern to him since the first Soviet atomic explosion in 1949, which had led to the administration's decision in 1950 to develop the hydrogen bomb. Russian possession of the atomic bomb had contributed to continued preventive-war talk in some circles in the United States. Truman shrank in horror from this idea; his solution was to seek more-powerful weapons of defense. He believed that the United States would have the ultimate weapon in the hydrogen bomb. Eben Ayers wrote that Truman had told him in August 1951: "It will settle everything." The president thought that two bombs would obliterate Moscow, and said, "That's a terrible thing." He believed that he had no choice, however, but to spur the development of the hydrogen bomb, especially as he understood that the Russians would not be far behind the United States in perfecting their own hydrogen bomb. Truman did not glory in the power that the bomb would give him; he told Ayers: "I never wanted power, only what is necessary to have so as to get some things done. I'd lay it all down and get out of here right off if I could settle all this now."[21] This he could not achieve.

Foreign affairs were not Truman's only burdensome worry with regard to communism. He also had to deal with the constant and savage criticism, led by Senator Joseph McCarthy, that the administration had failed to take care of subversion at home. In 1950 the president had sought to deal with this criticism by trying to discredit McCarthy, but he had failed in this. Indeed, McCarthy and other Republicans had effectively counterattacked in the November elections, which had led to losses among the administration's forces on Capitol Hill and an erosion of the courage of McCarthy's opponents there. Although the campaign to discredit the Wisconsin senator continued in 1951 and 1952, it had less and less force, as his antagonists feared his retaliatory powers. By

September 1951 only the short-term Democratic senator from Connecticut, William Benton, dared to engage McCarthy on the floor of the upper chamber. It was also Benton who sponsored the motion to expel McCarthy from the Senate; and on the subcommittee that considered the motion, only Democratic Senator Mike Monroney of Oklahoma pressed the matter. Clearly, the other members of the subcommittee either were McCarthy's defenders or had been intimidated. Indeed, Republican Margaret Chase Smith of Maine and Iowa Democrat Guy M. Gillette, chairman of the subcommittee, resigned from the panel rather than face McCarthy's awesome power. In a bizarre twist, in spring 1952, the Wisconsin senator persuaded the Senate to have the subcommittee investigate Benton as well as himself. Given McCarthy's clever exploitation of the country's widespread and hysterical fear of communism, it is no surprise that he was triumphantly reelected in 1952, while Benton was defeated at the polls.

Another tactic that the administration tried in order to legitimize its internal-security program was the establishment of a blue-ribbon commission on the subject. After the 1950 elections, Truman asked Herbert Hoover to accept the chairmanship of this bipartisan commission to inquire into the infiltration of Communists into the government, about which there "has been a great deal of misrepresentation and garbling of facts." Although Hoover was sympathetic to Truman's purpose, he wanted no part of an endeavor that he believed would not work, especially as "Congress itself is likely to be engaged in such investigations anyway."[22] Truman nevertheless proceeded, establishing the Commission on Internal Security and Individual Rights in January 1951, with Fleet Adm. Chester W. Nimitz as chairman. The commission soon became bogged down because its members insisted that they and the commission's employees be exempted by law from certain conflict-of-interest statutes. The House responded favorably to this idea, but the Senate Judiciary Committee refused to report the necessary legislation. In May, all members of the commission resigned, and in October, after an unsuccessful struggle with the Judiciary Committee, the president accepted the resignations and announced that he would make no replacement appointments. What Herbert Hoover had foreseen turned out to be a bigger fiasco than he had anticipated.

President Truman felt forced to turn to existing instrumentalities in trying to regain the credibility of the administration's internal-security program. The Loyalty Review Board had recommended that dismissal from federal service should be based on reasonable doubt about an employee's loyalty instead of on evidence of one's disloyalty. By late April, with criticism and pressure mounting, Truman accepted this new standard; but he continued to seek a better approach. Consequently, in July he asked the National Security Council for advice on improving the effectiveness of the internal-security program while making it more fair. In April 1952 the NSC recommended that he issue an executive order to accomplish these purposes. By the time that Truman issued the executive order in November, it was too late for it to be effective before the end of his presidency. The administration turned out to be better in showing its toughness than in following up on the president's concerns for individual rights. For example, in June 1951 the government arrested twenty-one more Communists under the provisions of the Smith Act.

However muddled his administration's record, Truman was concerned with the distinction between maintaining national security and protecting individual rights. He repeatedly spoke out against those who would violate personal liberties. Particularly, the president was disturbed by attacks in Congress and the press on Secretary of State Acheson and later on Defense Secretary Marshall and General Bradley, supposedly for being at least front men for traitors. On June 25 he said to an audience in Tullahoma, Tennessee: "That political smear campaign is doing this country no good. It's playing right into the hands of the Russians. . . . Lies, slander, mudslinging are the weapons of the totalitarians." That Truman had a broader conception of the problem was clear in his speech to the American Legion of August 14, in which he declared:

> We want to protect the country against disloyalty—of course we do. We have been punishing people for disloyal acts, and we are going to keep on punishing the guilty whenever we have a case against them. But we don't want to destroy our whole system of justice in the process. We don't want to injure innocent people. And yet the scurrilous work of the scandalmongers gravely threatens the whole idea of protection for the innocent in our country today. . . . And when even one American—who has done nothing wrong—is forced by fear to shut his mind and close his mouth, then all Americans are in peril.

Truman meant this. His dilemma—one that was shared by most concerned United States officials—was that he did not know how to protect the nation against whatever subversion there was and simultaneously to defend the Bill of Rights. Clearly, he compromised his position on the latter in an attempt to counter charges that his administration was weak on the former.

Additional evidence of Truman's compromising attitude came in 1951 with new standards pertaining to the security classification of federal records and to the dismissal of governmental employees. On September 25 the president issued Executive Order 10290, which applied uniform regulations for restricting information about national security. It also established, for the first time, procedures for the downgrading and declassification of certain records, although few people in the government were moved to undertake these tasks. Basically, however, the goal of the new order was to make more effective the restrictions on the use of federal documents. This led to a wave of protest from the press. The Associated Press Managing Editors' Association called EO 10290 "a dangerous instrument of the news suppression," and it demanded that there be a reexamination of the whole question of restricting information.[23] The press was filled with stories and editorials on the matter, but Truman's answer was that most information—95 percent of it—was available to the public. The controversy reinforced the president's irritation with the press. He wrote, in an unsent letter to Arthur Krock of the *New York Times:* "You newspaper men have a complex that anyone who tells you of any of your many shortcomings is either ambitious to be a dictator or else he is an ignoramus. . . . You find no trouble in suppressing news in which I'm interested. Why can't you do a little safety policing?"[24]

The standards regarding security-related dismissals from federal employment had also been changed in 1951. Consequently, the Loyalty Review Board (LRB) and the Justice Department had a field day when homosexuality and alcoholism were added to the grounds for investigation and when social advocacy of almost any kind became suspect. In December the LRB even began a review of those civil servants whom it had already cleared of charges of being disloyal. As was mentioned earlier, Truman was disturbed by this new zealousness to ensure the loyalty of federal personnel, but not so much so that he was able effectively to combat it. Only after the civil service had been sanitized and after the loyalty-security hysteria in the United States had run its course by the late 1950s would things calm down. Truman, as president, could fret and even rant about the problem of balancing the state's security interests against the rights of individuals. What he was unable to do, given the hysteria of the times and his hesitancy to buck it, was to solve the problem.

Truman had, of course, his regular duties to perform, in addition to various miseries to suffer. As usual, he had to make nominations to office. The most important in 1951 was to find a replacement for Defense Secretary George C. Marshall, who resigned in September because of illness and fatigue. The choice was Marshall's deputy, Robert A. Lovett, who would serve Truman effectively for the rest of his time in office. Not all of the president's nominations worked out as well, however. Truman appointed two district court judges in Chicago, but Senator Paul Douglas of Illinois opposed these appointments because his own recommendations had been ignored. The upper chamber, following the tradition of senatorial courtesy, rejected the president's choices. Because Truman and Douglas could never come to agreement on the matter, it fell to a Republican president, Dwight Eisenhower, to fill the judgeships. Truman also nominated Earl W. Beck, a black political ally from Kansas City, to be recorder of deeds for the District of Columbia. As much out of spite as anything else, the Senate refused to confirm the appointment. In 1952 Truman again nominated Beck for the job; but Congress responded by vesting the appointment in the D.C. commissioners instead of in the president. It was a bitter blow for Truman, his Kansas City backers, and blacks. The president encountered a similar problem with his nomination of a woman, that of Federal Communications Commissioner Frieda B. Hennock to a federal district judgeship in New York. In this case the opposition—the American and New York bar associations—was more prestigious if not fairer. After several months, Hennock asked Truman to withdraw her nomination.

The president's most-controversial appointment in 1951 concerned, not color or gender, but religion. Truman had inherited Myron C. Taylor from Roosevelt as personal representative to the pope, but this irregular position lapsed with Taylor's resignation in 1950. In seeking a way to strengthen the informal anti-Communist alliance between the United States and the Vatican, Truman accepted Taylor's recommendation that an ambassador be appointed to replace him. The president delayed making this move because of Dean Acheson's suggestion that it would provoke controversy, of which the administration already had an abundance. In October 1951, however, Truman moved ahead with the appointment without either consulting Acheson or paving the way for it on Capitol Hill. Truman apparently believed that his appointee, Gen. Mark W. Clark, would command enough respect to be confirmed. In this he was wrong. Many senators, especially southern Democrats, became apoplectic; Protestant worthies roared; Catholics roared right back; and another of the great American furors of 1951 had been unleashed. For the next three weeks, the White House mail room was hard-pressed to handle the resulting mail, which ran six-and-a-half to one against sending an ambassador to the Vatican. Clark, bewildered by the controversy, asked to have his name withdrawn, thus cutting the ground out from under the president. Truman's reaction to the whole affair was, "I think maybe the United States does have a monopoly on bigotry."[25]

There was also the issue of scandal in government in 1951. The president was, of course, no stranger to scandal. However unfairly, Truman had repeatedly been criticized for his links to the Pendergast machine. His refusal to sever his friendship with the Pendergasts may have been admirable, but it was hardly politic. And there was enough genuine scandal in Kansas City during his presidency to make his Pendergast connections a live issue. In 1946 Truman had opposed the renomination of Kansas City Congressman Roger C. Slaughter, whom he deemed to be disloyal to his policies. This spurred a successful effort by the Pendergast organization to defeat Slaughter in the primary election. In 1947 seventy-one people were indicted for stuffing the ballot boxes; but the impounded ballots were stolen, so the case never went to trial. Then, in 1950, two leaders of a rival Kansas City political group, who had criminal connections, were shot dead in gangland fashion under an old Truman poster. The press had a grand time with this. Indeed, it had become a journalistic truism that Kansas City and even Missouri were corrupt and so was their best-known citizen.

Things became worse in 1951. Democratic Senator Estes Kefauver's 1950 investigations of crime in America had struck pay dirt, in part because of probes that he conducted in Kansas City and St. Louis. Kefauver attracted considerable Republican support for his activities, at least because investigation of urban crime was bound to be linked chiefly to Democrats, who ruled most of the cities. Kefauver's bipartisan backing led Truman to question both Kefauver's judgment and his loyalty to the Democratic party. The Tennessee senator's investigations extended into 1951, and they had greater impact as they attracted national television coverage. An audience estimated at 30 million people watched as Kefauver exposed crime and its connections with politicians, especially Democrats. Though the senator's work led to few convictions, it did over the years lead to other probes and to legislation that led to convictions. For Kefauver, it led to fame, a best-selling book, and status in 1952 as a leading contender for a presidential nomination. For Truman and the Democrats, it resulted in a black eye; and for the Republicans, in one of their key campaign issues. Kansas City emerged from the investigation better than most cities, although Kefauver characterized it as "a place that was struggling out from under the rule of the law of the jungle."[26] This was enough to stick in the public's memory and in the president's craw, especially since the senator had failed to investigate Republican areas and also his own state of Tennessee. To Truman's way of thinking, Kefauver was not only exceedingly ambitious but was also "a peculiar person. He is ignorant of history, an ametuer [sic] in politics and intellectually dishonest."[27]

This was only part of the administration's encounter with scandal in 1951. A Senate subcommittee, headed by Democrat J. William Fulbright of Arkansas, had been investigating the Reconstruction Finance Corporation (RFC), and the subcommittee's interim report of February suggested that there had been improper activities in connection with the agency's operations. In particular, the subcommittee report indicated that White House aide Donald S. Dawson had received free hotel accommodations from those who wanted favors from the RFC. There was also pressure on President Truman to comment on members of Congress who had tried to exercise influence with the agency. His response was that he had never done anything like that, and he was not going to comment on what others might have done (he was already having enough trouble with Congress). Regarding Dawson, Truman would only say that the people around him were honorable. Fulbright's subcommittee was able, however, to show a pattern of questionable RFC loans and to present evidence that reinforced suspicions of political influence having been involved. Truman was infuriated by what he regarded as the subcommittee's jumping to conclusions. Therefore, he plunged into a battle of wits and pressures with the members of the panel. This only led to additional charges, this time aimed at him. Senator Douglas complained that the president had asked the Internal Revenue Bureau to harass him, and Senator Charles W. Tobey reported that Truman had indicated that he had uncovered embarrassing information about members of the subcommittee. Plainly, the president had taken the wrong tack. Fulbright's subcommittee redoubled its efforts, which finally led to the resignation in October of the chairman of the Democratic National Committee, William M. Boyle, Jr., in connection with the RFC scandal.

The investigation of the RFC encouraged other congressional probes, which turned up additional instances of influence peddling in government. Particularly stunning was the evidence that officials of the Bureau of Internal Revenue had accepted bribes for tax fixing. This led to the dismissal of a number of federal officials and to prison sentences for several of them. Moreover, by the end of 1951, Attorney General J. Howard McGrath was under pressure to resign because of his department's slowness in dealing with the tax scandal. Truman indicated on December 26 how bad the situation was:

> The collector of internal revenue in San Francisco was discharged for inefficiency. He was afterward indicted. . . .

The collector in Boston was fired because of irregularities in his office. The collector in St. Louis was asked to resign because he did not attend to the duties of his office. He was afterward indicted for irregularities in his office. The collector at Nashville was fired because he is a drug addict. The New York office was cleaned up because of irregularities.

[Assistant Attorney General T. Lamar] Caudle was discharged because he did not handle his office efficiently and [IRB's Assistant General Counsel Charles] Oliphant was allowed to resign for the same reason.[28]

Truman believed that the administration had cleaned its own house, while Congress only wanted to talk about scandal. After all, he had promoted and facilitated the reorganization of the RFC and had spurred the purging of the IRB (Internal Revenue Bureau). He had also urged federal agencies to adopt conflict-of-interest rules, while Congress had failed to enact any. Yet, talk of governmental scandals would get worse in 1952, and the Republicans would adopt "corruption" as one of their most-effective election issues. Truman's chief problem in handling the scandals of his presidency was his slowness in believing that some of those around him could be corrupt; adding to his problem was that he failed to ask for help from those Democratic critics, such as Senators Douglas, Fulbright, and Kefauver, who could have been useful. And those whom he did ask for help, such as Republican Senator Wayne Morse, regardless of their reasons, declined to assist him.

The president believed that in 1951 he had staved off, again, a Communist onslaught on the free world; had improved the lot of his fellow Americans; had administered the government well and faithfully; had handled scandals effectively; and had had many good ideas for further improvement. He knew, though, that the year had been a most difficult one (largely, he thought, because of widespread and stubborn resistance to his plans). As he wrote to a cousin on December 12, with regard to the state of the Union, "It's in a hell of a state!"[29] It would not improve, from Truman's standpoint, during his final year in office.

12

★ ★ ★ ★ ★

"WINDING DOWN"

On January 1, 1952, Harry Truman jotted down in his diary: "What a New Year's Day! 1952 is here and so am I—gloomy as can be." It is not surprising that one of his aides would later characterize the rest of his presidency as "tired" and "winding down."[1] And why not? The Truman administration was beset by scandal, McCarthyism, usually belligerent Republicans and often uncooperative Democrats in Congress, the unending war in Korea, business bucking for higher prices, labor lusting for higher wages, and the world threatening to burst out into brush fires of conflict or criticism. There was so much to be done, as Truman saw it, but the odds of accomplishing it were lessening as time ran out for him.

The president was not so tired or gloomy that he had lost interest in doing his job. Repeatedly, he entered the breach to fight for his administration's programs. Foremost was the struggle for peace, which meant not only fighting on in Korea but also shoring up the defenses of the non-Communist nations. Intimately connected with this were the efforts to keep the United States economically strong by stimulating production and restraining inflation. After this came those aspects of the Fair Deal program that Truman believed were vital and feasible, especially housing and schools—under the guise of emergency measures—and agriculture and Social Security. In making requests of Congress in 1952, he largely repeated what he had called for in 1951, except for a new offensive in connection with health care. He also reiterated his sense of crisis and of the need for national unity. Truman emphasized that the threat of war had not vanished. Therefore, he asserted in his State of the Union Message of January 9, 1952: "When everything is said and done, all of us—Republicans and Democrats alike—all of us are Americans; and we are all going to sink or swim together."

Economically, not everyone would be together even in the administration. For example, the Council of Economic Advisers warned against the dangers of inflation, while the Federal Reserve Board was concerned with the potential of deflationary pressures. The president called for continued controls on inflation, but in 1951 he had already compromised by allowing the FRB to reduce some of them. Whatever the results of this conflict, the administration's policies worked reasonably well in 1952, as inflation remained in check, while employment, income, and production grew larger. Indeed, what dwindled were federal controls. In June, Congress not only refused to expand the government's powers to restrain inflation; it also placed limits on existing price controls and crippled the restrictions on credit, rent, and wages. This was only part of the pattern, for the FRB suspended its control of consumer credit on May 7 and of real-estate credit on September 16. Moreover, less money was appropriated for the operations of federal stabilization agencies, which, along with other governmental organizations, were in spirited disagreement about what controls should be exercised. The stabilization agencies were also affected by frequent changes in leadership. In March, Charles E. Wilson resigned as director of defense mobilization, to be succeeded by John R. Steelman, who in turn was replaced by Henry H. Fowler. Economic Stabilization Administrator Eric Johnston left, to be succeeded first by Roger Putnam and then by Michael DiSalle. DiSalle, Ellis Arnall, and Tighe Woods served as price-stabilization directors in 1952; and Nathan Feinsinger and Archibald Cox served as chairmen of the Wage Stabilization Board. It is no wonder that during the year the question was often asked jokingly, "Who's boss this month?" Not surprisingly, the government's structure of controls on inflation fell apart before the end of Truman's presidency.

The administration was more consistent in pressing for increased appropriations. On January 21 Truman asked Congress for almost $85.5 billion, compared with some $71.6 billion a year earlier. His requests for the military services was up by almost $10 billion, and for international security, by more than $3 billion; he asked for little extra and occasionally for less for domestic programs. The president tried to balance off his request for higher appropriations by asking for some $10 billion less in new obligational authority for long-term projects. He hoped that Congress would increase taxes in order to balance the budget, but as he expected, the legislators did not do so. Truman anticipated, therefore, that the federal debt would rise from $260 billion during the year after June 30, 1952, to $275 billion. Although Congress had largely appropriated in sum total what he had requested in 1951, it granted $10 billion less in 1952 than what he demanded, chiefly in the areas of the military and international security. This did, however, have the advantage of keeping the federal debt from rising as much as the president had predicted it would. In its own way, Congress had kept the problems of debt and inflation from getting out of hand.

Uppermost in Truman's mind was the international confrontation with communism. He was not sanguine about settling the many issues between East and West, for the information that was reaching him bolstered his conviction that a grave world crisis existed. For example, there was the special estimate prepared by the Central Intelligence Agency in September 1951. This report was blunt and quite bleak. There seemed to be little chance that the Kremlin would fail to control its allies. The military strength, including atomic weaponry, of Communist powers should grow. Moreover, they would "continue to have extensive propaganda, subversive, and obstructive capabilities, both overt and covert." The growth of the economic, military, and political strength of non-Communist nations made victory for the Soviet Union doubtful in a general war. "Nevertheless, this consideration cannot be accepted as necessarily controlling the USSR's decision and the period through mid-1953 will be one of acute danger of global war." A greater short-run danger would be that the Kremlin would temporarily relax international tensions in order "to lull the West into a false sense of security and undermine growing Western strength."[2]

President Truman and his military and diplomatic advisers took this and similar intelligence as confirmations of the wisdom of continuing to develop the West's economic, military, and political power. Congress and America's allies, they hoped, would continue to support this policy. If administration leaders were additionally affected by the word that was circulating among key eastern-European officials that the aging and ailing Joseph Stalin was planning a general war by 1953, this did not show. It did not have to, however, for Truman and his advisers already believed in the possibility of a global war. Affairs were discouraging enough that the president could get bellicose. This was evident in a letter that he wrote to himself on January 27, 1952, in which he charged: "Communist governments . . . have no sense of honor and no moral code. . . . We are tired of these phony calls for peace when there is no intention to make an honest approach to peace." What this seemed to suggest was an ultimatum to Moscow along the lines of: "Get the Chinamen out of Korea. Give Poland, Estonia, Latvia, Lithuania,

Rumania, and Hugary [sic] their freedom. Stop supplying war material to the thugs who are attacking the free world and settle down to an honorable policy of keeping agreements which have already been made." The alternative was "all out war." This meant that major cities and "every manufacturing plant in China and the Soviet Union will be eliminated. This is the final chance for the Soviet Government to decide whether it desires to survive or not." During the acrimonious discussions over exchanging war prisoners in Korea, the president penned another highly belligerent ultimatum in his private diary on May 18. This contained the question, "Now do you want an end to hostilities in Korea or do you want China and Siberia destroyed?" It was signed "The C. in C."[3]

One can imagine how much Captain Harry, the war veteran, was tempted to take direct action to solve his country's foreign problems. As Truman the President, however, he did not yield to this temptation, and he followed a more-reasoned policy. It was not easy. Having built a far-flung anti-Communist alliance, Truman now had to keep it together, make it more effective, and retain leadership of it for the United States. This meant, among other things, conferring with foreign leaders, ranging from newly elected British Prime Minister Winston Churchill at the beginning of 1952 to Norwegian Prime Minister Oscar Torp during the election campaign. Moreover, the president's men, at home and abroad, were often in touch with men of authority, using persuasion, concessions, cajolery, and pressure to try to keep the latter in line.

Crucial to American efforts abroad was the firming up of the North Atlantic Treaty Organization. This was Secretary of State Dean Acheson's chief responsibility, and the key objective was to integrate western Europe's defenses. Churchill initially balked because of his fantasy of the impossibility of making an effective platoon out of a mixture of Dutchmen, Frenchmen, Germans, Greeks, Italians, and Turks, although no one was suggesting such units. And this was just one of many issues, relevant and irrelevant, on which the grand old war horse wanted his say. Thanks to Foreign Minister Anthony Eden, though, the British lined up reasonably well on questions of European defense.

The chief stumbling block was France, which led the opposition to integrating Germany into European defense. This had been an ongoing issue, one that Acheson believed was the greatest problem facing the North Atlantic alliance. West Germany, seeing its star rising, strengthened its conditions for participating in the defense of western Europe. France responded by demanding restrictions on the rearmament of its traditional enemy. This was complicated by the fear of other continental allies that the eventual result of the interplay between France and

Germany might be that these two powers would dominate the alliance. In January the French proposed not only that German arms and arms production be restricted but also that German military strength in Europe not exceed that of France, that there be an economic union between France and the Saar, and that West Germany be a member only of the European Defense Community, not of NATO, which would presumably make that country easier to control. The Germans would not accept these conditions, considering them to be humiliating. Germany might volunteer to accept certain limitations, but it refused to have them imposed. With this the Americans agreed, and they sought to break the impasse.

Acheson had his work cut out for him. He made America's position clear, and he was prepared to gamble in order to get his way. Acheson took advantage of the funeral of King George VI in London in February to soften up the British and French foreign ministers, Anthony Eden and Robert Schuman. Chancellor Konrad Adenauer of Germany later joined them in London, which helped in gaining concessions from the most-important powers involved. Finally, a compromise was reached. Among the agreements were that West Germany would not produce airplanes, atomic energy, large vessels, and missiles; that certain allies, as well as Germany, would not manufacture specified types of war material; that there would be joint sessions of the NATO and EDC councils; and that France and Germany would dispose of the Saar issue separately.

The meeting of the NATO council in Lisbon, beginning February 21, took up these and other problems. None of this was easy, but progress was made. Probably spurred on by fear of future German power, France agreed to increase its defense budget to proportionately the highest in western Europe. The Germans vowed not only to seek a larger defense budget but also to increase their contribution for supporting Allied troops on their soil. The council approved the establishment of the European Army and the lowering of the proportion of America's financing of NATO; it also endorsed the arrangements that were emerging relative to West Germany. Acheson considered the results of the Lisbon meeting as "pretty close to a grand slam." He later wrote: "We seemed to have broken through a long series of obstacles and to be fairly started toward a more united and stronger Europe and an integrated Atlantic defense system."[4] This assessment was in part illusory, because the agreements that were reached in London and Lisbon were not necessarily acceptable in other NATO capitals. A new Russian demand of March 10 for talks to dispose of the German issue was central to this. It fanned French interest in restricting Germany, and it led many Germans to think that they might eventually get something better than what they already had. Although the Soviet initiative found some sympathizers in the United States and Britain, Washington and London remained firm in their resolve to keep Russia out of West German affairs. This was not enough to overcome resistance in Paris and Bonn to the implementation of the London and Lisbon accords. It did, however, in May lead the United States, Britain, and France to give West Germany freedom in conducting its domestic and foreign affairs. Ultimately, Bonn was given a role in NATO itself, but only after years of negotiation.

Middle Eastern questions also faced the Truman administration. Most important, the touchy relations between Israel and its Arab neighbors threatened to erupt into war and to invite Russian intrigue. Washington spent much time in trying to soothe the heightened sensibilities of the Arabs, the Israelis, and even the British and the French, who considered themselves to be repositories of wisdom on Middle Eastern questions. The United States also poured economic and military aid into the area, partly as a form of baksheesh to help trading relations and partly to bolster everybody's defenses against everyone else. There were also contributions, made out of charity as well as diplomacy, to help take care of the Palestinian refugees. Americans were learning, if slowly, that in the Middle East, other peoples did not readily embrace the live-and-let-live concept, that the events of one year could have long-term consequences, and that agreements could be short-lived.

Egypt, which was groping its way toward independence from Great Britain, was becoming a challenge for the United States. One idea to meet this challenge was to align Egypt with the West by establishing a Middle East command in which that country would become a key element. In the fall of 1951 Egypt rejected the idea of a Middle East command and, in effect, unilaterally declared its independence. Neither the British nor the Egyptians were willing to negotiate their differences, despite United States encouragement. By January 1952 fighting had broken out between British and Egyptian troops. The immediate crisis was resolved when King Farouk dismissed the Egyptian government and the British took a more conciliatory line. This did not, however, get the two governments into harness toward resolving their differences. In July a military front, under the nominal leadership of Gen. Mohammed Naguib, overthrew Farouk. Naguib later gave some promise of negotiating with the British; but by then the Truman administration had left office, with Americans being frustrated by events in Egypt, although not as frustrated as they would become with the rise to power of Col. Gamal Abd-al Nasser.

Then there was the continuing problem of Iran. Great Britain would not concede its oil rights there, and the government of Mohammed Mossadegh would make no concessions. Although the United States sharply cut back its military aid to Iran in 1952, it did urge the British to be more reasonable, and it tried to arrange an Anglo-Iranian settlement through third parties. These efforts failed, as did an attempt by Britain to find satisfaction before the International Court of Justice. Meanwhile, Iranian politics and policies fluctuated wildly, thanks to the maneuverings between the forces of Prime Minister Mossadegh and those of Shah Reza Pahlavi. Fearing Soviet intervention and the cutting off of an important source of oil for the West, the Truman administration urged moderation upon both the British and the Iranians, but without effect. Whatever concessions were considered by one side were rejected by the other. This was of great concern to Washington. Truman wrote in November: "We held Cabinet meetings on it—we held Security Council meetings on it; and Dean [Acheson], Bob Lovett, Charlie Sawyer, Harriman and all the senior staff of Central Intelligence discussed that awful situation with me time and again." Nothing worked, according to the president, because the "block headed British" would not make "a fair deal with Iran."[5]

The administration made one more attempt after the 1952 election. This involved giving government financial backing to United States oil companies to join with the Anglo-Iranian company in settling the situation on a basis that would be acceptable to Mossadegh. This plan fell through, as the Iranian prime minister moved neither far nor fast enough in negotiations and as British Foreign Minister Eden was skeptical of the whole thing. Time would resolve the situation, and quickly, in 1953. Mossadegh fell into bitter disagreement with Iran's parliament, which he dissolved. A royalist coup d'état failed, and the shah fled his country. Then Communists in Iran made their move against Mossadegh. This gave the army an opportunity to act successfully against both the Communists and the prime minister, which led to the shah's return and the installation of a royalist government. The British and the Americans were then able to settle the oil dispute and to embrace Iran as an ally.

It was not only Iran that the Truman administration had to worry about in 1952. At the same time, as the president wrote: "We had Isreal [sic], Egypt, near east defense, Sudan, South Africa, Tunisia, the NATO treaties all on the fire. Britain and the Commonwealth Nations were and are absolutely essential if these things are successful. Then on top of it all we have Korea and Indo-China."[6] He could have added a great deal more. Trieste and Berlin had flared up again. There were riots in Paris and Tokyo, which Truman ascribed to the Communists. Much of Latin America complained because it believed that the administration was ignoring it. Canada joined India in making proposals to solve the Korean conflict in ways that were contrary to United States policy. By 1952 it had come to the point where there was no country in which the United States was not involved and where Washington usually viewed disagreement abroad as being prompted by stupidity, cupidity, or hostility.

There was, of course, abundant disagreement at home. This disagreement was not over the nature and danger of communism; instead, it dealt with the question of how to fight communism. And it seemed that the majority of legislators, out-of-office politicians, newspaper editors, and a variety of other influential Americans were vigorously asserting that they knew better than the administration what should be done. Senator Joseph McCarthy would purge treason within the United States; Senator Robert Taft would reduce expenditures and yet pursue more-effective means of combating international communism; former President Herbert Hoover would force America's allies to shoulder more of the burdens of defense; Gen. Douglas MacArthur would fight *and* beat the enemy; and Gen. Dwight Eisenhower, after he entered the 1952 presidential sweepstakes, would run Truman's policies correctly and yet satisfy the administration's critics. There were also many Democrats who agreed with one or another of these Republican strategies. This was often seen in Congress, where committees and subcommittees, headed and staffed by Democrats, probed and skewered administration proposals and leaders. The result during the Eighty-second Congress was that on no major issue did the Truman administration emerge unscathed by Democratic and Republican attacks.

The hostility between Capitol Hill and the White House continued to affect the operation and funding of foreign and military policies. Whatever the administration did in these areas was met in Congress with criticism, often of an ugly nature. And the consequences were mirrored in fierce battles over appropriations. In 1952 Truman pressed Congress to increase the budget for foreign-defense aid to some $7.9 billion, but the legislators cut it back by 25 percent. Yet, it was still almost 15 percent larger than the sum appropriated the year before. Much the same thing happened to his request for higher military expenditures, with the amount appropriated being almost 10 percent more than the year before.

Congress was in a cutting mood, and many of its members were vindictive toward the president. Nevertheless, no matter how much the administration would complain about Congress's short-sightedness, what had happened was striking. Congress had split the difference with the administration on defense appropriations; it had not reduced them. Truman told the reunion of his old army division, the Thirty-fifth, on June 7:

> Two years ago we had an Air Force of 48 wings, with 400,000 men on duty and less than 9,000 planes in active use. Now we have an Air Force of 91 wings, with almost a million men on duty and nearly 15,000 planes in active use. . . . The United States Army has been doubled in size these last 2 years. . . . As for the Navy, there are twice as many ships in full operation now as before Korea. . . . With our help there will be 60 wings in Europe under NATO command by the end of this year. . . . The story is the same with the land forces and the sea forces under the NATO command.

Yet, as much as Congress had done to support the development of a world-wide anti-Communist defense system, the president declared to his old comrades that more had to be done and spent before Americans could "feel that the world is safe. . . . The Kremlin is not going to take a vacation just because we are having a Presidential election in this country."

The Truman administration also pressed other defense matters with considerable success. The president celebrated Flag Day by attending the laying of the keel of the first atomic-energy submarine, and despite sometimes bitter arguments between Congress and the administration, appropriations for nuclear-energy projects continued to increase. One result of this by fall 1952 was the successful explosion of the prototype of the hydrogen bomb on Eniwetok, an atoll in the Pacific. Indeed, by the time Truman left office, $7 billion had been spent on the development of atomic energy, chiefly on increasing America's arsenal of nuclear weapons. The president was proud of this and also of the fact that "by 1953 atomic energy had been applied successfully in the fields of medicine and biology, and research was being pushed still further for economically feasible peacetime uses."[7]

There was also related action in 1952 on the mobilization of the domestic front, but with mixed success for the administration. Truman continued to call for the expansion of the raw materials needed to make the United States economically and militarily strong. He successfully sought legislation to facilitate further the development of the synthetic-rubber industry and to fund research on the purification of salt water. He secured passage of the Emergency Powers Continuation Act, which permitted him to exercise authority that would otherwise lapse upon ratification of the peace treaty with Japan. More pressing was Truman's struggle to renew and strengthen the Defense Production Act in order to promote production and stabilize the economy. What Congress enacted in late June continued most of the president's economic powers, but it seriously weakened his administration's controls on credit, prices, rents, and wages.

Truman also pressed the expansion of America's civil-defense program. Indeed he made a harum-scarum public statement in its support on January 12, 1952, saying: "You and I are now in a national emergency as grave as any we have ever faced. . . . We have no right to feel safe militarily or on the homefront. . . . I will be the first to tell you when urgency is no longer a grave problem in our security program. That is not now the case." The result was increased appropriations for his civil-defense program, though not as much as he had requested. In July the president inaugurated Operation Skywatch, wherein unpaid volunteers scanned the skies looking for the approach of low-flying enemy planes that might escape the nation's radar defenses. This was of questionable value, given the paucity of the training involved and the fact that most of the volunteers were governmental employees who were pressured into accepting the duty. Operation Skywatch was, however, one more screw turned into the country's emergency psychology. Yet another was the highly publicized initiation in December of the CONELRAD program, which was designed to control American radio transmissions in case of enemy attack.

If the president had his crises with Congress in 1952, he also had them with labor and management. He summed up his attitude pointedly at his May 8 news conference: "Conditions at the present time are very grave." The nation was confronted with strikes in the steel, oil, and, possibly, copper industries, which, he implied, Congress had encouraged by its negative attitudes toward the defense and foreign-aid programs. All this "is right down the alley of Mr. Stalin." As it turned out, the administration, using the many powers and influences at its command, was usually successful in preventing work stoppages. Occasionally, such situations did get out of hand, however. The worst was the dispute between the steel industry and its workers.

The steel crisis had been brewing since late 1951, when it became clear that the United Steelworkers wanted a large wage increase that would compromise the administration's anti-inflation program. The matter was referred to the Wage Stabilization Board, which on March 20, 1952, recommended a considerable wage increase and some additional fringe benefits. Although not happy with this report, the Council of Economic Advisers endorsed it, as a way of keeping the industrial peace, and suggested that price increases for steel be contained. Management found this recommendation unacceptable, although it gave more concessions on wages. At this point, April 1, "no one was fooling around," as Commerce Secretary Charles Sawyer wrote.[8] Director of Price Stabilization Ellis Arnall offered steel a price increase in excess of the law. It was not enough to move steel, whose wage offer was not enough to budge labor. Consequently, a strike was called for April 9, and the buck for dealing with the situation passed to the president.

Truman and his advisers had spent a great deal of time preparing for this eventuality. Unfortunately for him, the advice that he received was divided. Secretary of Defense Robert Lovett, presidential aides Charles Murphy and John Steelman, and representatives of the Justice Department had recommended that the government seize the steel mills, while Director of Defense Mobilization Charles E. Wilson, Democratic National Committee Chairman Frank E. McKinney, and informal adviser Clark Clifford had advised against this. Truman, man of action that he was, decided to test his inherent powers in what he considered to be an emergency situation. On April 8 he directed Secretary Sawyer, in Executive Order 10340, to take over and continue operation of the steel mills, because a "work stoppage would immediately jeopardize and imperil our national defense." The president took to radio and television that evening to tell the nation what he had done, assigning the blame for the situation to management. He made it clear that he was not using the Taft-Hartley Act, because the United Steelworkers had voluntarily delayed their strike beyond the time provided for in the law. Also, negotiations between labor and management were being renewed.

Gauntlets littered this field of industrial struggle. Charles Wilson had already resigned as director of defense mobilization in protest at how things were being handled. Philip Murray, as president of both the steelworkers and the Congress of Industrial Organizations (CIO), plainly was challenging the government's wage controls and testing one of labor's most implacable, grasping foes—steel management. Believing that the government and labor were ganging up on it, the steel industry attacked them as being power hungry and politically inspired. The president made it clear that he was exasperated by those who would ignore America's peril and that he was using his emergency powers as commander in chief in order to deal with such treachery. Much of Congress bridled over Truman's refusal to use the Taft-Hartley Act and the administration's support of labor's attempt to ignore legislative guidelines for wage increases. Plainly, the situation was a complicated test of constitutional, economic, and political power. It was also a test of lung power, because all of the parties involved and their many allies ranted and railed at one another. Cries of "reactionary," "Socialist," "emergency," "unconstitutional," and the like filled the air and the press. Resolutions for Truman's impeachment were introduced in the House, and attempts were made in the Senate to restrict the use of federal funds for operating the steel mills. Most significant, court suits were initiated to resolve the situation legally.

Among the suits filed, the key one was *Youngstown* v. *Sawyer*. This case was initially heard in the federal district court for the District of Columbia, where Judge David A. Pine on April 29 issued a temporary injunction against the seizure of the steel mills, holding that the government's action was unconstitutional. The United States Court of Appeals stayed this order the next day, after the steelworkers had walked off the job. Although administration leaders were divided in their advice to the president, the government decided to take the case to the Supreme Court for settlement. Truman, meanwhile, asked labor and management officials to meet with him on May 3 to try to work out an earlier settlement. This meeting came and went without any agreement being reached on fundamental issues, although the steelworkers did consent to return to work for as long as the government controlled the mills.

The Supreme Court began its hearings on the *Youngstown* case on May 12, but things did not proceed well for the government. All of the justices, except Sherman Minton, Truman's old friend, seemed to be hostile in questioning the administration's champion, Solicitor General Philip B. Perlman. Meanwhile, Congress and the press sustained their crescendo of criticism against the president, and the steelworkers and management continued to be hostile toward each other. They were not the only ones who were antagonistic. Vice-President Alben W. Barkley encouraged the combativeness of the United Steelworkers at their convention; Chairman Nathan Feinsinger of the Wage Stabilization Board accused the government of botching its handling of the situation; and when Secretary Sawyer called Philip Murray's attention to reports of industrial sabotage, the union leader charged Sawyer publicly with having an "unthinkable bias against the union."[9] Everyone's nerves were on edge, especially on the administration's side, which had not seemed to fare well in the courtroom.

The Supreme Court announced its decision on June 2. By a vote of six to three, the justices held against the administration. Justice Hugo Black, speaking for the court, declared that there was no federal statute that empowered the president to seize the steel mills. Moreover, it was up to the country's lawmakers, not its courts, to authorize the commander in chief of the armed services to seize private property in order to prevent industrial disputes from halting production. "Nor can," Black added, "the seizure only be sustained because of the several constitutional provisions that grant executive power to the President. In the framework of our Constitution, the President's power to see that the laws are faithfully executed refutes the idea that he is to be a lawmaker."[10] Seldom had the Supreme Court so soundly rebuffed a president. Truman had sought not only to resolve the steel crisis but also substantially to expand the president's powers in a single action that matched his sense of the gravity of the emergency that was confronting the nation. He had gambled badly, and he had lost badly.

Not surprisingly, Truman believed that everyone was out of step but himself. On June 4 he wrote about his Thirty-fifth Division comrades, those who "talk about how brave and great they were forty years ago are a pain in the neck to me. They should be using experience to meet present day problems." He added: "That's what is the trouble with the Senate and the High Court! Those two bodies are controlled by the past."[11] Grumble Truman might, and misunderstand he did. He did not, however, defy the Supreme Court, for the government immediately relinquished control of the steel mills. Yet the crisis of production in the steel industry had not vanished; the workers again had left their jobs. The president had to consult with his chief advisers, who were no more united on what to do than they had been before the Supreme Court had rendered its decision. Truman decided to go to Congress, as he had done earlier without success. On June 10 he did this, after a new round of labor-management negotiations had failed. He reported that the Taft-Hartley Act could not be used either in fairness to labor or, probably, effectively. Therefore, Truman requested the authority to seize the steel mills and to adjust wages and working conditions. Congress, which was not impressed with his unwillingness to use existing law, rejected his proposals. Indeed, the Senate adopted a resolution, forty-nine to thirty, asking the president to use his powers under the Taft-Hartley Act. This he refused to do. Truman's only hope now was that new negotiations between steel management and workers would lead them to settle their dispute, which they finally did on July 24. The result was that both wages and prices for steel increased substantially, violating the administration's anti-inflation guidelines.

The war continued, meanwhile, in Korea. Peace negotiations also continued, but they proved to be only an extension of the hostilities in the field. The Truman administration had become accustomed to the painful, expensive, and never-ending war. By 1952 the relative military positions of the UN and the Communist forces had largely been consolidated, although each would launch offensives in order to improve its situation. The truce negotiations seemed to go very much the same way. For Americans, the only consolation was that their casualties declined during the long, drawn-out negotiations. The United States suffered 12,300 killed from July 1951 to July 1953, compared to 21,300 during the first year of the war. The figures for those who were wounded, missing, or captured were less favorable, running, respectively, 50,900 to 57,500.

One bit of news regarding Korea that spring was that President Truman appointed Gen. Mark Clark to succeed Gen. Matthew Ridgway as commander in chief of the UN Command and of the United States Far East Command. Ridgway had been chosen to replace Dwight Eisenhower as Supreme Allied Commander in Europe. Other big news in 1952 concerned the occasional serious disorders in the prisoner-of-war camps, which held as many as 170,000 troops who had been captured by UN forces. Communist truce negotiators exploited this situation relentlessly, demanding that all prisoners be returned as a price for a truce. The UN negotiators resisted this on the ground that many of the prisoners whom they held would thus be returned to punishment or even death—the answer to the question of return should be up to individual prisoners. All this was complicated by the fact that the UN forces held many more prisoners than did the Communists and by reports of the extreme hardships that were being endured by prisoners in Communist camps. The stalemated war and peace negotiations continued beyond the end of Truman's presidency. It was not until July 1953 that terms, favorable to the UN, were reached and an armistice was signed, an armistice that would continue in lieu of complete peace into the 1980s. However accustomed American officials became to the war in Korea, it colored their every action on the world scene. The conflict was taken as proof of the aggressiveness and unreliability of Communist leaders. It was also a heavy drain on United States resources. Moreover, the war was the sharpest spur that led to the mounting of Truman's grand anti-Communist coalition, as well as to severe criticism of him that he was not doing his job well enough.

Questions of defense seemed to be so pressing in 1952 that they usually overshadowed everything else. Certainly, what remained of the Fair Deal program were only tatters and shadows. Truman again tried to use the issue of flood control to advance the cause of developing valley authorities, especially in the Missouri River Valley. In this he had far less success than he had enjoyed in 1951. As in so many other matters, the president had to be content with inching forward on the flood-control work of the Army Corps of Engineers, sponsoring a governmental report on the integrated development of the Missouri River basin, and proposing a national system of flood-disaster insurance. In another case, Truman also proposed less than he had requested before and received little or nothing from Congress. He had created the Commission on the Health Needs of the Nation at the end of 1951. The commission's exhaustive five-volume report, which began to appear in December 1952, argued the case that the government should promote good and reasonably priced health care for all Americans. This was less than the president had earlier recommended in his comprehensive health-insurance proposals, but it was far more than the medical profession and Congress were willing to accept. A dozen years would pass before the United States would respond affirmatively to any significant portion of Truman's concerns about medical care.

The president had some successes in 1952 on domestic matters, but they were small joys compared to what he had wanted. Congress and Truman agreed on a compromise farm program in July, giving farmers price supports based on 90 percent of parity, instead of a sliding scale, for corn, cotton, peanuts, and wheat. Thus was the most important piece of agricultural legislation since 1949 enacted, prompted by the exigencies of a presidential-election year. The same criterion was also involved in Truman's greatest triumph on domestic legislation in 1952— various amendments to the Social Security Act. These enactments not only raised benefits on old-age and survivors insurance and railroad retirement, but they also hiked the federal contribution to state public-assistance programs, increased the allowable earnings that a person could make without jeopardizing his retirement benefits, and gave Social Security credits to recent veterans of military service. This legislation, important as it was in fine tuning Social Security benefits, was not the landmark that Truman called it. Upon signing the amendments on July 18, he said that Congress should "consider the entire question of further extending and liberalizing the Social Security Act as a whole." The government usually proved reluctant, however, to deal systematically with the Social Security program.

Congress acted quickly in 1952 to approve the constitution that had been accepted by the people of Puerto Rico, which gave them self-government except in diplomatic and military affairs. This was President Truman's only significant legislative victory during this year in the broad area of civil rights. He had called upon Congress to extend civil rights, but he had anticipated little action, and little is what he got. This was not surprising, for resistance to civil-rights action had been growing across the land. In 1951 and 1952 it was fashionable for many Americans to display Confederate flags and insignia as symbols of protest. In 1951 the country's largest flag company reported that the demand for the Stars and Bars exceeded that for the Stars and Stripes. The flag fad would have been only annoying except that it was accompanied by a rising number of violent incidents, including the bombing of places that were identified with blacks, Jews, and Mexican-Americans. Truman also pressed, though unsuccessfully, for fair-employment-practices legislation and some self-government for the District of Columbia. Congress would only agree with him on granting Japanese-American civil servants the grade, pay, and seniority that they would have had if it had not been for security measures taken during World War II. In 1952 Truman continued to speak out for civil rights and to direct the government, wherever it had the authority, to intervene to protect the civil rights of minorities. This particularly was seen in the capital, where some federal officials had joined with civil-rights groups since 1950 in an effort to integrate public and private facilities through persuasion, protest, and legal action. If the results of this were far from satisfactory, a pattern of action had been set which would be built upon during the Eisenhower administration.

If progress had been made, however little, with respect to the status of some minorities, this was not true with regard to Indians since 1950. When Dillon S. Myer became commissioner of Indian affairs that year, he sought to withdraw the federal government as much as possible from Indian matters. He proposed a series of actions that would gradually have removed federal protection and appropriations from Indians in the cause of speeding their integration into American society. On most of these he was unsuccessful, although during the Eisenhower administration, Congress transferred criminal and civil authority over many tribes to state courts. Myer and the Truman administration did inaugurate a program, which Congress funded, to give Indians job training and to encourage them to relocate off their reservations in order to exploit their new skills. This program had mixed results, except that it outraged most Indians. Their champions had a field day in denouncing Myer for being, as Harold L. Ickes put it, a "little tin Hitler" and "Commissar" of Indian affairs.[12]

Despite Truman's substantial success in regard to appropriations for defense and military aid and despite his scattered victories on domestic legislation, 1952 was another year of intense disagreement between the administration and Congress. The president had been defeated on most of his favorite domestic requests, and he had endured endless wrangles on matters relating to military and foreign aid. This result was assured by the very conservative and, indeed, combative cast of the Congress that was elected in 1950. Republicans, whether of the McCarthy, Taft, or even moderate variety, sensed the high possibility of victory at the polls in 1952. People were growing increasingly tired of the stalemate in Korea, high taxes, and governmental intervention; and the Republicans were exploiting the public's fear of Communist infiltration and the reaction to tales of scandal in the administration. Furthermore, Truman, who was a natural scrapper, was not one to let controversy pass. He had an answer—usually a tart one—for almost any criticism of his administration. Easily goaded, he often went on record with statements that his enemies seized upon to goad him some more. Truman himself had become a prime issue, as the polls indicated. In the Gallup poll he had not received the approval of even a plurality of the respondents since September of 1950. Indeed, a majority consistently disapproved of his handling of the presidency during his last two years in office, and the percentage of those who approved of his performance never exceeded 32 during that period and dropped as low as 23 in December 1951.

The president's widespread unpopularity contributed to the frequent independence from and even hostility toward the administration that were evinced by many Democrats in Congress during 1951 and 1952. Truman had not helped the situation by his undisguised contempt for many Democratic senators and representatives whom he considered to be personally offensive, sometimes irrespective of their position on the issues. Thus he favored those who seemed to him most sympathetic and reasonable, for example, Senators Robert S. Kerr of Oklahoma and Lyndon B. Johnson of Texas, even though they might not go along on certain big issues. The same applied to interest groups. Their style and their support at crucial times warmed the president to them, usually more than did their overall position on his program. Charles Murphy, the chief White House aide, later said, "I think generally we tended to regard them as special interest groups if they were opposed to us, and if they supported us we tended to regard them as public interest groups."[13] Yet, often enough this was interpreted as meaning that if Truman thought one was decent about what one did, then occasional opposition was acceptable. Woe to anyone who did not measure up to the president's standards of decent conduct, however, even if that person was generally supportive of the administration's program. The effect of this was that Truman was unnecessarily antagonistic toward some Democrats, such as Senators Paul H. Douglas, J. William Fulbright, and Estes Kefauver, who might have responded well to courting from the White House.

The intense hostility between the administration and Congress and private interests came out in many ways. President Truman was rarely discreet in his private conversations and correspondence. Often he used his public speeches and, especially, his news conferences as vehicles for making attacks and counterattacks. His combativeness was even more evident in the many statements that he made on legislation. There were also his veto messages, which allowed him to be particularly biting in pointing out the failings of Congress. Truman only vetoed nine acts in 1952, partly because of Congress's increased ability to pass legislation containing equal amounts of wheat and chaff. Two of the president's vetoes were of great importance; one of these was overridden. His first veto, which was sustained, was of a bill that would have vested in the appropriate state the title to offshore lands and the natural resources contained in them. The issue here concerned offshore oil deposits and whether they should be owned by the federal government or by the adjacent state. Truman contended that these offshore resources were the property of all Americans, because the federal government had the primary jurisdiction over navigable waters and the land beneath. He was not about to give away the nation's patrimony to a few states and, in effect, to private business interests. The Eisenhower administration saw the matter differently and in 1953 approved a new version of the legislation in regard to offshore oil lands.

An even-more-significant veto message in 1952 concerned the McCarran-Walter Immigration Act. This measure codified and revised policies on immigration, naturalization, and nationality; and it reflected the strength of xenophobia and anticommunism in the United States. In his veto message of June 25, Truman conceded that the bill abolished, as he had requested, national and racial barriers to naturalization; but the defects of the measure were too great to overlook. Not only did the bill continue the severely discriminatory quota system based on national origin; it was also more restrictive in the proportion of people it permitted to immigrate from certain countries. It announced, in effect, that Americans not only feared immigrants, but especially those from nations that were quite unlike the United States. In addition, the president found objectionable the criteria for the administration of the proposed new law. These criteria, especially the ones regarding past affiliations, "would make it even more difficult to enter our country. . . . Admission to our citizenship would be made more difficult; expulsion from our citizenship would be made easier. . . . Seldom has a bill exhibited the distrust evidenced here for citizens and aliens alike." These were only some of Truman's objections to the measure. The fight to override his veto was fierce, though brief. At a time when fear of subversion and foreignness was peaking, the defenders of the McCarran-Walter Immigration Act were many and vociferous. They were not daunted by quotations from the Declaration of Independence, references to Christian belief, or appeals not to offend actual or potential allies. The House immediately overrode Truman's veto, 278 to 112; the Senate joined the House two days later, 57 to 26. Not until 1965 would Congress significantly liberalize the nation's immigration law.

The battle over questions of loyalty and security continued on other fronts, of course, with Truman often condemning those who saw subversion in anyone who disagreed with them. Yet the president and his administration were still concerned in 1952 with improving their record in dealing with security risks. The Justice Department, with Truman's approval, was eager to expand its wiretapping authority and to find ways to maintain microphone surveillance that would not involve trespass. But the president tightened up restrictions on congressional use of files from the executive branch in loyalty-security cases, probably more to keep federal agencies from being additionally burdened with work than to protect employees. He also indicated by word and deed that he was unclear as to how to root out security risks and yet protect the rights of civil servants. This indecision would plague him to the end of his presidency, for he was unable to satisfy anyone, whether among the hunters of subversives, the civil libertarians, or those who stood in between those two camps.

In 1952, conservatism and congressional obstinancy were important issues for the president, and communism and Korea were large issues for his opponents; but corruption grew into a bigger issue for everyone. Truman had worked hard in 1951 to deal with the scandals touching his administration, and his efforts would continue into 1952. On January 2 he announced a sweeping reorganization of the Internal Revenue Bureau (IRB). This included applying civil-service procedures to the selection of all of the bureau's officials except the commissioner, the consolidation of the bureau's some two hundred field offices into twenty-five district offices, and the creation of a strong inspection service. Congress approved Truman's reorganization plan by March, although the corruption exposed in the IRB in 1951 would continue to be an issue in the 1952 election campaign.

Rumors that Attorney General J. Howard McGrath would resign, because of his slowness in dealing with governmental corruption, continued into 1952. Moreover, the House Judiciary Committee voted to investigate him and the Justice Department. Truman sought to establish a commission to investigate corruption in government, in addition to what he hoped the Justice Department was doing; but no one seemed to want to get involved. So the president signaled, in his January 10 news conference, that he had abandoned the idea of appointing a commission, saying that "the Attorney General will carry out the job that is necessary." The problem with this was not only that public confidence in McGrath was rapidly declining but also that there were those who believed that he was blocking inquiries into corruption. The pressure to act became increasingly intense. Indeed, high officials of the Justice Department became harder to find: for example, Deputy Attorney General A. Devitt Vanech often nipped across the street to the National Archives to find respite by reading in the stacks of the Indian records unit. Truman had to do something. In February he brought in a prominent New Yorker, Newbold Morris, to be McGrath's special assistant to investigate corruption in government. Morris took his charge very seriously, and soon he had made a remarkable number of enemies, especially McGrath. Meanwhile, Truman refused to open the files of executive agencies to the subcommittee of the House Judiciary Committee that was investigating the Justice Department.

The situation came to a spectacular head on April 3, when Truman announced that McGrath had dismissed Morris, that McGrath had resigned, and that Judge James P. McGranery of Philadelphia would be nominated to be attorney general. The president later wrote this about the politically loyal but legally laggard McGrath: "When things became bad in Justice I had to ask for his resignation. It was hard to do." Truman believed that he had gotten what he wanted in McGranery, whom he later assessed as "doing an excellent job."[14] Despite the change, critics of the administration, regardless of party, were not disposed to close the matter. Legislation was introduced, indeed, to keep the issue hot: for example, Mississippi Senator James Eastland's bill to require agency heads to report to the Federal Bureau of Investigation any information or allegations about illegal acts performed by federal employees. The administration had no answer for this kind of legislation; in fact, the executive agencies were in serious disagreement about whether to support or to oppose Eastland's bill. Such legislation was not enacted, but there was continued agitation for action to police the operations of federal agencies. Republicans constantly exploited the issue during the election campaign, and the press found the whole matter enthralling.

One of the key questions about the 1952 election was whether Harry Truman would run again for president. It was rumored that Mrs. Truman was discouraging him, and he often favorably alluded to the two-term tradition. The president seemed to have made up his mind by April 16, 1950, when he wrote in his diary, "I am not a candidate for nomination by the Democratic Convention."[15] He occasionally pondered about who his successor should be. On May 8, 1950, he again turned to his diary, writing: "Now if we can find a man who will take over and continue the Fair Deal, Point IV, Fair Employment, parity for farmers and a consumers protective policy, the Democratic party can win from now on. It seems to me now that the Governor of Illinois has the background and what it takes. Think I'll talk to him."[16] It would be some time before Truman would chat with Governor Adlai E. Stevenson. Meanwhile, Truman considered other potential Democratic candidates, especially his friend Chief Justice Fred Vinson.

The president also thought about possible Republican nominees. He told his August 9, 1951, news conference that he had a candidate for the Republican ticket, Ohio's Senator Robert A. Taft, whom he thought almost any Democrat could beat. Yet, as 1951 wore on, Truman became edgy about the forthcoming presidential election, especially about rumors that Gen. Dwight D. Eisenhower might seek the Republican nomination. The signs were, nevertheless, that the president was not interested in renomination except in case of an emergency. Indeed, on November 19 he told some of his aides of his intention not to seek reelection. A few days later he sounded out Chief Justice Vinson about running for the Democratic nomination. The jurist's answer, though considerably delayed, was no. By January 9, 1952, the president apparently was firm in his own mind that he would not run again.[17] It was during this month that, at the suggestion of White House aides Charles Murphy and David D. Lloyd, Truman invited Adlai Stevenson to talk with him. The Missourian encouraged the Illinois governor to run for president. "I told him that if he would agree he could be nominated . . . that a President in the White House always controlled the National Convention. . . . But he said No! He apparently was flabergasted [sic]."[18] Truman and his aides pursued Stevenson at least until March, though with no positive result.

Truman was also approached by several Democrats who were interested in the presidential nomination. He encouraged all of them, though in different degrees, Senator Estes "Cow Fever" least of all.[19] Truman just could not get over Kefauver's investigation of crime, the damage that it had done to the Democratic party and Missouri, and the money that he believed the senator had made as a result of his probe. Of course, there were those—such as Vinson, Stevenson, and former aide Samuel Rosenman—who urged the president either to run again or not to rule out accepting a draft. On March 4 Truman wrote that even his "wife and daughter had said the same thing to me. . . . What the hell am I to do? I'll know when the time comes because I am sure God

Almighty will guide me.''[20] It was the senior White House staff that guided him as they upheld his wish to retire. Thus, at the Jefferson-Jackson day dinner in Washington on March 29, the president announced: ''I shall not be a candidate for reelection. I have served my country long, and I think efficiently and honestly. I shall not accept a renomination. I do not feel that it is my duty to spend another 4 years in the White House.'' That was it, though not until the Democrats had chosen a new presidential nominee did everyone believe him. There was, of course, the alternative question that was asked him: What was he going to do if he did not run for reelection? Truman's answer was, as he told the press on May 8, ''I am going to have a good time, . . . and do just as I damn please!''

The president had already begun to do as he pleased, at least in his comments about the contenders for the Democratic nomination, which made clear his lack of enthusiasm for Kefauver. And he regretted this, telling an aide on May 31, ''I wish I had kept my mouth shut about it.''[21] Truman stressed his neutrality to his news conference on June 5, although he did not fully convince the press. One reporter asked him, ''Mr. President, do you plan to be neutral in favor of people or neutral against *them*?'' Of course, Truman could no more have been neutral than he could have been nonpartisan. His speeches were increasingly passionate, even testy. This was evidenced in his remarks at Batesville, Arkansas, on July 2:

> There is not a man or woman in this audience who is not better off as a result of 20 years of Democratic rule. Now, if you want to throw that out the window and go off after false gods, that is your business, and I can't stop you. But just do a little thinking, and you will find that your interests are with the party that represents the people as a whole, and not special interests.

Truman became increasingly concerned with the business of presidential nominations. Although dismayed by General Eisenhower's decision to run for the Republican nomination, he believed that Senator Taft would control the GOP convention. He was surprised when Eisenhower was nominated in July, saying that Taft ''has beaten himself. Of all the dumb bunnies—he is the worst.'' It would not be long before he would view the general in equally low terms. Of course, the president's chief concern was who his own party's nominee would be, and his assessment of the Democratic contenders was far from rosy. Senator Richard Russell of Georgia had ''all the qualifications as to ability and brains. But he is poison to Northern Democrats and honest Liberals.'' As for Kefauver, ''What a President this demogogic dumb

13

bell would make!" Oklahoma Senator Robert S. Kerr was "a grand man, a good administrator. . . . But he has a gas record and a cloture record." As for Truman's beloved vice-president, Barkley, "I wish he could be 64 instead of 74. . . . My good friend Alben would be dead in three months if he should inherit my job!" The president believed that his master of many missions, Averell Harriman, was "the ablest of them all," but he asked, "Can we elect a Wall Street Banker and a railroad tycoon President of the United States on the Democratic Ticket?"[22]

The president believed that he had to get involved in convention politics in order to help his party. On July 13 he met with Barkley, Democratic National Committee Chairman Frank McKinney, and several White House aides. Their choice for the Democratic nomination was Barkley. The White House staff also prepared drafts of the party's platform, basically to try to persuade the resolutions committee and then the convention to endorse Truman's record and program. The presidential contingent at the Democratic National Convention in Chicago was largely successful in this effort. By the time of the convention in late July, it was plain that Barkley could not muster the support of a majority of the delegates. The president therefore shifted his backing to Harriman, although when Adlai Stevenson finally entered the contest, Truman encouraged him. Indeed, when Harriman failed to rally a large number of delegates, the president endorsed the candidacy of the Illinois governor. After the Democratic Convention had nominated Stevenson for president, Truman met with him, McKinney, and House Speaker Sam Rayburn to discuss their party's vice-presidential nomination. His account of this is unintentionally amusing, but it does point up how seriously the president took his role as a politician. "I told the Governor he had the right to choose" his running mate. "He favored Kefauver. I vetoed that." Stevenson ruled Barkley out because of his age and because of labor's unfavorable attitude toward him. Rayburn wanted Senator Mike Monroney of Oklahoma, but the president declared that Monroney could not carry Texas or the Dixiecrats. On and on into the night they talked. Truman finally asserted that Alabama Senator John Sparkman "is your best bet. I am going to bed."[23] And it was a Stevenson-Sparkman ticket.

Adlai Stevenson's urbanity, wit, and excellent record as governor of Illinois, in addition to his sympathetic positions on Truman's foreign policy, labor affairs, and urban issues quickly won him the favor of liberals. And there was nothing in his background that would upset southern White Democrats. Indeed he seemed to have little interest in civil rights. One black newspaper commented that Stevenson would turn race relations over to "his ghost writer, Arthur Schlesinger Jr., of

Harvard, who knows as much about Negroes as the King of Norway."[24] Senator Sparkman obviously was a sop to the South, though his record, except on civil rights, was liberal, and he was a staunch supporter of the administration's foreign policy. What remained to be seen was how good a campaign the Democratic national standard-bearers would run.

The president was prepared to help Stevenson and Sparkman run a good campaign. At Truman's invitation, they visited the White House on August 12 when, as he wrote, "I explained to them all the duties and obligations of the President, went into the budget, the legislative situation and told them that the Office of the President is the greatest and most powerful in the history of the world." After this lecture on civics, Truman gave Stevenson various written reports and talked about how they would campaign. This was followed by briefings by top federal officials, though the president could not resist pointing out to his guests "the duties of the men present." Later there was a meeting with Truman's and Stevenson's staffs. Truman "told the assemblage that our objective was to win the election, that I wanted to win as much as the Governor. He said he thought that I was more anxious . . . than he was to win."[25] Not surprisingly, strains quickly appeared between the president and his would-be successor. Truman thought that Stevenson's replacement of Frank McKinney as chairman of the Democratic National Committee by Stephen Mitchell was a mistake, and he was offended by Stevenson's wish that he limit his participation in the campaign. It became clear that the man from Missouri and the man from Illinois were not particularly compatible.

Truman was stung by reports later in August that Stevenson had promised to clean up the "mess" in Washington and that Sparkman had said that the administration had mishandled the steel strike. Truman already felt that he was being ignored by Stevenson and had written him an unsent letter, saying, "I have come to the conclusion that you are embarrassed by having the President of the United States in your corner in this campaign." Truman followed this up with another unsent missive to Stevenson, complaining that he and Sparkman "are trying to beat the Democratic President instead of the Republicans."[26] To Sparkman, apparently in another unsent letter, the president bewailed his "kicking the only friend who can cause your election, just as he caused the nomination of both you and Stevenson. . . . I can enjoy myself in a rocking chair . . . if that's what the Democratic Nominees want."[27]

Truman was even less happy with Eisenhower. He had also invited the general to the White House for a briefing, but Ike had declined, apparently believing that it would injure him politically. Truman was deeply offended. He wrote to the Republican nominee in August: "What I've always had in mind was and is a continuing foreign policy. You know that is a fact, because you had a part in outlining it. . . . You have made a bad mistake and I'm hoping it won't injure this great Republic."[28] This was just the beginning, for Truman would fume about many of Eisenhower's campaign positions, particularly his criticism of the administration's conduct of the Korean War. Truman was especially bitter when Eisenhower not only consorted with Senator Joseph McCarthy but also refused to defend Gen. George C. Marshall against Republican attacks on his integrity.

Stevenson may have wanted Truman to restrict his participation in the campaign, and the president may have been tempted to do so out of pique with the Democratic nominees. His fighting instincts won out, however, as did his keen desire to influence the course of the campaign and to defend his administration's policies. Furthermore, there just was not very much to do in Washington, with Congress out of session and his work load winding down. Truman therefore plunged into the campaign with gusto. Between September 1 and November 1 he made speeches in twenty-six states, from coast to coast, and in the District of Columbia. The president's message was familiar. His party was the party of all the people; the Republicans represented the special interests. His party was the party of truth; the opposition was the home of McCarthyism and the Big Lie. The people, as well as freedom and democracy world-wide, had benefited from the deeds of a Democratic administration; one could, at best, only be profoundly skeptical of what Republican government would bring. Truman was usually in good form, even if it increasingly appeared that most voters would subscribe to the Republican slogan of "I Like Ike." On election eve, November 3, the president joined the Democratic nominees on radio and television to state the issues. This he did succinctly:

> This election may decide whether we shall go ahead and expand our prosperity here at home or slide back into a depression. It may decide whether we shall preserve and extend our civil rights and liberties, or see them fall before a wave of smear and fear. Above all, it may decide whether we shall finally achieve lasting peace or be led into a third world war. . . .
> On the basis of the facts and the record, the people should choose the Democratic Party in this election.

America's voters did not take Truman's advice. Dwight D. Eisenhower and Richard M. Nixon handily defeated Stevenson and Sparkman by 33,936,234 to 27,314,992 popular votes and 442 to 89 electoral votes. The Republicans also swept to control of both houses of Congress and of a majority of the governorships. Truman immediately sent Eisenhower a telegram of congratulations. In private he was philosophical, though unhappily so. The president told Eben Ayers that perhaps it was just as well that those who had not lived under a Republican administration should experience it—the running rampant of big business, and a man like Nixon, whom Truman called a "crook."[29] Then, he mused, maybe people would appreciate what Franklin Roosevelt and he had been trying to accomplish.

Truman had one more innovation in him before he left office. He invited Eisenhower to meet with him to facilitate the orderly transfer of government business to the incoming administration. The general accepted this invitation, establishing a precedent for the cooperation of old and new administrations in the period between election and inauguration days. When the president-elect came to the White House on November 18 to begin the process, strains were evident. Several of Eisenhower's advisers had warned him to be wary, and he was cool; several of Truman's aides thought that Eisenhower and his retinue were presumptuous. Truman lectured Eisenhower on the functions of government, warning that "men in Congress are forever trying to take the President's powers as Chief Executive, Commander in Chief of the Armed Forces, and Foreign Policy Chief away from him." Another sensitive point was addressed in his advice that Eisenhower have an assistant to deal with ethnic, racial, and religious minority groups. "They can never be satisfied, but they must be listened to!"[30]

There was much else to be done during Truman's final weeks in office, largely by way of closing shop. The president continued to try to set a record for the future. He was delighted with a report from the Bureau of the Census that showed, as he commented in a public letter of January 5, 1953, "the American people are today better off than ever before in our history." Truman was also pleased to have the report of his Commission on Immigration and Naturalization; this he transmitted to Congress on January 11 in urging that the McCarran-Walter Act be overturned. Similarly, in January he used the report of his Water Resources Commission to prod Congress into adopting legislation to develop the nation's river basins. Such volleys were in addition to his 1953 State of the Union, Budget, and Economic Report messages, in which he justified his administration's policies and called for their extension. In his State of the Union message on January 7, the president said:

The Nation's business is never finished. The basic questions we have been dealing with, these eight years past, present themselves anew. That is the way of our society. Circumstances change and current questions take on different forms, new complications, year by year. But underneath, the great issues remain the same—prosperity, welfare, human rights, effective democracy, and above all, peace.

There were also actions to be taken. Truman left a gift for conservationists on January 6, by adding 47,753 acres to the Olympic National Park. In December 1952 he acted decisively to ward off a coal strike by approving a wage increase of $1.90 a day, which was negotiated by the coal operators and miners. This led to the resignations, in protest, of Chairman Archibald Cox and the industry members of the Wage Stabilization Board. The whole economic-stabilization apparatus was dying anyway, so it made little difference. It did, however, eliminate the likelihood of Truman's bequeathing a major industrial crisis to the country. More important, it signaled his determination not to strike out at labor—even if this involved the detested John L. Lewis—in a situation in which management was equally culpable. This was his farewell present to labor. The departing president also had something for America's blacks. This concerned the desegregation of the public schools, as the Truman administration in December 1952 intervened with an amicus curiae brief in the case of *Brown* v. *Board of Education of Topeka*. The Eisenhower administration carried on with this, though with less vigor, thus contributing to the Supreme Court's reversal of the separate-but-equal doctrine in education in 1954. In tidying up, Truman passed some things on to his successor. One item was the highly publicized case of Julius and Ethel Rosenberg, who had received death sentences for their involvement in transmitting atomic secrets to Russia. They had received a stay of execution in order to seek executive clemency, but their plea did not reach Truman in time for him to make a decision.

There was time, too, for mulling over old vendettas in 1952. Truman intensified his invectives against the press in his diary, and almost anything in public print set him off. He began the year indicting the *St. Louis Post-Dispatch*, the *New York World*, the *Kansas City Star*, the *Detroit News*, and the *Cleveland Plain-Dealer*. "The only thing that will save the Republic is the air and tellivision [sic] provided we do not let these same liars and blackmailers control that means of public communication too."[31] Even the Associated Press did not escape the president's scorn, for by May he had concluded that it no longer reported the news honestly. In August he was raving about Chicago publisher Robert R.

McCormick's being "a moron," the "anemic Roy Howard," and William Randolph Hearst's having "had no morals and no ethics. . . . the 87% opposition [of the press] never did and, of course, never will tell the truth!"[32] Among Truman's many maledictions on the opposition press was his diary entry of December 6: "To hell with them. When history is written they will be the sons of bitches—not I."[33]

In 1952 the president also took time to assess men in public life. He told Eben Ayers that James F. Byrnes, the former secretary of state, was the closest thing to a "political whore" and that Senator Paul Douglas was "something of a crackpot."[34] Truman recorded that he had "liked [Joseph Stalin] very much." The Soviet leader had changed, however. Why? "I don't know—I guess he got to thinking about it, and thought he had been cheated by a young man from Missouri." Yet, "We kept to the letter of every agreement we made with them."[35] Senator J. William Fulbright "has never recovered from his House Resolution which sent him to the Senate (Potomac Fever), nor has he forgiven me for telling him at a Press Club dinner that he'd been a better constitutionalist had he been educated in a land grant American College rather than at Oxford."[36] Sometimes the president went on record with his comments. In his December 31 news conference, a reporter asked him his opinion of Robert Taft's remark that the Republican legislative program would put the country "back on the track where we got off 20 years ago." Truman responded, "If Senator Taft has his way, that is what will happen."

Truman also evaluated his aides and agency heads toward the end of his presidency, concluding that most of them had served him and the nation well. He applied the word "great" to Dean Acheson, W. Averell Harriman, and Fred Vinson, in their respective cabinet posts at State, Commerce, and the Treasury. John Snyder, Vinson's successor, had been "able, efficient and right in his handling of the money matters of the government." Defense Secretary Robert Lovett had been "100% in his present position." Attorney General Tom Clark had done an "excellent job." Agriculture Secretary Charles F. Brannan was "the best one we've had since I've been in Washington." In his evaluations of White House aides, Truman rated Press Secretaries Charles Ross "a good one" and Joseph Short "loyal and efficient." Appointments Secretary Matthew Connelly was "in a class by himself." Counsel Clark Clifford was "as efficient as they come," and Assistant to the President John Steelman was "tops." Truman added that Harry Vaughan had been "slandered and misrepresented . . . but he's able and efficient and I'm satisfied with him." And these are only examples of what the president wrote.[37] Though he was generous in assessing most of his subordinates, he also knew that many of them had sometimes erred. Nevertheless, Truman accepted the ultimate responsibility for the conduct of the Executive Branch. In November 1952 he wrote: "The President must see the whole picture and make his decisions accordingly. Maybe I made some wrong ones—but I made them and I shall never run out on the men who carried them out."[38]

Truman's aides and agency heads usually knew what he thought of them, thanks to his candor. The many favored ones often reciprocated in kind. Indeed, the president and most of his subordinates would leave office as members of a long-lasting mutual-admiration society. When they said that their chief had been fair, spirited, decisive, sensible, considerate, appreciative, and supportive, they meant it. It was Truman who had kept so many of them going. Dean Acheson described their feelings by quoting from Shakespeare's *Henry V*:

> . . . every wretch, pining and pale before,
> Beholding him, plucks comfort from his looks. . . .
> His liberal eye doth give to every one . . .
> A little touch of Harry in the night.[39]

As the changing of the guard in Washington approached in 1953, there were many farewells. The best known was Truman's touching broadcast address to the people on January 15. It was a mixture of many things, including wishes for success to Eisenhower and a plea to the public to support the new president. Truman also took this opportunity to review—favorably, of course—what he and his administration had done. And he commented on his office: "The greatest part of the President's job is to make decisions. . . . He can't pass the buck to anybody. No one else can do the deciding for him. That's his job." Perhaps others were better qualified than he had been to do the job. "But the work was mine to do, and I had to do it. And I tried to give it everything that was in me." He thought that he had been successful, with the help of others and the people. "So, as I empty the drawers of this desk, and as Mrs. Truman and I leave the White House, we have no regret. We feel we have done our best in the public service."

Truman's last official act, on January 19, 1953, was to sign a letter of recognition of the seventieth anniversary of the federal civil-service merit system. This gave him the opportunity for a final presidential sally as he criticized "recent reckless attacks which can destroy that great asset," the civil service. Then, he had to wind up odds and ends and say additional goodbyes before he rode up to the Capitol with Dwight Eisenhower the next day for the inauguration of the new president. Their conversation was general. The water of Eisenhower and the oil of

Truman could not mix, however. The president-elect commented that Army Secretary Kenneth Royall had tried to order him home for the 1948 inaugural ceremony, but he would not attend because half of those who were cheering for Truman then were actually for Eisenhower himself. The outgoing president retorted, "Ike I didn't ask you to come—or you'd been here."[40] As Truman had quickly become a scrapper in the White House, so he returned to Independence as a scrapper. And he would remain one, as a concerned elder statesman, for the almost two decades of life that were left to him.

13

★ ★ ★ ★ ★

EPILOG

It is not too much to suggest that the Truman administration, along with the Franklin D. Roosevelt era, constituted the most important turning point in recent United States history. During the Roosevelt administration the American state system had changed dramatically. The federal government had rapidly become ascendant over state and local governments as Americans had increasingly looked to the nation's capital for assistance and as Washington had intervened unprecedentedly into previously private and local matters. Moreover, the Federal government had assumed a major role in international affairs, which had significant domestic consequences. As a result, the executive branch and particularly the presidency had become repositories of vast power.

Yet, as happened after World War I, some of these weighty changes could have been temporary. This did not occur after World War II, however. Most American voters were pleased with or accepted most of what the Roosevelt administration had wrought. Indeed, many of them sought more assistance from Washington, despite their criticism of specific federal programs. Much the same could be said about members of Congress and about state and local officials. Certainly, many of them talked of cutting the powers of the federal government; but when it came to acting, they found themselves unable or, for political reasons, unwilling to turn back the clock. Too many officials and their constituents enjoyed the bounty of the federal government too much for them to do so. As for the judiciary, it usually found ample reasons for justifying what existed, grumble though some judges did in the privacy of their chambers.

There were also foreign and military affairs to be considered. The nation's participation in the First World War had been too painful for most Americans to approve of having the United States play much of a part in world politics during the ensuing two decades. All that was changed by the coming of World War II, the activities of aggressive totalitarian societies, and the rapid rise of military technologies that threatened American security. Once again, Americans met the challenge of another world war. This time they emerged from it prepared to become a guarantor of the peace, even if this should mean maintaining a powerful military establishment. As it turned out, most Americans were willing to take step after step toward involving their country more deeply in international affairs than they had contemplated.

Harry S. Truman was crucial to all of these developments. Although he did not go as far as some wanted, he was instrumental in regularizing and expanding the new American state system. Governmentally, he played Augustus to Roosevelt's Caesar, and he was well prepared for such a role in terms of his experience, ideas, and temperament. Truman had caught glimpses of a new American state during the administration of Woodrow Wilson, and he had been disappointed with the retreat from Wilson's vision during the presidencies of Warren G. Harding, Calvin Coolidge, and Herbert Hoover. Never mind that Truman's reactions were partly born of his extreme partisanship or that his own vision was fragmented. He had, however imperfectly, been caught up in Wilson's rhetoric about using government to improve the people's lives, to make the world safe for democracy, and to secure perpetual peace. Truman was ready to see the power and the glory of his country develop under the guidance of a Democratic government in Washington. By the 1930s he was even envisioning a role for himself in these matters, either as a governor or as a congressman. As fate would have it, the part that he played was as a United States senator from 1935 until he became vice-president a decade later.

Truman's role as a senator was a modest one before World War II. Still, he was certain that the New Deal had demonstrated the effectiveness of a powerful federal government in dealing with a wide range of domestic problems. Truman believed that the government in Washington would have to do more, even though some of its activities required reassessment. If World War II disrupted some of the government's domestic activities, it also opened new reservoirs of federal power in connection with foreign and military matters. Truman largely favored these developments. Indeed, he took pride in their results, for his country's performance during the war displayed the abilities and resources of the United States to their best advantage.

When he became president in April 1945, Truman easily assumed custody of Wilson's grand dream—as amplified by Franklin D. Roosevelt—of America's championship of the right. After all, Truman accepted at face value the idea of the president's having a mandate to use federal power to improve the people's lot, to advance democracy, and to secure world peace. His way would not be Wilson's or Roosevelt's. He was different from them, and the times had changed. Truman would put his own particular stamp on the Wilsonian dream, just as Roosevelt had in laying the bases for its implementation. It remained for Truman to make the new American state system a permanent fixture at home and to define its role on the world scene. For better or worse, the American state system reached maturity during Truman's presidency. Very substantially, it would be the products of Truman's administration that his successors down to the present would have to work with, especially abroad.

Truman was far from being the sole author of his administration's works. Nor did he pretend to be, for he was a political realist. As a seasoned politician and officeholder, he had learned that a political leader in the United States is in effect the chairman of many boards, not the lord of the realm. Thus, as president, he knew that his job was to satisfy or to pacify a majority of the voters, political leaders, representatives of interest groups, and governmental officials, as well as to pursue his own concepts of the national interest. And this applied both to legislation and to administration. Truman knew, too, that Congress would play a very considerable role—indeed, more than he had anticipated—in shaping his administration, as would the various aides and administrators with whom he staffed the government. Moreover, if any activity had implications for foreign policy, there would be influences from abroad. The president, of course, still had tremendous power. It rarely seemed to be enough, however, to meet the challenges facing Truman, especially as there was always the risk of using it in such a way that it could upset some delicate alignment of forces. Once again, this meant that Truman could seldom be the sole master of what his administration did.

Truman's overall goals were clear from the beginning of his presidency, and he pursued them, though not without some confusion, throughout his two terms in the White House. These objectives embraced economic security and opportunity, domestic order, world peace, and the universal enhancement of freedom and democracy. Broad these aims were and had to be, for the details of their implementation would depend upon a multitude of factors in a rapidly changing world. And Truman had little time to spare in pursuing his dreams. Immediately upon his assumption of office, he was confronted with the problems of bringing a victorious end to World War II, plotting the peace that would follow, and devising policies for economic reconversion. Any one of these was a major challenge, but tackling all three simultaneously was an almost insuperable task, especially for a new president who had yet to decide on how to staff his administration.

Harry Truman would become adept at facing major challenges, for he was never long without one being at hand during his almost eight years in the White House. He could therefore hardly avoid having great impact on his time and the future. This was all the more true because of the vastly expanded jurisdiction of the federal government and the presidency during the Roosevelt years. True, some federal powers in domestic matters had been whittled away during World War II, and many of the government's emergency wartime powers would soon be terminated. Yet, most of the important New Deal programs survived. Even before the end of the war, steps had been taken to ensure that the government would play a large role on the world scene through participation in international organizations and agreements, arrangements for governing occupied lands, and attempts at world reconstruction. Then, too, few Americans seriously contemplated reducing United States military personnel to prewar levels any more than they contemplated replacing B-29 bombers with Ford Trimotors or forgetting how to split the atom. The question before the United States was not how to return to the days of Calvin Coolidge but, instead, how to use the government to promote economic security and democracy and to perform as a world power.

In terms of domestic policy, the result was that the fundamentals of the New Deal were confirmed during the Truman presidency. Thus, Social Security was broadened; labor policy was reformed, though from a conservative viewpoint; economy and efficiency were often applied to governmental operations; the movements continued, however haphazardly, to regulate the economy in terms of supplies, resources, growth, finances, prices, markets, and business practices; and public housing was extended. It is true that the Truman administration was not able to gain significant congressional approval for any of its major domestic initiatives, such as civil rights, health care, and aid to education. It is also true, however, that none of the major New Deal programs was seriously disturbed, and some were even expanded. From this vantage point, it is clear that one of the Truman administration's major domestic accomplishments was to preserve and even to help to reform the New Deal.

The Truman administration exercised major effects on American society in at least two other important ways. One, perhaps the most significant, was to make permanent the huge federal government, with its great powers. In part, this accompanied the confirmation of so much of the New Deal. This was also accomplished as a result of the care that the Truman administration exercised in handling fiscal and budgetary matters. Particularly, this included the stimulation of economic growth to ensure that there would be enough revenues to finance the activities of a powerful federal state while fostering increases in the purchasing power of the people. There was also the institutionalization of the presidency. This chiefly involved expanding the president's staff and their responsibilities; establishing or expanding advisory agencies, such as the Bureau of the Budget, the Council of Economic Advisers, and the National Security Council; relying more on ad hoc commissions, such as the President's Committee on Civil Rights; supporting the reorganization of the executive branch (most importantly through the work of the Hoover Commission); and promoting better management of federal affairs in dozens of relatively undramatic ways. Truman knew that the president could not make every important decision on his own, any more than the vastly expanded government could be operated as a ramshackle collection of satrapies. Structure had to be brought to the federal government, and Truman bent mighty efforts to do so. In this he had considerable success, so that well before he left office, the government had become better organized and better coordinated than ever before. It might not have been fully satisfactory, but there it was, resembling a pyramidical hierarchy in which reports, directives, and monitoring took on some semblance of order. Topping it all was Harry S. Truman, whose desk was decorated with a sign that was full of meaning in the institutionalized presidency: THE BUCK STOPS HERE.

Another important domestic activity of the Truman administration—especially for the future—was the spurring on of debate on the unfinished business of the New Deal and the issues that had been freshly raised by the Fair Deal. Whether it concerned civil rights, education, health, housing, migratory labor, natural resources, or a dozen other questions, the Truman administration constantly pressed the nation to consider making changes. Some of these issues would virtually be forgotten and would have to be raised much later. Most of them, however, became perennial issues that the federal government eventually would act upon. Truman may not initially have known of Theodore Roosevelt's idea of using the presidency as a "bully pulpit," but that did not prevent him from vigorously using his office as such. Indeed, Truman was outstanding in his efforts to inform his fellow

Americans of a broad range of problems that were confronting the nation, however palatable or unpalatable his proposed solutions might have been.

The regularization of the new American state system and Truman's vigor in airing issues also affected the development of the nation's foreign and military policies. It is in the implementation of these policies that the administration had its greatest impact upon its time and posterity, both at home and abroad. It was also on foreign and military matters that the administration had its greatest success in the formulation of policy. Most Americans and their representatives were less sure of themselves on such matters than they were on purely domestic affairs. Thus they were more willing to follow the Truman administration's prescriptions on military and foreign policies, especially as these Americans had come to believe that inaction would promise dire consequences for the United States and the world. International Communist leadership eschewed trying to calm the fears of the people, and many prospective allies of the United States encouraged those fears because they shared them. Soon after the war it became evident that the defeat of the Axis powers and the establishment of the United Nations were not automatically going to create an era of international peace, good will, and cooperation. Impatient and disappointed with the rising animosity between the East and the West, the United States could not condone what it saw as Soviet hostility and aggrandizement. Nor were Americans this time going to withdraw behind their oceanic barriers.

The Truman administration decided to act with increasing forcefulness and with mounting support from the American people. In 1945, Washington was using the carrot and the stick in dealing with the Russians, who seemed to be at the center of the deteriorating world situation. The Truman administration, almost from its beginning, made clear that although it was willing to extend assistance to and to negotiate differences with the Soviet Union, it would not allow Russian aggrandizement to go unchallenged. Mounting troubles in 1946 prompted United States leaders to talk more about the stick and less about the carrot in dealing with the USSR and its allies. In short, the situation was shattering the American dream of achieving international cooperation to secure peace, to extend freedom and democracy, and to foster world economic progress. A nightmare of incessant animosity and the threat of another, even-more-catastrophic world war rapidly was replacing the dream.

The United States responded, and with enormous consequences for the entire world. Just as most Americans could not condone Communist aggrandizement, so most of them would not contemplate engaging in a preventive war. Since by 1947 their leadership had also concluded—probably rashly—that no one could negotiate with Moscow and its allies, that left open only one course of action. This was to forge alliances to contain the expansion of Communist power. The first major step in this direction came in 1947 through the implementation of the Truman Doctrine and the accompanying aid programs to Greece and Turkey. The administration then proposed a massive European reconstruction program and the Rio Pact for a Western Hemisphere alliance. This defensive atmosphere also spurred the unification of the armed forces and the creation of the Central Intelligence Agency, the National Security Council, and the president's loyalty-security program. Clearly, the Cold War had begun in earnest, especially as Moscow devised a series of chilling responses.

The developments of 1947 were just the beginning, however. In 1948 came the implementation of the Marshall Plan, the tough Anglo-French-American response to the Soviet blockade of Berlin, and the laying of the foundations for the North Atlantic Treaty. The treaty itself was ratified in the following year, and the West German state was established. In 1950 the Truman administration laid plans, through NSC 68, for a massive, coordinated world-wide anti-Communist program, which included defense, propaganda, aid, economic, domestic-security, and intelligence activities. The Korean War also broke out that year, which clinched administrative and legislative approval of most of NSC 68 as well as demonstrating that the United States would not shrink from a military response to Communist aggression. By the end of the Truman presidency, the Cold War plainly was the dominant feature of world affairs and would remain so for a long time to come. Indeed, down to the present, no nation on earth has remained untouched by it.

The response of Americans to the threats that they perceived to be coming from Moscow during the Truman presidency was not uniform. Many Americans were disturbed by their government's actions or inactions. There was occasional talk of granting substantial concessions to the Soviet Union or of launching a preventive war; there was far more talk of tightening domestic security. Most of the discussion, however, concerned questions of the amount of money to spend, where to spend it, and how much authority to give the administration in pursuing the containment of communism. These debates, however intense, did not seriously alter the general trend of United States foreign and military programs after 1945, because most Americans and their representatives accepted, sometimes enthusiastically, the outline of the administration's anti-Communist policies. Plainly, neither appeasement nor preventive war was acceptable, and by 1947 the Truman administration had rejected the idea of relying on hard and relentless bargaining for American interests in negotiating with the Soviets. As for the Communist leaders, after the Potsdam Conference of 1945, they seldom gave believable signs that they were willing to cooperate in establishing a fair, just, and honorable peace; and this only confirmed the American determination to get tougher in the conduct of foreign affairs. This was the tragedy of the time, one that would beget other tragedies in the future. If the United States was not able to be more patient in bargaining determinedly for the achievement of its grand dream of securing peace and advancing democracy, personal freedom, and economic security, the Russians—and later China—were not able to allay their own nationalistic fears and ideological ambitions. Neither side could, consequently, win high marks in the court of history for far-sightedness, although each did succeed in winning many of its short-term objectives.

The Truman presidency long ago passed into history, but its consequences have not. Harry Truman himself gave a strong and far-from-incorrect impression of being a tough, concerned, and direct leader. He was occasionally vulgar, often partisan, and usually nationalistic. Moreover, he was a decisive man who was surrounded by men who knew exactly what they wanted him to be decisive about. Sometimes uncritical of the advice that they gave him, Truman occasionally acted hastily and on the basis of inadequate information. Nevertheless, he was a president whose positive characteristics would later come to be widely admired. He would never completely work himself out from under the shadow of his predecessor, for it was Franklin D. Roosevelt who had laid so many of the bases of what the Missourian had to deal with. Yet Truman partly commands our attention because he was the reasonably successful executor of Roosevelt's remarkable political estate. Truman also commands attention in his own right. He and his administration had to face four crises—more in number if not in their individual importance than were confronted by any other American presidency. He accelerated a victorious conclusion to World War II, even though the awesome atomic bomb was used in order to do so. With remarkable success he confronted the touchy problem of domestic economic reconversion with its prime goal of avoiding a depression. He led his nation to make substantial contributions to the reconstruction of a world that had been ravaged by war. And he responded aggressively to the threats to world peace that most Americans perceived to be emanating from Moscow. This marked departure from traditional American foreign and military policy was the most important aspect of his presidency. On his own terms, Truman can be seen as having prevented the coming of a third world war and as having preserved from

Communist oppression much of what he called the free world. Yet clearly he largely failed to achieve his Wilsonian aim of securing perpetual peace, making the world safe for democracy, and advancing opportunities for individual development internationally.

In handling these crises at home and abroad, the Truman presidency was instrumental in fostering the growth of the United States economy. This not only helped to finance the myriad activities of the federal government; it also improved the economic status of many Americans and raised the aspirations of people everywhere. And it also enhanced American involvement in world trade, making the United States by far the largest single international trader and investor. This reinforced the nation's position in world politics. Economic expansion was also related to the acceleration of the use of natural resources, which would eventually lead to an energy and raw-materials crisis in the United States and elsewhere. The Truman administration's concern for advancing economic security through private and public means was undeniable. In the United States, this contributed to the stabilization of society, and it was intended to do so in non-Communist lands at least through the Marshall Plan and the Point IV program.

The Truman administration's civil-rights initiatives at home and its spasmodic concern for human rights elsewhere were intended to serve the same purpose. Yet the government's loyalty and security programs and its increasing support for oppressive non-Communist regimes abroad encouraged contrary trends. The administration's confusion, with abundant help from Congress, was nowhere better demonstrated than in these areas. This was not unlike the clash of motives and interests that led to proposing greater regulation of the economy and greater preservation of natural resources while encouraging both large entrepreneurs and the increased exploitation of resources in pursuit of economic growth. In the welter of confusion and the rush of events, it is not surprising that the administration of government would be improved during the Truman presidency at the same time that the administration was becoming noted for the scandals arising from the corruption or ineptitude of some of its members.

Overall, as already indicated, Truman and his administration made big government a permanent and pervasive feature of the American scene. The administration also made the United States government an enduring and powerful presence in world affairs. These developments were almost predictable. After all, never before had a presidency had the means, the motives, and the opportunities to realize them. The Truman administration did, and it took full advantage of the situation, with substantial public and congressional support, to regularize its domestic authority and to expand its powers abroad. If the succeeding administration—that of Dwight D. Eisenhower—did not greatly develop the power of the federal government, it repealed little of significance from the Truman years. As for the proposals of the Truman administration that had been ignored or barely recognized, later administrations would implement many of them.

The Truman administration also entrenched the presidency as the centerpiece of the nation's government, largely by institutionalizing the trends in this direction that had been initiated under earlier presidents. Thus, under Truman, the effectiveness of the presidential office now depended less on the genius of the incumbent and more on the advisory, managerial, and power structures surrounding him. The institutionalized presidency offered no guarantee of outstanding performance. It did, however, ensure that the president would have impact, because the incumbent could mobilize resources as never before, just as he had the resources upon which to draw as never before.

This is not to say that Harry S. Truman was solely responsible for all of this; there were many others in the executive, legislative, and judicial branches who shared the responsibility. Furthermore, Truman's presidency was as much the occasion as the reason for what developed, given what Franklin D. Roosevelt had bequeathed to his successor and given the attitudes of most other American officeholders and of the public. Yet Truman's ego, his abilities, and his faith in what the government and the United States could accomplish enabled him to make a great deal of what he had inherited, regardless of the consequences. And this was true, even though he did not get all that he wanted during his presidency. Truman would often be disappointed as a result; but he was never disenchanted. He knew that, however irksome, mistakes would occur, compromises would be made, and disappointments would endure. As he saw it, he had "done his damnedest"—successes, failures, compromises, mistakes, and all. If this was not enough, the people were free to look elsewhere for leadership. They did this by 1952. In doing so, though, they repudiated more the man than his works.

NOTES

Consonant with the style of the American Presidency Series, only unusual materials, particularly quotations, are documented in this book. The author is, of course, indebted to a wide variety of other sources, the most important of which are cited in the accompanying Bibliographical Essay. It must be noted that undocumented quotations are drawn from *Public Papers of the Presidents of the United States, Harry S. Truman, Containing the Public Messages, Speeches, and Statements of the President, 1945–1953,* 8 vols. (Washington: Government Printing Office, 1961–1966). These quotations are dated in the text of this work.

CHAPTER 1
ARRIVING AT ARMAGEDDON

1. Harry S. Truman, *Memoirs by Harry S. Truman,* vol. 1: *Year of Decisions,* vol. 2: *Years of Trial and Hope* (Garden City, N.Y.: Doubleday & Co., 1955, 1956), 1:19.

2. Ibid., p. 119.

3. Ibid., p. 138.

CHAPTER 2
TO END A WAR

1. Robert H. Ferrell, ed., *Off the Record: The Private Papers of Harry S. Truman* (New York: Harper & Row, 1980), pp. 35, 29.

2. Ibid., p. 30.

3. Eben Ayers Diary, Sept. 14, 1945, Harry S. Truman Library, Independence, Mo. (hereafter cited as TL).

4. Ferrell, *Off the Record*, p. 174.
5. Ibid., pp. 24–25.
6. Ibid., pp. 37–38.
7. Franklin D. Roosevelt and Winston Churchill, *aide-mémoire*, Sept. 18, 1944, cited in Martin J. Sherwin, *A World Destroyed: The Atomic Bomb and the Grand Alliance* (New York: Alfred A. Knopf Co., 1975), p. 284.
8. Truman, *Memoirs*, 1:10.
9. Sherwin, *A World Destroyed*, p. 302.
10. Henry L. Stimson and McGeorge Bundy, *On Active Service in Peace and War* (New York: Harper, 1948), p. 637.
11. Vojtech Mastny, *Russia's Road to the Cold War* (New York: Columbia University Press, 1979), p. 283.
12. *Roosevelt and Churchill: Their Secret Wartime Correspondence*, ed. Francis L. Loewenheim, Harold D. Langley, and Manfred Jonas (New York: Saturday Review Press, 1975), p. 67.

13. Ibid., p. 705.
14. Robert J. Donovan, *Conflict and Crisis: The Presidency of Harry S Truman, 1945–1948* (New York: W. W. Norton & Co., 1977), p. 38.
15. Truman, *Memoirs*, 1:82.
16. Ayers Diary, May 4, 1945, TL.
17. Ferrell, *Off the Record*, p. 35.
18. Truman Longhand Notes File, May 23, 1945, President's Secretary's File (hereafter cited as PSF), TL.
19. Ibid., July 4, 1945.
20. Ferrell, *Off the Record*, p. 49.
21. Ibid., p. 55.
22. Truman, *Memoirs*, 1:392.
23. Ibid., p. 416.
24. Ibid., p. 412.
25. Henry A. Wallace, *The Price of Vision: The Diary of Henry A. Wallace, 1942–1946*, ed. John Morton Blum (Boston: Houghton Mifflin Co., 1973), p. 474; Donovan, *Conflict and Crisis*, p. 96.

CHAPTER 3
RECONVERSION

1. James F. Byrnes, *Problems of Mobilization and Reconversion, First Report of the Director of War Mobilization and Reconversion, January 1, 1945* (Washington, D.C.: Government Printing Office, 1945), p. 14.
2. Chester Bowles, *Promises to Keep: My Years in Public Life, 1941–1969* (New York: Harper & Row, 1971), p. 127.
3. *New York Times*, July 30, 1945.
4. Samuel B. Hand, *Counsel and Advise: A Political Biography of Samuel I. Rosenman* (New York: Garland Publishing Co., 1979), p. 226.
5. *New York Times*, Sept. 8, 1945.
6. Ferrell, *Off the Record*, p. 68.

7. Ayers Diary, Sept. 21, 1945, TL.
8. Ferrell, *Off the Record*, p. 86.
9. Allen J. Matusow, *Farm Policies and Politics in the Truman Years* (Cambridge: Harvard University Press, 1967), p. 36.
10. Ayers Diary, Jan. 12, 1946, TL.
11. Ibid., Jan. 24, 1946.
12. Truman Longhand Notes File, n.d., 1946, PSF, TL.
13. Donovan, *Conflict and Crisis*, pp. 212–213.
14. Daily Sheets, President's Appointments File, Sept. 27, 1945, PSF, TL.
15. Ayers Diary, May 24, 1946.

CHAPTER 4
THE IRON CURTAIN DESCENDS

1. Dean Acheson, *Present at the Creation: My Years in the State Department* (New York: W. W. Norton & Co., 1969), p. 113.

2. Arthur H. Vandenberg, *The Private Papers of Senator Vandenberg*, ed. Arthur H. Vandenberg, Jr. (Boston: Houghton Mifflin Co., 1952), pp. 218–219.

3. Carol Ann Briley, "George Elsey's White House Career" (M.A. thesis, University of Missouri-Kansas City, 1976), p. 19.

4. Daniel Yergin, *Shattered Peace: The Origins of the Cold War and the National Security State* (Boston: Houghton Mifflin Co., 1977), p. 76.

5. Ibid., p. 109.

6. James Forrestal, *The Forrestal Diaries*, ed. Walter Millis (New York: Viking Press, 1951), p. 96.

7. Wallace, *Price of Vision*, pp. 440–441.

8. James F. Byrnes, *All in One Lifetime* (New York: Harper & Brothers, 1958), p. 317.

9. John Foster Dulles, *War or Peace* (New York: Macmillan & Co., 1950), p. 30.

10. Bonner Fellers to Herbert Hoover, Oct. 3, 1945, Bonner Fellers File, Herbert Hoover Presidential Library, West Branch, Iowa.

11. James F. Schnabel, *The History of the Joint Chiefs of Staff*, vol. 1: *The Joint Chiefs of Staff and National Policy, 1945-1947*, 2 vols. (Wilmington, Del.: Michael Glazier, Inc., 1979), 1:73.

12. Ferrell, *Off the Record*, p. 74.

13. Acheson, *Present at the Creation*, p. 173.

14. Byrnes, *All in One Lifetime*, p. 334.

15. Truman, *Memoirs*, 1:551-552.

16. George F. Kennan, *Memoirs, 1925-1950* (Boston: Little, Brown Co., 1967), pp. 547-559.

17. Vandenberg, *Private Papers*, pp. 247-248.

18. Department of State, *Bulletin*, Mar. 10, 1946, pp. 355-358.

19. *Vital Speeches of the Day*, March 15, 1946.

20. Daily Sheets, President's Appointments File, Mar. 23, 1946, PSF, TL.

21. Forrestal, *Diaries*, p. 155.

22. Memorandum of May 16, 1946, Harry S. Truman File, Hoover Library.

23. Department of State, *Union of Soviet Socialist Republics, Policy and Information Statement, May 15, 1946*, pp. 2, 5, in Russia File, Papers of Clark M. Clifford, TL.

24. Byrnes, *All in One Lifetime*, p. 369.

25. Wallace, *Price of Vision*, p. 598.

26. Truman Longhand Notes File, Sept. 16, 1946, PSF, TL.

27. James F. Byrnes, *Speaking Frankly* (New York: Harper & Brothers, 1947), p. 242.

28. Truman Longhand Notes File, Sept. 19, 1946, PSF, TL.

29. "American Relations with the Soviet Union, A Report to the President by the Special Counsel to the President, September 1946," enclosed in Clark M. Clifford to the President, Sept. 24, 1946, Foreign Relations—Russia File, Papers of George M. Elsey, TL. See also Russia File, Clifford Papers, TL.

30. Margaret Truman, *Harry S. Truman* (New York: William Morrow & Co., 1973), p. 347.

31. Forrestal, *Diaries*, p. 215.

CHAPTER 5
THE EIGHTIETH CONGRESS AND THE
HOME FRONT

1. Ayers Diary, Dec. 7, 1946, TL.
2. Ferrell, *Off the Record*, p. 110.
3. Forrestal, *Diaries*, p. 220.
4. Matusow, *Farm Policies*, pp. 158–159.
5. Ayers Diary, Oct. 5, 1947, TL.
6. Ibid., Sept. 30, 1947.
7. Ibid., Oct. 15, 1947.
8. Ibid., Oct. 28, 1947.
9. Ferrell, *Off the Record*, pp. 118–119.
10. Harry S. Truman to Ruby Hurley, Oct. 27, 1949, Presidential Personal File 393, TL.
11. *New York Times*, Mar. 13, 1948.
12. *Chicago Defender*, July 31, 1948.
13. Clinton P. Anderson to John R. Steelman, Dec. 3, 1946, General Correspondence, Legislation, Office of the Secretary of Agriculture, Record Group (hereafter RG) 16, National Archives, Washington D.C.
14. Clinton P. Anderson to W. R. Ronald, June 9, 1947, ibid.

CHAPTER 6
THE COLD WAR COMES

1. Forrestal, *Diaries*, p. 239.
2. *Foreign Relations of the United States, 1946* (Washington: Government Printing Office, 1970), 7:235–237.
3. Lincoln MacVeagh, *Ambassador MacVeagh Reports: Greece, 1933–1947*, ed. John O. Iatrides (Princeton, N.J.: Princeton University Press, 1980), p. 712.
4. George M. Elsey, oral history transcript, pp. 375–376, TL.
5. Vandenberg, *Private Papers*, p. 339.
6. Acheson, *Present at the Creation*, p. 219.
7. Marx Leva to Secretary of the Navy, Mar. 8, 1947, enclosed in James V. Forrestal to Clark M. Clifford, Mar. 8, 1947, Presidential Speech File (Mar. 12, 1947), Clifford Papers, TL.
8. Ayers Diary, Mar. 12, 1947, TL.
9. Mark Ethridge, oral history transcript, pp. 36–37, TL.
10. James T. Patterson, *Mr. Republican: A Biography of Robert A. Taft* (Boston: Houghton Mifflin Co., 1972), p. 371.
11. Excerpted telephone conversation between James V. Forrestal and Carl Vinson, Mar. 13, 1947, enclosed in Forrestal to Clark M. Clifford, Mar. 14, 1947, Presidential Speech File, Clifford Papers, TL.
12. *Congressional Record*, 80th Cong., 1st sess., p. 4742.
13. *Wichita* (Kans.) *Beacon*, Mar. 22, 1947.
14. Adlai E. Stevenson, *The Papers of Adlai E. Stevenson: Washington to Springfield, 1941–1948*, ed. Walter Johnson, 8 vols. (Boston: Little, Brown, Co., 1973), 2:398.
15. Department of State, *Bulletin*, June 15, 1947, p. 1160.
16. Theodore A. Wilson, *The Marshall Plan*, Headline Series no. 236 (New York: Foreign Policy Association, 1977), p. 23.
17. Acheson, *Present at the Creation*, pp. 234–235.
18. Forrestal, *Diaries*, p. 288.

19. Wilson, *Marshall Plan*, p. 26.

20. Herbert Hoover to Arthur H. Vandenberg, Dec. 24, 1947, Vandenberg File, Hoover Library.

21. Central Intelligence Agency, *Review of the World Situation as It Relates to the Security of the United States* (Sept. 26, 1947), p. 5, Meeting 1 File, National Security Council Meetings, PSF, TL.

22. Vandenberg, *Private Papers*, p. 382.

23. Joseph W. Martin, Jr., *My First Fifty Years in Politics* (New York: McGraw-Hill Book Co., 1960), p. 193.

24. Dirk U. Stikker, *Men of Responsibility: A Memoir* (London: John Murray Co., 1966), p. 164.

25. Ayers Diary, Apr. 10, 1948, TL.

26. R. C. Mowat, *Creating the European Community* (London: Blandford Press, 1973), p. 37.

27. Forrestal, *Diaries*, p. 265.

28. Robert L. Dennison, oral history transcript, p. 5, TL.

29. Lucius D. Clay, *The Papers of General Lucius D. Clay: Germany 1945–1949*, ed. Jean Edward Smith, 2 vols. (Bloomington: Indiana University Press, 1974), 1:459.

30. CIA, *Review of the World Situation* (Nov. 14, 1947), p. 1, Meeting 2 File, NSC Meetings, PSF, TL.

31. Forrestal, *Diaries*, p. 432.

32. CIA, *Review of the World Situation* (Dec. 17, 1947), pp. 1–2, Meeting 3 File, NSC Meetings, PSF, TL.

33. Edward Fursdon, *The European Defence Community: A History* (London: Macmillan Press, 1980), p. 35.

34. Stanley E. Hilton, "The United States, Brazil, and the Cold War, 1945–1960: End of the Special Relationship," *Journal of American History* 68 (Dec. 1981): 604.

35. Ayers Diary, Dec. 2, 1947, TL.

36. Ferrell, *Off the Record*, p. 127.

37. CIA, *Review of the World Situation* (June 17, 1948), p. 1, Meeting 13 File, NSC Meetings, PSF, TL.

38. Clay, *Papers*, 2:697.

39. Forrestal, *Diaries*, pp. 454–455.

40. Vandenberg, *Private Papers*, p. 410.

41. Ferrell, *Off the Record*, pp. 148–149.

42. Forrestal, *Diaries*, p. 536.

43. *A Report to the National Security Council by the Executive Secretary* (Mar. 3, 1948), Meeting 9 File, NSC Meetings, PSF, TL.

44. Peyton Ford to James E. Webb, Feb. 27, 1948, ser. 47.1, E19-1/47.2, Bureau of the Budget, RG 51, National Archives. See also Elmer B. Staats to Attorney General, Mar. 8, 1948, ibid.

CHAPTER 7
PERSONALITY: PRESIDENT AND POLITICIAN

1. Ayers Diary, Dec. 24, 1948, TL.

2. Ferrell, *Off the Record*, p. 134.

3. Ayers Diary, Jan. 30, 1947, TL.

4. Ibid., Sept. 22–27, 1947.

5. Truman, draft of Gridiron Club remarks, Dec. 1947, Longhand Notes File, PSF, TL.

6. Charles Murphy, oral history transcript, p. 66, TL.

7. Dennison, oral history transcript, p. 176, TL.

8. Truman, list of cabinet members and White House aides with notes, n.d. [late 1952], Longhand Notes File, PSF, TL.

9. Ferrell, *Off the Record*, p. 133.

10. Ibid., pp. 145, 119, 124.

11. Ayers Diary, Dec. 31, 1947, TL.

12. Ferrell, *Off the Record*, p. 127.

13. Richard S. Kirkendall, "Election of 1948," in *History of American Presidential Elections, 1789–1968*, ed. Arthur M. Schlesinger, Jr., and Fred L. Israel, 4 vols. (New York: Chelsea House, 1971), 4:3104.

14. Donald R. McCoy and Richard T. Ruetten, *Quest and Response: Minority Rights and the Truman Administration* (Lawrence: University Press of Kansas, 1973), p. 97.

15. Vandenberg, *Private Papers*, p. 379.

16. Ferrell, *Off the Record*, p. 122.

17. Transcript of Conference of Southern Governors with Senator J. Howard McGrath, Feb. 23, 1948, Papers of J. Howard McGrath, TL.

18. Ferrell, *Off the Record*, p. 141.

19. Memorandum, "Should the President Call Congress Back?" June 29, 1948, app., Clark M. Clifford, oral history transcript, TL.

20. Ayers Diary, July 13, 1948, TL.

21. George M. Elsey, oral history transcript, p. 71, TL.

22. Ayers Diary, Oct. 6, 1948, TL.

23. Ferrell, *Off the Record*, p. 150.

24. Ayers Diary, Nov. 2–3, 1948, TL.

CHAPTER 8
THE FAIR DEAL

1. Clifford, oral history transcript, p. 332, TL.

2. Frank Pace, Jr., oral history transcript, p. 17, TL.

3. Paul H. Douglas, *In the Fullness of Time: The Memoirs of Paul H. Douglas* (New York: Harcourt Brace Jovanovich, Inc., 1971), p. 203.

4. Harry S. Truman to Francis Matthews, Nov. 29, 1948, Papers of Francis Matthews, TL.

5. Meeting of the President and the Four Service Secretaries with the President's Committee on Equality of Treatment and Opportunity in the Armed Services, Jan. 12, 1949, Official File 1285F, TL.

6. E. W. Kenworthy to Charles H. Fahy, July 25, 1950, Philleo Nash Files, TL.

7. *Afro-American* (Baltimore, Md.), June 17, 1950.

8. Ferrell, *Off the Record*, p. 166.

9. Douglas, *In the Fullness of Time*, p. 391.

10. Ayers Diary, Apr. 11, 1950, TL.

11. Ibid., Apr. 28, 1950.

12. Council of Economic Advisers to the President, Apr. 17, 1950, Papers of John D. Clark, TL.

13. Emanuel Celler, *You Never Leave Brooklyn* (New York: John Day, 1953), p. 147.

14. Richard Bolling, *Power in the House: A History of the Leadership of the House of Representatives* (New York: E. P. Dutton Co., 1968), p. 184.

15. David L. Marden, "The Cold War and American Education" (Ph.D. diss., University of Kansas, 1976), p. 457.

16. McCoy and Ruetten, *Quest and Response*, p. 185.

17. Congressional Quarterly News Features, *Congressional Quarterly Almanac 1949* (Washington, D.C.: Congressional Quarterly, 1950), pp. 269-270.

18. Ayers Diary, Sept. 15, 1950, TL.

19. Truman, Bound Diaries, Aug. 30, 1949, PSF, TL.

20. "Statement on Presidential Appointments," n.d. (probably 1949 or 1950), Longhand Notes File, PSF, TL.

21. Truman, Bound Diaries, Oct. 22, 1949, PSF, TL.

22. Ayers Diary, June 21, Aug. 8, 1949, TL.

23. Ibid., Aug. 1, 1949, TL.

24. Truman, Bound Diaries, Mar. 26, 1949, PSF, TL.

25. Truman, Longhand Notes File, Sept. 11, 1950, PSF, TL.

26. Ibid., Dec. 3, 1950.

CHAPTER 9
RAISING THE STAKES

1. Clay, *Papers*, 2:1137-1138.

2. Acheson, *Present at the Creation*, p. 327. It is interesting that Eben Ayers, in 1949, quoted Dean Acheson as having said, "Tito is an s. o. b., but he is our s. o. b." Ayers Diary, Sept. 15, 1949, TL.

3. CIA, *Review of the World Situation* (Nov. 17, 1948), p. 1, Meeting 27 File, NSC Meetings, PSF, TL.

4. Vandenberg, *Private Papers*, p. 536.

5. Herbert Hoover to William F. Knowland, Dec. 31, 1949, Knowland File, Hoover Library.

6. Vandenberg, *Private Papers*, pp. 499-500, 503-504.

7. Ibid., p. 508.

8. Ayers Diary, May 6, 1949, TL.

9. John W. Gibson to the Secretary, Mar. 7, 1949, General Subject File 1949, Administrative, Maurice Tobin, Office of the Secretary of Labor, RG 174, National Archives.

10. Philip M. Kaiser to Maurice Tobin, May 30, 1950, ibid., 1950.

11. Patterson, *Mr. Republican*, p. 438.

12. CIA, *Review of the World Situation* (Nov. 17, 1948), p. 1, Meeting 17

File, NSC Meetings, PSF, TL.

13. Ayers Diary, Aug. 25, 1950, TL.

14. *A Report to the President by the National Security Council on the Position of the United States with Respect to Asia* (Dec. 30, 1949), NSC 48/2, Meeting 50 File, NSC Meetings, PSF, TL.

15. "Report to the President by the Secretary of the Interior on His February-March 1947 Tour of the Pacific Islands," Official File 85-L, TL.

16. U.S., Senate, Committee on Foreign Relations, Hearings: *Trusteeship Agreement for the Territory of the Pacific Islands*, 80th Cong., 1st sess., on S.J. Res. 143, p. 5.

17. Stephen J. Spingarn to Clark M. Clifford, Sept. 22, 1949, OF 85-L, TL.

18. CIA, *Review of the World Situation* (Oct. 19, 1949), p. 1, Meeting 47 File, NSC Meetings, PSF, TL.

19. Acheson, *Present at the Creation*, p. 265.

20. Henry G. Gomperts to the Secretary, May 18, 1950, General Subject File 1950, Administrative, Maurice Tobin, RG 174.

21. Dennison, oral history transcript, p. 31, TL.

22. Lewis B. Hershey to Roger W. Jones, June 6, 1949, ser. 47.1, M14-7/49.1, RG 51.

23. Murray Green, "Stuart Symington and the B-36" (Ph.D. diss., American University, 1960), p. 307.

24. Thomas K. Finletter, oral history transcript, p. 30, TL.

25. NSC 68, quoted in *Containment: Documents on American Policy and Strategy, 1945–1950*, ed. Thomas H. Etzold and John Lewis Gaddis (New York: Columbia University Press, 1978), pp. 385–442.

26. Pace, oral history transcript, pp. 31–32, TL.

27. Acheson, *Present at the Creation*, p. 360.

28. Ferrell, *Off the Record*, p. 172.

29. Ayers Diary, Apr. 29, 1950, TL.

30. Ibid., June 28, 1950.

CHAPTER 10
THE FOCUS SHIFTS

1. Herbert Hoover to Bonner Fellers, June 12, 1950, Fellers File, Hoover Library.

2. Donald R. McCoy, *Landon of Kansas* (Lincoln: University of Nebraska Press, 1966), p. 545.

3. Ayers Diary, June 29, 1950, TL.

4. Ferrell, *Off the Record*, p. 185.

5. Matthew B. Ridgway, *The Korean War* (Garden City, N.Y.: Doubleday & Co., 1967), p. 29.

6. Council of Economic Advisers to the President, Sept. 26, 1950, Clark Papers, TL.

7. Harry S. Truman to the Secretary of Labor et al., Sept. 28, 1950, General Subject File 1950, White House, Maurice Tobin, RG 174.

8. Philip M. Kaiser to the Secretary, Jan. 5, 1951, General Subject File 1951, NSC, Maurice Tobin, RG 174.

9. CIA, *Review of the World Situation* (Aug. 16, 1950), Meeting 65 File, NSC Meetings, PSF, TL.

10. Douglas, *In the Fullness of Time*, p. 307.

11. Truman, Longhand Notes File, Aug. 27, 1950, PSF, TL.

12. Acheson, *Present at the Creation*, p. 451.

13. Ibid., p. 453.

14. Finletter, oral history transcript, p. 30, TL.

15. Pace, oral history transcript, p. 111, TL.

16. U.S., Senate, Committee on Armed Services and Committee on Foreign Relations, *Substance of Statements Made at Wake Island Conference on October 15, 1950, Compiled by General of the Army Omar N. Bradley*, 82d Cong., 1st sess., passim.

17. Truman, Longhand Notes File, Nov. 5, 1950 (misdated Oct. 5, 1950), PSF, TL.

18. *Public Papers of the Presidents of the United States, Harry S. Truman, 1950* (Washington, D.C.: Government Printing Office, 1965), p. 725.

19. Ridgway, *Korean War*, p. 62.

20. Ibid., p. 83.

21. Ferrell, *Off the Record*, pp. 201–202.

CHAPTER 11
CONFLICT AT HOME AND ABROAD

1. Herbert Hoover to Joseph P. Kennedy, Dec. 18, 1950, Kennedy File, Hoover Library.

2. *New York Times*, Jan. 12, 1951.

3. John Hersey, *Aspects of the Presidency* (New Haven, Conn.: Ticknor & Fields Co., 1980), p. 113.

4. Ferrell, *Off the Record*, p. 209.

5. Philleo Nash to George M. Elsey, May 23, 1951, Nash File, TL.

6. *Pittsburgh Courier*, Dec. 15, 1951.

7. Willard Cass, Lawrence Weiss, and Morris Weisz to the Under Secretary of Labor, Nov. 27, 1951, General Subject File 1951, Administration, Maurice Tobin, RG 174.

8. Ferrell, *Off the Record*, p. 201.

9. William F. Knowland to Herbert Hoover, Feb. 2, 1951, Knowland File, Hoover Library.

10. Douglas, *In the Fullness of Time*, pp. 495–496.

11. Joseph Short to the President, Apr. 2, 1951, General Subject File 1951, White House-General, Maurice Tobin, RG 174.

12. Martin, *My First Fifty Years*, p. 205.

13. Truman Bound Diaries, Apr. 5, 1951, PSF, TL.

14. Ferrell, *Off the Record*, p. 210.

15. Truman, Bound Diaries, Apr. 7, 1951, PSF, TL.

16. Ayers Diary, Apr. 16, 1951, TL.

17. Martin, *My First Fifty Years*, p. 212.

18. Ridgway, *Korean War*, p. 151.

19. Truman, Longhand Notes File, Feb. 8, 1951, PSF, TL.

20. Ferrell, *Off the Record*, p. 212.

21. Ayers Diary, Aug. 4, 1951, TL.

22. Harry S. Truman to Herbert Hoover, Nov. 25, 1950, and Hoover to Truman, Nov. 26, 1950, Truman File, Hoover Library.

23. *The Truman Presidency: The Origins of the Imperial Presidency and the National Security State*, ed. Athan G. Theoharis (Stanfordville, N.Y.: Earl M. Coleman Enterprises, 1979), p. 81.

24. Ferrell, *Off the Record*, pp. 218–219.

25. Ayers Diary, Oct. 24, 1951, TL.

26. Estes Kefauver, *Crime in America* (Garden City, N.Y.: Doubleday & Co., 1951), p. 141.

27. Truman, Longhand Notes File, Dec. 25, 1952, PSF, TL.

28. Ferrell, *Off the Record*, pp. 220–221.

29. Ibid., p. 219.

CHAPTER 12
"WINDING DOWN"

1. Ferrell, *Off the Record*, p. 224; Leon H. Keyserling, oral history transcript, p. 159, TL.

2. CIA, *Special Estimate, Probable Developments in the World Situation through Mid-1953* (Sept. 24, 1951), enclosed in S. Everett Gleason to the National Security Council, Oct. 12, 1951, Meeting 105 File, NSC Meetings, PSF, TL.

3. Truman, Longhand Notes File, Jan. 27, 1952, PSF, TL; Ferrell, *Off the Record*, p. 251.

4. Acheson, *Present at the Crea-*

tion, p. 626.

5. Harry S. Truman to Henry F. Grady, Nov. 27, 1952, Personal File, PSF, TL.

6. Ibid.

7. Truman, *Memoirs*, 2:314.

8. Charles Sawyer, *Concerns of a Conservative Democrat* (Carbondale: Southern Illinois University Press, 1968), p. 256.

9. Ibid., p. 268.

10. *Youngstown Sheet & Tube Co. et al. v. Charles Sawyer* (1952), 343 U.S. 579.

11. Ferrell, *Off the Record*, p. 252.

12. Harold L. Ickes to Oscar L. Chapman, Aug. 28, 30, 1951, Oscar L. Chapman Papers, TL.

13. Murphy, oral history transcript, pp. 462-463, TL.

14. Truman, list of cabinet members and White House aides with notes, n.d. [late 1952], Longhand Notes File, PSF, TL.

15. Ferrell, *Off the Record*, p. 177.

16. Truman, Longhand Notes File, May 8, 1950, PSF, TL.

17. "Mr. President" File, Jan. 9, 1952, PSF, TL.

18. Truman, Longhand Notes File, July 26 or 27, 1952, PSF, TL; Ferrell, *Off the Record*, pp. 244-245.

19. Truman, Longhand Notes File, Dec. 25, 1952, PSF, TL.

20. Ferrell, *Off the Record*, p. 245.

21. Ayers Diary, May 31, 1952, TL.

22. Ferrell, *Off the Record*, pp. 260-262.

23. Truman, Longhand Notes File, July 26 or 27, 1952, PSF, TL.

24. *Pittsburgh Courier*, Oct. 25, 1952.

25. Truman, Longhand Notes File, n.d. [1952], PSF, TL.

26. Ferrell, *Off the Record*, pp. 266, 268.

27. Harry S. Truman to John Sparkman, n.d. [1952], Longhand Notes File, PSF, TL.

28. Ferrell, *Off the Record*, p. 263.

29. Ayers Diary, Nov. 8, 1952, TL.

30. Truman, Memo for the President of the United States, n.d. [Nov. 1952], Longhand Notes File, PSF, TL; see also Ferrell, *Off the Record*, pp. 274-275.

31. Truman, Longhand Notes File, Jan. 18, 1952, PSF, TL.

32. Ibid., Aug. 21, 1952.

33. Ferrell, *Off the Record*, p. 279.

34. Ayers Diary, Apr. 14, May 31, 1952, TL.

35. "Mr. President" File, Jan. 9, 1952, PSF, TL.

36. Truman, Longhand Notes File, Feb. 6, 1952, PSF, TL.

37. Truman, list of cabinet members and White House aides with notes, n.d. [late 1952], Longhand Notes File, PSF, TL.

38. Truman to Henry F. Grady, Nov. 27, 1952, Personal File, PSF, TL.

39. Acheson, *Present at the Creation*, p. 730.

40. Ferrell, *Off the Record*, p. 287.

BIBLIOGRAPHICAL ESSAY

The number of historians, journalists, and political scientists who have produced books and articles dealing with Harry S. Truman and his presidency now reaches into the thousands. There is also a considerable amount of literature in print that was written by public notables of the period, as well as numerous master's theses and doctoral dissertations. Writing about Truman and his administration has indeed become a substantial business, spurred on in part by the significance of his presidency and in part by the character of the chief executive and many of the people associated with him. What follows, because of limitations of space, will necessarily be selective.

The raw material for so much of the writings on Harry Truman and his presidency is found in the unpublished materials deposited in scores of manuscript and archival repositories, most notably the National Archives in Washington, D.C., and the Harry S. Truman Library in Independence, Missouri. The basic key to unlocking the treasures of the National Archives is the *Guide to the National Archives of the United States* (Washington, D.C.: National Archives and Records Service, 1974). There are voluminous collections of manuscripts, oral histories, and microfilms in the Truman Library, the guide to which is *Historical Materials in the Harry S. Truman Library* (Independence, Mo.: Harry S. Truman Library, 1982). The library also contains pertinent collections of photographs, motion pictures, sound recordings, and artifacts.

Richard S. Kirkendall is the editor of the key bibliographical and historiographical treatments. These are entitled *The Truman Period as a Research Field* (Columbia: University of Missouri Press, 1967) and *The Truman Period as a Research Field: A Reappraisal, 1974* (Columbia: University of Missouri Press, 1974). It is expected that the centenary of Truman's birth, 1984, will see the publication of Richard D. Burns, ed., *Harry S. Truman, The Man and the Presidency: A Guide to References*.

There are a large number of volumes of pertinent printed documents. Among them are *Public Papers of the Presidents of the United States, Harry S. Truman, Containing the Public Messages, Speeches, and Statements of the President, 1945–1953*, 8 vols. (Washington, D.C.: Government Printing Office, 1961–1966); Barton J. Bernstein and Allen J. Matusow, eds., *The Truman Administration: A Documentary History* (New York: Harper & Row, 1966); Robert H. Ferrell, ed., *Off the Record: The Private Papers of Harry S. Truman* (New York: Harper & Row, 1980) and *Dear Bess: The Letters from Harry to Bess Truman, 1910–1959* (New York: W. W. Norton, 1983); and Monte M. Poen, ed., *Strictly Personal and Confidential: The Letters That Harry Truman Never Mailed* (Boston: Little, Brown, 1982). For interesting oddities see William Hillman, *Mr. President* (New York: Farrar, Straus & Young, 1952), and Merle Miller, *Plain Speaking: An Oral Biography of Harry S. Truman* (New York: Berkley, 1974).

For autobiographical material see Harry S. Truman, *The Autobiography of Harry S. Truman*, ed. Robert H. Ferrell (Boulder: Colorado Associated University Press, 1980), and the former president's pastiche of pride and prejudice, *Memoirs by Harry S. Truman*, vol. 1: *Year of Decisions* and vol. 2: *Years of Trial and Hope, 1946–1952* (Garden City, N.Y.: Doubleday, 1955, 1956). There is no first-rate biography of Truman. The best of those available is by his daughter, Margaret Truman, *Harry S. Truman* (New York: William Morrow, 1973). Also interesting are Charles Robbins and Bradley Smith, *Last of His Kind: An Informal Portrait of Harry S. Truman* (New York: William Morrow, 1979), and Alfred Steinberg, *The Man from Missouri: The Life and Times of Harry S. Truman* (New York: G. P. Putnam's Sons, 1962).

Robert J. Donovan is the author of the most-detailed work on the Truman presidency, *Conflict and Crisis: The Presidency of Harry S Truman, 1945–1948* and *Tumultuous Years: The Presidency of Harry S Truman, 1949–1953* (New York: W. W. Norton, 1977, 1982). Other accounts of Truman's presidency include Cabell Phillips, *The Truman Presidency: The History of a Triumphant Succession* (New York: Macmillan, 1966); Robert H. Ferrell, *Harry S. Truman and the Modern Presidency* (Boston: Little, Brown, 1982); and in effect, Harold F. Gosnell, *Truman's Crises: A Political Biography of Harry S. Truman* (Westport, Conn.: Greenwood, 1980), a solid conventional treatment. Two important, though contrasting, interpretations of the Truman presidency are Alonzo L. Hamby's *Beyond the New Deal: Harry S. Truman and American Liberalism* (New York: Columbia University Press, 1973) and Bert Cochran's *Harry Truman and the Crisis Presidency* (New York: Funk & Wagnalls, 1973). Arthur M. Schlesinger, Jr., *The Imperial Presidency* (Boston: Houghton Mifflin, 1973), contains a trenchant liberal critique of the Truman administration. Various aspects of the presidency are viewed from the standpoint of the New Left in Barton J. Bernstein, ed., *Politics and Policies of the Truman Administration* (Chicago: Quadrangle, 1970).

Insights and information on the operating techniques of the Truman presidency are found in Louis W. Koenig, ed., *The Truman Administration: Its*

Principles and Practice (New York: New York University Press, 1956); Francis H. Heller, ed., *The Truman White House: The Administration of the Presidency, 1945-1953* (Lawrence: Regents Press of Kansas, 1980); John Hersey, *Aspects of the Presidency* (New Haven, Conn., and New York: Ticknor & Fields, 1980); and Robert Underhill, *The Truman Persuasions* (Ames: Iowa State University Press, 1981). One should also consult Ronald T. Farrar, *Reluctant Servant: The Story of Charles G. Ross* (Columbia: University of Missouri Press, 1969); Samuel B. Hand, *Counsel and Advise: A Political Biography of Samuel I. Rosenman* (New York: Garland, 1979); and *Working with Truman: A Personal Memoir of the White House Years* (New York: Putnam, 1982), by Ken Hechler, another White House aide.

The number of works concerning high-ranking officials during the Truman presidency is legion. Those by or about department heads include Dean Acheson, *Present at the Creation: My Years in the State Department* (New York: W. W. Norton, 1969); David S. McLellan, *Dean Acheson: The State Department Years* (New York: Dodd, Mead, 1976); Gaddis Smith, *Dean Acheson* (New York: Cooper Square, 1972); James L. Forsythe, "Clinton P. Anderson: Politician and Business Man as Truman's Secretary of Agriculture" (Ph.D. diss., University of New Mexico, 1970); James F. Byrnes, *Speaking Frankly* (New York: Harper & Bros., 1947) and *All in One Lifetime* (New York: Harper & Bros., 1958); Richard L. Walker and George Curry, *E. R. Stettinius, Jr., and James F. Byrnes* (New York: Cooper Square, 1965); Patricia Dawson Ward, *The Threat of Peace: James F. Byrnes and the Council of Foreign Ministers, 1945-1946* (Kent, Ohio: Kent State University, 1979); Clayton R. Koppes, "Oscar Chapman: A Liberal at the Interior Department, 1933-1953" (Ph.D. diss., University of Kansas, 1974); James Forrestal, *The Forrestal Diaries*, ed. Walter Millis (New York: Viking Press, 1951); Robert H. Ferrell, *George C. Marshall* (New York: Cooper Square, 1966); Charles Sawyer, *Concerns of a Conservative Democrat* (Carbondale: Southern Illinois University Press, 1968); Elting E. Morison, *Turmoil and Tradition: A Study of the Life and Times of Henry L. Stimson* (Boston: Houghton Mifflin, 1960); Henry L. Stimson and McGeorge Bundy, *On Active Service in Peace and War* (New York: Harper & Bros., 1948); Edward L. and Frederick H. Schapsmeier, *Prophet in Politics: Henry A. Wallace and the War Years, 1940-1965* (Ames: Iowa State University Press, 1970); and Henry A. Wallace, *The Price of Vision: The Diary of Henry A. Wallace, 1942-1946*, ed. John Morton Blum (Boston: Houghton Mifflin, 1973).

Other important figures connected with the Truman administration are dealt with in George T. Mazuzan, *Warren R. Austin at the U.N., 1946-1953* (Kent, Ohio: Kent State University Press, 1977); Jordan A. Schwarz, *The Speculator: Bernard M. Baruch in Washington, 1917-1965* (Chapel Hill: University of North Carolina Press, 1981); Charles E. Bohlen, *Witness to History, 1929-1969* (New York: W. W. Norton, 1973); Chester Bowles, *Promises to Keep: My Years in Public Life, 1941-1969* (New York: Harper & Row, 1971); *The Papers of General Lucius D. Clay*, ed. Jean Edward Smith, 2 vols. (Bloomington: Indiana University Press, 1974); *Selected Papers of Will Clayton*, ed. Fredrick J. Dobney (Baltimore, Md.: Johns Hopkins University Press, 1971); Lawrence A. Yates, "John Foster Dulles and Bipartisanship, 1944-1952" (Ph.D. diss., University of Kansas, 1981); W.

Averell Harriman, with Elie Abel, *Special Envoy to Churchill and Stalin, 1941–1946* (New York: Random House, 1975); George F. Kennan, *Memoirs, 1925–1950* and *1950–1963* (Boston: Little, Brown, 1967, 1972); Wilson D. Miscamble, "George F. Kennan, the Policy Planning Staff and American Foreign Policy, 1947–1950" (Ph.D. diss., University of Notre Dame, 1980); *The Papers of Adlai E. Stevenson*, vol. 2: *Washington to Springfield, 1941–1948*, ed. Walter Johnson (Boston: Little, Brown, 1973); and William Manchester, *American Caesar: Douglas MacArthur, 1880–1964* (Boston: Little, Brown, 1978).

There are a number of useful books by and about members of Congress during the Truman period. These include Richard Bolling, *Power in the House: A History of the Leadership of the House of Representatives* (New York: E. P. Dutton, 1968); Emanuel Celler, *You Never Leave Brooklyn: The Autobiography of Emanuel Celler* (New York: John Day, 1953); Tom Connally, *My Name Is Tom Connally* (New York: Crowell, 1954); Paul H. Douglas, *In the Fullness of Time: The Memoirs of Paul H. Douglas* (New York: Harcourt Brace Jovanovich, 1971); Charles L. Fontenay, *Estes Kefauver: A Biography* (Knoxville: University of Tennessee Press, 1980); Anne Hodges Morgan, *Robert S. Kerr: The Senate Years* (Norman: University of Oklahoma Press, 1977); Joseph W. Martin, Jr., *My First Fifty Years in Politics* (New York: McGraw-Hill, 1960); James T. Patterson, *Mr. Republican: A Biography of Robert A. Taft* (Boston: Houghton Mifflin, 1972); and especially, Arthur H. Vandenberg, *The Private Papers of Senator Vandenberg*, ed. Arthur H. Vandenberg, Jr. (Boston: Houghton Mifflin, 1952). See also Kenneth D. Hairgrove, "Sam Rayburn: Congressional Leader, 1940–1952" (Ph.D. diss., Texas Tech University, 1974), and Susan Hartmann, *Truman and the 80th Congress* (Columbia: University of Missouri Press, 1971).

For insights into the work and thought of members of the Supreme Court see William O. Douglas, *The Court Years, 1939–1975: The Autobiography of William O. Douglas* (New York: Random House, 1980), and Felix Frankfurter, *From the Diaries of Felix Frankfurter*, ed. Joseph P. Lash (New York: W. W. Norton, 1975). An interesting and relevant study is David N. Atkinson's "Mr. Justice Minton and the Supreme Court, 1949–1956" (Ph.D. diss., University of Iowa, 1969).

Among works by foreign statesmen of the time are Konrad Adenauer, *Memoirs, 1945–53*, tr. Beate Ruhm von Oppen (Chicago: Henry Regnery, 1965); Clement R. Attlee, *As It Happened* (New York: Viking, 1954), and *Twilight of Empire: Memoirs of Prime Minister Clement Attlee* (New York: A. S. Barnes, 1962); Lester B. Pearson, *Mike: The Memoirs of the Right Honourable Lester B. Pearson, 1948–1957*, vol. 2 (New York: Quadrangle, 1973); and Dirk U. Stikker, *Men of Responsibility* (London: John Murray, 1966). See also the biography of Attlee (London: Weidenfeld & Nicolson, 1982), by Kenneth Harris.

In studying the Truman administration, scholars have been most concerned with the Cold War. William Appleman Williams, *The Tragedy of American Diplomacy* (Cleveland: World, 1959), led off the intense debate and intensive research that have characterized this study for a quarter of a century. Key inquiries that have dealt with the origins and some of the many manifestations of the Cold War include Gar Alperovitz, *Atomic Diplomacy: Hiroshima and Potsdam*

(New York: Simon & Schuster, 1965); Lloyd C. Gardner, *Architects of Illusion: Men and Ideas in American Foreign Policy, 1941-1949* (Chicago: Quadrangle, 1970); Herbert Feis, *From Trust to Terror: The Onset of the Cold War, 1945-1950* (New York: W. W. Norton, 1970); Thomas G. Paterson, ed., *Cold War Critics: Alternatives to American Foreign Policy in the Truman Years* (Chicago: Quadrangle, 1971); Robert W. Tucker, *The Radical Left and American Foreign Policy* (Baltimore, Md.: Johns Hopkins Press, 1971); Adam B. Ulam, *The Rivals: America and Russia since World War II* (New York: Viking, 1971); John Lewis Gaddis, *The United States and the Origins of the Cold War, 1941-1947* (New York: Columbia University Press, 1972); Joyce and Gabriel Kolko, *The Limits of Power: The World and United States Foreign Policy, 1945-1954* (New York: Harper & Row, 1972); Lisle A. Rose, *After Yalta* (New York: Charles Scribner's Sons, 1973); Thomas G. Paterson, *Soviet-American Confrontation: Postwar Reconstruction and the Origins of the Cold War* (Baltimore, Md.: Johns Hopkins University Press, 1973); Charles L. Mee, Jr., *Meeting at Potsdam* (New York: M. Evans, 1975); Martin J. Sherwin, *A World Destroyed: The Atomic Bomb and the Grand Alliance* (New York: Alfred A. Knopf, 1975); Walter La Feber, *America, Russia, and the Cold War, 1945-1975*, 3d ed. (New York: John Wiley, 1976); Daniel Yergin, *Shattered Peace: The Origins of the Cold War and the National Security State* (Boston: Houghton Mifflin, 1977); Vojtech Mastny, *Russia's Road to the Cold War: Diplomacy, Warfare, and the Politics of Communism, 1941-1945* (New York: Columbia University Press, 1979); Thomas G. Paterson, *On Every Front: The Making of the Cold War* (New York: W. W. Norton, 1979); Leon Martel, *Lend-Lease, Loans, and the Coming of the Cold War: A Study of the Implementation of Foreign Policy* (Boulder, Colo.: Westview, 1979); Gregg Herken, *The Winning Weapon: The Atomic Bomb in the Cold War, 1945-1950* (New York: Alfred A. Knopf, 1980); Robert L. Messer, *The End of an Alliance: James F. Byrnes, Roosevelt, Truman, and the Origins of the Cold War* (Chapel Hill: University of North Carolina Press, 1982); William Taubman, *Stalin's American Policy: From Entente to Detente to Cold War* (New York: W. W. Norton, 1982); and John Lewis Gaddis, *Strategies of Containment: A Critical Appraisal of Postwar American National Security Policy* (New York: Oxford University Press, 1982). A useful book of documents is Thomas H. Etzold and John Lewis Gaddis, eds., *Containment: Documents on American Policy and Strategy, 1945-1950* (New York: Columbia University Press, 1978). It is also instructive to read Joan Lee Bryniarski, "Against the Tide: Senate Opposition to the Internationalist Foreign Policy of Presidents Franklin D. Roosevelt and Harry S. Truman, 1943-1949" (Ph.D. diss., University of Maryland, 1972), and John T. Rourke, "Congress and the Cold War: Congressional Influence on the Foreign Policy Process" (Ph.D. diss., University of Connecticut, 1975). For treatments of views on the Cold War see Kenneth W. Thompson, *Cold War Theories*, vol. 1: *World Polarization, 1943-1953* (Baton Rouge: Louisiana State University Press, 1981); Robert J. Maddox, *The New Left and the Origins of the Cold War* (Princeton, N.J.: Princeton University Press, 1973); and Joseph M. Siracusa, *New Left Diplomatic Histories and Historians: The American Revisionists* (Port Washington, N.Y.: Kennikat, 1973).

For works on national situations pertaining to the development of the Cold War in the West see Bruce Kuklick, *American Policy and the Division of Germany: The Clash with Russia over Reparations* (Ithaca, N.Y.: Cornell University Press, 1972); John Gimbel, *The American Occupation of Germany: Politics and the Military, 1945–1949* (Stanford, Calif.: Stanford University Press, 1968); Earl Ziemke, *The U.S. Army in the Occupation of Germany, 1944–1946* (Washington, D.C.: Center of Military History, 1975); Edward N. Peterson, *The American Occupation of Germany: Retreat to Victory* (Detroit, Mich.: Wayne State University, 1978); Bruce Robellet Kuniholm, *The Origins of the Cold War in the Near East: Great Power Conflict and Diplomacy in Iran, Turkey, and Greece* (Princeton, N.J.: Princeton University Press, 1980); Fraser J. Harbutt, "The Fulton Speech and the Iran Crisis of 1946: A Turning Point in American Foreign Policy" (Ph.D. diss., University of California, Berkeley, 1976); Lincoln MacVeagh, *Ambassador Mac-Veagh Reports, Greece, 1933–1947*, ed. John O. Iatrides (Princeton, N.J.: Princeton University Press, 1980); Lawrence S. Wittner, *American Intervention in Greece, 1943–1949* (New York: Columbia University Press, 1982); Terry H. Anderson, *The United States, Great Britain, and the Cold War, 1944–1947* (Columbia: University of Missouri Press, 1981); Robert M. Hathaway, *Ambiguous Partnership: Britain and America, 1944–1947* (New York: Columbia University Press, 1981); Victor Rothwell, *Britain and the Cold War, 1941–1947* (London: Jonathan Cape, 1981); Marvin R. Zahniser, *Uncertain Friendship: American-French Diplomatic Relations through the Cold War* (New York: John Wiley, 1975); and Geir Lundestad, *America, Scandinavia, and the Cold War, 1945–1949* (New York: Columbia University Press, 1980).

Works dealing with the key points in the development of an anti-Communist alliance among Western nations include Alfred Grosser, *The Western Alliance: European-American Relations since 1945* (New York: Continuum, 1980); John Gimbel, *The Origins of the Marshall Plan* (Stanford, Calif.: Stanford University Press, 1976); Theodore A. Wilson, *The Marshall Plan, 1947–1951*, Headline Series no. 236 (New York: Foreign Policy Association, 1977); Avi Shlaim, *The United States and the Berlin Blockade, 1948–1949* (Berkeley: University of California Press, 1983); Nicholas Henderson, *The Birth of NATO* (London: Weidenfeld & Nicolson, 1982); Lawrence S. Kaplan, *A Community of Interests: NATO and the Military Assistance Program, 1948–1951* (Washington, D.C.: Office of the Secretary of Defense, Historical Office, 1980); Timothy P. Ireland, *Creating the Entangling Alliance: The Origins of the North Atlantic Treaty Organization* (Westport, Conn.: Greenwood, 1981); Robert McGeehan, *The German Rearmament Question: American Diplomacy and European Defense after World War II* (Urbana: University of Illinois Press, 1971); Edward Fursdon, *The European Defence Community: A History* (London: Macmillan, 1980); and R. C. Mowat, *Creating the European Community* (London: Blandford, 1973).

Much literature has been published on Cold War tensions in East Asia. General works include Robert M. Blum, *Drawing the Line: The Origin of the American Containment Policy in East Asia* (New York: W. W. Norton, 1982); Yonosuke Nagai and Akira Iriye, eds., *The Origins of the Cold War in Asia* (New

York: Columbia University Press, 1977); Akira Iriye, *The Cold War in Asia* (Englewood Cliffs, N.J.: Prentice-Hall, 1974); and Russell D. Buhite, *Soviet-American Relations in Asia, 1945–1954* (Norman: University of Oklahoma Press, 1981). A work dealing with the Philippines is Teodoro Villamor Cortes, "Interaction Patterns in a Big Power–Small Power Relationship: The United States–Philippine Experience, 1946 to 1971" (Ph.D. diss., University of Illinois, Urbana, 1972). The studies concerning China include Herbert Feis, *The China Tangle: The American Effort in China from Pearl Harbor to the Marshall Mission* (Princeton, N.J.: Princeton University Press, 1953); Russell D. Buhite, *Patrick J. Hurley and American Foreign Policy* (Ithaca, N.Y.: Cornell University Press, 1973); Michael Schaller, *The U.S. Crusade in China, 1938–1945* (New York: Columbia University Press, 1979); Kenneth S. Chern, *Dilemma in China: America's Policy Debate, 1945* (Hamden, Conn.: Archon, 1980); and Dorothy Borg and Waldo Heinrichs, eds., *Uncertain Years: Chinese-American Relations, 1947–1950* (New York: Columbia University Press, 1980). In *The Road to Confrontation: American Policy toward China and Korea, 1947–1950* (Chapel Hill: University of North Carolina Press, 1981), William Whitney Stueck, Jr., strives to bridge the problems perceived by Americans in China and Korea.

Concentrating on the prelude to the war in Korea are Bruce Cumings, *The Origins of the Korean War: Liberation and the Emergence of Separate Regimes, 1945–1947* (Princeton, N.J.: Princeton University Press, 1981); Charles M. Dobbs, *The Unwanted Symbol: American Foreign Policy, the Cold War, and Korea, 1945–1950* (Kent, Ohio: Kent State University Press, 1981); and James I. Matray, "The Reluctant Crusade: American Foreign Policy in Korea, 1941–1950" (Ph.D. diss., University of Virginia, 1977). Various aspects of the involvement of the United States in the Korean War are treated in Glenn D. Paige, *The Korean Decision, June 24–30, 1950* (New York: Free Press, 1968); Francis H. Heller, ed., *The Korean War: A 25 Year Perspective* (Lawrence: Regents Press of Kansas, 1977); James F. Schnabel, *Policy and Direction: The First Year*, vol. 3 of *United States Army in the Korean War* (Washington, D.C.: Government Printing Office, 1972); Joseph C. Goulden, *Korea: The Untold Story of the War* (New York: Times Books, 1982); Matthew B. Ridgway, *The Korean War* (Garden City, N.Y.: Doubleday, 1967); J. Lawton Collins, *War in Peacetime: The History and Lessons of Korea* (Boston: Houghton Mifflin, 1969); Mark W. Clark, *From the Danube to the Yalu* (New York: Harper & Bros., 1954); John W. Spanier, *The Truman-MacArthur Controversy and the Korean War* (Cambridge: Belknap Press of Harvard University Press, 1959); Ronald J. Caridi, *The Korean War and American Politics: The Republican Party as a Case Study* (Philadelphia: University of Pennsylvania Press, 1968); and Hornell N. Hart, comp., *The "Great Debate" on American Foreign Policy: Issues, Pros, Cons and Agreements* (Durham, N.C.: Duke University Consensus Project, 1951).

Special issues of interest to Americans during the Truman presidency existed in the Near East. Many of these are dealt with by Michael B. Stoff in *Oil, War, and American Security: The Search for a National Policy on Foreign Oil, 1941–1947* (New Haven, Conn.: Yale University Press, 1980); Irvine H. Anderson, *Aramco, the United States, and Saudi Arabia: A Study in the Dynamics of Foreign*

Oil Policy, 1933–1950 (Princeton, N.J.: Princeton University Press, 1981); John Snetsinger, *Truman, The Jewish Vote and the Creation of Israel* (Stanford, Calif.: Hoover Institution Press, 1974); Zvi Ganin, *Truman, American Jewry, and Israel, 1945–1948* (New York: Holmes & Meier, 1979); and Edward H. Buehrig, *The UN and the Palestinian Refugees: A Study in Nonterritorial Administration* (Bloomington: Indiana University Press, 1971).

On questions pertaining to the Western Hemisphere see Robert D. Cuff and J. L. Granatstein, *American Dollars—Canadian Prosperity: Canadian-American Economic Relations, 1945–1950* (Toronto and Sarasoto: Samuel-Stevens, 1978); David Green, *The Containment of Latin America: A History of the Myths and Realities of the Good Neighbor Policy* (Chicago: Quadrangle, 1971); Rita Ana Giacalone, "From Bad Neighbors to Reluctant Partners: Argentina and the United States, 1946–1950" (Ph.D. diss., Indiana University, 1977); Lester D. Langley, *The United States and the Caribbean, 1900–1970* (Athens: University of Georgia Press, 1980); and Surendra Bhana, *The United States and the Development of the Puerto Rican Status Question, 1936–1968* (Lawrence: University Press of Kansas, 1975).

Special issues touching on foreign affairs are treated by Evan Luard in *A History of the United Nations*, vol. 1: *The Years of Western Domination, 1945–1955* (London: Macmillan, 1982); Alfred E. Eckes, Jr., *The United States and the Global Struggle for Minerals* (Austin: University of Texas Press, 1979); Leonard Dinnerstein, *America and the Survivors of the Holocaust* (New York: Columbia University Press, 1982); Roger W. Gale, *The Americanization of Micronesia: A Study of the Consolidation of U.S. Rule in the Pacific* (Washington, D.C.: University Press of America, 1979).

A variety of works deal with matters concerning United States military power and its development during the Truman presidency. These include Richard F. Haynes, *The Awesome Power: Harry S. Truman as Commander in Chief* (Baton Rouge: Louisiana State University Press, 1973); Thomas F. Troy, *Donovan and the CIA: A History of the Establishment of the Central Intelligence Agency* (Frederick, Md.: University Publications of America, 1982); the four volumes in *The History of the Joint Chiefs of Staff* (Wilmington, Del.: Michael Glazier, 1979–1980): *The Joint Chiefs of Staff and National Policy*, vol. 1, *1945–1947*, by James F. Schnabel, vol. 2, *1947–1949*, by Kenneth W. Condit, vol. 3, *The Korean War*, by James F. Schnabel and Robert J. Watson, and vol. 4, *1950–1952*, by Walter S. Poole; Murray Green, "Stuart Symington and the B-36" (Ph.D. diss., American University, 1960); Harry R. Borowski, *A Hollow Threat: Strategic Air Power and Containment before Korea* (Westport, Conn.: Greenwood, 1982); Paolo E. Coletta, *The United States Navy and Defense Unification, 1947–1953* (Newark: University of Delaware Press, 1981); Clayton R. Koppes, *JPL and the American Space Program: The Jet Propulsion Laboratory* (New Haven, Conn.: Yale University Press, 1982); Michael Mandelbaum, *The Nuclear Question: The United States and Nuclear Weapons, 1946–1976* (New York: Cambridge University Press, 1979); and on the Atomic Energy Commission and its background, Richard G. Hewlett and Oscar E. Anderson, Jr., *The New World, 1939/1946* (University Park: Pennsylvania State

University Press, 1962), and Richard G. Hewlett and Francis Duncan, *Atomic Shield, 1947/1952* (University Park: Pennsylvania State University Press, 1969).

There is a substantial, though far from comprehensive, body of scholarship on economic questions faced by the Truman administration. See Francis H. Heller, ed., *Economics and the Truman Administration* (Lawrence: Regents Press of Kansas, 1981); Stephen K. Bailey, *Congress Makes a Law: The Story behind the Employment Act of 1946* (New York: Columbia University Press, 1950); Hugh S. Norton, *The Employment Act and the Council of Economic Advisers, 1946–1976* (Columbia: University of South Carolina Press, 1977); Edward S. Flash, Jr., *Economic Advice and Presidential Leadership: The Council of Economic Advisers* (New York: Columbia University Press, 1965); Craufurd D. Goodwin, ed., *Exhortation and Controls: The Search for a Wage-Price Policy, 1945–1971* (Washington, D.C.: Brookings Institution, 1974); Arthur F. McClure, *The Truman Administration and the Problems of Postwar Labor, 1945–1948* (Rutherford, N.J.: Fairleigh Dickinson University Press, 1969); R. Alton Lee, *Truman and Taft-Hartley: A Question of Mandate* (Lexington: University of Kentucky Press, 1966); Melvyn Dubofsky and Warren Van Tine, *John L. Lewis: A Biography* (New York: Quadrangle, 1977); Maeva Marcus, *Truman and the Steel Seizure Case: The Limits of Presidential Power* (New York: Columbia University Press, 1977); Allen J. Matusow, *Farm Policies and Politics in the Truman Years* (Cambridge: Harvard University Press, 1967); Murray R. Benedict and Oscar C. Stine, *The Agricultural Commodity Programs: Two Decades of Experience* (New York: Twentieth Century Fund, 1956); Darrel Robert Cady, "The Truman Administration's Reconversion Policies, 1945–1947" (Ph.D. diss., University of Kansas, 1974); William O. Wagnon, Jr., "The Politics of Economic Growth: The Truman Administration and the 1949 Recession" (Ph.D. diss., University of Missouri, 1970); Robert L. Branyan, "Antimonopoly Activities during the Truman Administration" (Ph.D. diss., University of Oklahoma, 1961); and Gale E. Peterson, "President Harry S. Truman and the Independent Regulatory Commissions, 1945–1952" (Ph.D. diss., University of Maryland, 1973).

Among other domestic issues, civil rights was a persistent and important one. Works on this subject include William C. Berman, *The Politics of Civil Rights in the Truman Administration* (Columbus: Ohio State University Press, 1970); Donald R. McCoy and Richard T. Ruetten, *Quest and Response: Minority Rights and the Truman Administration* (Lawrence: University Press of Kansas, 1973); Richard Dalfiume, *Desegregation of the U.S. Armed Forces: Fighting on Two Fronts, 1939–1953* (Columbia: University of Missouri Press, 1969); and Richard B. Craig, *The Bracero Program: Interest Groups and Foreign Policy* (Austin: University of Texas Press, 1971).

The presidential-election campaigns of 1948 reflected a great number of issues. Among the works dealing with this are Richard S. Kirkendall, "Election of 1948," in *History of American Presidential Elections, 1789–1968*, ed. Arthur M. Schlesinger, Jr., and Fred L. Israel, 4 vols. (New York: Chelsea House, 1971), 4:3099–3145; Jules Abels, *Out of the Jaws of Victory* (New York: Holt, 1959); Irwin Ross, *The Loneliest Campaign: The Truman Victory of 1948* (New York: New

American Library, 1968); Allen Yarnell, *Democrats and Progressives: The 1948 Election as a Test of Postwar Liberalism* (Berkeley: University of California Press, 1974); and Curtis D. MacDougall, *Gideon's Army* (New York: Mazani & Munsell, 1965). See also Richard Norton Smith, *Thomas E. Dewey and His Times* (New York: Simon & Schuster, 1982).

There are also works on a variety of other domestic matters during the Truman era. These include Davis R. B. Ross, *Preparing for Ulysses: Politics and Veterans during World War II* (New York: Columbia University Press, 1969); Keith W. Olson, *The G. I. Bill, the Veterans, and the Colleges* (Lexington: University Press of Kentucky, 1974); United States Commission on Organization of the Executive Branch of the Government, *The Hoover Commission Report on Organization of the Executive Branch of the Government* (New York: McGraw-Hill, 1949); William E. Pemberton, *Bureaucratic Politics: Executive Reorganization during the Truman Administration* (Columbia: University of Missouri Press, 1979); Elmo R. Richardson, *Dams, Parks & Politics: Resource Development & Preservation in the Truman-Eisenhower Era* (Lexington: University Press of Kentucky, 1973); Craufurd D. Goodwin, ed., *Energy Policy in Prospective: Today's Problems, Yesterday's Solutions* (Washington, D.C.: Brookings Institution, 1981); Richard O. Davies, *Housing Reform during the Truman Administration* (Columbia: University of Missouri Press, 1966); Monte M. Poen, *Harry S. Truman versus the Medical Lobby: The Genesis of Medicare* (Columbia: University of Missouri Press, 1979); Kenneth M. Jones, "Science, Scientists, and Americans: Images of Science and the Formation of Federal Science Policy, 1945–1950" (Ph.D. diss., Cornell University, 1975); David L. Marden, "The Cold War and American Education" (Ph.D. diss., University of Kansas, 1975); Jules Abels, *The Truman Scandals* (Chicago: Henry Regnery, 1956); and Andrew J. Dunar, "All Honorable Men: The Truman Scandals and the Politics of Morality" (Ph.D. diss., University of Southern California, 1981).

Last but far from least among the books documenting the Truman period are those dealing with the knotty questions of loyalty and internal security. The scope involved is indicated by Earl Latham, *The Communist Controversy in Washington: From the New Deal to McCarthy* (Cambridge: Harvard University Press, 1966); Alan D. Harper, *The Politics of Loyalty: The White House and the Communist Issue, 1946–1952* (Westport, Conn.: Greenwood, 1969); Richard M. Freeland, *The Truman Doctrine and the Origins of McCarthyism: Foreign Policy, Domestic Politics, and Internal Security, 1946–1948* (New York: Alfred A. Knopf, 1972); Athan Theoharis, *Seeds of Repression: Harry S. Truman and the Origins of McCarthyism* (Chicago: Quadrangle, 1971); Michal R. Belknap, *Cold War Political Justice: The Smith Act, the Communist Party, and American Civil Liberties* (Westport, Conn.: Greenwood, 1977); Allen Weinstein, *Perjury: The Hiss-Chambers Case* (New York: Vintage, 1979); Athan Theoharis, ed., *Beyond the Hiss Case: The FBI, Congress, and the Cold War* (Philadelphia: Temple University Press, 1982); Robert Griffith, *The Politics of Fear: Joseph R. McCarthy and the Senate* (Lexington: University Press of Kentucky, for the Organization of American Historians, 1970); Robert Griffith and Athan Theoharis, eds., *The Specter: Original Essays on the Cold War and the Origins of McCarthyism* (New York: New Viewpoints, 1974); Richard M. Fried, *Men against McCarthy* (New York: Columbia University Press, 1976); O. Edmund Clubb, *The Witness and I* (New York: Columbia University Press, 1974); Gary May, *China Scapegoat: The Diplomatic Ordeal of John Carter Vincent* (Washington, D.C.: New Republic, 1979); Thomas C. Reeves, *The Life and Times of Joe McCarthy: A Biography* (New York: Stein & Day, 1982); David M. Oshinsky, *Conspiracy so Immense: The World of Joe McCarthy* (New York: Free Press, 1983); and Ronald Radosh and Joyce Milton, *The Rosenberg File: A Search for the Truth* (New York: Holt, Rinehart & Winston, 1983). See also Athan G. Theoharis, ed., *The Truman Presidency: The Origins of the Imperial Presidency and the National Security State* (Stanfordville, N.Y.: Earl M. Coleman, 1979).

INDEX

Davidson, C. Girard, 152
Davies, Joseph E., 28, 34
Davis, William H., 45
Dawson, Donald S., 146, 159, 279
Dean, William F., 226
Defense, Department of, 116
Defense Mobilization, Office of, 247
Defense Production Act (1950), 230, 264–
265, 290
De Gaulle, Charles, 32
Denfeld, Louis, 212
Denmark, 30, 81
Dennison, Robert L., 146, 205
Dewey, Thomas E.: on Truman Doctrine,
122; and internal security, 141; and 1948
election, 156, 158–159, 161–162; on Ko-
rean War, 224
DiSalle, Michael V., 263
Displaced Persons, 74–76
Donaldson, Jesse, 148–149
Donovan, William J., 20
Douglas, Paul H.: quoted, 165, 174; and
military assistance, 198, 260; and internal
security, 234; and appointments, 277;
and Senate investigation, 279; evaluation
of, 308
Douglas, William O., 7–8, 157
Dulles, John Foster: on foreign policy, 72,
250; and Marshall Plan, 127; and Korean
War, 224–225; and Japan, 271

Early, Stephen T., 154
Eastland, James, 300
Economic Cooperation Administration,
128–129
Economic reconversion, 41–61
Economic Stabilization, Office of, 45–46, 58
Economic Stabilization Administration, 263
Eden, Anthony, 28, 284–285, 287
Edwards, India, 187
Egypt, 286
Einstein, Albert, 24
Eisenhower, Dwight D.: on foreign aid,
124; on Russia, 130; and 1948 election,
153–156; and European defense, 232,

259; and 1952 election, 301–302, 304–306;
as president-elect, 306, 309–310
Eisenhower administration, 180, 320
Election: of 1944, 7–8; of 1946, 66; of 1948,
99–100, 104, 112, 150–162; of 1950, 242,
273; of 1952, 300–306
Elsey, George M.: and foreign policy, 87–
89, 120, 209; and 1948 election, 159; and
MacArthur controversy, 263
Employment Act (1946), 61–62
Employment Service, 52, 106
Ethridge, Mark, 119, 121
Ewing, Oscar, 152, 173

Fahy, Charles H., 169–170
Fair Employment Board, 109, 169
Fair Employment Practices Committee,
106–107, 255
Fairless, Benjamin, 57
Farouk (king of Egypt), 286
Federal Power Commission, 176–177
Federal Reserve Board, 264, 282
Feinsinger, Nathan, 292
Fellers, Bonner, 73
Fine, Benjamin, 182
Finletter, Thomas K., 187, 211–214, 238
Flood Control Act (1950), 175
Foreign Assistance Act (1948), 110, 127–128
Foreign Economic Assistance Act (1950),
210
Forrestal, James V.: as secretary of the
navy, 19, 22, 63; on Russia, 29, 69, 82;
and China, 73–74; and Palestine, 75; on
defense efforts, 85, 88, 116, 120, 132–133;
on labor, 98; as secretary of defense, 116,
187; and Marshall Plan, 125–126; evalua-
tion of, 147–148
Foskett, James H., 144, 146
France: and World War II, 32, 28; and
Berlin Blockade, 137–139, 193–194; and
Indochina, 204–205, 240–241, 266; and
European army, 233, 266–267, 284–286
Franco, Francisco, 202
French Indochina, 204–205, 232, 240–241,
266
Fulbright, J. William, 231, 279, 308
Fulbright Act (1946), 83

and Security Council vetoes, 134; and Korean War, 222–224, 226–229, 237–238, 244–245
United States in the 1940s, 8–13
United States Steel, 52, 57
United Steelworkers, 50, 57, 290–292
Universal Military Training, 117–118

Valentine, Alan, 263
Vandenberg, Arthur H., 92; and industrial disputes, 50; on United Nations, 67; on Russia, 70, 79–80; and Truman Doctrine, 121–123; and Marshall Plan, 126–127; and collective security, 130, 139, 198–200; on 1948 election, 153; and cloture, 168; on China, 195–196
Vandenberg, Hoyt, 244
Vardaman, James K., Jr., 17, 64
Vatican, 277
Vaughan, Harry: and Truman, 1, 17, 64–65; described, 146; investigation of, 188–189; quoted, 212; evaluation of, 308
Venezia Giulia, 30–31, 82, 85, 130
Vinson, Carl, 122
Vinson, Fred M.: as secretary of the Treasury, 18, 49; as director of war mobilization and reconversion, 45, 64; as chief justice, 63; and 1952 election, 301; evaluation of, 308
Virgin Islands, 106
Vishinsky, Andrei Y., 267
Voice of America, 83, 130–131

Wage Stabilization Board, 263, 290, 307
Walker, Frank C., 19
Walker, Walton H., 226, 236–238, 245
Wallace, Henry A.: and 1944 election, 7–8; as secretary of commerce, 19–20, 44, 63–64; and foreign policy, 67–68, 82, 85–87; on Truman, 70; and 1948 election, 153–154, 158–159, 161–162
Wallgren, Mon, 173, 177
War Mobilization and Reconversion, Office of, 43, 45–46
War Production Board, 42, 45–46, 48–49
Warren, Earl, 156
Webb, James E., 133, 146, 211, 215
Weizmann, Chaim, 136
Western Union, 135
Wherry, Kenneth S., 65, 251, 259–260
Whitney, A. F., 59–60
Wickard, Claude R., 19
Willett, Edward F., 79, 82, 87
Wilson, Charles E., 107, 247, 264, 291
Wilson, Woodrow, 67, 70–71, 312–313
World War II, 15–16, 20–40
Wright, Fielding, 158

Yalta Conference, 24, 29
Youngstown v. *Sawyer* (1952), 292–293
Yugoslavia: and Venezia Giulia, 30–31, 82, 85; and Russia, 138, 195; and U.S. aid, 269–270

5324 077